AN INTRODUCTION TO AP SEMIOTICS

An Introduction to Applied Semiotics presents nineteen semiotics tools for text and image analysis. Covering a variety of different schools and approaches, together with the author's own original approach, this is a full and synthetic introduction to semiotics. This book presents general tools that can be used with any semiotic product. Drawing on the work of Fontanille, Genette, Greimas, Hébert, Jakobson, Peirce, Rastier and Zilberberg, the tools deal with the analysis of themes and action, true and false, positive and negative, rhythm, narration and other elements.

The application of each tool is illustrated with analyses of a wide range of texts and images, from well-known or distinctive literary texts, philosophical or religious texts or images, paintings, advertising and everyday signs and symbols. Each chapter has the same structure – summary, theory and application – and includes exercises and discussion questions, making it ideal for course use.

Covering both visual and textual objects, this is a key text for all courses in semiotics and textual analysis within linguistics, communication studies, literary theory, design, marketing and related areas.

Louis Hébert is a professor of literature at the Université du Québec à Rimouski (UQAR, Canada). His research focuses primarily on semiotics (textual and visual), interpretive semantics, the methodology of literary analysis, Magritte and Buddhism.

AN INTRODUCTION TO APPLIED SEMIOTICS

Tools for Text and Image Analysis

Louis Hébert

Translated from French by Julie Tabler

Routledge
Taylor & Francis Group
LONDON AND NEW YORK

First published 2020
by Routledge
2 Park Square, Milton Park, Abingdon, Oxon OX14 4RN

and by Routledge
52 Vanderbilt Avenue, New York, NY 10017

Routledge is an imprint of the Taylor & Francis Group, an informa business

British Library Cataloguing-in-Publication Data
A catalogue record for this book is available from the British Library

Library of Congress Cataloging-in-Publication Data
Names: Hébert, Louis, 1961– author. | Tabler, Julie, translator.
Title: An introduction to applied semiotics : tools for text and image analysis / Louis Hébert ; translated from the French by Julie Tabler.
Other titles: Dispositifs pour l'analyse des textes et des images. English
Description: 1. | New York : Taylor and Francis, 2020. | Includes bibliographical references and index. | Translated from French.
Identifiers: LCCN 2019038128 | ISBN 9780367351113 (hardback) | ISBN 9780367351120 (paperback) | ISBN 9780429329807 (ebook)
Subjects: LCSH: Semiotics. | Semiotics and literature. | Semiotics and art.
Classification: LCC P99 .H32513 2020 | DDC 401/.4—dc23
LC record available at https://lccn.loc.gov/2019038128

ISBN: 978-0-367-35111-3 (hbk)
ISBN: 978-0-367-35112-0 (pbk)
ISBN: 978-0-429-32980-7 (ebk)

Typeset in Berthold Akzidenz Grotesk
by ApexCovantage, LLC

CONTENTS

FIGURES

TABLES

SYMBOLS USED

The standard symbols shown in the table below are used to distinguish between (1) the sign (the word or lexia) "concrete"; (2) the signified that it conveys, 'concrete'; (3) the signifier associated with this signified, *concrete*, which is composed of the phonemes *k-o-n-k-r-E-t* and the graphemes (letters) *c-o-n-c-r-e-t-e*; (4) the seme /concrete/ (in 'knife', for example) or (5) the isotopy /concrete/ (in "steel knife", for example); and (6) the semantic class //concrete// (which contains the signifieds 'house', 'cat' and 'wind', for example).

Table 0.1 Symbols used

<table>
<tr><th></th><th>ELEMENT</th><th>SYMBOL</th><th>EXAMPLE</th></tr>
<tr><td>01</td><td>sign</td><td>"sign"</td><td>"water"</td></tr>
<tr><td>02</td><td>signifier</td><td>signifier</td><td>water</td></tr>
<tr><td>03</td><td>signified</td><td>'signified'</td><td>'water'</td></tr>
<tr><td>04</td><td>seme and isotopy</td><td>/seme/ and /isotopy/</td><td>/liquid/</td></tr>
<tr><td>05</td><td>case (relation between semes)</td><td>(CASE)</td><td>/woman/ → (ATT) → /beautiful/</td></tr>
<tr><td>06</td><td>semic molecule (when the relations between semes are not specified by cases)</td><td>/seme/ + /seme/</td><td>/dark/ + /negative/</td></tr>
<tr><td>07</td><td>class (semantic class, to be specific)</td><td>//class//</td><td>//times of day// (contains 'day' and 'night')</td></tr>
<tr><td>08</td><td>interpretive rewriting</td><td>|rewriting|
or source element → |rewriting|</td><td>rite → |right|
"draft" (current of air) → |"draft"| (military conscription)
'eagle' → |United States of America|</td></tr>
<tr><td>09</td><td>opposition</td><td>A / B</td><td>day / night</td></tr>
<tr><td>10</td><td>homologation</td><td>A : B :: C : D
(A is to B as C is to D)</td><td>day : night :: light : darkness</td></tr>
</table>

Introduction

Analytical tools: what they are and how they are used

The intent of this book is not to present one or more systems of theoretical semiotics, but to extract a few *tools for text and image analysis* from these systems, explain and refine them and illustrate their use.

The term "tool" refers here to a preestablished analytical device developed from a relatively simple concept network, which, despite its simplicity, can provide a rigorous, accurate analysis (although an admittedly segmented one).

Semiotics, which is concerned with the study of signs, is obviously more than just an inventory of these tools (see Chapter 20, this book, for a more complete overview of this field). While the basic functions of this field of study[1] are descriptive (the empirical approach, as in linguistics), formal (the logical approach), interpretive (the hermeneutic approach) and explanatory (the speculative approach, as in philosophy), we should point out that with analytical tools, the emphasis is on formalization.

Analytical tools appear to be underrated. Along with the postmodern decline of formalism – if not of rationalism – they have become suspect, partly because they arose in an environment of theoretical hegemony and dogmatism. This is easily addressed by isolating them from their original context and revising as needed. In an age of complexity, as we call it, analytical tools are seen as reductive. However, they are quite adequate for what they are and what they can do. Furthermore, analytical tools are worth using if for no other reason than they can often provide a rational and methodological initial approach to a text or an image.

Introduction to the tools

Our choice of analytical tools is somewhat arbitrary, defined by our reading, inclinations and analytical experiments. Most of the tools we have selected belong to four theoretical families: the school of semiotics established under A.J. Greimas's influence, the school of semiosemantics that developed under F. Rastier, the school of R. Jakobson, and the school of C.S. Peirce. Some of our tools are very general (e.g., homologation), and others are more specific (e.g., ontological and veridictory dialogics); some apply mainly to texts (e.g., the veridictory square), and others apply to images as well (e.g., semic analysis).

Each tool is the subject of a chapter, structured in the following way: (1) summary, (2) theory, (3) application(s).

Although our text is indeed addressed to students of semiotics, and more broadly, to those who want to know more about methods of text and image analysis, we believe there is also something of value in it for the specialist. Perhaps this would simply be the fact that we have often found it necessary to break with the status quo approach used in the theoretical systems where these tools originated in order to increase their functionality, either by eliminating traditionally used constraints that we have deemed unnecessary, or by adding substantial enhancements. The indented notes and the parallel use of technical and classroom terminology provide a way to use the text at different levels with varying degrees of difficulty. Within the limits of practicality, the presentation of each analytical tool is an autonomous entity, limiting the number of references to other chapters; as a result, a certain amount of repetition (whose educational value is well known) is inevitable. The index can be used for a more specialized reading of the text, to learn more about a concept or a term.

The texts we analyze are short and come from various genres (examples are poems, plays, fables, philosophical essays, short stories, *The new testament*, etc.), eras and countries; in some cases, we have constructed "laboratory texts" for illustrative purposes. We have included a variety of objects for image analysis: paintings, images from advertisements, logos, and Buddhist iconography.

Lastly, some chapters (1, 3–13) come from our book *Dispositifs pour l'analyse des textes et des images. Introduction à la sémiotique appliquée* (written in French; Presses Universitaires de Limoges, 2007a). These chapters were shortened slightly in the translation. However, the English version includes a chapter that has been completely revised and expanded (see Chapter 1) and eight new chapters, including Chapter 20, "A short introduction to semiotics". Among these new chapters are the following: four (15, 16, 17, 20) are the translations of chapters in *Cours de sémiotique* (Classiques Garnier, 2020); one (19) is the translation of a chapter in a collective work, *Magritte: perspectives nouvelles, nouveaux regards* (Nota bene, 2018); and one (14) is the translation of a chapter in *L'analyse des textes littéraires: une méthodologie complète* (Classiques Garnier, 2014). We supplemented some of these translations with new analyses: an analysis of Amazon's logo and three analyses of *Hamlet*.

* * *

I would like to express my gratitude to François Rastier, Jean-Marie Klinkenberg, Claude Zilberberg, Jacques Fontanille, Julie Tabler, Nicole Everaert-Desmedt, Lucie Guillemette, Cynthia Lévesque, and my students, who have taught me much.

I would like to thank the following institutions for financially supporting this research: Université du Québec à Rimouski (UQAR, Canada) and the Social Sciences and Humanities Research Council (Canada).

Note

1 As summarized by Pierre Ouellet in a paper presented at the colloquium *Théories et objets métissés*, Montreal, Société de sémiotique du Québec, May 2000.

1 Structural relations

Homologation

Summary

A structure is composed of at least two elements, known as terms, with at least one relation established between them. By formulating a typology of relations, we can predict various kinds of structures. Distinctions can be drawn between comparative relations (identity, similarity, alterity, opposition, homologation, etc.), presential relations (presupposition, mutual exclusion, etc.), and others. From among the many simple structures used to characterize the role of signifiers (elements of expression) and/or signifieds (content) in a semiotic act, we have chosen to focus on homologation. Homologation is the relation between (at least) two pairs of opposite elements, such that for two oppositions A/B and C/D, one can say that A is to B as C is to D. For example, in a particular text, life (A) is to death (B) as positive (C) is to negative (D).

Theory

Structure defined

We will posit that any signifying unit – except for signifying units that are considered impossible to break down, not from a purely methodological standpoint, but de facto – may be analyzed in terms of structure, and that any **structure** is an entity that may be broken down into at least two **terms** (or *relata* – *relatum* in the singular) linked by at least one **relation** (or function). Generally speaking, the inventory of terms is in opposition with the inventory of relations, in that the terms are a priori undefined in number, and the relations are a priori limited in number (although the inventory of relations can be partially open and can vary according to the analytical objectives and the type of objects being analyzed).

We will say that the **minimal structure** is composed of two terms linked by only one relation (one relation that we are describing, anyway). Thus, fire/water is a minimal structure (of the signified) in "firewater", whose terms are related by opposition. In "fire is luminous water", the oppositional relation is accompanied by a comparative relation (a metaphor).

NOTE: OTHER POSSIBLE DEFINITIONS OF THE MINIMAL STRUCTURE

Our definition of the minimal structure can be expanded to include cases in which the relation is established between a term and itself (a reflexive relation). Hjelmslev gives a more restrictive definition of the minimal structure than ours; he views a structure as "an autonomous entity of internal dependencies", i.e., a relation between relations. By this definition, the minimal structure would entail two relations linked by a third relation, and would customarily include four elements. A homology between two oppositions is in fact a minimal structure of this kind. However, other kinds of minimal structures are possible. Suppose that r = a relation and R = a relation between relations. A minimal structure might include only two elements. They will be linked either by two different relations: (A r1 B) R (A r2 B) or (A r1 A) R (A r2 B); or by a single relation: (A r1 B) R (A r1 B) or (A r1 A) R (A r1 B). Lastly, a structure could even theoretically comprise just one term, linked to itself, but probably only if the two relations are different: (A r1 A) R (A r2 A).

Structures composed of signifiers, signifieds and signs

With respect to the signifier/signified opposition (or expression/content) constituting any sign, there are three basic kinds of structural analysis one can perform, depending on whether the structure includes (1) only the signifier (e.g., an analysis restricted to the versification of a poem), (2) only the signified (e.g., a traditional thematic analysis), or (3) both the signifier and the signified (e.g., an analysis of the relations between the sounds and the meanings of the words used for rhyming in a poem).

A typology of relations

By formulating a typology of relations, we can predict various kinds of structures. A relation may be characterized according to numerous criteria. We will distinguish somewhat arbitrarily between what we will call **formal** criteria (reflexive/transitive, directional/non-directional, monadic/polyadic relations, and others) and what we will call **semantic** criteria (comparative relations, such as identity, similarity, alterity, opposition, homologation; presential relations, such as presupposition and mutual exclusion; and others).

The following diagram illustrates a few possible structures. They were produced by combining some formal criteria (such as direction and the number of elements linked together) and some semantic criteria (opposition and presupposition, among others) by which we can characterize the relations.

In order to increase the representational capabilities of our diagram, for the structures that include three terms or more (from S6 to S11), we have chosen to leave the directional status of the relations undetermined (as indicated by the dotted lines). We can give a profusion of specifications for these undetermined relations, such as non-directional, unidirectional, and so forth. We can have a structure S6a, for example, in which B and C are linked to A by a relation of simple presupposition (unidirectional, therefore). Likewise, we can derive numerous other structures from the ones given here by adding terms or by adding semantic relations. For instance, if we add a relation of opposition between D and E in structure 10, we obtain a new structure, in which an opposition between two terms is linked to an opposition between three terms.[1]

Formal typologies

MONADIC/POLYADIC RELATIONS

Depending on the number of terms linked together, we refer to a relation as **monadic** (S1) or **polyadic** (S2, S3, S4 and S5 are dyadic; S6 and S7 are triadic; S8 and S9 are tetradic, S10 is pentadic, and so on).

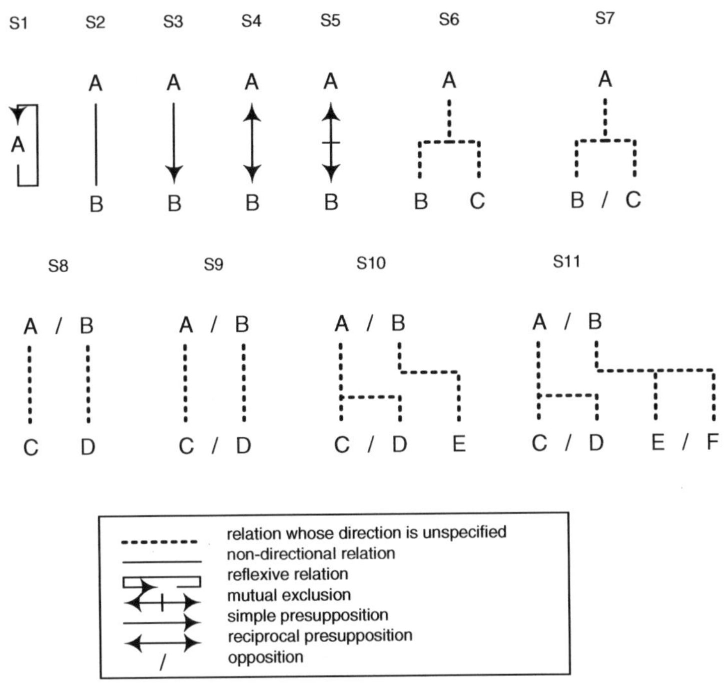

Figure 1.1 Diagram of some possible structures

REFLEXIVE/TRANSITIVE RELATIONS

A relation is said to be **reflexive** if it links a term to itself (S1). It is said to be **transitive** if it links a term to one (S2, for example) or more other terms.

To take a grammatical example, in "She dressed herself", "dressed" is a reflexive verb, in that the action of dressing starts and ends with "she", so to speak; conversely, in "She dressed her daughter", "dressed" is a direct transitive verb, since the action starts with "she" and crosses over to "her daughter", ending there. Another example is the poetic function – one of the functions of language as defined by Jakobson (see the chapter about Jakobson) – which consists of a reflexive relation in which the message refers to itself. All relations whose names use the prefixes "self-" and "auto-" are reflexive (self-definition, self-representation, autoreference, etc.). We will come back to this later.

NOTE: REFLEXIVE/TRANSITIVE RELATIONS AND MONADIC/POLYADIC RELATIONS

A monadic relation is necessarily reflexive (a single element is linked to itself); a polyadic relation is necessarily transitive (at the same time, it can be partly reflexive).

NON-DIRECTIONAL/DIRECTIONAL RELATIONS

A relation is said to be **non-directional** when it is established either by the facts or through methodological reduction (by intentional simplification, made explicit and justified) that it is not directed toward one of the terms involved (S2, for example).[2] A relation is said to be **directional** when it is said to go from one or more source terms to one or more target terms. It is said to be **unidirectional**, or asymmetrical, or non-reciprocal, if it goes from one or more source terms to one or more target terms, but not the reverse (S3, for instance); if the reverse is also true, then it is a **bidirectional**, or symmetrical, or reciprocal relation (S4 and S5, for instance).

Semantic typologies

We propose a methodological distinction between four basic kinds of semantic relations: (1) **comparative relations**: identity, similarity, alterity, opposition, homologation, etc.; (2) **temporal relations**: simultaneity and succession, etc.; (3) **presential relations**: simple presupposition, reciprocal presupposition and mutual exclusion; (4) **relations of inclusion**: set relations (involving classes and/or elements thereof), mereological relations (involving wholes and/or parts), and type-token relations (involving types and/or tokens); and (5) other semantic relations.

TEMPORAL AND SPATIAL RELATIONS

Simultaneity (or concomitance) is the relation between terms associated with the same initial and final temporal positions, and thus with the same temporal extent (duration). We can distinguish between strict simultaneity (1) (as in our definition) and the following kinds of **partial simultaneity** (2): **inclusive simultaneity** (2.1) (in which the first time period is entirely contained within the second, and is exceeded by it); inclusive simultaneity in which the initial positions coincide (2.1.1); inclusive simultaneity in which the final positions coincide (2.1.2); inclusive simultaneity in which the initial and final positions do not coincide (2.1.3); simultaneity-succession (2.2) (partial simultaneity and succession).

Succession (3) is the relation between terms in which the final temporal position of one term precedes the initial position of the other term. **Immediate succession** (3.1) implies that the initial position of the second term comes immediately after the final position of the first term; otherwise we have **mediate** or delayed succession (3.2). A distinction can be made between strict succession (3) (addressed in the preceding definitions) and simultaneity-succession (2.2), a form of partial simultaneity and succession.

The following diagram illustrates the main dyadic temporal relations.

These temporal relations have spatial correspondents, and thus, through generalization, they are relations of extent, whether the extent is spatial or temporal; but other spatial relations exist as well.

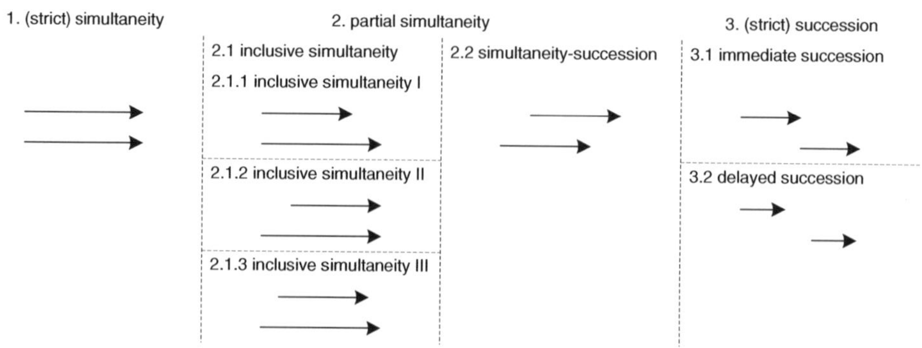

Figure 1.2 Dyadic temporal relations

PRESENTIAL RELATIONS

A **presential relation** is a relation in which the presence or absence of one term indicates the presence or absence of another term.

Presupposition is a relation in which the presence of one term (the presupposing term) indicates the presence of another term (the presupposed term). This type of relation can be described as "both . . . and . . ." (both one term and the other term). **Simple presupposition** (or unilateral dependence) is a unidirectional relation (A presupposes B, but not the reverse). For example, the presence of a wolf presupposes the presence of a mammal (since the wolf is a mammal), but the presence of a mammal does not presuppose the presence of a wolf (since the mammal could be a dog, for instance). **Reciprocal presupposition** (or interdependence) is a bidirectional relation (A presupposes B and B presupposes A. For example, the back side of a sheet of paper presupposes the front, and vice versa; in fact, there is no front without a back, and vice versa. We can represent simple presupposition by an arrow (A presupposes B would be written as: A → B, or B ← A) and reciprocal presupposition by an arrow with two heads (A ↔ B).

Mutual exclusion is the relation between two elements that cannot be present together. This type of relation can be described as "either . . . or . . ." (either one term or the other term). For example, in reality, a single element cannot be alive and dead at the same time (which does not necessarily apply in a semiotic act, such as a fantasy story).[3] We can represent mutual exclusion by using two arrows pointing toward each other (A →← B) or a vertical line (A | B).

If the presence of the terms is viewed not from a categorial standpoint (of all or nothing), but from a gradual (and thus quantitative) standpoint, two types of **correlation** may then be found between two terms. The correlation is said to be **direct** if (1) an increase in A leads to an increase in B and vice versa, and (2) a decrease in A leads to a decrease in B and vice versa. A direct correlation, thus, is a "more . . . more . . ." or "less . . . less . . ." type of correlation. For example, when the kinetic energy of a car increases, its speed also increases, and if its speed increases, its kinetic energy does, too.

The correlation is said to be **inverse** if (1) an increase in A leads to a decrease in B, and an increase in B leads to a decrease in A, and (2) a decrease in A leads to an increase in B and a decrease in B leads to an increase in A. An inverse correlation, thus, is a "more . . . less . . ." or "less . . . more . . ." type of correlation. For a constant quantity of gas at a constant temperature, pressure and volume are inversely correlated; i.e., if the volume is increased, the pressure decreases, and if the pressure increases, it is because the volume has decreased.

Direct and inverse correlation can be compared to reciprocal presupposition and mutual exclusion, respectively. That is, in a direct correlation, by raising the degree of presence of one term, I increase the presence of another;[4] in an inverse correlation, by raising the degree of presence of one term, I decrease the presence of another (or in other words, I increase its degree of absence). For more details, see the chapter on the tensive model.

A presential relation is not necessarily coupled with any **relation**, i.e., joining a cause to an effect, or a non-effect to a cause or the absence of a cause. The following is a presential relation not coupled with a causal relation: A few decades ago (perhaps it's still true), if you changed your altitude, you also changed your chances of dying of a lung disease; to be precise, the two variables were directly related. It would be wrong to think that altitude was harmful to the lungs; it was just that those who were seriously ill were advised to live in the mountains. The following is a presential relation coupled with a causal relation: An explosion is necessarily caused by an explosive substance, and it presupposes an explosive substance (but the explosive substance does not necessarily involve an explosion).

A presential relation is not necessarily coupled with any particular temporal relation: all presential relations can be combined with succession or simultaneity. For example, "wolf" presupposes "mammal", since a wolf is necessarily a mammal (but not the reverse: a mammal is not necessarily a wolf); therefore we can say that "wolf" and "mammal" are simultaneously present. (We can also take the view that there is a lack of temporal relation: a sort of atemporal logical present.) However, a bank robbery necessarily presupposes a previous stage, even reduced to the simplest terms, such as coming up with a plan (but the reverse does not hold: coming up with a plan does not necessarily imply that it will be carried out). This illustrates our view that presupposition is not correlated a priori with a temporal relation, despite the presence of the prefix "pre-"; however, in order to avoid violent semantic shocks, we can use the term "implication" when the presupposed element is temporally posterior (this is why we have said that coming up with a plan does not necessarily *imply* carrying it out). For examples of combinations of presential and temporal relations, see the chapter on the narrative program.

COMPARATIVE RELATIONS

Strictly speaking, identity is the relation between terms that have all identical characteristics. Alterity is the relation between terms that possess no identical characteristics. As we can see, this brings in the distinction between the whole (that which has characteristics) and the parts (the characteristics). Absolute identity does not exist for material objects: two "identical" sheets of paper will prove to be non-identical under a microscope. It is questionable whether it exists even for mental objects: two "identical" triangles with exactly the same spatial coordinates must be distinguishable (even just by "labeling" them "triangle A" and "triangle B"), which presumes some form of non-identity. In fact, identity in the strict meaning is certain only for ipsativity, an element's identity with itself (provided we subscribe to the thesis that a self-identity exists).

NOTE: COMPARABILITY

Given the possibility of strict identity and alterity, "**comparability**" is the name we will give to a relation of partial identity/alterity. **Similarity** is the term we will use for the sub-species of comparability in which identity prevails over alterity (but in which at least one unshared characteristic remains); it can be represented by the approximate equality sign (≅). Mathematically speaking, in minimum similarity we find 50 percent + 1 identities; in maximum similarity, we find 100 percent – 1 identities. **Dissimilarity** is the term we will use for the other sub-species of comparability, in which alterity prevails over identity (but in which at least one common characteristic remains); it can be represented by the unequal sign (≠). Mathematically speaking, in minimum dissimilarity we find 50 percent + 1 alterities; in maximum dissimilarity, we find 100 percent – 1 alterities. **Assimilarity** is the term we will use for the sub-species of comparability in which identity and alterity are equal, i.e., 50 percent identities and 50 percent alterities, mathematically.

Of course, through methodological reduction (i.e., intentional, made explicit and relevant), we can have identity in the broad sense and alterity in the broad sense. This reduction may be functional, in particular: it matters little which piece of blank paper I write on – they are "identical". In the broad sense, **identity** is then the relation between terms whose strength and/or number of identical characteristics predominate over the strength and/or number of non-identical characteristics. In the broad sense, **alterity** is the relation between terms whose strength and/or number of non-identical characteristics predominate over the strength and/or number of identical characteristics.

The relation of **similarity** can be placed in the vicinity of identity, as it is an attenuated form of identity. There is a distinction to be made between ordinary similarity and analogical similarity. The latter takes two forms: **quantitative analogical similarity** (as in mathematical proportions – 1 is to 4 as 10 is to 40) and **qualitative analogical similarity** (as in metaphors and homologies, either metaphorical or not – a woman is to a rose as the human order is to the plant order). We will treat homologation as a complex form of comparative relation. As we will see later, it involves relations of opposition, similarity, presupposition and mutual exclusion; however, on the whole, it can be regarded as a relation of similarity, or more accurately, of qualitative analogical similarity.

In theory, on the scale of alterity/identity, there is a zone where the alterities and identities between characteristics are equal in strength and/or number. In practice, no doubt, this neutral zone, defined by a relation that can be termed **identity-alterity**, emerges only rarely, since the adjacent zones of identity and alterity draw in the values likely to fit there by "rounding" them.

There is a distinction to be made between ordinary identity – or just identity – and **ipsative identity**, which is an element's self-identity (an element is identical to itself). **Transformation** is the process or operation whose outcome is to establish a comparative relation other than identity between what a term was and what it has become. The word also designates the result of this process. Transformation may be represented by an apostrophe, where *O'* indicates the transformation of an object *O*, for instance.

Opposition is a relation between terms that are more or less incompatible. We can distinguish two kinds of opposition: **contrariety** (e.g., true/false, life/death, rich/poor) and **contradiction** (e.g., true/not-true, life/not-life, rich/not-rich). For example, a contradiction occurs in *The treachery of images* by Magritte, a painting representing a pipe (pipe term) with the caption [translated]: "This is not a pipe". (non-pipe term). As we can see, the contradiction can be made between one semiotics and another. It can even occur within a non-linguistic semiotics, e.g., if a painting represents the same individual alive and dead. The **Aristotelian contradiction** presumes (1) the presence of a relation of contradiction (2) within the same object (3) seen from the same point of view. That is, supposing that empty and full form a contradiction, a piece of Swiss cheese (or a doughnut) is the scene of a relation of contradiction, but not an Aristotelian contradiction, since empty and full don't apply to the same parts of the cheese. Aristotelian contradictions often dissolve completely or partially through dissimilation, a differentiation of relationships. For example, "Your son [paternity] is not your son [property]" (Confucius), and "Black [emotional darkness] sun [physical brightness] of melancholy" (Nerval). Contrariety is a relation of opposition in which incompatibility is minimal, and contradiction is a relation of opposition in which incompatibility is maximal. Mutual exclusion can be seen as the most fundamental result of a relation of **incompatibility**, but it seems that not every case of mutual exclusion is built on an opposition (e.g., every time a character is chewing a carrot, he is not chewing a potato, and vice versa). **Compatibility** can take form as complementarity; but not every compatibility is a case of **complementarity**: e.g., two identical propositions (like "the earth is round") are compatible, but not complementary. Presupposition can be seen as the most fundamental result of a relation of complementarity (notably as a relation that, in a semiotic square, becomes established between not-true and false, to give an example).

In practice, how do we distinguish contrariety from contradiction, since not every contradiction is necessarily expressed with the privative "not-"? We will say that contradiction is categorial and that contrariety is gradual. For example, in classical logic, true and false are contradictories, since not-true equals false and not-false equals true; however, rich and poor are contraries, since not-rich does not necessarily equal poor, and not-poor does not necessarily equal rich.

Opposition can be viewed in several different ways: as a comparative relation at the same level as alterity and identity, or as a subspecies of alterity, or as a subspecies of similarity, among others. Actually, elements set in opposition are comparable, and therefore similar: for example, day and night are opposable because both are time spans in a day (a shared property). A forward slash represents a relationship of opposition between terms, such as life/death. The production of a contradictory term may be indicated by the logical negation symbol (e.g., ¬life means not-life).

In semiotics, when both terms of an opposition are co-present in a single semiotic act, it is termed a **contrast**. For example, for the opposition water/fire in "They get along like water and fire", we have contrast. We have **non-contrast** when one of the terms of the opposition remains virtual by not appearing in the semiotic act, e.g., "fire" in "I'm drinking water". Obviously, it is possible that none of the terms of the opposition will appear in the semiotic act, e.g., "I'm eating an apple". The contrast will vary in force depending on how close together the two terms are in the distribution of signs (if "life" is the first word of a linguistic sequence and "death" the second, the contrast will be forceful) and/or whether they relate ("this death-life") or do not relate to the same object ("this person is alive and this other one is dead"). For a more in-depth analysis of the notion of opposition, refer to the chapter on the semiotic square.

NOTE: COMPARATIVE RELATIONS AND RELATIONS OF COMPARISON

We must distinguish a comparative relation from the (metaphorical) **relation of comparison** that can be established within a semiotic act between a **comparing** term and a **compared** term. For instance, in Baudelaire's poem "The albatross", a metaphorical comparison is created between the poet (compared) and an albatross (comparing).

The following table gives the main comparative relations.

Table 1.1 Typology of comparative relations

RELATION FAMILY	*RELATION*		*ELEMENT 1*	*SYMBOL FOR THE RELATION*	*ELEMENT 2*	*EXAMPLE*
identity (broad sense)	self-identity (ipsativity)		A_1	=	A_1	this white = the same white
	(ordinary) identity		A_1	=	A_2	this white = the other white
similarity	(ordinary) similarity		A	≅	A'	this white ≅ the other white
	analogical similarity	quantitative				1 is to 4 as 10 is to 40 or, roughly, 1 is to 4 as 11 is to 40
		qualitative (including homologation)	A/B	::	C/D	rose is to woman as plant is to human
alterity (broad sense)	opposition	contrariety	A	/	B	white/black
		contradiction	A	/	¬A	white/not-white
	(ordinary) alterity		A	≠	C	white ≠ hippopotamus

RELATIONS OF INCLUSION

Three kinds of including/included states are distinguished here, along with the three families of relations and three families of operations that they define. **Mereological** or holistic inclusion involves **wholes** (such as a word) and **parts** (such as the letters in the word). **Set** inclusion involves **classes** (such as the class of words) and **elements** (such as a particular word). **Typological** inclusion involves **types** (models, such as the sonnet genre) and **tokens** (more or less complete manifestations of a model or type, such as a particular sonnet that is more or less regular).

NOTE: THE DIFFERENCE BETWEEN A CLASS AND A TYPE

What exactly is the difference between a type (e.g., the poetry genre) and a class (e.g., the class of poems)? Strictly speaking, a type is not a class because rather than *containing,* or *bringing together* the token units (the poems) governed by it, it generates them. We will distinguish between a class's **extension** (or enumeration) and its **intension** (or comprehension). For example, the extension of the class of positive whole numbers is: 1, 2, 3, 4, and so on. The intension – the definition of this class – is the principle that must be followed by the elements of this class, which in this case is to be a positive whole number. The distinction between a type and the **definition**, or intension, of a class may seem vague, but they are indeed two distinct things. Type and definition are necessarily abstract entities; token and element can be concrete (this poem as a representative of the poetry genre; this marble as a member of the class of the marbles in this bag) as well as abstract (this love, which is a manifestation of love; humiliation, a member of the class of negative emotions). The difference lies elsewhere. The type is an abstract "individual" that is the result of an induction made from what will become its tokens, relative to which it subsequently acquires the status of a **generative** entity (as opposed to **genetic**).[5] The definition of a class is not an individual entity, but rather an inventory of one or more properties, optionally accompanied by rules for evaluating the membership of the element. This does not keep us from optionally associating a type with a class. The prototype is the token that is considered by a specific observing subject to be the best and/or the most representative of the type (e.g., the apple or the orange for fruits); the other tokens are further removed (e.g., the star fruit and the lychee).

Including/included is a relative status, and including units can be included units elsewhere, and vice versa. That is, a part (e.g., the syllable as part of a word) may be seen as a whole (the syllable as a grouping of phonemes); an element (a mammal in the class of animals) may be seen as a class (a mammal as a class encompassing the class-elements Canidae, Felidae, etc.); and a token (e.g., the drama genre as a token of the generic field of theater) may be seen as a type (historical drama as a sub-genre of the drama generic type).

Of the various operations of including/included relations, there are a few that should be emphasized. **Partitioning** or **decomposition** is a (descending) operation that separates out the parts of a whole that was previously unanalyzed (e.g., by stipulating the semes that make up a given signified). **Classification** is an (ascending) operation by which we index/include an element in a class. The term "classification" also designates the result of classifying: a structure made up of classes and classified elements (e.g., the scientific taxonomies, such as vertebrate/invertebrate animals, etc.). **Typing** (or **categorization**) is an (ascending) operation by which a token is subsumed under a type, related to it, and recognized as its emanation or manifestation. These operations are also the basis of the relations. That is, there is a relation of decomposition between the whole and one of its parts, a relation of classification between the element and the class, and a relation of typing between the token and its type.

For each including/included relation, if we distinguish two including units, and two different included units belonging to each of them, we obtain the following relations: (1) between the two including terms; (2) between an including term and its own included term; (3) between an including term and an included term not its own; (4) between two included terms belonging to the same including term; (5) between two included terms, each belonging to a different including term (this relation gives rise to an indirect relation between the two including terms, just as the relation between including terms gives rise to an indirect relation between the terms included therein). Each of these relations can be followed in either direction. For example, the relation between an including term and its included term may go from including to included (**a descending relation**) and/or from included to including (**an ascending relation**). To these five dual relations, we can add the reflexive relation (6) between an including term and itself, and (7) between an included term and itself.

We will give an example using type relations established between genres and the texts that may belong to them. The typology is constructed as follows: (1) between one type and another (e.g., between two opposite textual genres); (2) between the type and its own token (e.g., between a genre and the text belonging to it); (3) between a type and a token other than its own (e.g., between a genre and a text belonging to the opposite genre); (4) between one token and another belonging to the same type; (5) between one token and another belonging to another type (e.g., intertextuality between two texts from different genres); (6) between a type and itself; (7) between a token and itself.

NOTE: INTERNAL (INTRA-) RELATIONS

The relations within a whole can be named using the prefix "intra-" (as in **intratextuality**, a relation between two parts of one text). A type or a class may be viewed from a mereological standpoint. In the case of a type, the parts can be the defining traits of the type (although it is not certain that a type is always equivalent to an inventory of traits, ranked or unranked). With the extension of a class, the parts are obviously the elements; with the intension of a class, i.e., its definition, the parts can be defining traits or parts of the rules for evaluating whether the elements fit within the definition. Relations within a type can be termed "intratype relations", and relations within a class can be termed "intraclass relations". Obviously, the tokens and the elements – as long as they are considered decomposable – may have relations between their parts; these can be called intra-token and intra-element relations, respectively.

On this basis, we will distinguish several sorts of relations involving text (meant in the broad sense of a semiotic act, such as a text, image, etc.) and generic type ("genre" is meant in the broad sense: genre, discourse, sub-genre, generic form, etc.): **autotextuality** (relation 7): a text is linked to itself; **intertextuality** (relation 4 or 5): a text is linked to another text or other texts; **architextuality** (type 2 or 3 relations): a text token is linked to a text type; **autogenericity** (a form of autotyping) (relation 6, not shown in the diagram that follows): a type is linked to itself; **intergenericity** (a form of intertyping) (relation 1, not shown in the diagram that follows): a text type is linked to another text type or other text types. These relations may be viewed as unidirectional, i.e., in one direction or the other (e.g., from the text to its genre or from the genre to the text), or as bidirectional (e.g., from the text to its genre and the reverse).

NOTE: INTERTEXTUALITY ACCORDING TO GENETTE

Genette (1982, p. 8) distinguishes five forms of **transtextuality**: (a) **paratextuality** (the relation a text has with its preface, for example); (b) **intertextuality** (citation, plagiarism, allusion); (c) **metatextuality** (text commentary by another party); (d) **hypertextuality** (when a text is grafted onto a prior text, not as commentary, but to transform it (a parody, misrepresentation, transposition), or imitate it (a pastiche, counterfeit, etc.), the former is the hypertext, and the latter is the hypotext); and (e) **architextuality** (the relation between a text and the classes to which it belongs, such as its genre). Depending on the status assigned to them, Genette's paratextual elements will participate in an intertextual relation (in the expanded sense that we give the term) if one views them as external to the text, or in an intratextual relation if one views them as being internal to the text, or in a strictly paratextual relation. The debate over the intra- or extra-textual nature of the title illustrates the various typological possibilities. For ourselves, we have defined intertextuality in a broader sense than Genette has, one that encompasses what he calls intertextuality, metatextuality, and hyper/hypotextuality; obviously, Genette's distinctions are nonetheless relevant. For details on intertextuality, see Hébert and Guillemette (2009).

NOTE: TEXTUALITY AND INTRATEXTUALITY

Autotextuality may take several forms: from the text as a whole to itself as a whole, from the whole to a part, from a part to the whole, and lastly, from a part to the same part. When the relation is between a part and another part of the same whole, we have **intratextuality**. Intertextuality and architextuality may be viewed either as including relations (established between wholes), or as included relations (established first between parts, and indirectly between wholes); in the latter case, the source term is viewed as part of the text, and the target term as part of another text (intertextuality) or part of a text type (architextuality). Moreover, there are included-including relations: e.g., part of a text may evoke the whole of another text or genre (such as the sentence (part) in a novel that says "I've read *Hamlet*" (whole).

Autotextuality is closely related to the other reflexive relations.

Since **autoreference** involves a referent – the third part that we often attribute to the sign, and which we generally define as "the thing we are talking about", the first two parts being the signifier and signified – it is at once broader than autotextuality (it can involve a sign of any range, and not necessarily a text or complete semiotic act) and also narrower (there is no doubt that not every autotextuality can be considered as an autoreference); if the word "reference" is meant in a broad sense of any referral of one unit to another (which can be itself), then autotextuality is a specific case of autoreference.[6]

Self-representation (an act represents itself in itself) and **self-reflexivity** (an act "reflects" on itself in itself) presuppose a relation of autotextuality: that which represents itself or reflects on itself necessarily refers to itself in doing so. Moreover, self-reflexivity presupposes a relation of self-representation: in order to "reflect on itself", the act must somehow present itself as the object of its own discourse. However, not all self-representation is automatically self-reflexive. For example, the Laughing Cow – the trademark for a well-known cheese – is self-represented in her earrings, but it is difficult to see this as any kind of reflection). Finally, autotextuality – or self-reference – may be found by itself, without self-representation or self-reflexivity. For example, the famous political slogan "I like Ike" attracts attention to itself by its sounds, without having any self-reflexivity or actual self-representation.

In summary: all self-reflexivity presupposes self-representation, and all self-representation presupposes autotextuality; however, not all autotextuality is self-representation, and not all self-representation is self-reflexivity The diagram overleaf illustrates the main textual relations. For the sake of simplicity, we have made the relations unidirectional, but they can also be viewed as unidirectional in the other direction or as bidirectional.

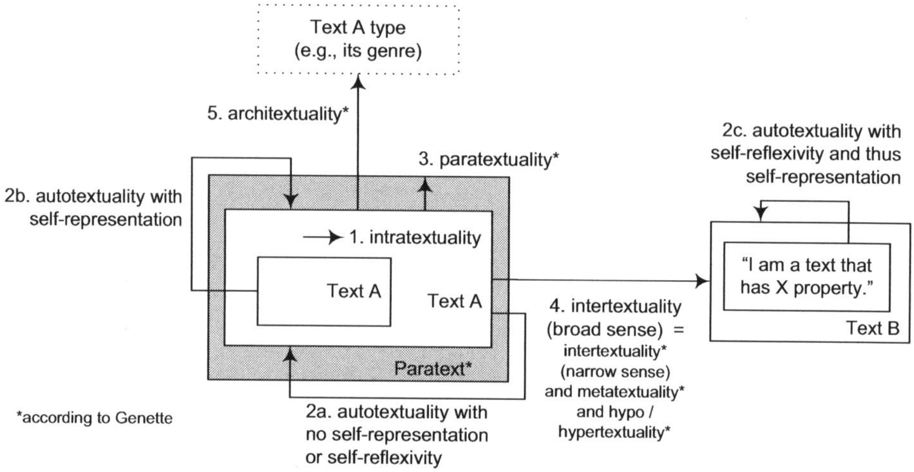

Figure 1.3 The main textual relations

OTHER SEMANTIC RELATIONS

We should mention some of the other possible semantic relations, including (1) **case** relations, which are used in semantic graphs (cause, effect, agent, patient, etc.; see the corresponding chapter), what we will call (2) **systemic** relations (symbolic, semi-symbolic and semiotic relations; see the chapter on figurative, thematic and axiological analysis); and what we will call **sign** relations (a symbol, index, or icon of something).

Categorial/incremental relations

Some relations are **categorial**: they either are or are not, with no possible intermediate position. For instance, in theory, two terms are either opposite or they are not; there is no possible intermediate position. Other relations may be considered from either a categorial or an **incremental** perspective. From a categorial standpoint, for example, there is a relation of mutual exclusion between two terms if and only if *each time* one of the terms appears, the other term is absent, and vice versa; from an incremental standpoint, there is mutual exclusion if this situation applies *nearly always*, *usually* or *most of the time* (the mathematical limit being half of the cases plus one. Thus, from an incremental perspective, a homologation does not fall apart because one of the elements of the opposition sometimes appears without its counterpart from the other opposition in the homology. Moreover, quantitative considerations are not the only ones, and in order to determine whether a relation is active or not, one must consider the quality, or significance, of the elements that express it.

Decidability, the observing subject, and time

All properties, relations or otherwise, are either **decidable** – e.g., we may judge that two terms are identical – or **undecidable** – e.g., we may not be able to say whether two terms are identical or not.

All properties can vary according to the **observing subject** and **time**. The same applies to relations established between terms. This means that: (1) from one observer to another, different or even incompatible relations may be established between the same terms, rightly or wrongly; (2) the nature of the terms or their interaction may change over time; or (3) they can remain the same while the knowledge we have about them changes (a particular character may view particular terms as linked by a relation of identity, and then realize his mistake and change his mind). In a literary text, the observers can be the following, among others: the real or empirical author, the implied author (the impression that the text gives of its author), the narrator, the narratee, the character, the implied reader (the impression that the text gives of its expected and unexpected readers), the real or empirical reader. For details on this typology of observing subjects, see the chapter on thymic analysis.

The structure of homologation

At least one other device beside homologation could rightfully have fit into this chapter on structures: the semiotic square (which deals with relations of opposition and implication). Instead, we have chosen to devote a separate chapter to the semiotic square, and here we will examine homologation in more detail. For another analysis with homologations in it, consult the chapter on figurative, thematic and axiological analysis.

Homologation defined

Homologation is the relation between (at least) two pairs of opposite elements, such that for two oppositions A/B and C/D, one can say that A is (usually or always) to B as C is (usually or always) to D.[7] The formal notation of a homology is written in the following manner: A : B :: C : D. For example, in our culture, white : black :: life : death :: positive : negative (white is to black as life is to death, as positive is to negative, and so on). The following notation can also be used: A/B :: C/D.

NOTE: SOME DIFFICULTIES WITH ANALYSES USING HOMOLOGATION

When identifying a homologized structure, there are some common pitfalls to avoid:

1 Uncoupling the terms in an opposition (such as life/positive :: death/negative instead of life/death :: positive/negative).
2 Inverting the relations between terms (such as positive/negative :: death/life instead of positive/negative :: life/death).
3 Bringing oppositions together without checking and demonstrating that there is homologation; in particular, concluding that an opposition Z is homologized with an opposition X just because Z is homologized with Y and Y is homologized with X.
4 Unintentionally using "compound oppositions", we might call them, whose terms define more than one opposition. For example, the pairs gain/loss or excess/lack would be preferable to a less precise opposition such as profusion/loss.
5 Unintentionally confusing synthetic approaches (e.g., governing the opposition cave/moon) and analytic approaches (governing the opposition low/high in which the objects cave and moon are participants). In other words, the homologation of characteristics (low/high) should not be confused with the indirect homologation of the elements that possess these characteristics (cave and moon).

The constituent relations of homologation

We shall say that a relation of similarity is established between the terms of one opposition of a homology and the corresponding terms of the other opposition (between A and C and between B and D). In addition, a relation of qualitative analogical similarity is established between the two oppositions themselves. Lastly, a relation of simple or reciprocal presupposition is established between the corresponding terms. For example, there is a relation of simple presupposition if each time the theme of life comes up in a text, it is put in a positive light, but that other themes besides life are associated with a positive value. (In other words, life necessarily presupposes a positive value, but a positive value does not necessarily presuppose life). There is a relation of reciprocal presupposition between life and positive if life is positive and nothing else is. Furthermore, the association life-positive excludes the association life-negative, and the association death-negative excludes the association death-positive.

Homology and counter-homology

We will use the term **counter-homology** for a homology that reverses the terms of one of the two constituent oppositions of a homology. For example, a text in praise of suicide values death and devalues life; it takes the opposite view from the usual homology, and transforms the homology life : death :: positive : negative into a counter-homology life : death :: negative : positive.

A homology and its counter-homology may belong to identical or different **system levels**. We will distinguish particularly between the following system levels for texts, and with adjustments for other semiotic acts, from the higher to the lower levels: (1) the **dialect**: the language system; (2) the **sociolect**: the usage of a dialect and other standards specific to a particular social practice (rather than a particular social group), which defines the discourses (literary, religious, etc.) and genres (novel, poetry, etc.) of semiotic acts; (3) the **idiolect**: the particular usage of a dialect, a sociolect and other, strictly idiolectal regularities, which defines the style of a producer. (4) the **textolect**: the particular usage of the three aforementioned systems and other, strictly textolectal regularities in a particular semiotic act (e.g., a particular text by a particular author); and lastly, (5) the **analect**: the elements of a semiotic act that don't come from any system. The minimal condition for a unit to be systematic in nature is to be repeated at least twice. For example, while a topos (or sociotopos) – such as being absent-minded from falling in love – is not a dialectal unit, it is found in at least two texts (or semiotic acts) by different authors. While an idiotopos is not a dialectal or sociolectal unit, it is a semantic unit found in at least two texts by the same author. While a textotopos is not a dialectal, sociolectal or idiolectal unit, it is repeated at least twice in a single text by a single author. An anatopos is a semantic unit that is found just once in a single text by a single author.

Homology and counter-homology are symmetrical categories. However, we can reserve the term "counter-homology" for marked homologies, i.e., less frequent ones (whether they come from the same system level as the homology or a different system level). For example, the homology virtue : vice :: positive : negative, which is very common in literature, has a counter-homology, virtue : vice :: negative : positive in libertine literature, particularly in the works of the Marquis de Sade.

Application: *The battle of the Argonne* by Magritte

The battle of the Argonne (1959) by Magritte brings together – in a polemical manner, if we are to believe the title, which evokes a battle, or a group of famous battles of the first world war – two opposite objects, as shown by the homologized oppositions presented in the table opposite. The characteristics listed in this table relate to a point of comparison (e.g., the characteristic "on the left" relates to the point "horizontal position").[8]

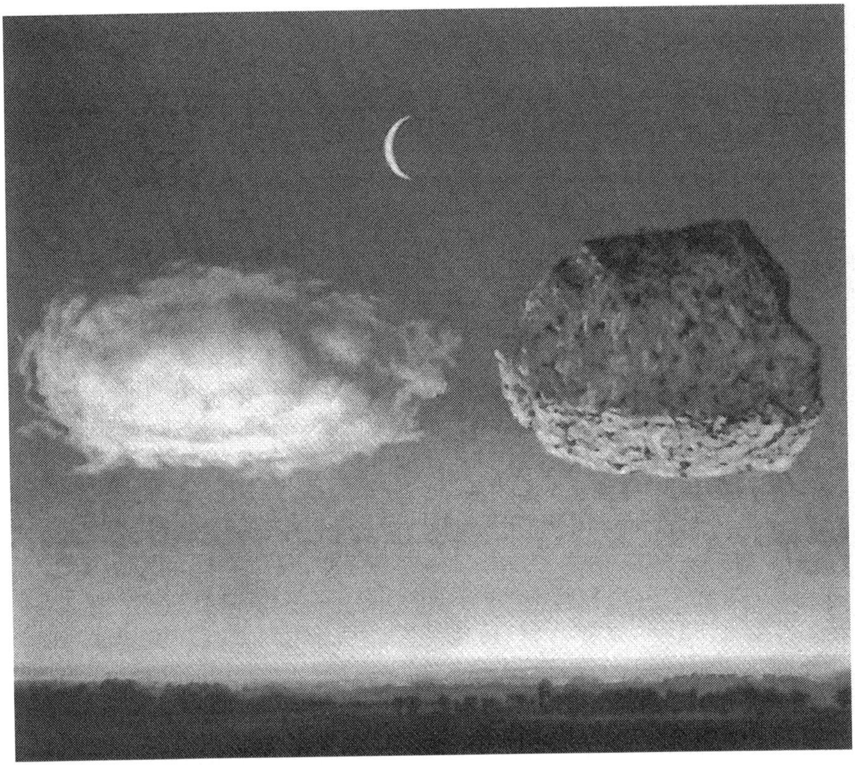

Figure 1.4 The battle of the Argonne

Source: Magritte (1959)

Table 1.2 The main homologized oppositions in *The battle of the Argonne*

		CLOUD	ROCK
	POINT	CHARACTERISTIC	CHARACTERISTIC
1	Horizontal position	on the left	on the right
2	Matter	gaseous	solid
3	Weight	light	heavy (normally)
4	Form	wispy	chunky
5	Outline	indistinct	distinct
6	Color	mostly white	mostly gray
7	Properties	normal	abnormal (a levitating rock)
8	Realm inhabited	sky	earth (normally)

Although numerous oppositions keep the main figures of the painting far removed from each other, what paradoxically emerges from the comparison is the astounding overall resemblance between a cloud and a rock, simply from surrealistically suspending the heaviness inherent to the rock.[9] The results of the analysis depend on the objective and the degree of precision of the analysis. Since the objective was to identify and homologize oppositions, in order to increase the contrast between the two objects being analyzed, we have said that the rock is normally heavy and belongs to the earthly realm. These properties are virtualized in the painting – neutralized, but not absent, as the surrealistic effect of the painting testifies – in favor of the opposite properties in common with the cloud. Each time, we have selected the degree of precision most suited to our objective: for example, while a detailed analysis would classify the cloud as wispy and the rock as chunky, a more general analysis would view them as similar elliptical shapes.

The moon at the top of the canvas seems to be mediating between the cloud and the rock[10]: for one, it is in a somewhat intermediate horizontal position; For another, it is simultaneously white on the left – just as the cloud is generally white and located on the left – and dark on the right (so dark that it merges with the sky) – just as the rock is generally dark and located on the right. The moon and the rock have other shared properties: the moon is also a mass of levitating rock with an irregular surface; like the moon, and like the cloud on the canvas, this rock has a lit side (toward the earth) and a dark side (toward the sky). While the moon has only two levels of luminosity – light and dark – the cloud and the rock have three: actually, the part facing us has an intermediate level of light; in their luminosity, then, the cloud and the rock reproduce the triadic nature of the three-figured composition within themselves.

Notes

1 Oppositions are not always dyadic, and one sometimes finds triadic and tetradic oppositions, among others; for instance, in French Canadian rural legend, the three following spaces form a triadic opposition: forest / countryside / city (see the chapter on figurative, thematic and axiological analysis).

2 Can we consider a non-directional relation to be equivalent to a bidirectional relation? Probably not. Admittedly, if A is linked to B, this implies that B is linked to A; but, to use an electrical metaphor, this simply means that the terms are in contact, not that there is necessarily any "energy" running through this contact in either direction.

3 Alternation is a relation of mutual exclusion in which one of the terms must necessarily be present (the absence of all the terms is excluded); the terms are said to be alternating. We will give an example involving two terms, but remember that an alternation can involve more than two terms: in a realist text, if a human being cannot be alive and dead at the same time, (s)he *must* be one or the other.

4 As for simple presupposition, it can be seen as a correlation that is categorial (the element's presence has a status of 0 or 1, with no other possibility) and asymmetrical (operating in just one direction).

5 We will give a simple example of generative and genetic viewpoints: If we isolated the world view governing the production of a work of literature, we would be isolating a hypothetical, abstract form that generated the work; if we studied the notes and the rough drafts for this work, we would be looking from a genetic viewpoint.

6 Greimas and Courtés (1982, p. 259) distinguish four types of "*références*": (1) those established within the utterance (e.g., in syntactic anaphorae ("he" anaphorizing "soldier" in "The soldier stood up. He took my hand.") and semantic anaphorae ("do" anaphorizing "sew" in "Are you going to sew it? – Yes, I'll do it."); (2) those established between the utterance and the enunciation (through deictics); (3) those existing between two discourses (for which they suggest the term "intertextuality" instead); (4) those established between the utterance and the natural world. Certainly a more suitable term to encompass these various unidirectional and other relations is "referral" [Fr. "renvoi"]. One of the acceptations for the [French] term "*référence*" seems to correspond to Greimas's and Courtés's fourth type of reference, but not all theories of reference view it or view it exclusively as referring to the objects of the natural world. For *référence* [Fr.] strictly speaking, we can use the term "reference" or, to avoid polysemy, the term "referentiation."

7 According to Greimas and Courtés (1982, p. 144), in a homologation, the relation between A and B on the one hand, and between C and D on the other, "is identical and can be recognized as one of the elementary logical relations (contradiction, contrariety, complementarity)." For example, if I say that life is to death as not-life is to not-death, the relation between the two oppositions is contradiction. It is at least clear that homologation has as its basis a relation of similarity between the corresponding terms of each opposition and between the oppositions themselves. According to Rastier (1997, p. 38): "Matrices of homologation play an eminent role in the methodology of the social sciences (in Dumézil and Lévi-Strauss, for example): they found in fact qualitative analogical reasoning." We should add that quantitative analogical reasoning is most rigorously manifested in the mathematical proportions that make the rule of three work (e.g., 10 is to 100 as 100 is to 1000).

8 In logical terms, a point is a subject (what we are talking about) to which we apply a characteristic, which is a predicate (what we are saying about the subject); a characteristic and the point to which it relates together form a predicate applied to a subject, which here is the cloud or the rock. The relation between the compared object and a point of comparison is a mereological relation, more precisely, a relation between a whole (e.g., the cloud) and one of its parts (e.g., its horizontal position).

9 The painting can be viewed as a rhetorical figure: metaphorical comparison; note that a commonly used function of comparison, especially surrealistic comparison, is to bring out the previously unnoticed resemblance between two very disparate elements.

10 This mediation by the moon may be compared to that of the bottle-carrot present in another of Magritte's works, *The explanation* (1952). It is analyzed in the chapter on the semiotic square.

2 Operations of transformation[1]

Summary

Operations, along with relations and terms, are the units that make up a structure. An operation is a process, an action by which an operating subject characterizes or transforms an object (whether the object is a relation, a term, or an operation). Operations of characterization isolate properties of an object by decomposition (mental), classification, typing or categorization, comparison, and other processes. Operations of transformation (1) produce objects (through creation ex nihilo, emanation from a type, or construction from materials known to be pre-existing), (2) destroy them (through annihilation, i.e., with no remaining trace, or through complete deconstruction) or (3) transform them. Continuance is what we have when a given operation (of either characterization or transformation) does not occur. (From a dynamic standpoint, either the operation lacks strength or a counterforce of equal or greater strength is applied.) If one superposes three typologies of transformational operations (Groupe μ's, Zilberberg's and Rastier's), a typology with nine operations is obtained. Firstly, there will be six operations of extensity (on substances): (1) addition (or blending: e.g., A becomes A, B); (2) deletion (or sorting: e.g., A, B becomes A); (3) substitution (e.g., A, B becomes A, C); (4) permutation (e.g., A, B becomes B, A); (5) displacement (e.g., an eye displaced onto the belly of a monster) and (6) continuance (e.g., A, B remains A, B). Secondly, there will be three operations of intensity (on intensities): (7) increase (e.g., from low to high intensity), (8) decrease (e.g., from high to low intensity), and (9) continuance (e.g., an intensity that remains medium).

Theory

Operations of characterization and transformation

Operations, along with **relations** and **terms**, are the units that make up a **structure** (see the chapter on structural relations). An **operation** is a process, an action by which an operating subject characterizes or transforms an object (whether the object is a relation, a term, or an operation). **Operations of characterization** isolate properties of an object by decomposition (mental), classification, typing or categorization, comparison, and other processes. **Operations of transformation** (1) produce objects (through creation ex nihilo, emanation from a type, or construction from materials known to be pre-existing), (2) destroy them (through annihilation, i.e., with no remaining trace, or through complete deconstruction) or (3) transform them. Operations of transformation introduce dynamism into a structure. Continuance is what we have when a given operation (either characterizing or transforming) does not occur. (From a dynamic standpoint, either the operation lacks strength or a counterforce of equal or greater strength is applied.) Since the result of continuance is to not change the object (or in partial continuance, to not change it completely), it maintains the ipsative relation between the object and itself, with the object remaining equal (or partially equal) to itself. Henceforth, when we talk about operations of transformation, unless we state otherwise, we will include continuance, even though continuance, in this context, is actually a non-transformation.

A metatypology of operations of transformation

With a brief discussion of their distinguishing features, three typologies of transformational operations will be merged (which is an operation of transformation): (1) Groupe μ (or Groupe mu, 1982, pp. 45–49; Klinkenberg, 1996, pp. 259–361), whose typology identifies addition, deletion, substitution, and permutation; (2) Zilberberg (2000, 2006), whose typology distinguishes blending, sorting, increase and decrease, and proposes four degrees of blending/sorting: separation, contiguity, mixing and merging; and (3) Rastier (1987, p. 83), whose typology distinguishes insertion, deletion, insertion-deletion, and continuance. Each of the typologies is supplemented by being superposed with the others, producing a metatypology. In addition, we will fill out the metatypology in various other ways.

As follows are the operations we have selected in merging the three typologies; we have excluded some operations, and added one: displacement (although implicit, it is new).

Operations of extensity (on substances)

1 **Addition** or blending: switch → switcharoo, merde → merdre (Alfred Jarry);
2 **Deletion** or sorting: I am → I'm;
3 **Substitution** (type 1 coordinated deletion-addition): do the dishes → do the gishes;
4 **Permutation** (type 2 coordinated deletion-addition): infarction → infraction;
5 **Simple displacement** (simple deletion-addition): an eye displaced onto the belly (see our application in following sections);
6 **Extense continuance**: merde → merde (in a text by Jarry, instead of "merdre").

Operations of intensity (on intensities)

7 **Increase** (intensity): rich → super-rich
8 **Decrease** (intensity): blue → bluish
9 **Intense continuance**: poor → poor (for someone attempting to become rich).

Details of the metatypology

It is not the point of this text on applied semiotics to explain the particulars of the metatypology, the conceptual and terminological choices we have made, or the numerous additions we have planned.[2]

It will serve the purpose to give just the most crucial explanations for understanding and applying the theory.

Addition/deletion and substitution/permutation

Substitution can be viewed as a coordinated deletion-addition: one element is actually deleted and replaced by adding another. Similarly, permutation can be seen as another form of coordinated deletion-addition: an element located in a position X is deleted, and added in a position Y. Consequently, addition and deletion are the basic operations from which substitution and permutation are derived. This means that simple operations can be combined, either simultaneously or successively, to create a structure.

Addition/deletion and blending/sorting

In our view, the opposition addition/deletion is equivalent to the opposition blending/sorting. Of course, the word "addition" evokes an asymmetrical operation, unlike the word "blending" (with addition, X is added to Y, but not Y to X). But our view is that the operations of addition and deletion are a priori neither symmetrical nor asymmetrical. That is, deletion can be symmetrical, as in the breakdown of an atom into its constituents, or asymmetrical, as in the deletion of a letter from a word. The label "sorting" implies a selection, of course, and therefore a classification (or typing or categorization), but sorting should simply be viewed a priori as an un-blending. Whatever the case, addition and deletion presuppose classification, except in random blending and sorting, but even so, these operations also classify, even if they do it by no criterion other than chance.

Intense substitution, permutation and displacement

Intense addition and deletion correspond respectively to increase and decrease. We are not including intense substitution, permutation or displacement, as they can be seen more readily as specific extense operations that apply to intensities as substances (e.g., as semantic features, or semes). For example, if one replaces "very polite" with "not very polite", this can be understood as an extense substitution of the feature (seme) /low intensity/ for the feature /high intensity/. It should be noted that any increase or decrease can be viewed as an operation of substitution, of a higher intensity for a lower intensity or a lower intensity for a higher intensity, respectively.

Extensity/intensity as a relative concept

As in any description, depending on the observing subjects (and on the time of observation, of course), descriptions of intensity and extensity for the same phenomenon can be identical (an interpretive consensus) or different (an interpretive conflict).

The intense or extense nature of any given phenomenon is not absolute, but relative; it can vary according to the universes being described and the observers who found or "inhabit" them – observers whose point of view is being reported. We will use a genocidal person as an example. Compared to a normal human being, does he result from the addition (of cruelty, for example) and/or deletion (of pity, for example) of properties, or from a variation in the intensity (through increase and/or decrease) of properties that any average man possesses (e.g., an increase in cruelty and a correlated decrease in pity)? The answer to this depends on the observer's conception of a human. For Freud, the difference between a normal person and a psychotic person is a matter of varying degrees, not varying natures, and he would no doubt opt for an intense conception of the genocidal person. To take another example, a giant (such as we will see in our application) can be understood as either the result of adding organic matter or of intensifying size. This means that, ultimately, extensities can be "converted" into intensities and vice versa.

Displacement and placement

One of the operations that apparently Groupe μ did not directly envisage is **simple displacement**. A permutation presupposes a coordinated double displacement at minimum (e.g., A, B becomes B, A; where B is now in position 1, and A in position 2). While a displacement of the graphemes (letters, roughly), or phonemes is necessarily a permutation, the same does not necessarily apply in semiotic acts that are not a priori temporal and linear, such as pictorial ones. It is also far from certain that permutation occurs in all displacements of phonemes or graphemes (or more generally, in displacements in the temporal semiotics). For example, if the word "End" is placed at the beginning of a novel rather than at the end, one will sense the underlying displacement, but certainly not the permutation, i.e., the shifting of all the words that follow.

A displacement implies a source space and a target space. Many deletions, additions, and substitutions presuppose displacements (e.g., a marble is deleted from this bag and added into another, or X's heart is replaced with Y's heart, and X's heart is discarded); but others do not (death can be seen as the deletion of life, with no displacement). Both spaces can be situated within tokens (as in our example of a heart transplant) or one of them – the source space – can be within a type. For example, adding an eye to the palm of the hand of a token Tibetan deity (such as Tara) can be considered as an addition with displacement with respect to the humanoid type, in which eyes are located only on the face.

A displacement presupposes a **placement**, with "placement" simply being another name for "**arrangement**" (see our chapter on rhythm and arrangement). A placement may be the result of a prior displacement, or not: e.g., the letter that I have put in this word was not located elsewhere previously.

Continuance

While studying the potential semic transformations between a type signified (the model) and its token (the complete or to some degree deviant manifestation of the model), Rastier predicted the more or less exact counterpart of three operations defined by Groupe μ : addition, deletion[3] and substitution. Rastier's typology excludes permutation, which is not relevant, because the semes within a single signified have no position. As for continuance, it occurs when the token signified is completely identical to the type signified (when the meaning of a morpheme in context in a text is exactly the same as the meaning of the morpheme in language). When a token arises from a type, there is the addition of the token, of course; however, if this token is identical to the type, it is a continuance (or perfect reduplication), because it does not constitute a transformation of the type. We will return to this point later.

Rastier's typology differs from the other two in that it is not general. We have considerably generalized the notion of continuance. For Rastier, continuance is in fact the production of a token identical to the type from which it emanates, as we have just seen. In addition, Rastier's transformations are limited to those between a type sememe (the signified of a type morpheme) and a token that belongs to it (this is a type x → token x relation). However, there is no rule against extending them to other kinds of semiotic elements (even though, in our opinion, a continuance always involves a type-token relation as well, as we will see), and to other kinds of relations between types and tokens: type x → type y, type x ← token of x, etc. We will look at a typology of these relations in the next section.

Additionally, we are adding the distinction between marked continuance and **unmarked continuance**. "**Marked continuance**" is what we will call the operation by which a unit which, according to the expectations (founded or not) of an observing subject, should have been transformed, but was not. This means that the unit did not match the target type associated with it by the observer. A type is a standardized form defined within a system. We will distinguish the following system levels in particular, for texts, and with adjustments for the other semiotic acts. Going from the higher levels to the lower levels (we are enriching a typology introduced by Rastier, 1989): (1) the **dialect** (the language system); (2) the **sociolect**: the usage of a dialect and other standards specific to a particular social practice (rather than a particular social group), which defines the discourses (literary, religious, etc.) and genres (novel, poetry, etc.) of semiotic acts; (3) the **idiolect**: the particular usage of a dialect, a sociolect and other, strictly idiolectal regularities, which defines the style of a producer. (4) the **textolect**: the particular usage of the three aforementioned systems and other, strictly textolectal regularities in a particular semiotic act (e.g., a particular text by a particular author); and lastly, (5) the **analect**: the elements of a semiotic act that do not arise from any system. The minimal (but not necessarily sufficient) condition for a unit to be systematic is to be repeated at least twice.

We will give a simplified example. When Jarry writes "merdre" instead of "merde" in the play *Ubu roi* the first time, he creates a discrepancy between the token ("merdre") and the type ("merde"), which we expected it to match. This discrepancy is obviously produced with respect to the dialectal system, since the morpheme "merdre" (or "merdr-", to be more exact) does not exist in the language. When the second "merdre" occurs, the observer can consider that this unit is part of the textolect, i.e., the text's system. He will assume – rightly – that the third token will match the type "merdre" (actually, he could make this assumption for the second token as soon as the first token occurs). When he reads *Ubu cocu* by the same author and finds a first occurrence of "merdre", he will conclude that this unit is defined as a type in the author's idiolect. Ultimately, each "merdre" of Jarry's is the result of an addition to the dialectal unit, but is a continuance of the textolectal or idiolectal unit. Now if, in some other *Ubu* sitting in a dusty attic, Jarry had written a thunderous "merde" (instead of "merdre"), this would be a case of deletion with respect to the idiolectal unit, but marked continuance with respect to the dialectal unit. Obviously, the issue of marked continuance would not arise in the case of ordinary French folks writing "merde" in their diaries (especially before Jarry's time), since this unit is expected. Henceforth, unless we indicate otherwise, we will use the word "continuance" by itself to mean "marked continuance".

Continuance takes a variety of specific forms, depending on which transformational operations have not taken place. Thus, continuance might be: non-addition, non-deletion, non-substitution, non-permutation, non-displacement, non-increase, non-decrease (or non- any of the sub-species we will look at, such as non-separation and non-contiguity), and so forth. Clearly, for any one object, a specific form of continuance may have occurred, but not some other.

A problem arises in the typology of operations that has to do with the relations and operations between a type and its token. Strictly speaking, a type is never identical to a token, since they do not have the same status. So technically, a type cannot be said to be conserved [continuance], or reduplicated, or transformed in its token. The same principle applies to operations in the opposite direction, from the token to the type. Whether "identical" or transformed, a token is an emanation from its type. This being the case, we can use methodological reduction (intentional, relevant simplification, explicitly stated) to talk about a type that is conserved, reduplicated (wholly or partially), or transformed in its token, depending on the circumstances.

Types and tokens

The main operations of transformation are applied to one or more **source elements** in order to obtain one or more **target elements**. Target and source elements can correspond to **types** (models) or **tokens** (more or less complete manifestations of the model). Operations can thus act: (1) within a token; (2) within a type; (3) from a type to its token; (4) from the token to its type; (5) from one token to another (of the same type or of a different type); (6) from one type to another. We will give a few examples with patterns, or rhythmic structures. (For more details, see the chapter on rhythmic analysis). The type pattern can simply be kept as is in the token (or from a different point of view, perfectly reduplicated in the token): a particular text might manifest a perfect chiasmus (A, B, B, A). But the type pattern can also be transformed in its token: in A, B, C, B, A, the C can be seen as a delaying element inserted into a chiasmus. The token can be seen as the site of an internal transformation operation: for example, a particular token chiasmus can be seen as the result of a reduplicative addition through reverse permutation (the A, B is followed by the B, A). Clearly, operations can act between a type pattern and another type pattern. For example, groupings (e.g., A, A, B, B) can be seen as the result of a permutation starting from an embedding (the two embedded Bs are simply permuted with the second A in the source pattern A, B, B, A).

Generative/genetic perspectives

We will distinguish two perspectives on production: genetic and generative. The **generative perspective** explains the token as an emanation from a type, or model, which is either complete (when continuance or reduplication is applied) or transformational (when other transformation operations are applied). The **genetic perspective** conceives the unit as the result of operations on this unit or on parent units.

For example, from a generative perspective, with respect to the type "woman", a siren is produced by substituting the lower body of a fish for the lower body of a woman. From a genetic perspective, we might say the siren is produced through the mating of siren parents, or of one human and one fish parent, or through some very special genetic evolution. Although the meaning of the word "genetic" is also biological in our last example (as in "genetic engineering"), this is not usually the case. For example, a hammer is genetically produced by adding a handle to a head. Although a type is necessarily the starting point for emanations, and thus for generative acts, it can also undergo genetic processing. For example, by producing a male siren and some reverse male and female sirens (i.e., with a fish upper body and a human lower body) the painter Magritte transformed the type "siren", creating new types that emanate tokens.

Sub-species of operations

We have already looked at some sub-species of operations for continuance (non-addition, non-deletion, etc.). Obviously, other sub-species are identifiable for other operations, which we do using various criteria. Here we will present some other typologies of sub-species.

Sub-Species Proposed by Groupe µ

We can distinguish **partial deletion** (e.g., an apheresis, such as "phone" for "telephone") and **complete deletion** (e.g., deletion of a whole word).

We can distinguish **simple addition** (or singulative addition, e.g., epenthesis, such as "merdre" for "merde") and **repetitive addition** (or iterative addition). We can add to Groupe µ's sub-species by distinguishing between addition by repeating an element already present (e.g., modifying "changes" to "ch-ch-ch-ch-changes" (David Bowie)) and addition by repeating the added element (e.g., modifying "baby" to "little baby"). A repeated element is necessarily a **reduplication** (a copy) of another. We propose adding **negative (or oppositive) addition**. This would be the addition of an element that is the opposite of one already present (e.g., modifying "a good deed" to "a bad good deed" (Balzac)). Contrary to Groupe µ, we take the view that negative operations can occur, not just in substitution, but also in addition and even in permutation. Moreover, we would say that negative operations can apply not just to signifieds, but also to signifiers (for example, in traditional French versification, by adding a feminine rhyme to a masculine rhyme by replacing one with the other, or by permuting them).

We will distinguish between **partial substitution** (e.g., "do the gishes" for "do the dishes", in which a single grapheme is replaced) and **complete substitution** (e.g., "body" for "corpse", in which all of the graphemes are replaced). **Negative substitution** (or oppositive substitution) consists in replacing an element with its opposite (e.g., "What a *great* idea!" instead of "What a *bad* idea!" (irony)).

We will distinguish **any permutation** (e.g., an anagram, such as "lives" for "Elvis" = letters 2, 4, 3, 1, 5 for 1, 2, 3, 4, 5) and **permutation by inversion** (e.g., "amor" for "Roma" = letters 4, 3, 2, 1 for 1, 2, 3, 4). Negative permutation consists in permuting opposite elements (e.g., changing "big little man" to "little big man").

Addition, deletion, substitution, permutation (more generally, displacement and placement), and continuance can also be characterized according to where the operation is concluded. In this case, the operation is described as initial, medial, or final (occurring at the beginning, in the middle, or at the end of a word, respectively).

Sub-species proposed by Zilberberg

The distinction addition/deletion can be considered from an **incremental perspective** or from a **categorial perspective** (an element is added or deleted, or it is not, with no intermediate position). But this perspective says nothing about the **intensity of the blending/sorting** operation. In fact, different **degrees of blending/sorting** must be distinguished. Zilberberg proposes a scale with four intensities; but of course, there is no reason why we could not invent typologies with fewer or more degrees. The diagram opposite illustrates naïvely, as Zilberberg put it (2000, p. 11), the four degrees of blending/sorting. (The arrows indicate the direction of blending; they must be reversed for the sorting operations).

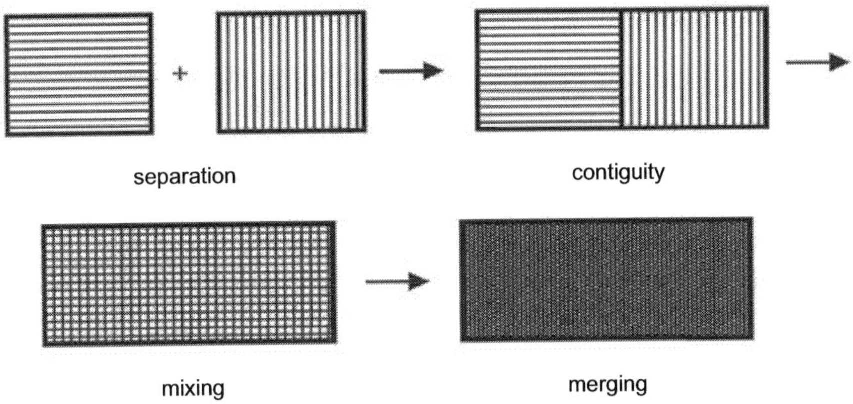

Figure 2.1 The four degrees of blending/sorting according to Zilberberg

The four degrees of blending/sorting do not act a priori on any specific kind of elements. For example, the elements can be material (e.g., atoms) or immaterial (e.g., semes). So even though a graphic metaphor was used to illustrate the degrees, the elements involved clearly are not necessarily graphic or even spatial.

From a static point of view, four degrees of blending/sorting can be distinguished: **separation**, **contiguity**, **mixing**, and **merging**. These elements are organized into super-contraries (a strong opposition between tonic or powerful elements) – separation and merging – and sub-contraries (a weak opposition between atonic, or weak, elements) – contiguity and mixing. The opposition super-contraries/subcontraries was proposed by Zilberberg (2006). It should be distinguished from the opposition contraries/subcontraries found in the semiotic square (see the chapter on the semiotic square).

In **absolute merging**, the source elements have "disappeared", at least in appearance: (1) through perceptive inability (e.g., no one can see the atoms that constitute an object); (2) through unintentional interpretive reduction (e.g., by someone who does not know that water is made up of oxygen and hydrogen); (3) through intentional interpretive reduction (e.g., pretending as though meringue is not a merging of egg whites and sugar, but an object with no "parts"). There are blends in which the source elements disappear (but their constituents may remain, except in systems that produce complete annihilation): oxygen and fuel disappear in the blend known as fire (undoubtedly a merging).

We will give a simplistic example using a woman and a fish. The simple copresence of a woman and a fish, say, at an outdoor market, is a separation. A chainsaw maniac who juxtaposes a woman's upper body and a fish tail produces a contiguity. A siren would be the mixing of a woman and a fish. A woman with the genetic code of a fish, with no visual clues of her fish nature, would be an example of merging.

A phenomenon's positioning at one stage or another is relatively relative. Consider Magritte's work titled *L'évidence éternelle* (1930), which consists of five paintings, each showing different parts of the same woman, hung on the wall from top to bottom so as to reconstitute the woman: the first reproduces her head; the second, her chest; the third, her lower torso; the fourth, her thighs and knees;

the fifth, her lower legs and feet. A normal representation of the woman in a single painting would constitute a merging of Magritte's piece, which then acquires the status of a separation. However, if instead of being hung together, the five paintings were distributed among five different rooms of a museum, then Magritte's original work would be a contiguity or a mixing, and the transformed work would be a separation.

From a dynamic standpoint, a blending/sorting operation is a trajectory that goes from an **initial stage** to a **final stage**. The typology of elementary trajectories of blending/sorting includes: 1) six elementary trajectories of blending: from separation to merging, from separation to mixing, etc.; 2) six elementary trajectories of sorting: from merging to separation, from mixing to separation, etc.; and (3) four elementary trajectories of continuance: from separation to separation, from merging to merging, etc.

Obviously, trajectories can combine with one another, in succession and/or simultaneity, to form a group, i.e., a **structure of elementary trajectories** (e.g., from separation to separation + from separation to merging).

A typology of **expanded trajectories** can be produced if the twelve main elementary trajectories (not including the trajectories of continuance) are used with the two terms of a given opposition placed in the initial stage and final stage (e.g., monster/non-monster or pretty/ugly). This produces 52 expanded trajectories. For example, going from separation to mixing with a man (non-monster) and a horse (non-monster) produces a centaur (monster). Combining expanded trajectories creates a structure of these trajectories. For example, if we combine a trajectory that yields a minotaur (man (non-monster) + bull (non-monster) = minotaur (monster)) and a trajectory that yields a centaur (man (non-monster) + horse (non-monster) = centaur (monster)), we will get a second-generation composite monster, a minotaur-centaur (minotaur (monster) + centaur (monster) = minotaur-centaur (monster)).

The same elements that we have just used to examine blending/sorting operations can be used to look at increases/decreases. From a static perspective, a scale with three degrees could be used: low, medium, and high intensity. From a dynamic perspective, we would then distinguish six **elementary trajectories of increase/decrease**: from low to medium (increase), etc.; from high to medium (decrease), etc. To these trajectories we can add three trajectories of continuance: from medium to medium, etc. Trajectories can be grouped, either in simultaneity or in succession, in order to define structures. For example, an immediate succession of two trajectories that defines three temporal positions (beginning, middle, end) can take 27 forms: from low to medium + from medium to low, etc. We presented a typology of this sort in the chapter on the tensive model, with intensity being applied to aesthetic euphoria, in that case.

Other sub-species

BALANCED/UNBALANCED OPERATIONS

One aspect that analysis of additions/deletions can incorporate is that of the **weighting of the added/deleted elements**. In a **balanced addition** (with no positive connotation), the number of added elements is the same as the number of elements to which the elements are added. The same principle applies to a balanced deletion. The weighting of the elements can have a qualitative impact on the result of the operation. So to give a trivial example, the weighting of oil relative to eggs can make it so that the result will not be mayonnaise.

CATEGORIAL/INCREMENTAL OPERATIONS

Like any property (including relations) or any process (including operations), a transformation operation, whether simple or made of a combination of simple operations, can be seen from a categorial or an incremental perspective by any given observer. In the first case, it is considered to be done or not done, with no possibility of partial completion. In the second case, partial completion is possible. For example, while it is possible to add a complete "r" to "merde" and thereby create "merdre", it is not possible to add half of an "r", unless a special graphic game is being played. So the addition and deletion of letters is in fact categorial. Conversely, a chapter of a novel can be partially deleted if some sentences are kept. Any operation that is not fully completed (e.g., an addition) is inversely correlated with a continuance of the same category (e.g., a non-addition): that is, the more transformation there is, the less continuance, and the less transformation, the more continuance.

MINIMUM/MAXIMUM OPERATIONS

The minimum transformation operation involves the addition, deletion, displacement, increase, decrease, or continuance of a single unit, or the substitution or permutation of two units. The maximum possible deletion and decrease – when they are total – respectively create the deletion of the relevant unit (e.g., a word is struck out) or its complete attenuation (e.g., a sound whose volume is reduced to zero). Total deletion and decrease are expressions of what we are calling semiotic silence (which is always relative, since there are always elements present). And as for extreme deletion and decrease, they occur just at the boundary before total deletion and decrease; but we should keep in mind that this boundary is always relative as well. If only the head of a character remains in a drawing (there is an example of this in our application), we could call this extreme deletion with respect to the large body parts, but not with respect to the small body parts (like ears, eyes, etc.) : the monster could have been reduced to an eye, or the eye to a pupil, etc.

Application: iconography of mythical beings from Tibetan Buddhism

Corpus

For our analysis we are using the corpus of mythical beings of Tibetan Buddhism illustrated in black and white in Tcheuky Sèngué's book (2002; other references to the book will mention only the date and page).[4] From among the rich depictions of these beings, we will simply look at how the bodies are put together, with some exceptions. And out of the factors of corporeal make-up, we will concentrate on heads, faces, eyes, arms, and legs (or lower bodies).

The corpus contains 270 images in which at least one fantastic being appears. Some beings are represented in many different images (e.g., the Buddha during different periods of his life). Some images include several deities (e.g., the Buddha and his entourage of Bodhisattvas). The same being can take different forms in different images (e.g., a peaceful form and a wrathful or semi-wrathful form, or a peaceful form with two arms and another with four). In addition, we will sometimes mention beings who do not have an iconographic depiction in our reference book, but only a physical description.

In the corpus, the depictions are sociolectally defined within the generic form "iconography of Tibetan Buddhism". We postulate that idiolectal manifestations in this work are relatively rare, since the Tibetan artist, unlike the western artist, does not seek to express a personality, or to improve and/or contest the generic forms. What's more, the drawings in our corpus are clearly not signed, nor even contextualized with a date or place, etc., which makes it problematic to identify idiolectal manifestations, or even more specific generic manifestations (sub-genres).

NOTE: THE TYPOLOGY OF MYTHICAL BEINGS

The mythical beings of Tibetan Buddhism that are represented in the iconography specifically include: (1) the "historical" Buddhas, or Manushi Buddhas, i.e., those who incarnated (as opposed to the "Celestial" Buddhas), among them Shakyamuni (the historically attested founder of Buddhism), the Buddhas who founded the Dharma (Kanakamuni, Kashyapa, etc.) prior to Shakyamuni, and those who come after him (Maitreya, etc.); (2) the other incarnate enlightened beings, some of whom are from legend, and others who are historically attested (Padmasambhava, Milarepa, etc.); (3) the primordial, or Adi Buddhas (Samantabhadra, Vajrasattva, etc.); (4) the five victors, or Dhyani Buddhas (Vairochana, Akshobya, Ratnasambhava, Amitabha, Amoghasiddhi), each of which presides over a "family" of Buddhas; (5) the celestial bodhisattvas, or Dhyani Bodhisattvas (Avalokiteshvara, Manjushri, Tara, etc.); (6) the protectors of the Dharma, some enlightened (Mahakala, Shri Devi, etc.) and some not (Vajrasadhu, Péhar, etc.); (7) some classes of spirits and demons (asparas, asouras, etc.); (8) mythical animals (Kirtimukha) and classes of mythical animals (dragons, garudas, makaras, etc.); (9) the pretas (or hungry ghosts), the asuras (or demigods or Titans), and the narakas (the damned). Devas (worldly gods), asuras, humans, animals, pretas and narakas constitute the six main forms of existence in samsara. Samsara is the conditioned world, and thus the source of suffering, from which one "escapes" through non-abiding (static) nirvana, or which one overcomes through dynamic (unfixed) nirvana, or full enlightenment.

Addition

There is no denying the fact that the corpus favors operations of addition. A goodly number of beings have more than one head and face, more than two eyes, two arms or two legs. The figure of Sitatapattra (2002, p. 258) wins the prize, with 1000 heads, 1000 faces (each of which has three eyes), 1000 arms, and 1000 legs; but 1000-armed Avalokiteshvara is not to be outdone, as we will see.

Faces are added: (1) to a given head (there are no faces without heads); (2) horizontally (there are no faces added vertically to the top of the head); (3) to a principal, central face, and (4) usually, symmetrically on both sides of the central face (e.g., a face on the right, and another on the left, for a total of three faces). Chakrasmavara (2002, p. 204) (and others, like Kalachakra (2002, p. 220)) is a counter example, since he has two faces to the right of his central face and only one to the left.

As for heads, they are added vertically, seemingly the opposite of multi-headed western monsters, whose heads are usually added horizontally. The added heads are always smaller than the head below, e.g., the first head is larger than the second, and the second is larger than the third.

There are seven fantastic beings in the iconographic corpus – all deities – who have multiple, stacked heads. Whereas the volume of the stacked heads can only decrease from one head level to the next, the number of faces will remain stable or decrease from one level to the next, but it will not increase in any case. In other words, the combinatorics here – as elsewhere – is pretty tightly constrained. In the simplest case, apart from the decreases by deincrementing from one level to the next, all of the heads are identical or nearly identical, even if the number of faces varies. Sitatapattra (2002, p. 258) has ten heads with multiple faces, which seem to be topped off with an eleventh identical head that has only one face (however, this would bring the number of faces to 1001, or it simply indicates that the number 1000 is symbolic). Yamantaka's first head (2002, p. 335) is a bull's head, but the three faces on the right are human. The second and third heads are human with only one face, but they appear different. However, these last two heads appear semi-wrathful, and their faces similar or identical to the human faces of the first head, which creates continuity between the three levels.

The numbers of elements of any one kind are clearly symbolic (2002, pp. 38–40). For example, the three eyes, which are seemingly always present on angry (or wrathful) deities, with one exception that we will see later, indicate "simultaneous knowledge of the three times (past, present and future)" (2002, p. 47). The proliferation of body parts on beneficent deities indicates their desire and ability to help all beings.

Operations of addition that affect parts of the body have several other interesting characteristics. Let's look at some of them.

Corporeal additions may consist in adding parts that are absent in the general humanoid type that generates the deity, such as a ring of fire, or wings. Or they may simply add parts that already exist in the type: e.g., two more arms, another eye, etc. Also, the added parts tend to be either identical to the "pre-existing" ones in the original specific type, or almost identical. For example, two more faces identical to the first are added, a second head identical to the first, but smaller, a third eye similar to the other two, but vertical. (But sometimes the eye is not rotated; along with displacement, rotation is one of the possible spatial operations. This is actually a permutation, to be more precise.) However, the faces added to one head are not always identical to the central face; sometimes the difference is minor (Vajrakilaya's different noses (2002, p. 354)) and sometimes the difference is major, such as that between peaceful and angry or humanoid and animal faces (we will come back to this).

Of course, one can distinguish referential adaptations, which alter the actual being who is depicted, and iconic adaptations, which are due to iconographic constraints and conventions. One-thousand-armed Avalokiteshvara's undersized arms may belong to the second category: under-proportioning them makes it possible to show the 1000 arms in an image that is not too large (in actuality, the 1000 arms are not all shown). Under-proportioning the additional heads, on the other hand, seems to be a referential adaptation. That is, even when just one head is added, and not 10 or 11, as in the extreme case of Sitatapattra (2002, p. 258), it is under-proportioned, even though from a pictorial standpoint, two superposed heads of the same size will fit into an image, even if it is small. Whether referential or iconic, we would say that under-proportioning is an intense operation, or more precisely, a decrease.

Moreover, wrathful and semi-wrathful deities always seem to be oversized; we view over-proportioning as resulting from an operation of increase. Increase clearly goes in the same direction as adding arms, heads, etc.: it indicates both the character of the being, and his or her power and desire to help. Over-proportioning is used most notably each time a deity tramples a human body (the corpse symbolizes the death of the ego or the conquest of the negative emotions brought about by the deities). Vajravahari (2002, p. 262) and Kurukulla (2002, p. 254) are obvious cases: Together, the head and the trunk of the trampled corpse are the same size as the deity's foot. The same goes for Vajrayogini (2002, p. 267, see Figure 2.2). Even so, the proportions in Tibetan iconography are no doubt more expressive than they are "realistic".

Three main types should be distinguished, to which the operations are applied and can be characterized. The first type corresponds to the normal human being; relative to this type, the token – i.e., the

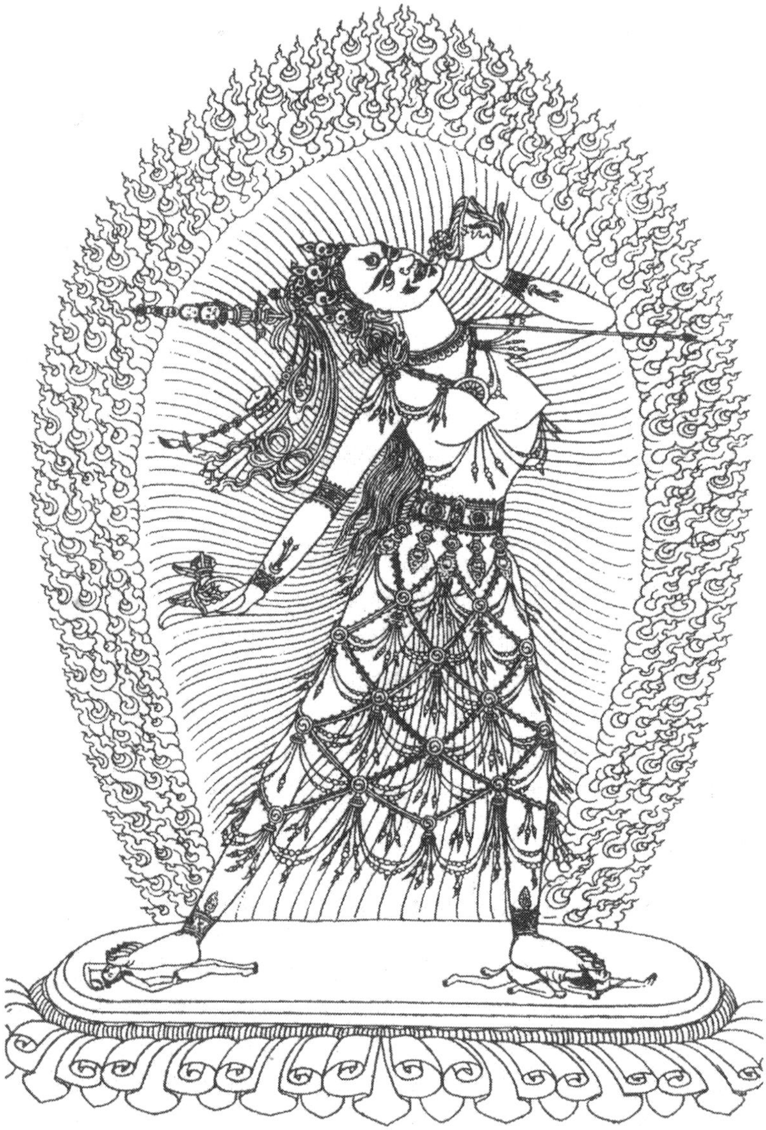

Figure 2.2 Vajrayogini
Source: (2002, p. 267)

fantastic being – may add two wings, two legs, etc. The second type corresponds to a class of deities (e.g., wrathful, semi-wrathful, peaceful; masculine, feminine; etc.). The third type corresponds to the "monster" itself, but minus the operations in question, and elevated to the rank of a type. With respect to this type, in the token there might be, for example, a head added that is identical to the first.

Like any sub-species of operation or any operation, reduplication can be categorial or incremental. From a categorial standpoint, there is reduplication if the added unit (e.g., a left arm) is exactly the same as a unit (the main left arm) found in an encompassing unit (the deity). From an incremental standpoint, a reduplicating unit (e.g., an under-proportioned head) is essentially identical to a reduplicated unit (a head that is not under-proportioned). Reduplication can be simple (e.g., one head or one eye is added) or repetitive (more than one head or more than one eye is added).

We observe that when additions apply to arms or legs, they are made in multiples of two (in our corpus, producing 4, 6, 8, 10, 12, 16, 24, 34 or 1000 arms; 2, 4, 16 or 1000 legs). When faces are added to one head, on the other hand, it is usually done in even numbers, but occasionally in odd numbers (e.g., giving Chakrasamvara four faces for a single head (2002, p. 204)). Heads are added in either odd numbers (which yields four heads on 1000-armed Avalokiteshvara) or even numbers (which yields five heads on 11-faced Avalokiteshvara (2002, p. 182)). The total number of faces is either odd (1, 3, 5, 9, 11 or 1000 faces) or even (4, 8 or 1000).

The added elements have the same characteristics as the elements that they are copying (as in copy and paste) when the elements are eyes (although they may be oriented vertically), arms, or legs. We have mentioned that there can be an adjustment in the form of iconographic (non-referential) under-proportioning.

However, faces are not treated in the same way. They can be added along two axes. On the vertical axis, the faces added above the original face are generally different from it. However, 1000-armed Avalokiteshvara (2002, p. 178, see Figure 2.3) has three identical heads vertically stacked (but they are decreased by successive deincrementation). However, the fourth head is wrathful, and the fifth head, which is peaceful, depicts the Buddha Amitabha, whose spiritual son is Avalokiteshvara (2002, p. 179). On the horizontal axis, the faces added on both sides of the central face have exactly the same properties as the latter. Some exceptions to this rule can be found: for Yamantaka (2002, p. 335), the faces on the right side (which are human) are not like the central face and the left-side faces (which are bull faces); and one of Rahula's heads (2002, p. 367) has a peaceful main face flanked by two seemingly wrathful faces.

Note that it is less common to have additional legs than additional arms; sometimes the contrast between the addition operation for arms and the continuance operation for legs is striking; this is the case for one thousand-armed Avalokiteshvara, who has two legs.

A third eye always seems to be added to the faces of wrathful deities (except for Ekajati, whom we will soon see), but some peaceful deities are given the same treatment (e.g., Paripurana Tara (2002, p. 252)). The addition of eyes elsewhere on the body seems to be more restricted. One thousand-armed Avalokitheshvara has two eyes for each face, and one eye in the palm of each hand. In addition to the three eyes in her single head, White Tara (2002, p. 242, see Figure 2.4) has an eye in the palms of her hands and on the soles of her feet. In contrast to faces, arms and legs, which are squeezed in near the elements that they reduplicate, eyes can be added to parts of the body that normally have none (the palms, the soles of feet, the forearms, the nipples, and the belly). Of course, one could say that the eye on Tara's hand is simply added, but relative to the humanoid type, and even relative to the peaceful female Tibetan deity type, there is a displacement from the head to the hand.

Operations of addition for eyes, arms, legs, heads, and faces take place on a core, a recognizable type that is a being of human form, or at least anthropomorphous, as opposed to an animal being, for example. (The outer aspect of many wrathful deities is based on that of the rakshasas, which are beings related to our ogres (2002, p. 439).) Operations of substitution proceed in similar fashion; for example, although the Garuda (Figure 2.5) is highly composite, nonetheless an original core is still identifiable: a human torso. However, there are strange instances of a being created by pure addition, almost without any basis on which to graft the additions (the additions are then completely

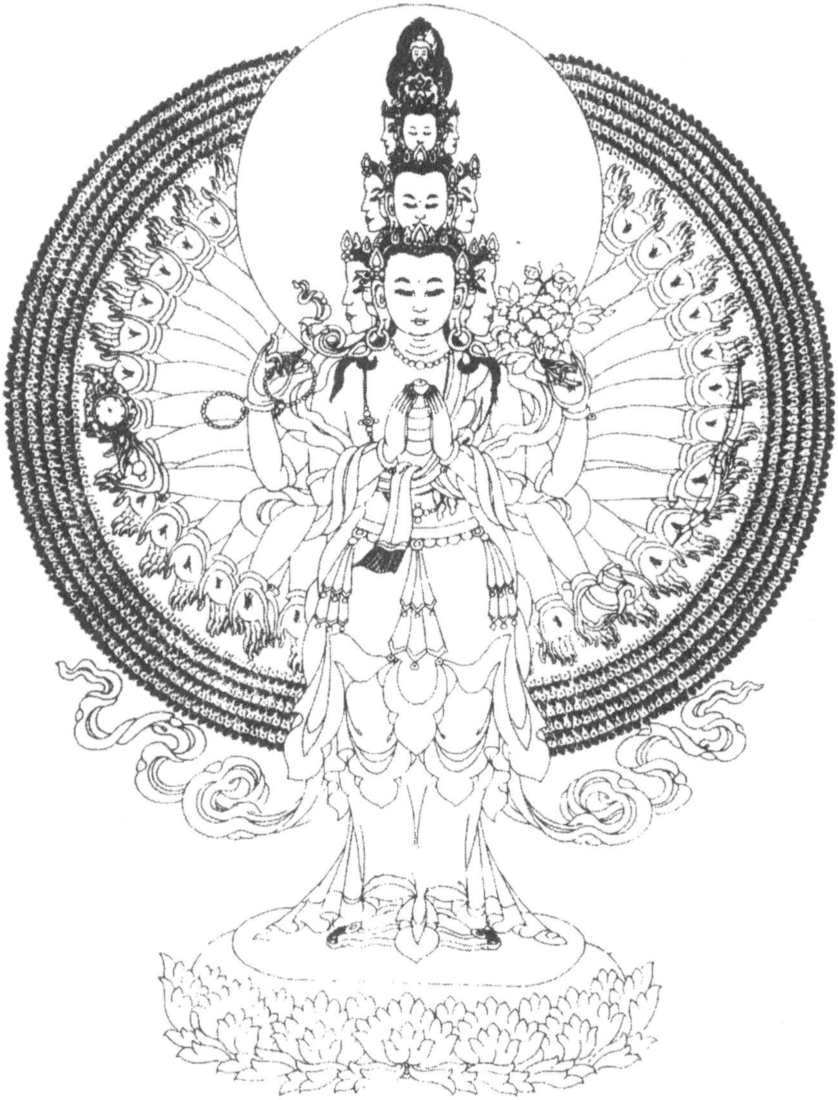

Figure 2.3 One thousand-armed Avalokiteshvara

Source: (2002, p. 178)

symmetrical, a blending of this and that, rather than an addition of this to that), such as the makara, "a sea monster related to the crocodile, but whose composite anatomy is borrowed from a plethora of animals: the lower jaw of a crocodile, the rather long trunk of an elephant, the ears of a wild boar, the eyes of a monkey, the scales of a fish, the mane of a lion, the horns of a deer, etc." (2002, p. 444, see Figure 2.5). This animal is close to a pure composite; i.e., it is difficult to find a being from which it could have been simply modified (its classification as a crocodile seems rather arbitrary (2002, p. 502)). Moreover, the makara is itself used to produce a monster by substitution. The deity Simha-vaktra (2002, p. 334) is created from a human form, but with the head of a makara.

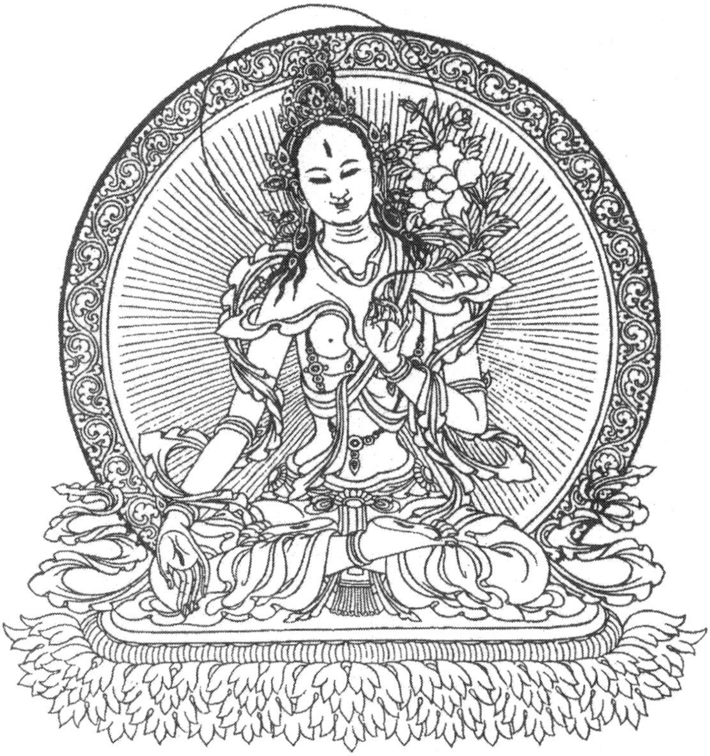

Figure 2.4 White Tara

Source: (2002, p. 242)

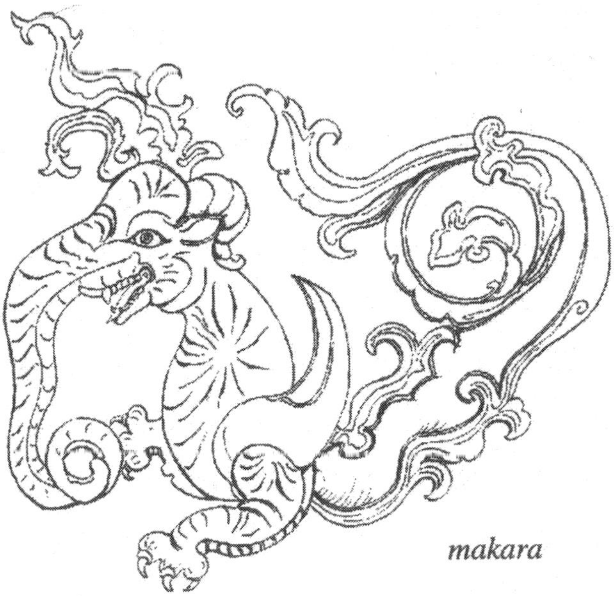

Figure 2.5 The makara

Source: (2002, p. 444)

In the ultimate example, the makara is combined with a conch to form a more composite monster yet, elliptically called a "makara" (2002, p. 502). Actually, this makara-conch belongs to a very specific class of animals. In Tibetan Buddhism, three animals symbolize victory over disharmony and disagreement. These mythical animals are forms resulting from a happy resolution of opposites, uniting two animals known to be enemies into one body. They are the otter-fish (known as the "furry fish"), the garuda-lion (known as the "eight-limbed lion"; the garuda is a mythical bird), and the makara-conch (elliptically called the "makara", but which we will call the "makara-conch", and which supposedly feeds on conches) (2002, p. 501). If a Minotaur-centaur is a second-generation composite monster created by combining two beings that are themselves composite, then the garuda-lion and the makara-conch are partly second-generation composite monsters, since just one of the two blended elements in each case is composite itself: the garuda and the makara.

Deletion

Operations of deletion are underused in the corpus, at least with respect to the aspects that are of interest to us: for example, there is no being with just one eye (with one exception), just one arm, or just one leg (we know that there is a form of one-legged demon, but it is seemingly not pictured or described in our corpus). However, there are two noteworthy exceptions.

In contrast to the figures of reduction that we have seen, there is an astonishing figure of vigorous deletion (the counterpart of vigorous addition), or to be more exact, of extreme deletion. That is, she is right at the boundary before the complete deletion of identical elements (from another standpoint, this would be weak continuance). We are referring to Ekajati. "She is characterized by bodily attributes reduced to oneness: a single braid of hair that stands up, a single eye, which gives her the appearance of a Cyclops, a single tooth resting on her lower lip, and a single breast. Her yellow mustache further reinforces the impression of strangeness that emanates from her". (2002, p. 365). While reducing her to a single eye comes across somewhat like a "mutilation" (which is a genetic operation, occurring directly in the token, since in the depiction there remains a sort of creasing in place of the left and right eyes), the single breast is in the center, which attenuates the effect of deletion that would have resulted from the presence of a single right or left breast. The same principle applies for the centered single tooth.

The mustache has had its natural color (black, brown, etc.) replaced with a color that is supernatural, because it is impossible (yellow). By comparison with Groupe μ's negative substitution (e.g., in irony, where a seme is replaced with the opposite seme), the mustache can be seen as part of a negative addition – i.e., semantically opposed – since a typically masculine feature is being added to a feminine being. Zilberberg would call this concessive blending (of elements that are mutually exclusive), as opposed to implicative blending (of identical or complementary elements): although the deity is feminine, she has a moustache. The internalization of masculine and feminine in the body of a single character is pushed to greater extremes in Maning Nakpo. Also there is nothing in the portrayal of this deity that would reveal it, "Maning Nakpo" signifies "the black eunuch": "By his eunuch nature, which is neither male nor female, he transcends the two sexes, thereby symbolizing the ultimate nature" (2002, p. 348, see Figure 2.6). This nature, which by tradition is considered to transcend oppositions through the neutral term (= neither one) rather than through the complex term (= both) (see the chapter on the semiotic square), is also found in Shri Devi's mount – a mule: "born of the mating of a donkey and a mare, she is neither one. In this sense, she represents the

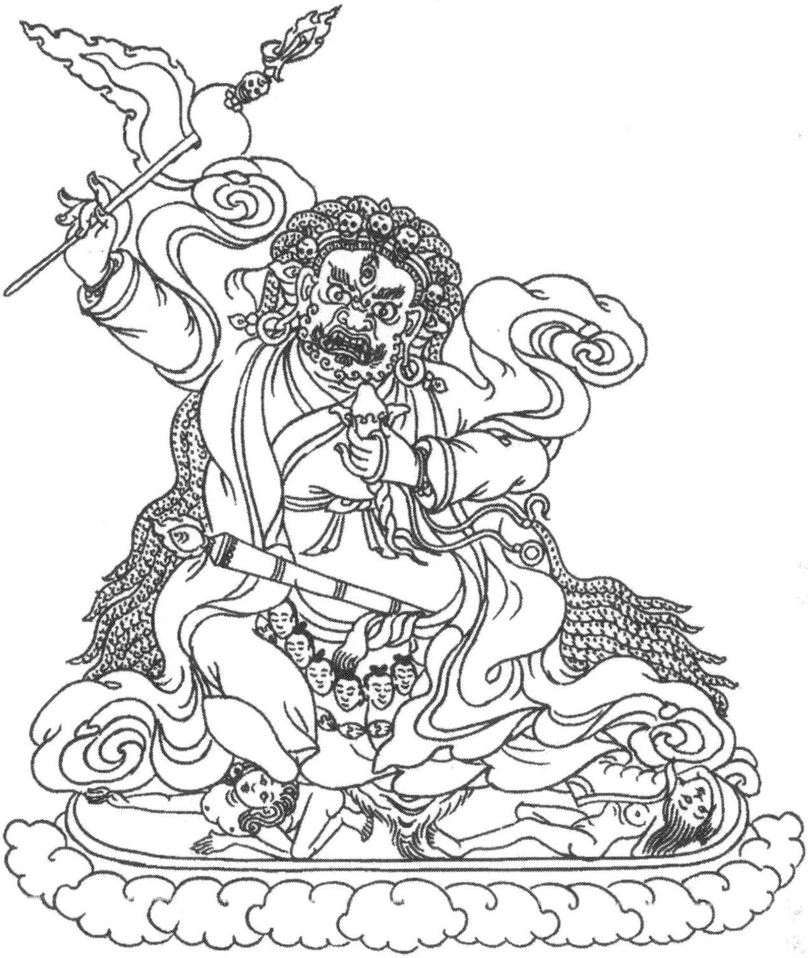

Figure 2.6 Maning Nakpo

Source: (2002, p. 347)

madhyamika, or middle way, which strays neither toward eternalism [the belief in the intrinsic existence of phenomena] nor toward nihilism. What's more, just as a mule is always sterile, the middle way yields no production [karma] in the samsara [our conditioned world]" (2002, pp. 328–329). We would add that since the eunuch is also sterile, he shares the same symbolic interpretation.

The other noteworthy exception using deletion is Kirtimukha, "an animal of which only the head remains (not including the jaw). The Shivaite legend from which he was born informs us that at one time he found himself so deprived of food that he could find no other solution than to consume his own body. Shiva gave him his name, which means "glorious face", and made him the guardian of the threshold of his door.[5] (2002, p. 444, see Figure 2.7). Note that in the image given of this monster, his hands are seen holding "a golden crest-bar that goes through his mouth" (Beer, 2006, p. 132), so it is not just the head that survived the generalized/maximum deletion (or the weak/minimum

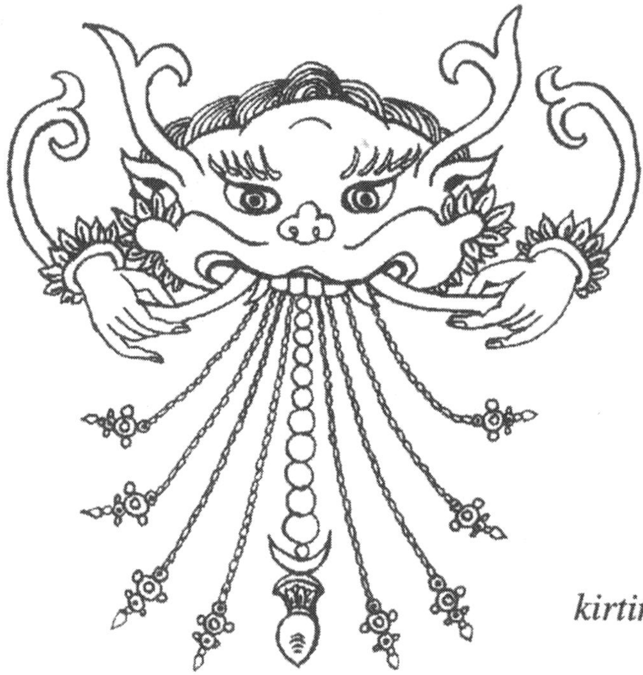

Figure 2.7 Kirtimukha

Source: (2002, p. 444)

continuance). Self-consumption is the result of those operations of transformation in which the operator is the same as the transformed object (as in suicide, self-mutilation, etc.).

Substitution

There are a few substitution operations found in the elements we are studying. The lower body of certain beings has been replaced with the hind part of a snake in the case of Rahula (2002, p. 367) and the nagas (spirits "related to snakes, but also to sirens" (2002, p. 438)), or with a ritual knife (*kila*) in the case of Guru Drakpur (2002, p. 298). This last substitution is surprising. While it is relatively common to have part of an existing or mythical animal used in substitution, this is the only substitution of an inanimate element for an animate element. Just one other metallic substitution is found in the corpus: one of the pictures of the garuda is titled "Garuda with metal horns" (2002, p. 435). This is not a case of substituting a metallic object for an organic, animate object (a lower body), but of substituting a metallic material for an organic, and – we would say – inanimate object (the horn).

Other deities, and even some classes of spirits, e.g., the sadaks (2002, p. 440), have had their human heads replaced with animal heads. According to our compilation, these substitutions include the following animals: deer, chamois, horse, goat, dog, owl, crow, cuckoo bird, crocodile, dragon, elephant, hawk, garuda, frog, hoopoe, leopard, lion, wolf, mongoose, bird, bear, brown bear, pig, fox, scorpion, snake, tiger, vulture, and yak. One deity has both humanoid and animal faces: Yamantaka, whose main face and left face are that of a bull (2002, p. 335). Others have one humanoid head, and in their hair, one animal head. For example, Vajravahari has a sow's head in her hair (2002, p. 262). In Maning Nakpo's case (2002, p. 347, see Figure 2.4), his humanoid hair is what is replaced – with snake tails that go all the way to the ground. This reminds us more than a little of Medusa. One thing seems clear from these two animal additions: that hair is associated with animality.

In theory, a substitution can be localized (e.g., by applying to the head or the lower body), or it can be generalized. The garuda represents this sort of generalized substitution: it is made of a human body whose arms and hands have been kept, but whose head and legs have been replaced with a bird of prey's head and talons, respectively, and to which a bird of prey's tail and wings have been added. This is not exactly a human form with animal influence, but rather an animal form with human influence.

Lastly, a being's seeming can be replaced by some other, while its being remains the same. This substitution is carried out either by changing the temperament status of a single deity (peaceful, semi-wrathful, wrathful), or by changing some other status[6] (e.g., peaceful two-armed, four-armed, or 1,000-armed Avalokiteshvara; the different aspects of Padmasambhava for a single temperament (2002, pp. 289–298)); or, lastly, by temporarily obscuring their actual seeming. The stories of many deities mention that they temporarily took the form even of particular demonic or evil spirits so as to subjugate them more effectively. This is what Vajrapani, Vajrakilaya, Hayagriva, and others did (2002, p. 196).

Notes

1 This text is an augmented version of Hébert, 2011 (but the conclusion was deleted).

2 Further details are found in Hébert, 2008, a text that we are correcting, clarifying, and supplementing here.

3 In a token, the deletion of a seme present in the type creates a state somewhere between presence and absence for this seme, known as virtualization (of an inherent seme, to be more precise).

4 Our thanks go to Éditions Claire Lumière (http://www.clairelumiere.com/) for graciously authorizing us to reproduce the illustrations in the book.

5 We take the view that "Kirtimukha" is the name of a unique being, and is thus a proper noun, but that "makara" is a common noun that designates a class of beings (thus the lower case letter).

6 Another modal series distinguishes the enlightened deities in terms of the particular "body" in which they are represented, of the three bodies they possess: in the nirmanakaya, or emanation body (like Sakyamuni); in the sambhogakaya, or body of glory (like the great majority of the corpus); in the dharmakaya, or absolute body (like Samantabhadra). The resemblance to the Christian deity's three persons is striking, but for lack of space and especially of theological knowledge, we cannot give the points of similarity and difference here.

3 The semiotic square

Summary

The semiotic square, developed by Greimas and Rastier, is a tool used in oppositional analyses. It allows us to refine an analysis by increasing the number of analytical classes stemming from a given opposition from two (e.g., life/death) to four – (1) life, (2) death, (3) life and death (the living dead), (4) neither life nor death (angels) – to eight or even ten.

Theory

The actantial model, isotopy and the semiotic square are undoubtedly the best-known theoretical models that have emerged from the Paris School of semiotics, a group of scholars with A. J. Greimas as their central figure (Courtés, Coquet, Floch, Fontanille, Zilberberg and others). The popularization of these models as "gadgets", to use Floch's language (1985, p. 197), in a goodly number of more or less "semiotic" texts attests to this.

Like the actantial model, the canonical narrative schema and the veridictory square, the semiotic square is designed to be both a conceptual network and a visual representation of this network, usually depicted in the form of a "square" (which actually looks like a rectangle). Developed by Greimas and Rastier (1968), the semiotic square may be defined as the logical articulation of a given opposition (this definition is adapted from Courtés's (1991, p. 152)).[1] The semiotic square is used to refine an oppositional analysis by increasing the number of analytical classes stemming from a given opposition from two (e.g., life/death) to four – (1) life, (2) death, (3) life and death (the living dead), (4) neither life nor death (angels) – to eight or even ten.

Opposite is an empty semiotic square (unlabeled, with no specific opposition mapped out).

Table 3.1 Structure of the semiotic square

		5. (=1 + 2) COMPLEX TERM		
	1. TERM A	9. (=1 + 4)	2. TERM B	
7. (=1 + 3) POSITIVE DEIXIS				8. (=2 + 4) NEGATIVE DEIXIS
	3. TERM NOT-B	10. (=2 + 3)	4. TERM NOT-A	
		6. (=3 + 4) NEUTRAL TERM		

Legend:
The + sign links the terms that are combined to make up a metaterm (a compound term); for example, 5 is the result of combining 1 and 2.

Constituent elements

The semiotic square includes the following elements:

1 Terms
2 Metaterms (compound terms)
3 Relations (between the terms)
4 Operations
5 Observing subject(s) who do(es) the classifying (the real author, implied author, narrator, character, etc.; see the chapter on thymic analysis)
6 Object(s) classified on the square
7 Time (of observation)
8 Transformations and/or successions (in time) of subjects and objects

The terms

The semiotic square is composed of four terms, each corresponding to a position on the square:

Position 1: (term A)
Position 2: (term B)
Position 3: (term not-B)
Position 4: (term not-A)

The first two terms form the basic opposition of the square, and the other two are obtained by negating each term of the opposition.

The metaterms

The semiotic square includes six metaterms. The metaterms are compound terms created by combining the four simple terms. Some of the metaterms have been named. (The complex term and the neutral term, despite their names, are indeed metaterms).

Position 5: A + B, the complex term
Position 6: not-B + not-A, the neutral term
Position 7: A + not-B, the positive deixis
Position 8: B + not-A, the negative deixis
Position 9: A + not-A, positive schema
Position 10: B + not-B, negative schema

Relations

The following relations have been established between the terms on the square:

1 Contrariety: the relation between term A and term B, and between term not-A and term not-B
2 Contradiction: the relation between term A and term not-A, and between term B and term not-B

The term "opposition" encompasses both contrariety and contradiction in this text.

3 Implication or complementarity (Fontanille's term, 2003, p. 60): the relation between term not-B and term A, and between term not-A and term B

Contrariety, contradiction and complementarity are bidirectional relations (that is, A is the opposite of B and vice versa), whereas implication is unidirectional, from not-B to A and from not-A to B.

Because of the relation between them, terms A and B are called the "contraries" and terms not-A and not-B are the "subcontraries" (because they are contrary terms located "below" the contraries); terms A and not-A are the "contradictories", and terms B and not-B are "contradictories" as well.

NOTE: THE LOGICAL STATUS OF CONTRARIETY AND CONTRADICTION

According to Courtés (1991, p. 153), contrariety does not have a formal logical status (which contradiction does: it is defined by a privative relation; we will come back to this later): the contraries are simply givens in any particular society. Courtés goes on to say, however, that Greimas "postulates that two terms may be said to be contrary when the presence of one presupposes the presence of the other, and when the absence of one goes hand in hand with the absence of the other. More generally speaking, two terms (s1 and s2) are said to be contrary if the negation of one implies the affirmation of the other, and vice versa" (1991, p. 153). By our observations, the contraries vary not just from one culture to another, but also from one type of semiotic act to another: "The novel, in contrast with poetry, sets Love in opposition with Ambition – a theme that is missing from poetry".

(Rastier, 2001, p. 206)

Operations

The following operations describe movements on the semiotic square, that is, movements from one position on the square to another (the arrow indicates the direction of movement):

1 Negation: term A → term not-A; term B → term not-B;
2 Assertion (affirmation): term not-B → term A; term not-A → term B.

An example of a semiotic square

We now have enough background to show an example of a semiotic square filled in and labelled. This one uses the traditional opposition masculine/feminine:

Table 3.2 An example of a semiotic square: masculine/feminine

		Masculine + Feminine "androgyne" "hermaphrodite"		
	Masculine "man"		Feminine "woman"	
Masculine + Not-feminine "real man", "macho"		Masculine + Not-masculine ? Feminine + Not-feminine ?		Feminine + Not-masculine "ultra-feminine", "vamp"?
	Not-feminine "mannish", "macha"		Not-masculine "effeminate"	
		Not-feminine + Not-masculine "angel"		

The words in quotation marks are examples of concepts that can be classified under a term or a metaterm (certain words may be offensive, and we wish to emphasize that they do not reflect our views). These concepts may be represented by the words used here or by others (for example, the concept 'androgynous' could be manifested in a text by the word "androgynous", but also by the expression "he was as masculine as he was feminine"). The question marks in positions 9 and 10 illustrate how difficult it can be to find actual phenomena that correspond to these metaterms. We will look at this square in more detail later.

Three levels of analysis

There are ultimately three levels of analysis that should be distinguished:

1 Do the objects covered by a given position on a given square actually exist in reality? That is, in reality, one cannot be dead and alive at the same time, a state exemplified by our worst horror, the vampire.
2 Can a position on the square be lexicalized more or less adequately; that is, can it be named with an existing word or expression in standard usage.[2] For example the neutral term 'neither

euphoria nor dysphoria' (that is, neither positive nor negative) can be lexicalized in the word "indifference", or better yet, with a technical neologism, "aphoria" (where the prefix "a-" indicates an absence of). In other cases, lexical choices may be lacking, which appears to be the case with the metaterm composed of euphoria and not-dysphoria.

NOTE: NAMING THE BASIC OPPOSITION ON THE SQUARE

One should not be unnecessarily restrictive in naming the basic opposition of the square. For example, one can just as well use the opposition life/not-life instead of life/death. The subcontraries would then be not-life (whose meaning is different from the first not-life) and not-not-life. The names of the classes on a semiotic square, like those for any analytical class, are labels and conventions more than anything else.

3 Is each position on a given square realized in the corresponding semiotic act? Generally speaking, only some of the possible positions are manifested in a semiotic act. Our masculine/feminine square is an abstract one; it does not describe a specific act.

Homogeneity in the square

As with any analytical tool, a semiotic square should be explicitly coherent (the square should describe a homogeneous universe (Floch, 1985, p. 200)). The analyst is naturally the one who defines what type and what degree of homogeneity are adequate, depending on the corpus and the objectives (all of which are open to discussion, of course).

For instance, in our masculine/feminine square (which is based on Floch's, 1985, p. 199), we chose to represent only the "natural", "spontaneous" states of masculinity/femininity (in a general sense, that is, not just biological), despite having to refer to unreal beings (angels). In order to increase or decrease the number of phenomena it covers, a square may be made more general or more specific. Generalizing will allow us to include in our square the "artificial" phenomenon of transsexuality. A transsexual who was originally a man has gone through the state of not-manhood (castration, etc.) to reach the state of womanhood. Depending on the descriptive stances required, one can say that the transsexual is a woman in some respects (legal, for example) and a man in others (chromosomal, for example). In other words, by changing the focus from the parts to the whole or from one part to another, we can make the classification vary. Classifications may also vary depending on whether one has a class of objects in mind or a specific object. For instance, a radical feminist may consider men in general to be dysphoric (negative), but her life partner would be excluded from this overall judgment. (For details on part-whole and class-element relations, refer to the chapters on structural relations and thymic analysis.)

The semiotic square and veridictory status

Veridictory status (true/false) can and sometimes must be included in the analysis, and therefore so must the observing subjects. For the apostles (observing subjects), Jesus (the object being observed) truly did pass from life to death, and then to life. (Later on, we will see that the trajectory is more complex in reality.) For the non-believers (observing subjects), if he existed, Christ simply passed from life to death, like everyone. Because of this, we will distinguish between reference positions or trajectories, which are defined by the observing subject who determines the ultimate truth of the text (usually the narrator), and assumptive positions or trajectories, which may be contradicted by the reference elements. For example, when stating the believers' (assumptive subject) thesis and the non-believers' (assumptive subject) thesis, the narrator (the reference subject) of a Christian essay will validate the former and invalidate the latter.

Changes in beliefs may be represented as a sequence of positions on the square, as long as we indicate the veridictory status (true/false) that applies to each position taken by each object on the square. Thus, for Thomas, after the crucifixion, Christ was in death, which he mistakenly believed until he touched his wounds and then realized that Christ was actually in life.

NOTE: ANOTHER EXAMPLE OF THE DYNAMICS OF VERIDICTORY STATUS

The transsexual provides another example of how the veridictory categories work. In terms of the veridictory square (see the chapter on this subject), one might say that the transsexual's being has not changed, and that her trajectory, like the transvestite's (which, of course, can play on an ambiguous, simultaneously male and female appearance) affects only her seeming. We can see that using the veridictory square entails moving from one part (being) of the observed object to the other (seeming).

Further details on the metaterms

Metaterms 9 and 10

Metaterms 9 and 10 are not really used in classical semiotics, undoubtedly for the sake of observing the Aristotelian principle of non-contradiction.[3] However, at least from a theoretical and deductive perspective, given that one can describe a zombie with assertions like "he was dead and not dead" as opposed to "he was dead and alive", we ought to consider the possibility that these metaterms exist, so long as we can rule out the possibility that the two are simply different names for the same thing ("not-dead" being equivalent to "alive").[4]

However, it is a fact that the apparent contradiction in many "absurd" utterances is neutralized to some degree by dissimilation of meanings (see Rastier, 1987, p. 143 and following). This seems to be the case with the usual opening statement in Majorcan folk tales: "Axio era y no era" (it was and was not) (see Jakobson, 1963, p. 239) and the Confucian maxim "Your son is not your son", where the dissimilations hinge on the oppositions imaginary/real ("it was"/"it was not") and filiation/property ("your son"/"is not your son").

Metaterms 7 and 8

There are two fundamental ways to conceptualize the positive and negative deixes (metaterms 7 and 8). One way is to think of them as intensifying a term by affirming a semantic value and simultaneously negating the opposite of that value (for example, white and not-black). This is the perspective we used in designing our square of the feminine/masculine opposition. (A "macho" man would thus overstate the so-called virile personality traits, and simultaneously attenuate the supposedly feminine traits). This principle also applies to the opposition glory/humiliation in *The red and the black* by Stendhal: Julien Sorel seeks glory while at the same time he shuns humiliation; the object of his quest should therefore be placed at the positive deixis.

On the other hand, when one integrates a dimension of quantity or intensity in the analysis, the negation of a term may be interpreted as that term at a weaker intensity (for example, not-life is still life, but at a lesser intensity, as in agony). Then the deixes can be viewed as representing a higher intensity of term A or B from which they are derived. For instance, life + not-death would correspond to an intense state of life, as in the prodigious vitality of some of the characters in *One hundred years of solitude* by Gabriel Garcia Marquez. However, this interpretation disagrees with the quantitative principle, which says that by combining a given element (such as life) with a corresponding element of less intensity (not-death), one obtains an element of intermediate intensity.

Metaterm 6

By virtue of the semiotic square's principle of homogeneity, the neutral term (metaterm 6) contains only those elements *marked* as 'neither one', not the elements that simply belong to the residual class of the square. For example, normally a concept like 'wealth' is simply absent from a square like life/death and does not enter into its neutral term. The "residual" class of the semiotic square incorporates all elements put into positions other than those selected by the analyst and, of course, all other elements.

The metaterms: positive/balanced/negative

Metaterms 5, 6, 9 and 10 are said to be positive or negative, depending on which of the two contrary or contradictory terms is dominant. For example, relative to the opposition prose/poetry, the expression "poetic prose" is a positive complex term, whereas "prose poem" is a negative complex term (in that the primary feature, poetry, is only partly deflected by the first word). One can also anticipate dominance in the other metaterms, at least in theory. When there is no dominance, we call it a balanced metaterm.[5] If there is no indication whether a metaterm is positive, balanced or negative, one cannot assume that it is balanced; this only indicates that the analysis has made no determination (as of yet) with respect to balance. One can also use a reductive methodology, that is, an intentional simplification, and choose not to specify whether the metaterms are positive, balanced or negative.

The metaterms and successive/simultaneous apprehension

How one distinguishes between terms and metaterms depends on whether two terms judged as distinct and different are apprehended successively or simultaneously. The oxymoron "black sun" (Gérard de Nerval) can be counted as a complex term (light + darkness) by predication (there exists a sun that is black); conversely, in the linear (tactical) construction of meaning, it would count as two contrary terms in succession. To give another example, the title *Goat parasol* (Saint-John Perse) illustrates, as does the text, the clash between culture and nature (in the anthropological sense of the word "culture", as that which is produced by man). If we consider "parasol" and "goat" in isolation and successively, then we have a succession of opposite terms (culture, then nature). Conversely, if we consider the syntagm without breaking it down (a parasol made of goat skins), a complex term emerges (culture + nature).[6]

NOTE: THE RELATIVITY OF OPPOSITIONS AND METATERMS

Within a single semiotic act, one element may occupy different positions, simply depending on the point of reference adopted. Thus, an opposition "has no substance; it is merely a rapport, and a single variable may be associated with one pole, the opposite pole, or somewhere between the two, depending on the context" (Courtés, 1991, p. 170). Consider the opposition nature/culture: In a well-known tripartite division of spaces, French-Canadian rural legend opposes the forest to the land, as well as the land to the city. Thus, the term "land" successively occupies the position of culture relative to the forest (the "land" is organized by man), and the position of nature relative to the city. One can also consider "land" to be a metaterm (a complex term, to be precise) if one thinks of the three terms "forest", "land" and "city" all together, and not in terms of the two binary relations (see the chapter on figurative, thematic and axiological analysis).

Typologies of oppositions

Since the semiotic square deals with oppositions, it will no doubt be helpful to formulate a typology of oppositions.

The most important kinds of oppositions in semiotics are categorial, incremental and privative (Courtés, 1991, pp. 70–71). (1) Oppositions described as categorial (true/false, legal/illegal) do not allow for an intermediate term. (2) Incremental oppositions take a given semantic axis with more than two divisions and project it onto a scale. For example, the semantic axis ranging from burning to frozen may be set out as follows: burning *vs.* hot *vs.* warm *vs.* cool *vs.* cold *vs.* frozen. (3) Oppositions described as privative (life/death, animate/inanimate, relevant/irrelevant, and so on), commonly used in phonology and lexical semantics, are defined by the presence of a given feature in one of the terms of the opposition and its absence in the other; according to Courtés, they are non-incremental. For instance, death is described in all the dictionaries as the termination of life.[7]

NOTE: RELATIVITY IN THE TYPOLOGY

Let us say that a given opposition's classification is relative in the typology we have just presented. True/false is a non-incremental opposition in classical logic, but fuzzy logic admits intermediate values (quantifiable or not): For instance, on a scale of 0 to 1, if a proposition is 0.7 true, then it is 0.3 false.

(see Martin, 1983)

The semiotic square can undoubtedly map out all of the types of oppositions.[8] However, it imprints its own dynamic on the oppositions that constitute it. Oppositions that are considered as non-incremental in the system being described – those with no intermediate term, in theory (like true/false in classical logic) – somehow manage to acquire an intermediate zone on the semiotic square: the two subcontraries, positions 3 and 4 on the square. No matter what the nature of the original opposition, a privative relation is set up between positions 1 and 4 of the square, and between positions 2 and 3. In our opinion, these two privative relations are not necessarily non-incremental (we are applying the same principle of possible gradation to these two relations as we have to the relations on which the other metaterms are established). A question arises regarding the relation between the underlying oppositional structure of the square, which we have just summarized, and the underlying structure of the object being described. For example, in the case of a text that belongs to a non-incrementalist system because of its main theme, its genre or its age, is it relevant to apply incrementalism to its metaterms, other than to evaluate the possible "paradoxical" nature of the object being described?

Semantic and syntactic approaches to the square

The square may be used on a *semantic* ("static") level or a *syntactic* ("dynamic") level (distinguished by the changes in position of each object over time).[9] In Greimasian semiotics, syntax is the sequencing or succession of semantic values. The syntactic approach to the square shows the successive positions occupied by one object or several objects.

The semantic approach

For a semantic approach, we proceed as follows:

1 Set up any opposition, that is, two contrary terms (e.g., life/death).
2 Project the sub-contraries (e.g., not-life/not-death).[10]
3 Create the various metaterms (life + death, not-life + not-death, etc.) by finding satisfactory lexical labels for them where possible (for example, masculine + feminine = "androgyne").
4 Examine the semiotic act in question for all ten semantic possibilities (the four terms and six metaterms). To each of the ten classes, assign the elements that manifest these possibilities. A single semiotic act – even an elaborate one like a novel – will not necessarily use all ten of the possible classes. The most frequent ones are the two contrary terms ('one or the other'), the complex term ('both') and the neutral term ('neither one').

In textual analysis, one cannot be bound by lexical labels. For example, an element may fall under the class 'death' without actually appearing as the word "death". "Deceased", "last journey" and similar expressions will do just as well. Conversely, a figurative expression like "dead tired" (or "dead battery") will not fit under 'death' unless the text is playing with double meanings – a frequent occurrence in literature – such as a vampire who claims to be "dead tired".

The syntactic approach and time

The syntactic approach entails examining the successive positions occupied by the objects on a square. Increasing numbers indicate the sequencing of the various positions occupied (by a single object or from one object to the next as one progresses through the text). As with any analysis that focuses on content, one can take into account three fundamental kinds of time: time as represented in the story, narrative time (the order in which the events of the story are presented), and tactical time (i.e., the linear sequencing of semantic units from one sentence to the next).

We also offer a representation of the semiotic square in table format. This allows us to easily represent both the movements on the square in terms of the selected temporality and the possible interplay between the observing subjects (the narrator, characters, etc.) who are apt to see things differently.

Table 3.3 An example of a semiotic square in table format

No	*Time*	*Object(s) (element placed on the square)*	*Object's position on the square (1–10)*	*Observing subject*

Applications

Application I: the passion of Christ

We shall adapt an example from Courtés (1991, pp. 152–154): in the *Bible*,[11] with respect to the opposition life/death, Christ goes through the following stages:

1 Not-life + not-death: the divine existential state, beyond life and death.
2 Life: the Nativity, which makes Jesus a human.
3 Not-life: the agony of crucifixion.
4 Death: he is pierced by the spear, confirming his death, and placed in the tomb.
5 Not-death: the process of resurrection. (Is it instantaneous or does it occur over time? In the latter case, there would be an ellipsis: why, and with what effect on the narrative?)
6 Life: emerging from the tomb. Other interpretations are possible: The resurrection brings Jesus back to not-life + not-death, right here on Earth, or it grants him boundless life, liberated from death (life + not-death). To simplify the picture, we shall say that Jesus is in life, and that the Ascension is what brings him back to not-life + not-death.
7 Not-life + not-death: beginning with the Ascension.

Notice that this syntactic description has the advantage of eliciting some much-debated theological positions and pinpointing them within a framework. These debates are interpreted in terms of "conflicts" over different classifications on the same semiotic square. For instance, some people maintain that when Jesus was placed in the tomb, he was not actually dead, but in a state of not-life (agony), thus explaining the seeming resurrection. Changes in beliefs may be represented as syntactic movement on the square, as long as one applies the appropriate veridictory status (true/false) to each position that is taken. Thus, for Thomas, Jesus is in death, not in life, which he mistakenly believes until he touches Jesus' wounds.

Application II: **The explanation** *by Magritte*

Using the semiotic square, we will give a brief analysis of *The explanation* by Magritte. The basic opposition for our square will be carrot/bottle. Note that, unlike other oppositions we have presented (masculine/feminine or life/death), this one is specific to the image being analyzed, and therefore has a solely contextual value. The opposition between these two wholes is reinforced, if not recognized, by the oppositions between some of their parts, and each one of these oppositions could be the basis of a semiotic square (for example, edible/inedible). However, between other parts a relation of identity is established, showing a possible connection between the two objects, a connection that appears to be justified to some extent (both of them have an oblong shape, for instance).

We shall make use of three of the analytical classes of the semiotic square: the two contraries, where the carrot (position 1) and the bottle (position 2) are situated, and the complex term, where we have the carrot-bottle (position 5).

Is this complex term balanced, or does one of the contraries dominate? In other words, is it a CARROT-bottle or a BOTTLE-carrot, or is it equally a carrot-bottle and a bottle-carrot? Clearly, everything depends on what criteria are used. If we use "realism" and scale-based criteria, we could conclude that the bottle is dominant. Between the bottle and the bottle parts of the carrot-bottle, there

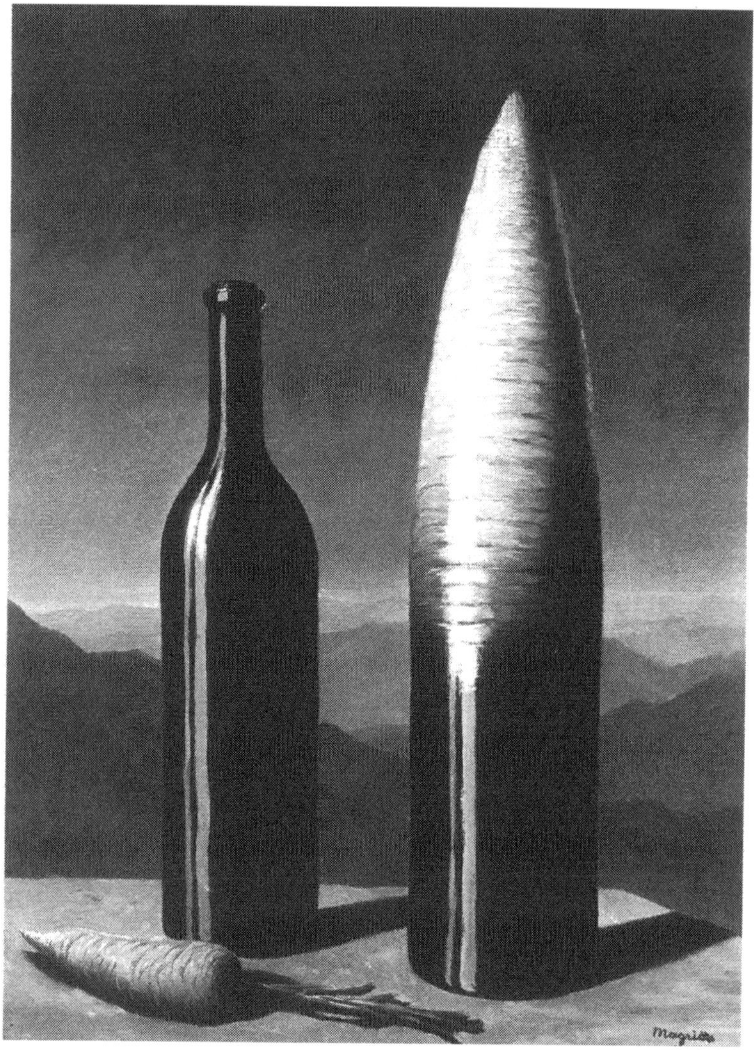

Figure 3.1 The explanation

Source: Magritte (1952)

is a consistency of scale, which is not the case between the carrot and the carrot part of the hybrid object. The effect could indeed be a prevalence of the bottle object over the carrot object, a sort of "real" bottle with a deformed, "fictitious" part added on – a disproportionate carrot.

Let us briefly distinguish two ways of producing complex terms corresponding to objects: fusion and juxtaposition. In *The explanation*, Magritte proceeds by fusion, as shown in the intermediate zone of the hybrid object, where the colors and textures of the two objects are intermixed. The painter also uses fusion in some other works (the boot-feet in *The red model* (1937), for example), but he also uses juxtaposition (the various pieces on different scales that make up the woman in *Delusions of grandeur II* (1948) can be seen as simply being placed on top of each other).

The series established by the term, its contrary, and their "merging" into the complex term is correlated with another series that is significant in the West: the custom of "reading" from left to right. The hybrid object is to the right of the objects from which it is composed. In this story consisting of three "time" units, the synthesis arrives "after" the thesis and the antithesis.[12] In other paintings, Magritte gives only the hybrid object, leaving it to the mind of the viewer to create the confrontation between the initial objects. (For an analysis of Magritte's and other hybrid objects, see the chapter on the semantic graph.) In this painting, Magritte dots his *i*'s and gives the genetic explanation, as the title indicates, for the fictitious shape.

We shall conclude by summarizing the main relations of identity and opposition between the three objects in the painting (the characteristics already mentioned are not included, such as the small, medium and large objects).

Table 3.4 Relations of identity and opposition between the objects in the painting

CARROT	*BOTTLE*	*CARROT-BOTTLE*
oblong shape	oblong shape	oblong shape
cylinder-cone	cylinder-cone	cylinder-cone
horizontal position	vertical position	vertical position
textured material	smooth material	smooth and textured material
bright color	dark color	bright and dark color
bipartite shape (root and top)	bipartite shape (base and neck)	bipartite shape
narrow upper part	narrow upper part	narrow upper part (that becomes thinner)
wide lower part	wide lower part	wide lower part
organic item	inorganic item	?
edible item	inedible (but designed to contain an edible element)	?
unbreakable object	breakable object	?
natural item	manufactured item (artifact)	?
existing object	existing object	fictitious object

Notes

1 The semiotic square was developed gradually, Courtés tells us (1991, p. 152), by building on Lévi-Strauss's research in anthropology and the linguistic theories of the Prague School (or Circle), which brought in the Russian linguists Jakobson and Trubetskoy in the late 1920s.

2 There are elements of content that have not been lexicalized in any language; one must speak in paraphrases to talk about them. This is presumably the case with the semic molecule /yellow/ + /viscous/ + /harmful/, which is present in Zola's *L'assommoir [The drunkard]* (see Rastier, 1989, pp. 167–170).

3 The classical model does not foresee combining a term and a metaterm, either (ex.: life and not-life + not-death). It seems we must allow for the existence of meta-metaterms. And we have in fact found an example, composed of a complex term and a neutral term: In the eleven-level "scale of thinking" proposed by Zen master Albert Low (1992, p. 62), one of the levels, the dilemma, is described as: "both YES and NO, but neither Yes nor NO."

4 In order to maintain that the principle of non-contradiction applies to the semiotic square – which would need to be demonstrated – one could argue that there are no "natural" units that combine contradictory elements (as far as the linguistic realm goes, we are talking about lexicalized units, that is units that exist as

morphemes, words or expressions). Nevertheless, the fact remains that we can create a profusion of units that combine these contradictories. (In the linguistic realm, we would be working at levels of complexity above the word or expression level, that is, the sentence and the text).

5 A balanced metaterm is obviously less plausible in theory. Given a scale from 0 to 0.9 with increments in tenths, there are more possibilities for dominance (all of the positions from 0.1 to 0.9, except 0.5) than for balance (position 0.5). The notions of dominance and balance pave the way for quantification within the qualitative classification of the square. The relations between the semiotic square and the tensive model (see the corresponding chapter) remain to be established. If we overlay the tensive model on the semiotic square, we can more accurately account for quantitative variations in the elements that make up a metaterm, typically the complex term. For example, the tensive model can be used to describe not just those terms in inverse relation – which already allows for the notion of balance/dominance – but also terms that are conversely related (or directly related), where an increase in the strength of a term goes hand-in-hand with an increase for the other term, and likewise for a decrease. For the purposes we have just described, the tensive model has a broader application than does the semiotic square, since it does not require elements in opposition; they must be describable in terms of intensity and extent, however.

6 In fact, whether the units involved are assimilated or dissimilated depends on the level on which the analyst is working (morpheme, word, expression, syntagm, etc.).

7 Life could also be described as the absence of death, but it is not, at least in lexicography (the field that handles the production of dictionaries). It generally seems to be the valued term – if there is one – that plays the pivotal role (life, in this case).

8 According to Courtés, incremental oppositions pose some problems when it comes to the syntactic progression allegedly dictated by the semiotic square. The semiotic square supposedly dictates a strict trajectory (here S1 = A, s2 = B, -s1 = not-A and –s2 = not-B): "In contrast to the Klein 4-group, the semiotic square dictates a set trajectory, from s2 to s1 via -s2, and from s1 to s2 via -s1" (Courtés, 1991, p. 153). Other theorists believe that the required trajectory is from s1 to -s2 and from s2 to -s1. However, Courtés minimizes the fixed nature of this trajectory: "two terms, s1 and s2, are said to be opposite if and only if the negation of one term *can* bring about the affirmation of the other term, and the reverse" (Courtés, 1991, p. 157). For instance, in the opposition rich/poor, not-rich does not necessarily imply poor. Courtés attributes this behavior to the incremental nature of this opposition. In a 4-group such as the veridictory square (see the chapter on this subject), movement will occur in all directions, but the trajectory will not be completely without limitations. According to Courtés (1991, p. 145), one cannot bypass a metaterm by going directly from illusion to secret, for instance, in the veridictory categories. Fontanille formulates a typology of trajectories (2003, p. 62) and identifies prohibited progressions (from A to B or B to A, from not-A to not-B or not-B to not-A), canonical progressions (from A to not-A to B or from B to not-B to A) and non-canonical progressions (from A to not-B to B or from B to not-A to A). Our position is the following: If a required trajectory on the semiotic square can be a valid notion in a model that generates opposite meaning from a source term – and this remains to be proven – then these trajectories and restrictions on trajectories should not be fixed a priori for the semiotic square or the 4-group. For example, there is no reason to preclude a text that goes directly from position S1 to S2 (from A to B) with no narrative ellipsis.

9 The μ Group (1977, pp. 58–62) would call these the tabular and linear approaches.

10 Visually speaking, note that the contradictory terms (A and not-A, B and not-B) are not placed one under another, but on the diagonal.

11 In Greimasian semiotics, in the theory of the generative trajectory of meaning, the deep structure of any semiotic act is simple and abstract; the surface structure is concrete and complex. Thus, on the deep level, the category life/death can describe the story of Christ, but by necessarily condensing it. On the surface level, this story is manifested by a multitude of other semantic values.

12 Another series is superposed onto the first two: small object, medium object, large object.

4 The veridictory square

Summary

An analytical tool developed by Greimas and Courtés, the veridictory square (or square of veridiction) may be described in simple terms as the semiotic square built on the opposition being/seeming. It can be used to examine the dynamics of veridiction (truth and falseness) in a semiotic act, particularly a text. The factors it takes into account are the following: (1) the evaluating subject, (2) the object being evaluated, (3) the specific characteristic evaluated in the object, (4) veridictory status: true (being + seeming), false (not-being + not-seeming), illusory (not-being + seeming) and secret (being + not-seeming), (5) the time of the evaluation and (6) transformations or changes in one or more of these factors. For example, when a cabaret Elvis goes into his dressing room after the show and then comes out, he goes from seeming + not-being Elvis (illusion) to not-seeming + not-being Elvis (falseness).

Theory

The square of veridiction, developed by Greimas and Courtés, which we will refer to as the *veridictory square*, can be used to examine the dynamics of truth/falseness in any semiotic act, particularly a text. In simple terms, we will consider the veridictory square as the "opposition" being/seeming projected onto the semiotic square. The veridictory square applies especially to texts in which truth/falseness is a prominent theme (the primary theme or at least an important one), for example *Tartuffe* (Molière), *The game of love and chance* (Marivaux), or *Each in his own way* (Pirandello). However, any reasonably long text implies a dynamic between truth and falseness, as do certain morphemes, words and expressions, such as "pseudo-", "crypto-", "so-called", "supposed", etc.

NOTE: THE VERIDICTORY SQUARE AND KLEIN'S 4-GROUP

As it turns out, the veridictory square is not actually a semiotic square, but a structure related to Klein's 4-groups (see Courtés, 1991, pp. 114–120, 137–141; Greimas and Courtés, 1982, pp. 310, 369; Greimas and Courtés, 1986, pp. 34–37, 105). This model, taken from the logic of mathematics, has been used in psychology by Piaget. The primary differences are the following: Klein's 4-group maps out two elements that are not necessarily in opposition (seeming and being, or wanting and doing, for instance). And since it addresses all of the possible combinations between two variables and their respective privative terms (for example, not-seeming and not-being, not-wanting and not-doing), it is composed solely of metaterms (compound terms).

In the theory we are discussing, any element subjected to interpretation (interpretive doing) is composed of and within the conjunction of a being and a seeming. Being is always accompanied by seeming and seeming is always associated with being. An element's being and seeming can be identical (for instance, a monk's seeming and being when he is wearing the robe) or opposite (for example, a layman will appear to be a monk with the robe as a disguise).[1]

NOTE: DIFFERENT WAYS TO INTERPRET THE RELATIONS BETWEEN BEING AND SEEMING

Clearly, there are several ways to conceptualize being, seeming and the relations between them. Each of these entails a different philosophical position, some of which are: (1) A being may not have a seeming and a seeming may not have a being. (2) Any being possesses a seeming, which is operative at the beginning, middle and end of its appearing, and which may or may not match its being. (3) Being exists, but is only accessible in its seeming. (4) Being is only an abstract reconstruction derived from seeming, which is the only accessible reality.

Being and seeming can each change through transformation. However, the transformation is not always accompanied by a corresponding transformation of the other variable: seeming may change without a change in being, and being may change without a change in seeming. For example, an honest citizen may become a wealthy drug dealer without any difference in his seeming.

In contrast with seeming, the knowledge one has about being may change without any difference in being (if, for example, you think someone is honest because he appears to be, and then you realize that despite appearances, he is not).

NOTE: BEING/SEEMING AND RECIPROCAL PRESUPPOSITION

Since seeming does not necessarily match being, and since being can change without any change in seeming and vice versa, then there is no a priori relation of reciprocal presupposition between being and seeming, even though this sort of relation can be established in certain semiotic acts (for instance, in Manichaean narratives, the bad guys always look bad and the good guys look good, except in cases of betrayal and deception).

The constituent elements of the veridictory square

The main constituent elements of the veridictory square, with the author's additions, are the following:[2]

1 The observing subject (S1, S2, . . .) (the real author, implied author, narrator, character, etc.; see the chapter on thymic analysis).
2 The object being observed (O1, O2, . . .)
3 The characteristic of the object being observed (C1, C2, . . .).[3]

NOTE: OPPOSITE CHARACTERISTICS

If the characteristic placed on the veridictory square has an opposite (good/bad, for instance), it can be used; in this case the positions on the square are reversed (1 becomes 3 and 2 becomes 4, or the reverse). Following the principle of homogeneity in description (Floch, 1985, p. 200), one should avoid switching from a characteristic to its opposite within one square (for example, one would put "good" for being and not-seeming rather than "good" for being and "bad" for seeming).

4 The marker(s) for seeming and being (M1, M2), that is, the elements that support a designation of seeming or being. The markers may be omitted in the analysis.
5 The four terms: being and seeming and their privatives, not-being and not-seeming.
6 The four metaterms[4] (or compound terms) that define the four veridictory statuses:

- True or truth (being + seeming),
- Illusory or lie (not-being + seeming),
- False or falseness (not-being + not-seeming),
- Secret or dissimulation[5] (being + not-seeming).[6]

Since the lexical labels for the metaterms (true, illusory, false, secret, etc.) are only indicators, one must not be misled by them. To take an example, when a cabaret Elvis goes into to his dressing room after the show and then comes out, he goes from seeming + not-being Elvis, which is illusion, to not-seeming + not-being Elvis, which is falseness. Intuitively one might argue the opposite: that he should be in the "true" position when he becomes himself again; This would indeed be the case for another characteristic: "himself" rather than "Elvis". Neither of the two characteristics is preferable in and of itself, but the analyst must take care not to switch unthinkingly from one to the other.

NOTE: THE ROLE OF THE CHARACTERISTIC

Vandendorpe (1994, p. 9) summarizes the originality of the Greimasian veridictory square in the following way, but also signals a possible shortcoming: "Truth is thus no longer seen as that which is implicit in language, nor is it in a transcendent position as one of the fundamental conditions of existence: It is only the flip side of falseness, with which it maintains a perfect symmetry, a point on which the authors are quite explicit (Greimas and Courtés, 1982, p. 116). However, we must say how regrettable it is that this definition is not expressed in terms of some category pertaining strictly to enunciation: By structuring truth and falseness as a conjunction between *being* and *seeming*, Greimas sanctions the interpretation of this category on an ontological level instead of a simple discursive level, despite all the cautionary statements he has made. This lack of vigilance is what prompts Claude Bremond to deride the veridictory square, objecting vehemently that the result of combining not-seeming with not-being can only be "absolutely nil"." From a theoretical standpoint, the veridictory square does in fact appear to lean towards ontologism. As far as veridictory status is concerned, the philosophical presuppositions (which are found in every analytical tool and every theory) of dialogics seem to have fewer epistemological consequences (see the chapter on dialogics). However, from a functional standpoint, Bremond's objection can be put aside so long as we include the structural features that we are proposing to enhance the veridictory square: This is a matter of relating not-seeming and not-being to a characteristic, which is itself related to an object. In this way, anyone could not seem to be a monk and not be one without vanishing into the philosophical void.

7 The four possible positions an object may occupy on the square, each of which corresponds to one of the four metaterms (1: true, 2: illusory, 3: false, 4: secret), and if applicable, the sequence of positions occupied by a single object (for example, 1 → 3).

NOTE: MOVEMENTS ON THE VERIDICTORY SQUARE

The conventional veridictory square appears to harbor several other useless aprioristic limitations. In our opinion, one of these is the notion that it must be composed solely of metaterms; another is the principle that movement may take place only between adjacent positions (for example, from 1 to 2, but not from 1 to 3 without going through 2) (see Courtés, 1991, p. 145). We prefer to leave open the assuredly marginal, but real possibility of a being with no seeming or a seeming with no being, if for no other reason than to be able to describe the present text, which demonstrates these possibilities. We have adopted these words from Floch (1985, p. 200), emphasizing the deductive value of the semiotic square: "As we can see, the point of the square is to give structure to the coherence of a conceptual universe, even if that universe is not recognized as "logical"; we can use the square to predict the trajectories that meaning can take, and the logically present, as-yet-unused positions that it can occupy". We also prefer to leave room for the possibility of nonadjacent trajectories, however rare they may be. We might add that Greimasian semiotics shows a predilection for simple trajectories, with no feedback loops or short circuits: unitary generative trajectories in which no stage can be short-circuited (although they can be interrupted prematurely, for example in abstract semiotic acts) and narrative trajectories biased in favor of the unicity of what has been done (as in reverse-chronological, unitary logic, where a narrative program generally presupposes one and only one trajectory) rather than the multiplicity of future possibilities (a logic of possibilities).

8 Time (T).

As with any analysis that focuses on content, three main kinds of time can be taken into account: time as represented in the story, narrative time (the order in which the events of the story are presented), and tactical time (e.g., the linear sequencing of semantic units from one sentence to the next). While reading the text, for example, one may come across position 2 followed by position 3, whereas the chronological order in the story might be 3 followed by 2.

Temporal segmentation can be based on various criteria. In a veridictory analysis, the most pertinent criterion for demarcating temporal intervals is, naturally, a change in one of more key beliefs (for instance, time interval T1 would last until a change in the key belief initiates interval T2).[7] Naturally, one can establish relations between this temporal segmentation and some other segmentation based on some other criterion, such as time in the usual sense (belief interval T1 might last from Monday to Wednesday morning; T2 from Wednesday noon to Thursday evening), or actions (T1 might last from action 1 to the beginning of action 3; T2 from the middle of action 3 to action 7) or tactical segmentation (paragraphs, chapters, scenes and acts or sequences, and so on).

An example of a veridictory square

We will first describe a veridictory square without giving a visual representation of it. In Molière's play *Tartuffe* (*The imposter*), with respect to the characteristic 'devout' (element C), Tartuffe (element O) goes from seeming devout + being devout (time 1, position 1: truth) to seeming devout + not-being devout (time 2, position 2: illusion) in the eyes of Orgon (element S) when the ostensible markers of religious devotion (the black habit, the anointed speeches, the omnipresent breviary, etc.) no longer carry as much weight as the opposite markers (the attempt to seduce his protector's wife, among others).

Visual representations

Strictly speaking, there is a distinction to be made between the veridictory square as a conceptual network and the visual representation of the network. (The same principle applies to other analytical tools, like the semiotic square, the actantial model, etc.) The conceptual network is usually represented visually as a "square" (which is usually rectangular). The veridictory square as a network is unitary in principle (one subject, one object, one characteristic, but one or more time intervals). The veridictory square as a representation may include one or more of these veridictory networks (a single subject and several objects, several subjects and a single object, and so on).

Square format

This how we represent the modified veridictory square:

Table 4.1 The modified veridictory square

	Position 1 TRUE		
According to subject S at time T	O BEING C	O SEEMING C	
Position 4 SECRET			Position 2 ILLUSION
	O NOT-SEEMING C	O NOT-BEING C	
	FALSE Position 3		

Legend: S: subject; O: object; C: characteristic; T: time

"X" Format

Greimas and Courtés also use an X-shaped diagram to represent the veridictory square (and to represent other 4-groups) (*b* indicates being; *s* is for seeming; the minus sign indicates not-being or not-seeming; the numbers indicate the corresponding positions):

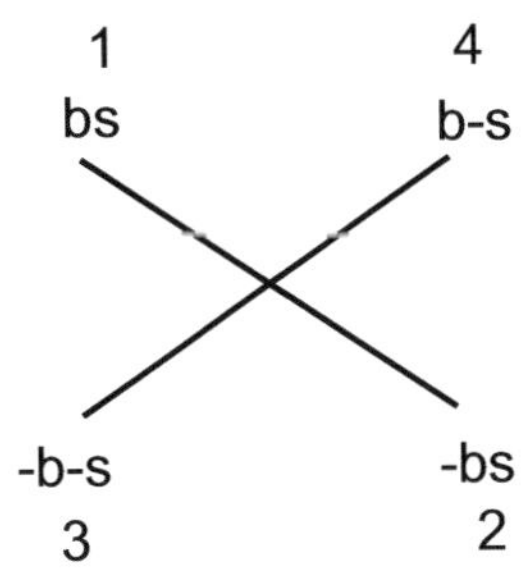

Figure 4.1 X-shaped diagram of the veridictory square

Table format

We also advocate the use of tables, for this tool as for other analytical tools with visual representations. Consider the following story: *A man buys a supposed Cartier watch and realizes later that it is an imitation.* We would create something like the below table:

Table 4.2 The modified veridictory square represented in table form

NO	*TIME T*	*SUBJECT S*	*OBJECT O*	*SEEMING*	*BEING*	*CHARACTERISTIC C*	*POSITION*
1	t1	man	watch	seeming	being	Cartier	1
2	t2	man	watch	seeming	not-being	Cartier	2

Beliefs: change and relativization

Decidable/undecidable and real/possible

An observing subject (for example, the analyst, the narrator or a character) may be unable to specify one or another of the terms that determine veridictory status. In this case, the term or the status would be undecidable; if the relevant term has not (yet) been specified, then the term or status is undecided. Decidable terms and statuses (those that are neither undecidable nor undecided) fall into two broad divisions, depending on which ontological status (status relative to existence) of the following two they are marked for: real (certainty) or possible (possibility, doubt).[8] In order to represent the category of possibility (cases where the subject is in doubt about being and/or seeming), one can use a question mark (?).[9] In this case, another symbol is necessary to distinguish the observing subject's doubts from the analyst's (who is also an observing subject, apt to be led by the author down a veridictory alley or to make up his own incorrect veridictory interpretation).

Seeming may be based on one marker (the seven tongues of the beast, for instance, as we will see later) or more (the clothing and breviary for Tartuffe). There may be variations in the degree to which a marker can be associated by the subject with its corresponding being. For instance, in the tale "The beast with seven heads", the false hero who brought back the seven heads of the beast as evidence of his exploit was unmasked by the real hero, who countered him with the seven tongues. Two interpretations are possible: the false hero's seeming has collapsed (he is in not-seeming + not-being a hero) or the seeming is there, but everyone knows that the being does not correspond to it (he is in seeming + not-being a hero). Unlike the heads in the case of the false hero, for Tartuffe, certain markers retain the power to evoke their corresponding being, but they become secondary in quantity and/or quality compared to other markers indicating the opposite being (he can wear all of the monk's clothing he wants; what matters is that his behavior is assuredly not that of a monk).[10]

Assumptive/reference veridictory evaluations

A veridictory evaluation is always subject to relativization: The supposed being may turn out to be only seeming, and not, in fact, actual being. However, in any given semiotic act, one generally finds reference evaluations that determine the ultimate truth. As a consequence, one needs to distinguish relative elements, which are called assumptive, from absolute elements, known as reference elements, since the first are judged by the second. Assumptive evaluations are subject to contradiction by the reference evaluations. Reference being and relative being can agree: In this case the being that a character presumes is correct would be confirmed, or at least not contradicted, by the reference subject (such as the omniscient narrator).

For example, Mary (S1, assumptive) thinks that in his robe (M), Peter (O) is and appears to be a monk (C). John (S2, assumptive) thinks the opposite. The narrator (S3, reference) eventually tells us that although Peter appears to be a monk, he is not. Mary's and John's evaluations are assumptive. The two evaluations are in opposition: there is a conflict in beliefs (the reverse would be a consensus in beliefs). The first evaluation is erroneous and the second one correct, because it corresponds to the reference evaluation (meaning the narrator's). Obviously, a given subject's belief may change. A "conversion" may or may not be preceded by doubt, during which the belief and the counter-belief confront each other, or by verification, whose purpose is to select one belief according to specific tests and criteria.

NOTE: THE DYNAMICS OF OBSERVING SUBJECTS

The standard veridictory square needs an additional feature, in our opinion, to address the dynamics of the observing subjects' viewpoints. At least in its most common usages, the veridictory square combines a stable, reference being, linked to the point of view of a subject associated with a universe of reference, and a seeming that changes, linked to the point of view of a subject associated with a universe of assumption. For example, in *Little Red Riding Hood*, the big bad wolf does not seem bad (along the pathway), but he is; later he seems bad (when he reveals his identity and says: "The better to eat you with . . ."). The reference being is nothing more than a being that, unlike the others, is not subject to relativization (mere seeming instead of actual being), and the analyst needs a way to describe this dynamic. In our opinion, one must be able to establish being as relative (initially, for Red Riding Hood, the wolf *is* not bad), and to express this belief, not just as a conjunction between not-seeming bad and being bad (which is the absolute point of view, since it is never contradicted in the story), but also as a conjunction between not-seeming bad and not-being bad, as formulated and applied to the wolf by Red Riding Hood. In this respect, the veridictory square seems to suffer from the same general inadequacy found throughout the interpretive component of Greimasian semiotics: Corresponding to the abstract subject at the source of the generative trajectory are two subjects: an interpreter whose position has not been very thoroughly worked out, and, for thematized interpretation within the text, a reference hermeneutic who possesses the ultimate knowledge of the text and thereby has continual access to the being of being.[11]

One veridictory evaluation embedded in another

As in any evaluation, one subject's point of view can be integrated into or embedded in another's: thus, a veridictory evaluation can be made about a veridictory evaluation. For instance, Mary (S1) might believe, wrongly or rightly, that Peter (S2) believes that John is and appears to be a monk (see also the analysis of *Tartuffe* that follows). The simplest solution is to include the second subject in the characteristic. In this example, the subject is Mary; the object is John; the status, seeming + being; and the characteristic "a monk, in Peter's opinion". There is another possibility: The subject is Mary; the object is "John is and seems to be a monk, in Peter's opinion"; the status is being + seeming; and the characteristic, "true".

Part vs. whole and element vs. class dynamics

As with other analytical tools, it can be helpful to include mereological (whole vs. part relations) and set dynamics (class vs. element relations), whether they apply to subjects (as in the case of a dual personality), objects or markers. For instance, for a person disillusioned with love, all people of the opposite sex (or possibly same sex) appear to be nice, but are not. Or the markers may suggest a particular evaluation overall (the whole), while some of them (the parts) may support the opposite evaluation (he looks like a monk, even though he swears at times). For more details on mereological and set dynamics, see the chapter on structural relations and the chapter on thymic analysis.

Application: Molière's *Tartuffe* (*The imposter*)

Consider the following synopsis of the primary veridictory plot in Molière's play *Tartuffe*:

T1: Orgon's entire entourage does not believe that Tartuffe is devout, except his mother.
T2: Orgon believes in Tartuffe until the moment when, hiding under the table, he hears Tartuffe trying to seduce his wife, Elmire.
T3: Armed with the truth, Orgon tries to convince his mother, Madame Pernelle, but she defends Tartuffe rather than believing Orgon.
T4: Orgon's mother obtains proof of Tartuffe's deceit when Mr. Loyal comes to seize Orgon's property for Tartuffe.
T5: The Prince seems to be in support of Tartuffe, because one of his emissaries, the exempt [sub-lieutenant] accompanies the scoundrel to go evict Orgon by force, or so Tartuffe believes.
T6: The exempt reveals to everyone that the Prince knows who Tartuffe is. Tartuffe is arrested.

Below is a "veridictory table", rather than a square, which illustrates this rendition of the play:

Table 4.3 An example of a veridictory square: *Tartuffe*

NO	*TIME T*	*SUBJECT S*	*OBJECT O*	*SEEMING*	*BEING*	*CHARACTERISTIC C*	*POSITION*
1	T1	Orgon's entourage except his mother	Tartuffe	seeming	not-being	devout	2
2	T1	Orgon	Tartuffe	seeming	being	devout	1
3	T2	Orgon	Tartuffe	seeming	not-being	devout	2
4	T1–T3	Orgon's mother	Tartuffe	seeming	being	devout	1
5	T4	Orgon's mother	Tartuffe	seeming	not-being	devout	2
6	T1-T6	Tartuffe	Tartuffe	seeming	not-being	devout	2
7	T5	Prince and exempt	Tartuffe	seeming	not-being	devout in the Prince's view	2
8	T5	everyone except the exempt and the Prince	Tartuffe	seeming	being	devout in the Prince's view	1
9	T6	everyone	Tartuffe	seeming	not-being	devout in the Prince's view	2

Note: The reference evaluation is the one on line 6. In addition, you will notice that in order to accommodate the surprise ending of the play, we have changed the characteristic in mid-analysis by integrating the Prince's point of view. (Thus, there is a veridictory evaluation within a veridictory evaluation, or more accurately, within the characteristic of the evaluation.)

Notes

1 Veridictory evaluations thus operate along the axis of immanence (being *vs.* not-being) and the axis of manifestation (seeming vs. not-seeming (Courtés, 1991, p. 114). According to Greimas and Courtés (1982, p. 130), these categories should not be seen as ontological ones, since it is simply a matter of characterizing a state in terms of being and seeming in the context of a modal categorization.

2 Where appropriate, we will show transformations in the subject, object or characteristic using a prime (S', O', C') in the notation.

3 In logic, the characteristic (C) and the object (O) correspond to the notions of predicate (the given characteristic) and subject (that which possesses the characteristic), respectively.

4 For the sake of simplicity, we are excluding the contradictory metaterms being + not-being and seeming + not-seeming, which are theoretically possible in a complete combinatorial analysis. To our knowledge, no semiotician has proposed the existence of contradictory metaterms, although we can predict their existence by deduction (see the chapter on the semiotic square).

5 Courtés explains (1991, p. 115): "In actuality, the negation of /seeming/ required for a /secret/ is never more than partial, as the person for whom the /secret/ exists must at least sense that something is being hidden from him; if there is a total negation of /seeming/, the subject involved would not be placed in the /secret/ position, but simply in a position of /not-knowing/, or ignorance. This means that all the while hiding something, a /secret/ must give a few indications that might prompt the subject to make inquiries or find out more." In our opinion, this restriction is not useful, and it stems partly from the influence of the lexical item chosen to express the conjunction between being and not-seeming ("secret"), and partly from the all-inclusive nature of the standard Greimasian veridictory square, which mixes the various points of view involved (in this case, that of the dissimulator and that of the person confronting the dissimulation). Per Aage Brandt (1995) has proposed these names for the four metaterms, in order: evidence, simulation, non-pertinence, and dissimulation. Bertrand (2000, p. 152), who combines Fontanille's proposals (in Greimas and Courtés, 1986, pp. 34–35), suggests an approach in which the relations of governance between being and seeming are modulated so that modal structures can be specified, depending on whether seeming governs (determines) being (self-evident truth), being governs seeming (a proven or revealed truth or a mark of authenticity), being governs not-seeming (an arcane secret), or not-seeming governs being (dissimulation, secretiveness). In this way, the relation between being and seeming, which is initially non-directional (despite the transition from seeming to being, from the interpretive standpoint), gives way to a relation that will either be balanced ("neutral" truth, illusion, falseness, or secret) or oriented in one direction or the other.

6 The semiotic square built on the opposition true/false must be distinguished from the semiotic square of veridiction, which maps out being versus seeming, and produces the metaterms true, false, illusory and secret. For that matter, as far as we know, the relations between this particular square and the square of veridiction have not yet been examined. Briefly, the complex term (true + false) on the semiotic square corresponds to an element classified simultaneously in positions 1 and 3 of the veridictory square. The neutral term (not-true + not-false) on the semiotic square is akin to secrecy or illusion. It remains to be seen how the notion of undecidability in logic (see Martin, 1983, for instance) is to be reconciled with the neutral term or the absence of a position on the semiotic square. (For example, in logic, elements separate from any proposition may be undecidable: *apple* and *red* taken separately are undecidable, but *This apple is red* may be decidable). One final possibility is to have gradations on the true/false axis, thereby obtaining ± T and ± F in an inversely proportional correlation, which would correspond to some form of complex term.

7 In a thymic analysis, the criterion is a change in the thymic evaluations, and so on.

8 It seems that in practice, the conventional Greimasian veridictory square only dealt with actuality as an ontological category, and did not take into account the modal category of possibility.

9 Although one might think otherwise, there can actually be doubt about seeming/not-seeming as well as doubt about being/not-being. For example, Tintin might wonder if his disguise really makes him look like a woman, and his duped victim may wonder at the virility of this strange woman.

10 A "marker" is what Courtés calls anything that can change seeming into not-seeming or vice versa. For example, the seven tongues allow the real hero – the one who really did kill the beast with seven heads – to reveal his identity before the king and to confound the traitor who presented the seven heads of the beast as proof of his victory (1991, p. 116). We use the term in a broader sense: a marker is any element that helps to designate being and/or seeming, accurately or not.

11 In Greimasian theory one finds a lack of symmetry: sometimes the focus is on the source element, such as the source of the generative trajectory, and sometimes it is on the target element, such as the choice of backwards-chronological logic over consecution for the sequencing of narrative programs (see the chapter on the narrative program).

5 The tensive model

Summary

The tensive model, an analytical tool used in post-Greimasian semiotics, was introduced by Fontanille and Zilberberg. In the tensive model, any given value is constituted by combining two "valencies" (dimensions): intensity and extent (range). Extent is the range over which intensity applies; it corresponds to quantity, variety, and the spatial or temporal range of phenomena. Intensity and extent are each subject to variation on a continuous scale from zero to the maximum (or even infinity). The tensive model is generally represented visually by a graph: intensity is placed on the ordinate, and extent on the abscissa. On this graph, any given phenomenon may occupy one or more positions. Two types of correlation exist between intensity and extent. The correlation is said to be converse, or direct, if (1) an increase in one of the two valencies is accompanied by an increase in the other and (2) a decrease in one valency leads to a decrease in the other. The correlation is said to be inverse if an increase in one of the two valencies is accompanied by a decrease in the other, and vice versa.

This model can be applied to knowledge. If intensity refers to the depth of knowledge and extent to the scope of the field of knowledge, and if one distinguishes high and low for both valencies, one obtains four different kinds of "knowers" or knowledge: (1) low intensity and extent (a little knowledge about a few things), (2) high intensity and low extent (a lot of knowledge about a few things), (3) low intensity and high extent (a little knowledge about many things), (4) high intensity and extent (a lot of knowledge about many things). It is generally accepted that the intensity of knowledge can only decrease if its extent is increased, and vice versa (an inverse correlation). A person going into medicine, for example, must choose between a specialty (2) and general practice (3). Note that the general practitioner's depth of knowledge is described as limited only as compared to the specialist's, not to the average person's, which is disastrously limited.

Theory

Values and valencies

The tensive model is an analytical tool used in post-Greimasian semiotics, introduced by Jacques Fontanille and Claude Zilberberg.[1] In the tensive model, any given value is constituted by combining two "valencies" (or dimensions): intensity and extent (range).[2] Extent is the range over which intensity applies; it corresponds to quantity, variety, and the spatial or temporal range of phenomena.[3] Both valencies are quantitative in nature; the first has to do with the measurable, the second with the countable.[4]

The strength of the valencies

Intensity and extent are each subject to variation on a continuous scale from zero to the maximum (or even infinity).

As with other analytical tools (the semiotic square, the veridictory square, the actantial model, etc.), the tensive model is simultaneously a network, a conceptual structure and a visual representation of this structure.[5] If we place intensity on the ordinate of a graph and extent on its abscissa, then we obtain a visual representation with two axes.

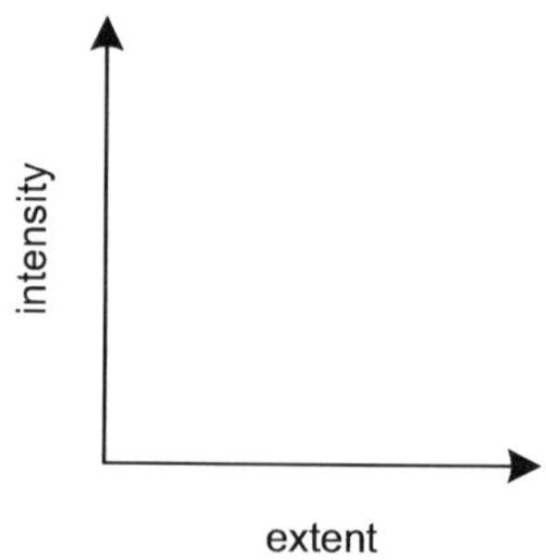

Figure 5.1 The two axes of the tensive model

Any given phenomenon will occupy one or more positions on this graph, depending on the degree of intensity it exhibits and the extent over which it ranges.[6] The model may also be represented in table form (we will give an example later).

Valency sectors and zones in the tensive model

The tensive scales can be divided into different sectors, which can vary in number.

Dyadic partitioning

If we distinguish two sectors for each valency, a low sector (an inactive sector) and a high sector (or dynamic sector), then we obtain four possible combinations of valencies, which define four zones:[7]

Zone 1: Low intensity and low extent
Zone 2: High intensity and low extent
Zone 3: Low intensity and high extent
Zone 4: High intensity and high extent

This yields the following diagram:

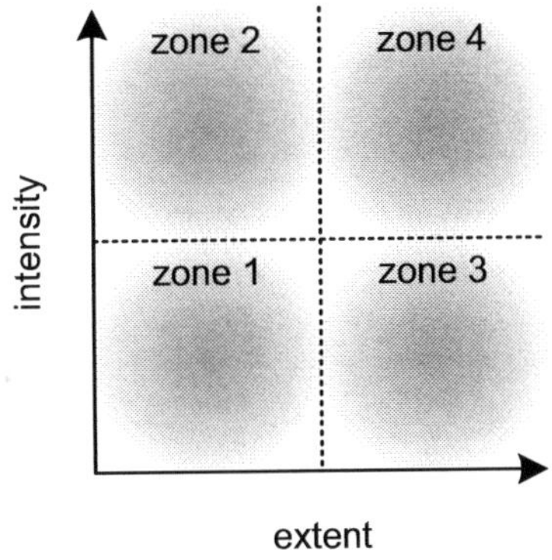

Figure 5.2 The four zones of the tensive model

Let us analyze a group of emotions associated with attachment to other beings. We will distinguish the emotions in this group solely in quantitative terms, although we are aware that a qualitative approach might conclude, for example, that between love and friendship, there is a difference in quality and not (just) quantity. The axis of intensity indicates the intensity of the emotion, and the axis of extent the number of beings toward which a given subject feels this emotion. By partitioning the graph into four zones, we will distinguish four fundamental kinds of emotions. In zone one, we have (a) love (ordinary love); (b) in zone two, "true love", or "the love of a lifetime"; (c) in zone three, we have friendship; and (d) in zone four, "universal love" or compassion. To refine our analysis, if we distinguish in terms of extent, true love generally applies to fewer beings than ordinary love, and conversely, universal love, as the name indicates, generally applies to more beings than friendship. Then if we distinguish in terms of intensity, friendship is generally a less intense feeling than love, and we consider universal love to be absolute compared to true love, not just in terms of extent but also intensity. This more exact analysis can be represented as follows:

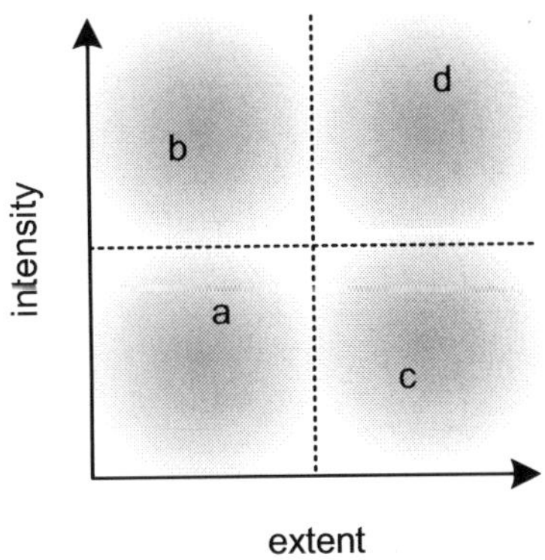

Figure 5.3 The tensive configuration of feelings of attachment

Other fine distinctions could be drawn, for instance, between Christian compassion and Buddhist compassion, which is greater in extent. It radiates not just toward humans, but other living creatures as well (so much for rocks and other inanimate "beings"!). The dominant Christian discourse places nature under the dominion of humans, who have no qualms, for example, about eating the flesh of animals even when they could do otherwise. In contrast, compassion as practiced by Francis of Assisi, who deeply loved animals, is similar to that of Buddhist discourse.

Other ways of partitioning

We have given an example of dyadic partitioning, which, when mapped onto both axes simultaneously, generates four zones. However, other methods of partitioning can be used. For example, triadic partitioning might distinguish low, medium and high on one or both axes; and pentadic partitioning would distinguish five levels, for example: zero, low, medium, high and maximum (or even infinite). Tetradic partitioning on two axes would allow us to attribute a specific zone to each of the four emotions we examined; some of the other twelve zones created by this partitioning might be appropriate for describing other feelings of attachment. In the application given, we address the issue of "translating" a diagram partitioned in one way into a diagram partitioned in another way.

Dynamic aspects of the tensive model

In this section we discuss the dynamic aspects of the tensive model.

Direct and inverse correlations

Two types of correlation exist between intensity and extent. The correlation is said to be converse, or direct, if (1) an increase in one of the two valencies is accompanied by an increase in the other and (2) a decrease in one valency leads to a decrease in the other. This could be described as "the more . . . the more . . ." or "the less . . . the less . . .". The correlation is said to be inverse if an increase in one of the two valencies is accompanied by a decrease in the other, and vice versa. This would be described as "the more . . . the less . . ." or "the less . . . the more . . .".

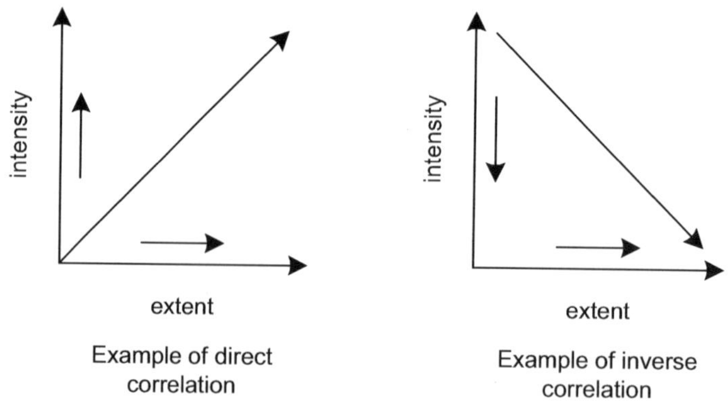

Figure 5.4 Examples of direct and inverse correlations

The two kinds of correlation are used to define zones of correlation, which can be approximately represented as follows:

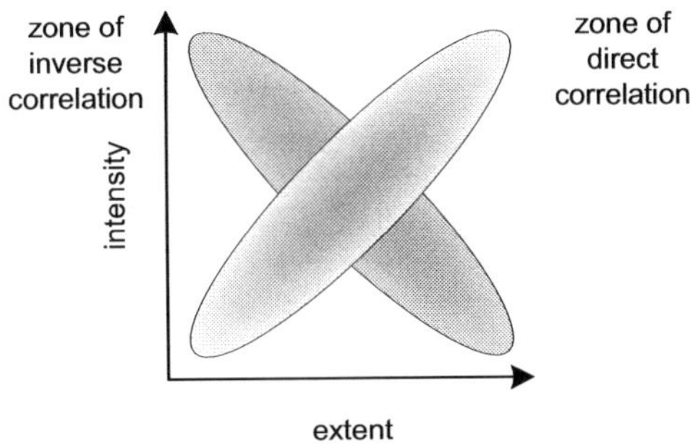

Figure 5.5 Zones of correlation

NOTE: THE RELEVANCE OF THE FOUR ZONES

All of the points on the graph may correspond to values for the same phenomenon. However, two organizing principles can be identified: firstly, the difference between direct and inverse correlation produces two basic directions of variation; secondly, "the end zones are determined by combining the strongest and weakest degrees on both axes. All of the points inside the space are relevant; but the zones at the two ends of each correlation are the most typical zones in the category being examined. By combining these two principles, we can identify four main zones that are typical for that category" (Fontanille, 2003, p. 74). Dyadic partitioning is admittedly an obvious choice; but in our opinion, while other ways of partitioning are less probable, they should not be dismissed out of hand (especially triadic partitioning) – only if they are not relevant to the phenomenon being described.

To return to our example of feelings of attachment, the average person is generally subject to an inverse correlation in which the more intense an emotion, the fewer the number of beings to which it applies. For him, universal love is unknown territory.

Elementary tensive models

By plotting the converse or inverse nature of tensive correlation as a function of time, we obtain four elementary tensive models:[8]

NOTE: THE TENSIVE MODEL AND GEOMETRY

The representations of the tensive model are inspired by geometry, but not derived from it. This explains certain graphical liberties and variations. For example, in representing direct and inverse correlation, Zilberberg uses modified ellipses that meet the zero points on the ordinate and the abscissa (2002, p. 118); however, Fontanille uses elliptical curves for inverse correlation and a straight line for direct correlation. Technically, Fontanille's ellipses (2003, p. 74) should be modified, which he does point out: "In a case of direct correlation, the variations in position generally follow the direction of the bisector; in a case of inverse correlation, the variations in position follow a path perpendicular to this bisector, a path that can also be represented by an arc whose two ends meet the two main axes". Most likely because it makes the diagrams easier to read, his graphs of inverse relations in his declining and ascending models do not show the curve going all the way to the axes (Fontanille, 2003, p. 111). As for our graphs, in order to keep them readable and consistent, we have not drawn them with the curves or the straight lines touching the axes, as they should.

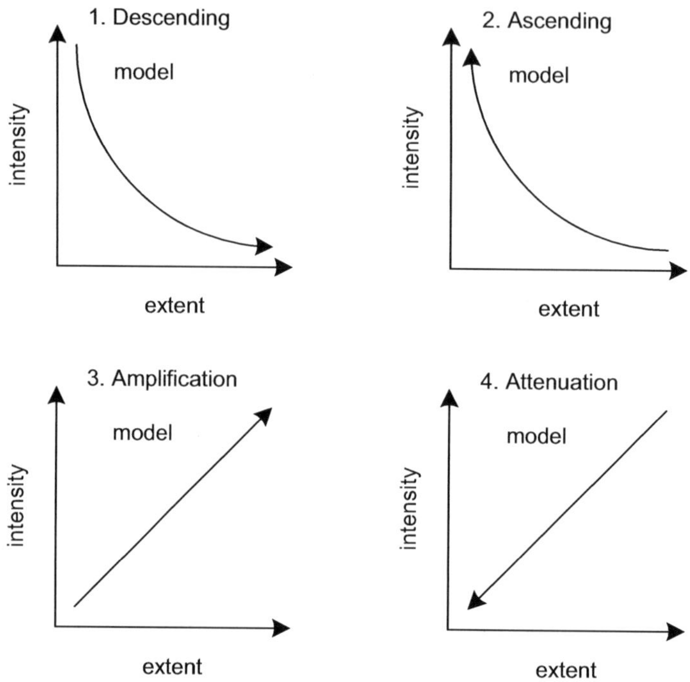

Figure 5.6 Elementary tensive models

NOTE: EFFECTS OF THE ELEMENTARY TENSIVE MODELS

According to Fontanille (2003, p. 110), the elementary tensive models are defined as variations in the balance between perception (intensity, affect, etc.) and understanding (dispersion over a range, measurability, comprehension). These variations lead "either to an increase in affective tension, or a decrease in cognitive tension. An increase in intensity brings tension; an increase in extent eases tension" (Fontanille, 2003, p. 110). As a result, (1) the declining model produces cognitive relaxation; (2) the ascending model produces affective tension; (3) the amplification model produces affective and cognitive tension; (4) the attenuation model produces overall relaxation, both affective and cognitive.

(Fontanille, 2003, pp. 111–112)

The declining model

An example of the declining model (or descending model) may be found in the transition between what advertisers call the "hook" (which is strongly affective, but often limited in extent) and the rest of the ad (Fontanille, 2003, p. 112).

The ascending model

An example of the ascending model may be found in literature in the transition between the body of a short story and its ending (the climax), which is more limited in extent, but has a higher intensity). The same phenomenon occurs between the body of a sonnet and its ending (or resolution) (Fontanille, 2003, p. 113).

The amplification model

The amplification model is exemplified in the majority of symphonic structures, which lead from the barely audible line played by one or just a few instruments into repetitions of growing intensity with more and more instruments (Fontanille, 2003, p. 113). Ravel's *Bolero* is an example of this.

The attenuation model

An example of the attenuation model is a drama with a happy ending or a comedy, where the number and intensity of problems decreases at the end, although they may not disappear entirely.

Combinations of elementary tensive models

Two or more tensive models may appear in succession in a semiotic act. When the sequence is a stereotyped one, we use the term "canonical tensive model" (Fontanille, 2003, p. 110). For example, from the fourth to the fifth act of a classical French tragedy there is an attenuation model (conflicts decrease in number and subside) followed by an amplification model (catastrophe arrives and becomes widespread).

NOTE: CANONICAL TENSIVE MODELS

Fontanille defines "canonical tensive models" as compound tensive models "that arrange several tensive models in a sequence according to a set configuration that is immediately recognizable in a given culture" (2003, p. 110). "Since they are characteristic of a type or a genre, they direct the interpretation of the discourse a priori, which gives them the status of cultural models, set by convention or inherited through tradition: this is why we call them *canonical models*" (Fontanille, 2003, p. 116). Our combinations of tensive models are more general, in that they do not have to be fixed or stereotyped, at least in theory, and when they are, it can be at the individual level and not necessarily at the level of an entire culture.

In terms of scale, there seem to be two ways of interpreting the elementary tensive models. The first approach takes the view that strictly speaking, elementary tensive models must cover all existing positions on at least one of the axes. To return to the French tragedy, if intensity is viewed as going from high to medium during the appeasement phase, then the graph that represents this appeasement is not the whole curve of the attenuation model, but only part of it. The second approach, which we have adopted, simply views this as a variation of scale within one integral elementary tensive model. Thus, the pointed figure known as a "cusp[9]", regardless of its size, is regarded as a combination of two elementary tensive models, such as the amplification model followed by the declining model.

Orthogonal models

None of the elementary tensive models allows for one valency to remain constant while the other changes; this would result in graphs with horizontal or vertical orthogonal straight lines. But deductively one can predict the existence of phenomena that would need to be described by plotting a line with one constant. (If need be, we could say that the existence of such a phenomenon is attested simply by raising the possibility.) What's more, we will see an example of this sort of phenomenon in our analysis of Pascal's theory of knowledge. How many of these orthogonal straight lines might we expect? In dyadic partitioning, we find: two vertical lines, one where extent is at a constant low and the other where it is at a constant high, and two horizontal lines, one of constant low intensity and the other of constant high intensity. Since each of these straight lines may be followed in two different directions (for a constant intensity, extent may be on the increase or the decrease, for instance), this gives us eight new trajectories, for a grand total of 12 kinds.

In our opinion, these lines with one constant are necessary, if not proven, and it is essential to integrate them into the description in one way or another. There are several possible ways of doing this. We have identified the two main ones as follows:

1 We can distinguish between elementary tensive models and elementary tensive movements.[10] This is a solution similar to the one we proposed in dealing with the succession of positions on a semiotic square (see the corresponding chapter). We recognize that the constraints generally placed on the sequencing of these positions on a semiotic square (i.e., the requirement that entails moving from one term through its negation to get to the contrary term) may be useful in producing a model to describe how this category (two elements related by contrariety) is generated. However, we maintain that a semiotic act can arrange these positions in any sequence it cares to (e.g., going directly from a term to its contrary, say, from beautiful to ugly, without going through not-beautiful). In short, the elementary tensive models represent ways of generating elementary values and movements, and their sequencing in a given semiotic act. Four of the twelve types of movement correspond to an elementary tensive model.
2 With dyadic partitioning, we have four elementary tensive models and eight elementary non-tensive models with which to structure a new analytical tool that is separate from the tensive model, although it is derived in the same way, using two axes. This tool can account for all kinds of combinations, tensive or not, between two intensive or quantitative variables. We can use it to represent variations in the intensities of two distinct phenomena, such as ambition (on the abscissa) and love (on the ordinate), to which Julien Sorel is prey in *The red and the black* by Stendhal. We can also represent variations in the range of two distinct phenomena, such as Eugénie Grandet's (Balzac) cash money (money in liquid form) and scriptural money (such as fixed-term credit notes).[11] This new tool places all of the following a priori on equal footing: non-tensive relations (with a constant), tensive relations and "semi-tensive" relations, that is, non-symmetrical ones. In fact, converse and inverse relations are not always symmetrical in the kind of variation they exhibit (increase/decrease) and/or the factor that varies (element X or element Y). We can conceive of a relation that is converse from X to Y, but not from Y to X, where an increase in X leads to an increase in Y, but an increase in Y does not lead to an increase in X (or it leads to a decrease in X). Of course, the typical converse and inverse relations are symmetrical.[12]

The tensive model and the curves of aesthetic euphoria

The curves of aesthetic euphoria, which we have presented in detail elsewhere (Hébert, 2005),[13] constitute a (1) cognitive and (as their name indicates) visual representation of (2) the variations (3) over time in the (4) intensity of the euphoric aesthetic effects that a (5) semiotic act (or semiotized event, such as a sunset seen as entertainment) generates (or could have/should have generated)

(6) in one or more agents of reception (such as the empirical reader or spectator). (For more details on agents of production and reception, see the chapter on thymic analysis.)

The curves of aesthetic euphoria can account for the variations in aesthetic intensity for any aesthetic phenomenon occurring or made to occur over time: semiotic acts in which the succession of units to interpret is strongly constrained (as in a written text) or absolutely constrained (as in performance art); but also semiotic acts that are regarded (wrongly or rightly) as having little or no temporality (such as a painting), which we then temporalize by inserting or recognizing some succession of units (e.g., by organizing an interpretive trajectory that arranges the figures of the painting into a series).

NOTE: AESTHETIC CURVES AND OTHER CURVES

If we drop the adjective "aesthetic" or use some other adjective, the same curves can also be used (a priori, at least) to describe non-aesthetic phenomena which involve (1) the passing of time, (2) a measurement of some type of intensity, and (3) the progression to which they apply. In this way, we could have a thymic curve (non-aesthetic), a dramatic curve, an orgasmic curve, a curve for an artisan at work hammering, and many others.

By using triadic partitioning (low, medium and high intensities; initial, midway and final temporal positions) and using irreversible time, we have produced a typology of 27 aesthetic curves. For example, while Ravel's *Bolero* is intended to produce an ascending straight-line effect for the listener, and in fact it succeeds, other semiotic acts with the same aspirations only succeed in generating the effect of a dull straight horizontal line for the receiver, at the lowest level of intensity.

NOTE: TENSIVITY AND THE CURVES OF EUPHORIA

A question arises as to whether our curves of aesthetic euphoria are based on the tensive model. The tensive model correlates elements belonging to two specific classes: on the ordinate we have intensity, and on the abscissa we have extent or range. It is evident that the ordinate of our curves does correspond to what tensive semiotics means by "intensity". What we have is not just intensity, but the intensity of a phenomenon that truly typifies the axis of intensities: axiology. As for our abscissa, it can be reduced to a form of temporal extent. However, we should distinguish cumulative time from successive time, or more accurately, time as duration from locative time (just as in grammar we distinguish cardinal from ordinal). Our curves are based on locative time, which allows us to define the boundaries of a duration. Tensive curves can obviously be based on time as duration, but, in the minds of those who designed them, can they be based on locative time? Is this still a matter of range, of extent? Even when time is not on the abscissa, tensive curves are not limited strictly to atemporal analyses. The typology of the four tensive models is in fact based on having a succession of tensive positions (with any succession occurring, at least theoretically, over time). Thus, tensive models – like tensive movements – combine three variables: intensity, extent and temporal position. Can we say that our curves are restricted to two variables, or must we say that the bidirectional movement that is possible a priori is not being used because it does not apply to the type of temporal substrate involved?

At the very least, our typology can serve as a point of departure for a typology of tensive models and movements using triadic partitioning. To round it out, we would have to add three "curves" that would be vertical straight lines (located at low, medium and high extent), and allow for bidirectionality on all of the curves: for example, curves 7 and 8 are identical, but with opposite temporal orientations; curves 25, 26, and 27 and the three vertical straight lines are each bidirectional. This typology would allow us to distinguish between ascending models with different temporal curves, such as 11, 15, 16 and 23.

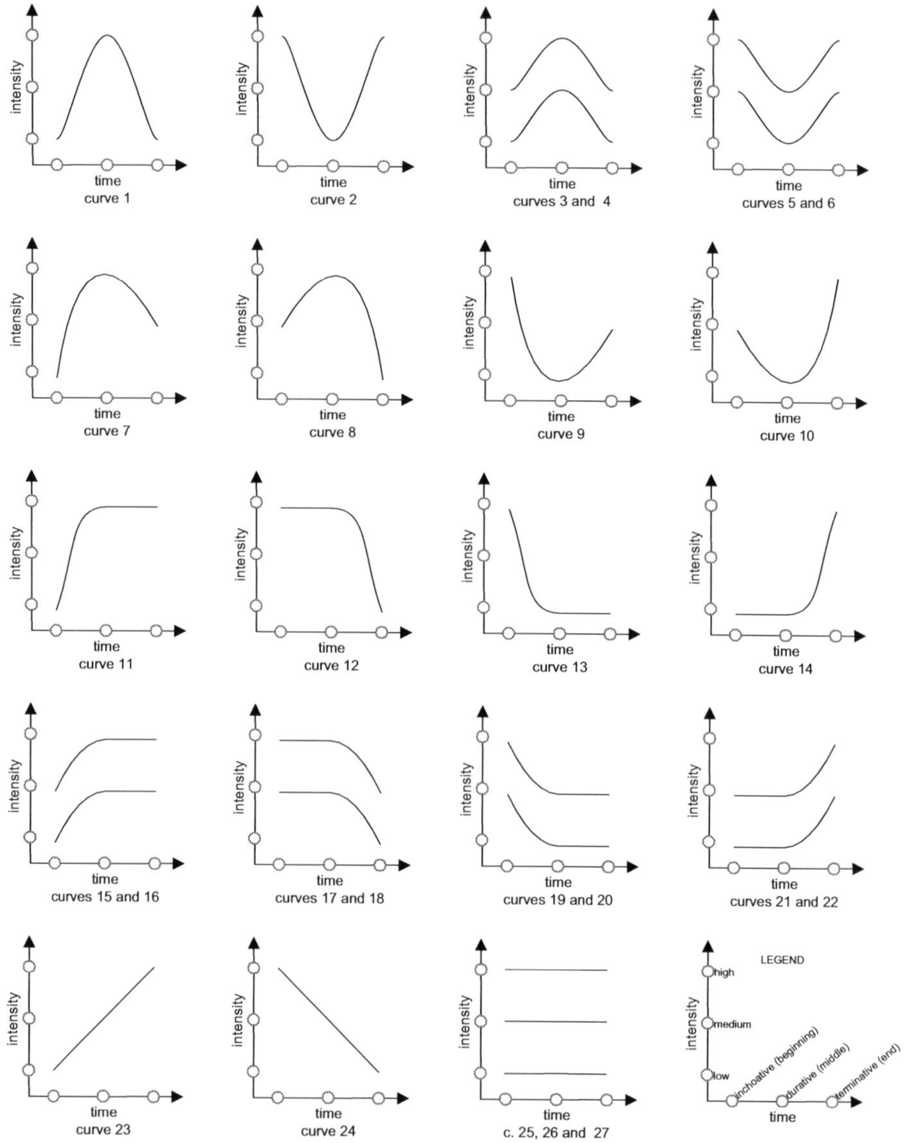

Figure 5.7 Typology of curves of aesthetic euphoria

Theoretical postulates

There is no need to discuss all of the theoretical postulates associated with the tensive model. What we are primarily interested in is its overall functionality, so to speak. However, for the record, we have listed the most important of these postulates:

1 Intensity and extent make up the content plane (the plane of signifieds) and the expression plane (the plane of signifiers), respectively (Fontanille, 2003, p. 72). Since any sign originates from the junction of these two planes, any sign is theoretically describable in tensive terms.[14]

2 Intensity is a matter of perception (that is, perception and/or affective feeling, to be discussed later); extent is a matter of understanding (Zilberberg, 2002, p. 115; Fontanille, 2003, p. 110).
3 Intensity refers to states of mind (passions); extent to states of affairs (Zilberberg, 2002, p. 115).[15]
4 Intensity has to do with interoception (sensitivity to stimuli originating inside the organism); extent has to do with exteroception (sensitivity to stimuli originating outside the organism) (Fontanille, 2003, p. 72).
5 Intensity corresponds to *visée* [intentionality, aim, focus, sighting]; extent corresponds to *saisie* [capture, the act of seizing or grasping] (Fontanille, 2003, pp. 73, 98). *Visée* and *saisie* are defined as follows: "this tension directed toward the world [. . .] is the concern of *visée intentionnelle*; in contrast, position, range and quantity characterize the boundaries and the properties of the field of relevance, that is, of *saisie*. Presence thus involves both elementary operations [. . .]: a *visée* of some level of intensity and a *saisie* of some extent" (Fontanille, 2003, p. 39).
6 Intensity corresponds to "feelings" (passions); extent to cognition (Fontanille, 2003, p. 110).
7 Intensity governs or controls extent (Zilberberg, 2002, pp. 114–116).
8 Intensity and extent are each broken down into two sub-dimensions: tempo and tonicity for the first; temporality and spatiality for the second (Zilberberg, 2002, p. 116).
9 The two basic functions of intensity are increase and decrease; the basic functions of extent are sorting (which increases diversity and/or number) and blending (which decreases diversity and/or number) (Zilberberg, 2006).
10 Implication derives from intensity and concession from extent (Zilberberg, 2006).
11 The tensive model belongs to a semiotics of continuity (and is complementary to the semiotics of discontinuity) (Zilberberg, 2002, p. 112), a semiotics of intervals (complementary to a semiotics of relations between terms) (Zilberberg, 2002, p. 125), and a semiotics of events (complementary to a semiotics of states) (Zilberberg, 2002, pp. 139–141).

NOTE: HOMOLOGIES BETWEEN THE POSTULATES

Most of the postulates that we have just listed belong to a series of homologies, that is, relations in which the first and second terms of an opposition are correlated with the first and second terms of other oppositions within the homology. The following is a list of these homologized oppositions: signified/signifier, content plane/expression plane, perception/understanding, internal/external, *visée/saisie*, feeling/cognition, states of mind/states of affairs, and interoception/exteroception. Fontanille establishes several of these homologies in the following quotation (2003, p. 72): "*intensity* defines the *internal, interoceptive* realm, which becomes the *content* plane; *extent* defines the *external, exteroceptive* realm, which becomes the *expression* plane; the *correlation* between the two realms is the result of a *position taken* by the body proper; this body is the abode of the perceptible effect of presence; therefore, the correlation is *proprioceptive*".

With the postulate concerning perception/understanding [*sensible/intelligible*] a question arises concerning Zilberberg's and Fontanille's use of the French word "*sensible*" [perceptible or sensitive in English]. Are we to interpret it according to its usual meaning, "perceptible", which places it in the commonly used opposition between what is perceived or taken in by the senses and what is only conceived in the mind; or should we interpret it according to its passional meaning (e.g., we say that a person is "sensitive" or "feels" a particular emotion), thereby placing it in the opposition between the heart and the head?[16] In Fontanille's work, both acceptations of the word seem to coexist: "substance is perceptible [*sensible*] – perceived, felt, intuited –, form is intelligible – understood, signifying", he explains (2003, p. 40), and later, he associates "*sensible*" explicitly with affect (2003, p. 110).

Taking this idea a bit further, we observe that while perception is generally said to be a matter of intensity, one of its specific forms, exteroception, is related to extent. It is common practice to classify an element as a whole in one of the terms of an opposition, and to classify the subtypes of the same element in both terms of the opposition. For example, in another area of Greimasian semiotics, one finds the following structure: discursive signifieds, like all signifieds, derive from understanding, but certain ones, the figurative signifieds, suggest perceptions (e.g., the signified for the word "red"), while others, such as the thematic signifieds, do not (e.g., the signified for the word "glory"). However, in our opinion, the general correlation of perception with intensity and understanding with extent creates a problem of coherence within the homologies. For although the signifier and the signified are both mental constructs, we must allow that signifiers (e.g., phonemes, the subject of phonology) have direct correlates in the physical world (e.g., when phonemes take form as particular sounds, which is the subject of phonetics), and as such, are part of perception. One could simply counter that the distinction between signifier/signified is entirely relational: that an expression plane can become a content plane in another semiotics, and a content plane can become an expression plane in another semiotics. The fact remains that the typical signifier arises from perception. A few additional points follow: The opposition between states of mind/states of affairs appears to be naturally homologous with understanding/perception. The mind is traditionally associated with the imperceptible and is set in opposition with the body and with material things in general. And then, temporality and spatiality, presented as sub-dimensions of extent, are properties of perceptible elements, more so than of cognitive elements. Of course, one cannot ignore metaphorical usages: One can talk about the "extent" of knowledge, for example, even if it concerns only abstract objects; however, literal usage is what should determine the elements that are typical of extent.

Application: Pascal's theory of knowledge

Consider the following thought by Pascal on knowledge (*Thoughts*, 37): "Since we cannot be universal and know all that is to be known of everything, we ought to know a little about everything. For it is far better to know something about everything than to know all about one thing. This universality is the best. If we can have both, still better; but if we must choose, we ought to choose the former. And the world feels this and does so; for the world is often a good judge".

The words "all" and "everything" in this reflection should not always be understood literally or absolutely, but sometimes in the sense of "a lot". For Pascal, man is caught between the Infinite and Nothing (*Thoughts*, 72), and cannot reach either one, as this second thought illustrates:

> "For in fact what is man in nature? A Nothing in comparison with the Infinite, an All in comparison with the Nothing, a mean between nothing and everything. Since he is infinitely removed from comprehending the extremes, the end of things and their beginning are hopelessly hidden from him in an impenetrable secret; he is equally incapable of seeing the Nothing from which he was made, and the Infinite in which he is swallowed up. [. . .] These extremes [the Nothing and the Infinite] meet and reunite by force of distance, and find each other in God, and in God alone. Let us then take our compass; we are something, and we are not everything. The nature of our existence hides from us the knowledge of first beginnings which are born of the Nothing; and the littleness of our being conceals from us the sight of the Infinite. [. . .] This is our true state; this is what makes us incapable of certain knowledge and of absolute ignorance".

If intensity applies to the depth of knowledge and extent to the scope of the field of this knowledge, we can establish four different kinds of "knowers" and knowledge.

Table 5.1 Tensive model of knowledge

INTENSITY \ EXTENT	*LOW*	*HIGH*
HIGH	2. A lot of knowledge about a few things	4. A lot of knowledge about many things
LOW	1. A little knowledge about a few things	3. A little knowledge about many things

Pascal makes use of these four zones and ranks them. Since the best zone – the fourth – is inaccessible to men, we must choose the third over the second; the first zone, which is implicit, is held to be of little value; it depicts man's initial state, which he must leave ("we *ought to* know a little about everything"). A person whose knowledge is at the junction of high extent and low intensity (but above the average person's) corresponds to the classical ideal in which Pascal believed. In contrast to the enlightened man, whose ideal is universal knowledge (for example, the extremely learned Pico della Mirandola), the classical "gentleman" should know, and can only know, a little about everything.[17] The classical conception is based on cognitive pessimism; the humanist conception on cognitive optimism, in which man must somehow compete with a God who knows all about everything.

On another level, two conceptions of knowledge seem to work together in Pascal's philosophy. The first conception, which relates to man's cognitive potential, postulates a constant level of cognitive energy, as it were, and establishes an inverse correlation between the two axes: Just as the pressure of a gas decreases if one increases the volume of space it occupies, so does the intensity of knowledge decrease if one increases the number of objects it encompasses. A converse correlation, in which cognitive energy would vary, is theoretically possible, but is implicitly assumed to be impossible in practice. The second conception, which relates to knowledge capital, postulates a possible increase in knowledge by increasing one of the two valencies at a time, either intensity or extent. (A loss of knowledge is not even considered.)

None of the elementary tensive models anticipates a situation where one valency remains constant while the other varies. We could argue that the line going from zone one to zone three is sloped: that the limited intensity of the latter is higher than the limited intensity of the former; in other words, that the apparently horizontal line turns out to be diagonal if we increase the precision of the analysis by allowing for the possibility of multiple positions within one zone. Whatever the case, it is more difficult to make this objection about the line going from zone one to zone two. Increasing the depth of one's knowledge cannot bring about an increase in extent if the increase applies to something already included in the limited initial knowledge. To return to our initial question: How do we integrate a description of these orthogonal straight lines into the tensive model? To present just one of many conceivable solutions, let us make a distinction – here and elsewhere, and perhaps even in all tensive descriptions – between elementary tensive models, which necessarily imply a converse or inverse relation, and elementary tensive movements, which cannot exhibit this sort of relation. Pascal uses only two of these non-converse, non-inverse movements; more specifically, he does not anticipate a transition from zone two to zone one, or from zone three to zone one.

We have chosen not to give any lexical labels, or names, for the zones in our table. In most of the tensive models, problems arise when selecting lexical labels for the zones: firstly, valid names do not always exist for a given zone, and secondly, several names and categories may be appropriate for the same zone, primarily because of the recursivity of tensive relations.

For example, in the pair ignoramus/average man, the first term belongs to the first zone and the second term belongs to the third zone; but in the pair average man/cultivated man, the first term belongs to the first zone and the second term belongs to the third zone. What happens if we want to account for the entire triad? If we are still opting for a model with four zones, we will classify two elements in the same zone, but in slightly different positions on one of the two axes, and the third element will be in a zone by itself. Then we would have (1) the ignoramus and the average man in the first zone, with the cultivated man in the third zone, or (2) the ignoramus in the first zone and the average man and the cultivated man in the third zone.

Now we will use a model with more than four zones. We will set up low, medium and high divisions on both axes. In this case, the ignoramus would be located at the junction of low intensity and low extent; the enlightened man would be at the junction of high intensity and extent. As for the other "knowers" we identified in the previous model, several alternate classifications are possible, and we propose the following: The cultivated man can be placed at the junction of medium intensity and high extent; the average man at the junction of medium intensity and medium extent; and the specialist at the junction of high intensity and medium extent. Our guideline in classifying these three "knowers" is that it would not be right to say that the specialist's knowledge is less extensive than the average man's, nor would it be right to say that the cultivated man's knowledge is of lower intensity than the average man's. Out of the nine zones in this model, there are four left for classifying other kinds of "knowers" and knowledge, if need be. The appropriate number of zones depends on what is being described. For example, two of the zones delineated in a dyadic partitioning are adequate to describe the kinds of doctors: the specialist (specialized doctor) resides in zone two, and the general practitioner (generalist) is in zone three. This inter-definition does not take into account non-medical knowledge and it excludes non-doctors. While the general practitioner knows "a little" about each field of medicine, this is relative to the specialist, not the man on the street, who knows "very little".

This next thought about knowledge by Pascal (*Thoughts*, 327) brings another level of complexity to our analysis:

> "The world is a good judge of things, for it is in natural ignorance, which is man's true state. The sciences have two extremes which meet. The first is the pure natural ignorance in which all men find themselves at birth. The other extreme is that reached by great intellects, who, having run through all that man can know, find they know nothing, and come back again to that same ignorance from which they set out; but this is a learned ignorance which is conscious of itself. Those between the two, who have departed from natural ignorance and not been able to reach the other, have some smattering of this vain knowledge, and pretend to be wise. These trouble the world, and are bad judges of everything. The people and the wise constitute the world; these despise it, and are despised. They judge badly of everything, and the world judges rightly of them".

In contrast to the first excerpt, this third thought by Pascal attributes a certain value to zone one, at least the part of zone one (located in the lower left corner) that corresponds to the absolute natural ignorance in which men are born. As in the second thought, we notice that the two extremes are valued, while the person in the intermediate position, the half-learned man, is devalued, having left natural ignorance forever, and never able to attain learned ignorance.[18]

Let us suppose that the transition from vast knowledge to natural ignorance is categorial rather than incremental[19] (with no transition when moving from one to the other), and that the knowledge leading one degree further to natural ignorance is located in zone three in the upper right corner. That leaves us with one position to identify: learned ignorance. As the name implies, learned ignorance is not a return to natural ignorance; it does not trace a circular path, but a spiral. What distinguishes it from ignorance, in addition to the high level of accumulated knowledge, is the paradoxical awareness of knowing that it does not know. Pascal attaches great importance to reflective consciousness, the knowing that is aware of its own self, the thinking subject. He writes (*Thoughts*, 347): "Man is but a reed, the most feeble thing in nature, but he is a thinking reed. The entire universe need not arm itself to crush him. A vapour, a drop of water suffices to kill him. But, if the universe were to crush him, man would still be more noble than that which kills him, because he knows that he dies and the advantage which the universe has over him; the universe knows nothing of this". To paraphrase Pascal, we would say that man's greatness lies in knowing (or having the capacity to know) that he does not know.

One possible response to our question is that the transition from vast knowledge to learned ignorance occurs not by jumping from zone three to zone one, but by transforming the knower's awareness of the map on which he finds himself: rather than remaining stable, the axes lengthen (like a horizon that is always at the same distance, or like a horizon that becomes more and more distant?) so that the knower finds himself in a relative position of natural ignorance. The learned ignorant man has truly taken the measure of what he does not know. This is a reminder that any classification is done in the estimation of an observer. Thus, a naturally ignorant person believes himself to be at the junction of a higher intensity and extent than he really is, because he is unaware of the extent of what he could know, but does not.

Notes

1 This chapter is loosely based on Fontanille, 2003, pp. 69–77, 109–116; Zilberberg, 2002.

2 In logic, a concept's intension or comprehension (i.e., the set of attributes that define it; for example, a human is a mammal, a biped, and so on) is opposed to its extension (the set of elements it covers, such as the set of humans). While extent has strong semantic similarities to extension, the same clearly does not apply for intensity and intension.

3 According to Zilberberg (2002, p. 116), tempo and tonicity are the two sub-dimensions of intensity, whereas temporality and spatiality are the two sub-dimensions of extent; The functives, or constituent elements, of each dimension are weak/strong for intensity, and concentrated/diffuse for extent (Zilberberg, 2006). In our opinion, temporality and spatiality neglect certain elements that should be covered by extent. In addition to spatial and temporal range, extent has to do with the quantity and variety of phenomena involved, and these things are not always reducible to spatial notions, unless the term is taken metaphorically, in which case it could include things such as concepts (this would apply to the "extent" of knowledge, for instance). Moreover, when we describe extent as diffuse or concentrated (see Fontanille, 2003, p. 46), thereby implying density, we are implicitly combining two aspects of extent: the quantity of phenomena and their spatial or temporal range. Fontanille (2003, p. 110) gives intensity and affect, along with an "etc.", as elements that can be plotted on the axis of intensity. So the question arises: Can one put a composite valency on an axis? If so, then there is a distinction to be made between analytic and synthetic approaches to using the tensive model. A synthetic approach allows for the placement of a composite valency on one axis: in this way one can use the axis of intensity to plot the intensity of some element other than the one found on the axis of extent. For example, the intensity of a positive evaluation attributed to knowledge (a compound valency, whereas the intensity of the knowledge itself would be a simple valency) may increase relative to the scope of the knowledge (a simple valency).

4 Zilberberg (2006) says this about the tensive description of units: "the unit must be measurable and/or countable, measurable in intensity, countable in extent." Farther on, he states that tensive semiotics allows

for "a reconciliation of quality and quantity, which is peculiar to the concept of measurement, allowing us to qualify quantity and to quantify quality at the least expense."

5 Although the tensive model is known as the "*schéma* [diagram, model] *tensif*" in French, this term does not allude so much to its visual representation as a diagram as it does the technical meaning of "schematism", a term that "in the Kantian tradition refers to the mediation between concept and image, and more generally, between the categories of understanding and perceptible phenomena" (Fontanille, 2003, p. 110). In fact, one of the theoretical postulates of the tensive model deals with how mediation occurs between understanding (intensity) and perception (extent).

6 Certain phenomena, like the curve of a French tragedy, to be discussed later, must be represented by combining several diagrams.

7 Zilberberg (2006) opts for a partitioning into two areas separated by the bisector of the graph. Above the bisector is the area of absolute values, and below it is the area of universal values: "As one begins to focus on discourse, what matters is not what each order signifies in isolation, but what each one represents "in the view" of the other: (1) From the perspective of universal values, which are influenced by valencies of extent, the absolute values are certainly intense, but they have a serious flaw in that they are concentrated [narrow in extent]; the universal values themselves are weak [in intensity], but have the superior advantage (from their perspective) of being diffuse [broad in extent]; (2) from the perspective of absolute values, which are strongly influenced by valencies of intensity, the universal values are diffuse, but weak; the absolute values themselves are certainly concentrated, but their brilliance [strong intensity] compensates overwhelmingly for this flaw. Thus, each order of values necessarily disqualifies its counterpart by following its own valency preferences." Note that typically, the areas occupied by absolute values and universal values are zones two and three, respectively.

8 As we can see, even when time is not on the abscissa, tensive graphs are not limited strictly to atemporal analysis. The typology of the four tensive models is in fact based on having a succession of tensive positions (with any succession occurring, at least theoretically, over time). Thus, tensive models include three variables: intensity, extent and temporal position.

9 For another example of a cusp, see Fontanille, 1999, p. 155.

10 We prefer the term "movement" to "trajectory", since the latter is associated with a succession of more or less obligatory stages in Greimasian semiotics, such as the "generative trajectory of meaning."

11 Zilberberg sometimes creates tensive models in which a type of element placed on one axis belongs a priori to the other axis. For instance, while he defines speed and slowness as part of tempo, and thus belonging on the axis of intensity, Zilberberg (2006) has a diagram with speed on the axis of intensity and slowness on the axis of extent. Does slowness necessarily have more extent than speed? Is this still a tensive model? In another case, Zilberberg also equates the minimum and maximum points on the tensive axes with the absence (represented by zero) and presence (represented by one), respectively, of the variable placed on either axis. The same question arises: Is this still a tensive model?

12 If there is a correlation, it is not necessarily a strict one: "We do not require a strict correlation to be strict, since it cannot be. In fact, correlation actualizes a trend, whose realization is impeded by resistance, obstructions, and as a consequence, delays" (Zilberberg, 2006). For the sake of symmetry, we are tempted to add that anticipatory effects may arise as well.

13 We have made our conclusions about the non-tensive nature of the curves of aesthetic euphoria noticeably less definitive here as compared with the previous publication.

14 In Zilberberg's work, any sign – or at least any discursive sign – seems to be describable in tensive terms: "any discursive entity is characterized in terms of intensity and extent" (2002, p. 115).

15 Zilberberg writes (2002, p. 115): "tensivity is the imaginary place where intensity (i.e., states of mind, the perceptible) and extent (i.e., states of affairs) are brought together."

16 Pascal uses this opposition when he writes: "There is internal war in man between reason and the passions" (*Thoughts*, 412).

17 Fontanille believes that today's "cultivated man" is bound by the same obligation: he is supposed "to know a little about everything, to have breadth of knowledge but without being too high-minded or making himself a specialist" (2003, p. 186).

18 Pascal also values the intermediate position in this passage (*Thoughts*, 378): "To leave the mean is to abandon humanity. The greatness of the human soul consists in knowing how to preserve the mean."

19 If the transition from vast knowledge to learned ignorance is incremental, then we must ask when it starts (that is, where on the chart), and whether it happens in equal increments or with an acceleration at the end.

6 The actantial model

Summary

The actantial model, developed by A.J. Greimas, can be used to break an action down into six facets, or actants: (1) The subject (for example, the Prince) is what wants or does not want to be conjoined with (2) an object (the rescued Princess, for example). (3) The sender (for example, the King) is what instigates the action, while (4) the receiver (for example, the King, the Princess, the Prince) is what benefits from it. Lastly, (5) a helper (for example, the magic sword, the horse, the Prince's courage) helps to accomplish the action, while (6) an opponent (the witch, the dragon, the Prince's fatigue, a hint of terror) hinders it.

Theory

Origins and function

During the sixties, A. J. Greimas proposed the actantial model (1966, pp. 174–185, 192–212), based the theories of Vladimir Propp (1970).[1] The actantial model is a tool that can theoretically be used to analyze any real or thematized action, but particularly those depicted in literary texts or images. In the actantial model, an action may be broken down into six components, called actants.[2] Actantial analysis consists of assigning each element of the action being described to one of the actantial classes.

Six actants and three axes

The six actants are divided into three oppositions, each of which forms an axis of the actantial description:

The axis of desire: (1) subject/(2) object. The subject is what is directed toward an object. The relationship established between the subject and the object is called a *junction*. Depending on whether the object is conjoined with the subject (for example, the Prince wants the Princess) or disjoined (for example, a murderer succeeds in getting rid of his victim's body), it is called a conjunction or a disjunction.
The axis of power: (3) helper/(4) opponent. The helper assists in achieving the desired junction between the subject and object; the opponent hinders the same (for example, the sword, the horse, courage, and the wise man help the Prince; the witch, the dragon, the far-off castle, and fear hinder him).[3]

The axis of transmission (the axis of knowledge, for Greimas): (5) sender/(6) receiver. The sender is the element requesting the establishment of the junction between subject and object (for example, the King asks the Prince to rescue the Princess). The receiver is the element for which the quest is being undertaken. To simplify, let us interpret the receiver (or beneficiary-receiver) as that which benefits from achieving the junction between subject and object (for example, the King, the kingdom, the Princess, the Prince, etc.).[4] Sender elements are often receiver elements as well.

NOTE: SENDER AND HELPER

Traditionally, the sender is considered to be that which initiates the action; anything that occurs along the way to stir up desire for the junction to be achieved will be assigned to the helper class instead[5] (the same logic applies for the anti-sender and opponents). This problem – where position in a narrative sequence and function in this sequence are mixed up – has been worked out in the canonical narrative schema, Greimas's subsequent model that is more developed than the actantial model (see the chapter on this model). The sender (more accurately called the sender-manipulator) has been redefined as that which prompts the action by manipulating either wanting-to-do or having-to-do, no matter when the inducement occurs.

NOTE: STEPS FOR CREATING AN ACTANTIAL MODEL

In simple terms, the steps for performing an actantial analysis are as follows: (1) Select the general action. (2) Convert the action into an actantial model by first selecting the subject and the object (since the other actants are defined relative to this axis), specifying the type of junction between the subject and the object (a conjunction or disjunction) and saying how and whether the junction is achieved (completely or partially, with certainty (a real junction) or doubt (a possible junction)). (3) Select the other actants. Each selection must be justified. (Where is the element found in the text? Why is it considered to be a subject, a helper, etc.?) It is a common error to lose sight of the particular subject-object axis identified by the analyst, and to designate senders, receivers, helpers or opponents that actually pertain to a different subject-object axis. The helper is not allied to the subject, but to the object-subject junction. For example, if a character's best friend helps him in every action except the one addressed by the model, then he is not a helper in that particular model.

Sets of actantial models

In theory, any real or thematized action may be described by at least one actantial model. Strictly speaking, *the* actantial model for a text does not exist. For one thing, there are as many models as there are actions; for another, the same action can often be seen from several different perspectives (for example, from the subject's point of view, or his rival, the anti-subject's).

Although one generally chooses the action that best summarizes the text, or lacking that, some key action, there is no rule against analyzing a group or a set of actantial models. A set involves at least two actantial models with at least one relation established between them. Relations may be temporal (complete or partial simultaneity, immediate or delayed succession) and/or logical (simple presupposition (for example, cause and effect) reciprocal presupposition, mutual exclusion (between incompatible actions), or a relation between type-model and token-model and so on). More details on these relations can be found in the chapter on narrative programs.

NOTE: COMPARING ACTANTIAL MODELS

In a short analysis, it is often best to examine a single actantial model, but two related models can also be compared. When we bring several actantial models into the picture, we can give them all the same emphasis, or we can develop one model more exhaustively (by focusing the analysis on one model, but making brief comparisons between it and other models). Some models may only be referred to in passing.

Visual representations

Technically speaking, the actantial model as a conceptual network should be distinguished from its visual representation. The conceptual network is generally depicted as a diagram, given in formats like the following:

Table 6.1 Actantial model represented as a square (I)

Sender	————>	Object	————>	Receiver
		↑		
Helper	————>	Subject	<————	Opponent

Table 6.2 Actantial model represented as a square (II)

SENDER			RECEIVER
	SUBJECT	OBJECT	
HELPER			OPPONENT

We have developed a table format, where we have included the additional features that we are proposing (explanation to come later) to the standard actantial model:

Table 6.3 The actantial model represented in table format

No	*time*	*observing subject*	*actant name*	*actant class s/o, send/rec, help/opp*	*actant sub-class: real/ possible*	*actant sub-class: true/ false*	*other actant sub-classes (active/passive, etc.)*
1							
2							
Etc.							

Since the actantial model and the visual representation thereof are two different things, a single diagram may be used to combine several actantial models, each of which refers to a different action or reflects a subsequent state of the same model. In this case, the elements of each model are distinguished by using conventional symbols (regular type for the elements of the first model and italics for the elements of the second actantial model, for instance).

Character/non-character actants

An actant does not always correspond to a character in the traditional sense of the term.[6] The concept of the actant is derived by broadening or generalizing the concept of the character, if you will. From the standpoint of natural ontology (which defines what kinds of beings, broadly speaking, make up reality), an actant may correspond to: (1) an anthropomorphic being (for example, a human, an animal, a talking sword, etc.) (2) a concrete, inanimate element, including things (such as a sword), although not limited to the concrete (such as the wind, the distance to be traveled), (3) a concept (courage, hope, freedom, etc.). An actant may be individual or collective (society, for instance).

In theory, the six actants may belong to any of the three ontological categories. In actual application, there are some common exclusions: subjects, senders and receivers tend to belong to the category of anthropomorphic beings. (An inanimate element or a concept must be personified in order to fill this role.) However, if one defines the sender as the element that acts, voluntarily or not, to elicit either wanting-to-do or having-to-do the action, then it can belong to any of the three ontological categories (see the chapter on the canonical narrative schema).

Actantial syncretism

A single element may be found in one, several, or even all actantial classes. Actantial syncretism occurs when a single element, known as an actor (such as a character in the traditional sense of the word), "contains" several actants from different classes (for example, subject and helper simultaneously) or several actants from the same class that have separate actions in the analysis.

NOTE: IS EVERY TEXTUAL ELEMENT AN ACTANT IN AT LEAST ONE ACTANTIAL MODEL?

Is every textual element an actant in at least one actantial model? No. Setting aside any limiting criteria that we might establish (for example, taking into account only those actants that are characters), we should point out firstly that actantial analysis occurs at the text level (the discourse level), and that each and every element of the lower levels (sentence and word levels) does not necessarily enter directly into this level (such as a definite article). Secondly, even elements at the text level may be designated as external to the actantial model, either on a general basis or relative to a specific actantial model, for example, elements that are judged as circumstantial (such as time and space) or simply descriptive (details deemed to be irrelevant in the analysis of a specific action, such as the color of the bridle on the prince's horse).

There is a quantitative issue to be addressed, similar to the previous one. In theory, for any specific action being described, one actantial class may contain one element, several, or none. In actual practice, it seems that empty actantial classes are not found, except in extremely brief texts (such as a proverb or an aphorism). In order to keep the analysis homogeneous, subjects and objects usually contain only one element (which can be a collective, like humans or society). In fact, the best strategy is to distinguish subjects clearly from each other and objects as well, even it they are closely related, in order to draw distinctions in the descriptions (for example, in the extreme case where two allied subjects who want the same object have all the same helpers except one).

Observing subjects

Actantial description must include observing subjects, since they influence how the elements are arranged within the actantial classes (and within the actantial sub-classes, as we will see later).

Classification is generally based on the reference observing subject: the one associated with the ultimate truth of the text (usually the narrator, especially if he is omniscient, but one can also assume the point of view of other observers, known as "assumptive observers", meaning those whose classifications may be refuted by the reference observer. For example, an observer-character (an assumptive observing subject) may believe, mistakenly from the narrator's standpoint (the reference observing subject), that a certain other character is a helper in a certain action. The observing subject may correspond to the subject of the action described in the actantial model, to another actant in the model, or to a simple witness-type observer who is outside the model. For example, he might be a helper who indicates, wrongly or rightly, who are the opponents in an action.

Time of observation

Classifications may vary, based not only on the observer, but also as a function of time. Thus one can (and sometimes must) set up an actantial model for each observer and each relevant temporal position of a single specific action. There are several kinds of time, or temporality: time as represented in the story (the chronological order of events in the story), narrative time (the order in which events of the story are presented), and tactical time (the linear sequencing of semantic units, for example, from one sentence to the next). To illustrate, there are cases where a helper goes further ahead in time in the story than an opponent, and vice versa. In summary, over time actants may integrate, leave the actantial model or change classes (or sub-classes).

Actant sub-classes

We shall now examine a few actantial sub-classes that can enhance an analysis. These sub-classes are also useful in the other actant-based models: the narrative program and the canonical narrative schema (see the corresponding chapters).

True/false actants

We will begin with the sub-classes derived from veridictory evaluations (true/false); later we will look at ontological evaluations of actuality vs. possibility (for more details on these modal categories, see the chapter on dialogics). We touched on veridictory evaluations in our discussion of observing subjects. The analysis can adopt the reference evaluations straight away (those deemed to be definitively correct in the text), or it can show the dynamics between the reference and assumptive evaluations. For example, if the observing subject mistakenly believes that a certain character is a helper, then this helper would be true for this observer, but false for the reference observer.

NOTE: ACTANTS AND THYMIC VALUES

There are other modal structures besides the ontological and veridictory categories, such as the thymic and deontic systems. For instance, thymic values apply especially to the object (which will generally be positive from the subject's point of view if he wants the object, and negative if he wants to get rid of it), the helper (positive from the subject's perspective) and the opponent (negative from the subject's perspective).[7] To give an example that involves veridictory and thymic evaluations, in "Lanval" by Marie de France, if we select King Arthur's wife as the subject, and her love for Lanval as the object, then it is possible to position Lanval as a sender. The queen mistakenly believes that Lanval would benefit from her love; from Lanval's perspective (which corresponds to the reference perspective), the Queen's love holds no attraction, and the hero prefers the love of his mysterious mistress.

Actants and antactants

If we map out an actantial class onto a semiotic square (see the chapter on the semiotic square), we obtain at least four types of actants: the actant (term A), the anti-actant or antactant (term B), the negactant (term not-B) and the negantactant (term not-A) (Greimas and Courtés, 1982, p. 5).[8] Studying the actantial subclasses is a complex matter. We will attempt to shed some light.

The relevant antactants for use in analytical practice, by our observations, are the following: the anti-sender, the anti-receiver and the anti-subject. For example, consider the subject *Prince* and the object *save the Princess*. The ogre is the anti-subject (he and the Prince are in contention for the same object), the anti-sender (he is certainly not asking the Prince to save the Princess) and the anti-receiver (he will in no way benefit from the rescue of the Princess – quite the contrary). Obviously, antactant positions are relative: We have only to select the ogre as the subject, and then the Prince becomes the anti-subject, and so on. As an obvious corollary to the connection we have established between the receiver and the beneficiary, we propose that the anti-receiver and the *maleficiary* are connected as well. The maleficiary is defined as the actant whose interests are thwarted by the attainment of the junction (for example, the ogre who kidnapped the Princess will be the maleficiary if the subject is the Prince and the object is to save the Princess). In the canonical schema, the model's anti-sender is defined as the actant who manipulates the subject's (the receiver-subject's) not-wanting-to-do and/or not-having-to-do. The anti-object does not seem to correspond to anything in particular in descriptive practice. (The anti-object is not the object for the anti-subject, because the latter theoretically has the same object as the subject); the anti-helper and anti-opponent seem to correspond to the opponent and the helper, respectively.

We have found that a better alternative for expanding our study of negactants (and negantactants) is to use the following actantial subclasses instead: actant/non-actant, possible/real and active/passive actants.

Actants/non-actants, real/possible actants and active/passive actants

The actant/non-actant (negactant) distinction is related to the distinctions between real/possible actants (based on ontological status) and active/passive actants. A friend who could have (and should have) helped but did not may be classified at Time 1 not as an opponent, but as 1) a non-helper (a type of non-actant) or as 2) a possible helper (a type of possible actant) who did not become a real helper (a type of real actant) as he should have at Time 2.

We shall now consider the distinction between active and passive actants. It is one thing not to help a person who is drowning (the non-action is what causes harm); it is quite another to hold his head under water (the action is what causes harm). In the first case, one could call this (1) a non-helper (a type of non-actant), or (2) a possible but unactualized helper (a type of possible actant that will not become real), or yet again (3) a passive opponent (a type of passive actant). In the second case, he may be (1) a possible but unactualized helper (a type of possible actant that will not become real) or (2) an active opponent (a type of active actant), which is undoubtedly a more adequate description. A being need not be anthropomorphic in order to be classified as passive/active: an alarm that does not go off when it should, thus allowing a robbery to occur, is a passive helper.

Intentional/unintentional actants, whole/part, class/element

Let us introduce some other useful actantial sub-classes. An anthropomorphic actant will play its role either intentionally or unintentionally. Thus, a character may not know that he is a helper, sender, etc. relative to a certain action.

Actantial analysis also makes use of the mereological opposition between the whole and its parts. Usually, the more specific the actant (with respect to the parts rather than the whole), the better the analysis. Thus, it is more accurate to say that the prince's courage is a helper in his own cause than to state that the prince is an overall helper. Otherwise stated: An analysis done at the level of the parts helps to reveal the differences that emerge between a description of the whole and that of its parts. For example, it could reveal that the Prince, who is an overall helper in his own cause, also harbors characteristics that act as opponents (for example, if he is a tiny bit lazy or fearful). The analysis can benefit in a similar way from the distinction made in set theory between class and element. For instance, a witch is always an opponent in traditional fairy tales; but in some "perverted" texts, it does happen that a witch may intentionally and voluntarily support the hero.

Applications

Application I: Hamlet

The main actantial model in *Hamlet* is represented in Table 6.4. Alternative analyses of the play can be found in the chapter on semantic graphs and the chapter *Analysis by classification*.

The main action in *Hamlet* in Hamlet clearly revolves around Hamlet's revenge for his father's murder. Thus, Hamlet is the subject and the main objective is revenge. By the end of the work, other objectives come into play: revenge for his mother's death and for his own imminent death. In killing Claudius, Hamlet achieves his three objectives at once. Claudius, for his part, achieves his objective of killing Hamlet after a failed attempt in England that leads to the demise of Hamlet's "friends". Similarly, Hamlet fails in his attempt to kill Claudius at prayer, slaying, instead, poor Polonius, in a tragic mixup. He intentionally fails at (carrying out) another attempt – killing Claudius at prayer – by postponing the act until a more favorable moment (not wanting to secure redemption for the soul of the praying Claudius).

Hamlet's objective is achieved not merely belatedly but *in extremis* – indeed, as he lies dying. This is the narrative topos, the narrative cliché of *in extremis* action at the last possible moment. The converse, here, is the immediate action taken in response to the request made by the ghost of Hamlet Sr. The other possibilities, theoretically speaking, are acting prematurely, at the right moment, at the best moment, somewhere in between, belatedly (but not *in extremis*) over-tardily, etc. In summary, Hamlet's acts effectively (he does take revenge) but hardly efficiently (he wastes much time and energy in doing so). Laertes, on the other hand, moves to avenge his father's death quickly – in fact, he wants to act even more hastily, but is made to wait by Claudius – but dishonorably by poisoning Hamlet with a sword in a "friendly" duel. But ultimately, he dies – poisoned by his own contrivance, hoist by his own petard, a fate which soon overtakes Claudius – renouncing his misdeed and asking for

Table 6.4 Actantial model of *Hamlet*

SENDER Father's ghost Hamlet Honor (avenge a crime) Filial duty (duty to avenge his father) Filial love (desire to avenge his father) Filial obedience (duty to avenge his father at the latter request) Eye-for-an-eye, tooth-for-a-tooth principle Morality (punish a wrongdoer)			RECEIVER Father's ghost Hamlet Honor Filial duty Filial love Filial obedience Eye-for-an-eye, tooth-for-a-tooth principle Morality (punish a wrongdoer)
	SUBJECT	OBJECT	
	Hamlet	Avenge the murder of his father by killing Claudius	
HELPER To overcome the uncertainty about the murder: the play-within-the-play To tackle Claudius as he prays: awaiting an opportune moment Opportune moment: the swordfight with Laertes Instrument: the poisoned sword and the poisoned wine Claudius's increasing crimes: he kills the queen and Hamlet (following the failed attempt in England): vengeance is all the more justified Reappearance of the ghost to urge Hamlet into action Love for the father (sender also?) Father's stature (majestic) relative to that of Claudius (pitiful) Incestuous relationship (Claudius marries his sister-in-law) At least partly feigned madness that gives Hamlet the leeway to act while disguising the true cause of his inner turmoil Horatio etc.			OPPONENT Uncertainty about the nature of the ghost (he could be a minion of the devil) Claudius, generally Claudius at prayer Exile (dispatched to England by Claudius) Possible death (beheading, twofold poisoning: sword and wine) Mistake: he kills Polonius, mistaking him for Claudius Queen: potential opponent, since she loves Claudius and would not wish him dead; would that change, however, if she learned of the regicide? Passage of time: the weakness of man's resolves, his inconstancy, an idea associated with women (as mentioned in the play) etc.

forgiveness. Hamlet implicitly eschews the type of underhanded vengeance chosen by Laertes, who purpose is to get the killing done – by whatever means – without hesitation. Hamlet procrastinates, justifiably – for example, he refuses to kill Claudius at prayer – or not. Only in Act 5 does he do what he ought to have done in the first place. The act is carried out properly and – as if to make amends for his dithering and the worsening crimes of Claudius – by two means: poisoned wine and poisoned sword. The poison (on the blade) and not the blade itself kills the King (Claudius), who tells those who come to his aid that he is merely wounded): the sword, thus, does not fulfill its primary function. What is basically a friendly, entertaining, and harmless duel ultimately turns into mortal combat, like the wartime combat between Hamlet Sr. and Fortinbras Sr. Here, however, both combatants – not just one (Fortinbras Sr.) – die.

Hamlet wants to take his own revenge. Besides, he is the only person in his family capable of exacting revenge. Laertes, who also initially seeks to personally take revenge, later accepts assistance from Claudius. Claudius, having unsuccessfully delegated the murder to the King of England, wishes to kill Hamlet himself – as he did Hamlet Sr. – this time with poisoned wine as well as the poisoned sword – and the help – of Laertes. This unsuccessful double poisoning attempt, since it succeeds only once, reprises the double poisoning of the play-within-the-play. In fact, the act of murder in *Hamlet*'s play-within-the-play, which starts out as dumb-show, is thereafter performed in the normal way, with speeches.

Avenging a father's death is a recurrent theme of the play. Hamlet gets revenge by killing Claudius; Laertes wreaks vengeance by slaying Hamlet, and Fortinbras – who could, in principle, obtain revenge by killing the son of his father's killer – procures vengeance by reclaiming his rightful lands (and more, by thereto annexing Denmark) lost in the mortal combat between Fortinbras Sr. and Hamlet Sr. By contrast, Ophelia, Polonius's daughter, exacts revenge on herself, perhaps through her suicide, but definitely through her eventual madness (whereas Hamlet madness is at once partly real, partly feigned). Symbolically: incapable of bringing herself to kill Hamlet on account of her love for him, and rather than kill someone (else) to restore her balance, she decides to take her own life.

Hamlet's procrastination has both positive and negative consequences. First, the negatives: his extreme temporizing leads to the death of many "innocent" persons (Polonius, Ophelia, the queen, Hamlet's two "friends"); Horatio's despair (he is the positive counterpart to Hamlet, also having an 'H' name). The positives include: Hamlet takes the necessary action. Hamlet Sr. and Heaven are appeased. Moral order has been restored, to the benefit of Fortinbras; the order destroyed by the duel between Hamlet Sr. and Fortinbras Sr. has been restored. Claudius's death is symbolic in that he is himself falls victim to poisoning (and twice!), having poisoned Hamlet Sr. The fictitious vengeance augured in the play-within-the-play comes to pass in reality: in fact, the regicide who carries out the act of poisoning in the play-within-the-play is the King's nephew, as is Hamlet, who poisons his uncle, the King. All the main actors die, save Horatio, who would be inclined to take his own life on witnessing the death of his friend Hamlet, but for latter's dissuasion. In addition, Ophelia perhaps takes her own life, Hamlet himself contemplating the same fate (like all human beings, he says). The queen is accidentally killed; like Polonius, victim of a tragic mistake – for it is Hamlet that the king desires to poison – but she is innocent of the murder of her husband (but guilty, perhaps, of adultery while he lived, see Act 1, Scene 4). Laertes accidently falls victim to the poison he intended for Hamlet: his is the guilt of attempting a murder that succeeds by other means (though he delays somewhat at the point of carrying out the act as Hamlet is wont to do). Paradoxically, Hamlet Sr., expiating his sins in a purgatory of sorts – overtaken by death without a chance to confess his sins: thus comparable to Claudius, who repents and confesses but holds out little hope – asks his son to commit a crime; thus, vengeance is not considered a crime, and an anomaly among Christian moral values. Why does suicide deny one paradise and burial on holy ground (see the discussion between the two gravediggers about Ophelia's burial) whereas committing murder does not?

Lastly, the evil Claudius performs a sort of reverse transubstantiation in an unholy eucharist: instead of transforming the wine into the blood of Christ from whence one drinks eternal life, he transforms it (by dropping therein a poisoned pearl) into a cup of death. This variation on the Eucharistic theme was generally apparent and comprehensible to Shakespeare's contemporaries, who were steeped in Christianity. Without the poison, the pearl would symbolize what transforms ordinary wine into the precious blood of Christ. However, it is also a symbol; of the transmutation of aggression – the aggression of the sand in the oyster, of the duel – into beauty. It is thus a symbol of the play itself – as an aesthetic work – and is one of the numerous *mise en abymes* in Hamlet.

Application II: The new testament

Our second application is taken from *The new testament*. We shall have to simplify the analysis by focusing primarily on the anthropomorphic actants, which provide abundant and complex subject matter from both literary and theological perspectives. As we shall see, using the actantial model, we can identify and describe several theological issues with clarity and integrate them into a complex system.

Subject and object

As the primary actantial model of *The new testament*, we have selected the action in which Jesus must save mankind.

Senders

The senders in our model are the following:[9]

God, who sends his only son for this purpose.

Jesus, who we can assume has a "personal" desire to save mankind in addition to the duty imposed by God.

Mankind, which is hoping and yearning for the coming of Christ. One could say that the "believers" are intentional senders and that the others are unintentional senders (their souls, although mute, yearn for salvation).

Receivers

If one interprets the receiver as the element that benefits from the desired junction between subject and object, mankind is clearly the receiver of the action. What about God and Jesus? Here a theological problem arises. Two points argue in favor of excluding these characters as receivers. For one thing, if that which is perfect neither needs nor benefits from anything whatsoever, then God and Jesus, who were conceived as perfect, cannot be receivers. For another, in Christian ideology, the best "good deed", if we may say, is one for which the subject receives no personal benefit. If we refer back to the semiotic typology that distinguishes an altruistic action (in which the subject is not a beneficiary of his own action) from an egoistic action (with no pejorative connotation; the subject is the only beneficiary of his action or one of them), then we would say that a Christ-like action – and the instincts that God gave him as a sender – must be completely altruistic.

Helpers and opponents

In order to sort out the helpers and opponents in this actantial model, we must distinguish between several important and related actions, meaning that these actions will form a set of actantial models. In order to obtain salvation for mankind, Jesus must rise from the dead; in order to rise from the dead, he must die, or more accurately, be executed; in order to be executed, he must be arrested and judged. (We shall interrupt the sequence of actions here; obviously, in order for this series of actions to occur, Jesus must be born among men: For our analysis, we shall select the following three actions: (1) Jesus is arrested and crucified; (2) Jesus rises from the dead; (3) Jesus saves mankind. The third action presupposes the second, which presupposes the first. The first and second actions are sequential in time, while the second and third are simultaneous.

As helper characters in action 1, we have: Judas, who sells Jesus; the judges; the people, who choose to liberate Barabbas rather than Jesus; and the soldiers, who carry out Jesus' arrest and execution. The opponent characters seem to be fleeting and fewer in number: the apostles do try to oppose Jesus' arrest, but none of them intervenes directly during the trial (Peter shirks this role with his denial) or the crucifixion. In short, the possible opponents just don't turn into real opponents. Pontius Pilate, who refuses either to condemn or liberate Jesus – by washing his hands of the matter – thus refuses to occupy any position on the helper/opponent axis. He plays the role of a non-helper-non-opponent. Seen in a different light, one could say that by not intervening, he promotes the harsher course – in this case, Jesus' death – making him a passive helper. (For a more detailed account of Pontius Pilate's role, refer to the note in this chapter.) As for Jesus, he falls more clearly within the passive helper class: he actually asks the apostles to stop resisting his arrest; and he does not defend himself directly before the judges. On the cross, he has a "moment of weakness", in keeping with his temporarily half-human, half-divine nature, and laments the fate in store for him; but he does not interfere personally with that fate (and perhaps at that point he has been deprived of his ability to perform miracles, a theological hypothesis), earning him the jeers of the bad thief: The son of God must be powerless! However, Jesus appeals to his father to take this cup from him, thereby asking God to be an opponent to his death, or at least his suffering. Lastly, let us assume that Satan knows the divine plan (even if the ways of God are said to be impenetrable, at least for mortals), and has every reason to try to divert Jesus from his death; he had also tempted Jesus in the wilderness to divert him from his destiny.

In action 2, the helper characters are God and Jesus, or perhaps only God if it is solely his power that makes his son rise from the dead. There are no opponent characters that appear directly, although Satan, the general enemy, would interfere in the completion of the miracle if he could. There is one non-character opponent that is fundamental in this action: matter, which by its very nature resists the breaking of a rule that generally tolerates no exceptions. That which is dead cannot rise again.

Now we come back to action 3. This is a cumulative action, resulting from the outcome of a series of actions. The most important of these are: Jesus' birth as a man, his death and his resurrection. This means that any helper or opponent in one of these crucial actions is also a helper or opponent in the cumulative action. This produces astounding results from a theological point of view: Judas is indeed a helper, and Satan was inconsistent and ill-advised when he gave Judas the idea of betraying Jesus by turning him over to the law. However that may be, even disregarding this point of the analysis, we can say that the main helper and opponent characters are God and Jesus on the one hand, and

Satan on the other. The actantial model thus takes on a predominantly metaphysical dimension, with human characters involved only as senders and receivers. However, their role will become crucial in the model of individual salvation: with collective salvation ensured by the redemption Jesus offers, it is now up to each man to "earn his way to heaven" through his good deeds – help yourself and heaven will help you – and by divine grace. In order to accomplish this, the role of the apostles is a major one: they announce the good news of redemption, they teach about individual salvation, and through the *Bible*, they give their example and their instruction to show the way.

The following table gives an overview of the helper and opponent characters associated with action three.

Table 6.5 Actantial model of *The new testament*'s primary action

No	*actant*	*actant class*	*actant sub-class*
01	God	sender	
02	Jesus	sender	
03	mankind	senders	intentional (believers) and unintentional (non-believers)
04	mankind	receivers	intentional (believers) and unintentional (non-believers)
05	God	helper	
06	Jesus	helper	
07	Satan	opponent	

Notes

1 For a comparison of Greimas's and Propp's models, see Simonsen, 1984, pp. 51–54, 57–58.

2 As with any classification, in addition to the six actants there is a residual class, a sort of "wastebasket category" for elements that do not fit into any of the selected analytical classes, or elements that belong to another action than the one chosen for analysis.

3 Greimas (1966, p. 178) views the helper as aiding in the completion of the quest and/or the transmission to the receiver; the same logic applies for the opponent.

4 In actuality, the receiver is not necessarily always the beneficiary, and the anti-receiver is not always the "maleficiary." (An analogous problem, found in semantic graphs, concerns the relations between the dative and the benefactive-malefactive; see the chapter on semantic graphs.) For example, if God is the one who asks Jesus to save mankind, many theologians would argue that he is the receiver, but not the beneficiary, since divine love is completely disinterested and moreover, nothing can add to or subtract from that which is perfect.

5 This is how Fontanille (2003, p. 121) can maintain that: "when the subject goes into action, he can appear to be independent from the sender. The latter can still intervene, but only in a diminished, ancillary capacity, that of the Helper, who supplements or strengthens the subject's competence."

6 The word "actant" (like the word "actor") carries an entirely different meaning in Rastier's work, where the Greimasian actants seem to correspond to particular cases of stereotyped agonists.

7 For an analysis combining conjunction/disjunction and euphoria/dysphoria, see the chapter on the canonical narrative schema.

8 Greimas and Courtés (1982, p. 5) do not say whether the negactant and the negantactant correspond to term not-B and term not-A respectively on the semiotic square, or the reverse. We have opted for the first possibility. We will supplement Greimas's and Courtés's system by adding the actant subclasses corresponding to the four (or six) metaterms of the square. As with the first four classes, some problems arise, concerning either

the understanding of the semiotic square, or more specifically, the subclasses identified. For example, what is a neutral actant (the neutral term of the square), that is, a character who is neither helper nor opponent? If one follows the principle that in order to be the neutral term, an element must be marked as neutral, not simply as being outside the opposition mapped onto the square, then a character who is neither a helper nor an opponent must be both a party to the action and marked as neither a helper nor an opponent. Take Pontius Pilate as an example: In relation to the object *to not condemn Jesus*, he seems to represent the idea of a neutral actant: as neither a helper nor an opponent, he washes his hands of the matter, he says. Now we can introduce the modal category real/possible: Is Pontius Pilate a possible, but unactualized helper (who did not become a real helper) and/or a possible, unactualized opponent? If he is indeed both at once, then he corresponds to the complex term within the modal category of possibility (he is both a possible helper and a possible opponent) and to the neutral term within the modal category of actuality (he is neither a real helper nor a real opponent). And finally, we can introduce the modal category probable/improbable: Now Pontius Pilate appears to be a real opponent, because, without his help, Jesus will most likely be condemned. From a probabilistic standpoint, passivity is far from being neutral; it seems like an accomplice to the status quo or the harsher course.

9 The Trinity – "The dogma and mystery of one God in three persons, coexisting, consubstantial and co-eternal", meaning God the Father, Jesus and the Holy Spirit (trans. from *Le petit Robert*) – is not without implications for actantial description. For insofar as he is also God, Jesus is assuredly the sender, even without bringing his "personal" will into the picture.

7 The narrative program

Summary

The narrative program (NP), developed by Greimas, is an abstract formula used to represent an action. Doing (action) is defined as a temporal succession from one state to the opposite state, effected by any agent (S1: the subject of doing). A state may be broken down into a subject of state (S2) and an object of state (O) and the junction between them, which is either a conjunction (n: the subject with the object) or a disjunction (u: the subject without the object). The long formula of the narrative program is:

$NP = F\{S1 \rightarrow [(S2 \text{ u } O) \rightarrow (S2 \text{ n } O)]\}$ (the conjunctive NP) or
$NP = F\{S1 \rightarrow [(S2 \text{ n } O) \rightarrow (S2 \text{ u } O)]\}$ (the disjunctive NP).

For example, in the fable "The crow and the fox", we have:

$NP = F\{\text{Fox} \rightarrow [(\text{Fox u Cheese}) \rightarrow (\text{Fox n Cheese})]\}$.

The abbreviated formula, which is the most commonly used, gives only the second state:

$NP = F\{S1 \rightarrow (S2 \text{ n } O)\}$ (the conjunctive NP) or
$NP = F\{S1 \rightarrow (S2 \text{ u } O)\}$ (the disjunctive NP).

This would give us, for example:

$NP = F\{\text{Fox} \rightarrow (\text{Fox n Cheese})\}$.

An array of NPs is composed of at least two NPs between which at least one temporal relation (succession, simultaneity) or one presential relation (presupposition, mutual exclusion, etc.) is described. For example, the previous NP describing appropriation by the Fox and the (short form) NP of dispossession, $NP = F\{\text{Fox} \rightarrow (\text{Crow u Cheese})\}$, presuppose each other reciprocally, in that one does not exist without the other; the temporal relation is simultaneity.

Theory

Elements of the narrative program

A product of Greimas's semiotics, the narrative program (NP) is an abstract formula used to represent an action (see Courtés, 1991, pp. 69–98, summarized here with our additions). Doing (action) is defined as a temporal succession from one state to the opposite state, effected by any agent (the subject of doing) and affecting any patient (the subject of state). A state may be broken down into a subject of state and an object of state and the junction between them, which is either a conjunction (the subject is with the object) or a disjunction (the subject is without the object). The two opposite states of a single action include the same subject and the same object; the opposition consists solely of the difference in the junction between them (conjunction becomes disjunction or the reverse).[1]

Table 7.1 Relations between actions, time and states in the narrative program

TIME	T1 (before)	→	T2 (after)
STATES	s1	→	s2 (= ¬s1)
STATES BROKEN DOWN	S n O	→	S u O
EXAMPLE: "The crow and the fox"	Crow with Cheese	→	Crow without Cheese
STATES BROKEN DOWN	S u O	→	S n O
EXAMPLE: "The crow and the fox"	Fox without Cheese	→	Fox with Cheese

Legend: T: time, s: state, S: subject of state, O: object of state, n: conjunction, u: disjunction, ¬: negation.

The formulas of the narrative program

The narrative program proper is presented as a long formula or a short formula. The formula for the narrative program, long or short, can be verbalized or explained as follows: the function by which a subject 1 (subject of doing) causes a subject 2 (subject of state) to be conjoined with (or disjoined from) an object (object of state). Here is the long formula:

$NP = F\,\{S1 \rightarrow [(S2 \text{ u } O) \rightarrow (S2 \text{ n } O)]\}$ (the conjunctive NP) or
$NP = F\,\{S1 \rightarrow [(S2 \text{ n } O) \rightarrow (S2 \text{ u } O)]\}$ (the disjunctive NP).

To give an example of a (conjunctive) NP in the long form, in the fable "The crow and the fox", we have:

$NP = F\,\{\text{Fox} \rightarrow [(\text{Fox u Cheese}) \rightarrow (\text{Fox n Cheese})]\}$.

The short formula of the NP, which is more commonly used, gives only the second state. This is based on the idea that only the second state need be mentioned, since the first state is its opposite (only the junction is different):

$NP = F\,\{S1 \rightarrow (S2 \text{ n } O)\}$ (the conjunctive NP) or
$NP = F\,\{S1 \rightarrow (S2 \text{ u } O)\}$ (the disjunctive NP).

Here is an example of a (conjunctive) NP in the short form:

$NP = F\,\{\text{Fox} \rightarrow (\text{Fox n Cheese})\}$.

The subject of doing may or may not correspond to the subject of state; in other words, what accomplishes the action may or may not be what is affected by it. When the subject of doing is identical to the subject of state (SD = SS or S1 = S2), it is called reflexive action or performance; otherwise, the action is transitive (SD ≠ SS or S1 ≠ S2). For example, if we take the view that the crow is the one who (unintentionally) gives the cheese to the fox, then we have the following transitive action: NP = F {Crow → (Fox n Cheese)}.

NOTE: ACTANTIAL SYNCRETISM

In Greimas's theory, actantial syncretism occurs when a single actor, such as a character, corresponds to two or more different actants. If we take the subject and object actants – the only actants directly involved in narrative programs (there are others in the actantial model and the canonical narrative schema) – we obtain the following syncretisms: (1) S1 = S2 (performance), (2) S1 = O (e.g., a professor who "dedicates himself" to his students), (3) S2 = O (e.g., a psychologist who enables a subject to "find himself"), (4) S1 = S2 = O (the injunction "Know thyself", for example). And lastly, there are some cases in which the actors fulfilling the actantial functions remain unknown (Courtés, 1991, p. 80). For example, a lucky find (finding an object by chance) could be transcribed in this way: ? → S n O. But it is usually possible to describe these "unknown" elements in one way or another, in terms of luck, chance or even Providence in the case of the lucky find.

NOTE: VARIANTS OF THE NARRATIVE PROGRAM

Some of the following variants of the narrative program may be useful:

1. NP of manipulation (causing-to-do): NP = F1 [S1 → F2 {S2 → (S3 n O)}]. The equivalents are as follows: F1 and F2: Action 1 and Action 2, S1: the subject of manipulation (or sender-manipulator) and S2: the subject of the action (or receiver-subject). Manipulation (this term has no pejorative connotations in semiotic) is the function by which a subject manipulates another subject's wanting-to-do and/or having-to-do to prompt him into action. Manipulation is one of the components of the canonical narrative schema (see the chapter on this analytical tool), along with action, competence, performance and sanction.
2. NP of exchange: NP = F1 {(S1 → S2 n O1)} ↔ F2 {(S2 → S1 n O2)}. F1 and F2 represent the two actions involved in the exchange (for instance, the consumer gives money to the merchant who gives him an item in exchange).
3. NP of participatory communication: NP = F {S1 → [(S1 n O u S2) → (S1 n O n S2)]}. S1 keeps what he gives to S2 (the professor retains the knowledge that he transmits to others, for instance).

Simplified formulas for narrative programs

To make them easier to read, in the narrative programs we use, we will replace the variables in the formula with the corresponding actors. We will also eliminate the parentheses and brackets. For "The crow and the fox", this would give us:

Fox → Fox n Cheese.

We can even reduce the formula to just the second state and use very minimal notations for the actors. This would give us:

F n C (F = fox and C = cheese).

When doing this, we need to be careful not to include a state as part of an action if it was not preceded by the opposite state in the story, in other words, if it is not the direct result of an action. For example: Crow n Ugly (since the crow did not in fact change from beautiful to ugly; there are not two states pertaining to ugliness).

Combinatorial analysis at work in the narrative program

The narrative program is essentially based on a combinatorics using the elements of the following oppositions: subject/object, state/doing (or action), and conjunction/disjunction:[2]

States: s1 (initial state): S2 u O; s2 (final state): S2 n O
The subject of state: S2
The object of state: O
The junction:[3] disjunction: u, conjunction: n
Doing: the whole narrative program (or in the restrictive sense, the change from the initial state to the final state)
The subject of doing: S1
The object of doing: the change from the initial state to the final state

Table 7.2 Summary of the elements of the narrative program

				T1	→	*T2*
				s1	→	*s2 (= ¬s1)*
NP with OD, OS, SD, SS	NP = F	{SD	→	[(SS J OS)	→	(SS ¬J OS)]}
				|----------------------	OD	------------------------|
Long formula NP	NP = F	{S1	→	[(S2 u O)	→	(S2 n O)]}
ex., S1 = S2: reflexive NP (= performance)		Fox	→	Fox u Cheese.	→	Fox n Cheese
ex., S1 ≠ S2: transitive NP		Crow	→	Fox u Cheese	→	Fox n Cheese
NP (short formula)	NP = F	{S1	→			(S2 n O)}
ex., S1 = S2: reflexive		Fox	→			Fox n Cheese
ex., S1 ≠ S2: transitive		Crow	→			Fox n Cheese

Legend: NP: narrative program, T: time, s: state, F: function, OD: object of doing, OS: object of state, SD: subject of doing, SS: subject of state, J: junction, ¬J: opposite junction, n: conjunction, u: disjunction. In those cases where the kind of junction is specified, only conjunctive NPs are represented (where the subject is conjoined with the object in state 2), and not disjunctive NPs (where the subject is disjoined from the object in state 2).

Arrays of narrative programs

A NP array is composed of at least two NPs between which at least one temporal relation (succession, simultaneity) or one presential relation (simple or reciprocal presupposition, mutual exclusion, comparing/compared, etc.) is identified.[4] We will give a few examples.

The following NPs are in reciprocal presupposition, in that one does not exist without the other, and the temporal relation is simultaneity.

NP1 = F {Fox → (Fox n Cheese)}
NP2 = F {Fox → (Crow u Cheese)}

Conversely, the following NPs are in mutual exclusion simultaneously, but not successively, in that they cannot be realized at the same time. (According to the logic of the story, only one of the two protagonists can take possession of the cheese at a time):

NP1 = F {Fox → (Fox n Cheese)}
NP2 = F {Crow → (Crow n Cheese)}

In the following example, the second narrative program presupposes the first in succession, but not the reverse. (Carrying out an action presupposes the idea of carrying it out, but the idea of carrying it out is not necessarily followed by its realization.)

NP1 = F {Fox → (Fox n idea of stealing)}
NP2 = F {Fox → (Fox n cheese stolen)}

An example of a simple narrative array

In order to represent temporal succession and simultaneity, we propose using the rows and columns of a table. The following table represents one of the NP arrays that may be used to describe this story: *Paul, who is an expert swimmer, rescues Andy from drowning, and then Bernard. (While rescuing Bernard, Paul thinks about the most beautiful moment of his life.) He does not get to Sasha in time to save him.*

Table 7.3 An example of a simple narrative array

	T1 (NP1)	*T2 (NP2)*	*T3 (NP3)*
A	P → A n rescue	P → B n rescue	(P → S n rescue)
B		P → P n thought	

We will use alphanumeric codes for the NPs to make them easier to find on the chart. (For example, P → P n thought is NP2b.) The parentheses around NP3a indicate that it was possible, but did not become real; it was not realized (we will come back to the possible/real status of NPs). Amongst the NPs we have selected, there is no specific logical relation on the axis of succession, such as presupposition (simple or reciprocal) or mutual exclusion; on the axis of simultaneity, there is a relation of mutual exclusion, in that any one of the three rescue NPs excludes the other two (the expert swimmer can only save one person at a time).

Relations of presupposition and mutual exclusion

We will address the relations between simultaneous and successive NPs in more depth, that is, simple presupposition, reciprocal presupposition and mutual exclusion.[5] We can refer to the absence of presential relations between NPs as "parataxis".[6]

All of these relations, or the absence thereof, are given in terms of the text being described. Thus, they could be different from the relations that would normally be established in reality. Taking just the example of reciprocal presupposition between simultaneous NPs, consider a text in which each time someone walks (whether just once or several times), he chews gum; or it even stipulates that in order to walk, one must necessarily chew and vice versa. Even if there are one or more cases in the text where one happens without the other, of course one could conclude that walking and chewing presuppose each other mutually, by using concepts such as the exception to the rule, bending the rules, general trends and approximation.

Table 7.4 Examples of relations of presupposition and mutual exclusion between narrative programs

	Examples of simultaneity	*Examples of succession*	
No particular relation (parataxis)	NP1a: Paul n turn on the lamp NP1b: Paul n sneeze	NP2: Paul n read	NP3: Paul n whistle
Simple presupposition	NP4a: Paul n food NP4b: Paul n roast chicken	NP5: Paul n money	NP6: Paul n buy
Reciprocal presupposition	NP7a: Fox n cheese NP7b: Crow u cheese	NP8: Seller n money	NP9: Buyer n product
Mutual exclusion	NP10a: Player x n ball NP10b: (Player y n ball)	NP11: Paul n divorce	NP12: Paul n traditional Catholic wedding

Comments:

We have listed only the final state of the action in the table, with no mention of the subject of doing.

The relation between NP4a-NP4b: The example in the table illustrates the relation between a general NP and a specific NP. This is a relation of simple presupposition, so long as there are at least two specific NPs associated with the general NP. Thus, in the story relating to this example, roast chicken is one possible food, but every food in the story is not necessarily roast chicken.

The relation between NP5-NP6: Presupposition is not reciprocal, in that having money does not necessarily presuppose buying, but buying presupposes having money (at least in the realistic story we have invented).

The relation between NP7a-NP7b: The fox's appropriation of the cheese implies dispossession for the crow and vice versa, since, according to the logic of this fable, the cheese must necessarily be in the possession of one of the protagonists.

The relation between NP8-NP-9: This is a specific type of exchange. In the case of a purchase that must be paid in advance, the second narrative program only occurs if the first program has already been realized. Of course, there are exchanges in which the two NPs are realized simultaneously (especially if the two parties involved distrust each other, as in a case of ransom).

The relation between NP10a-NP10b: In a baseball game, one ball is in play at a time, so that when it is in one player's possession, it cannot be in another player's possession (at certain times, it is not in any player's possession).

The relation between NP11-NP12: If Paul gets a divorce, he cannot enter into another Catholic marriage afterwards, and, by correlation, if he gets married in the Catholic Church, he cannot have been divorced previously.

NPs and modal categories

A NP is marked for various modal categories, either implicitly or explicitly.

Virtualized/actualized/realized narrative programs

A NP is marked implicitly or explicitly for ontological status (status with respect to existence). Greimasian semiotics distinguishes between the following modes of existence (however, "ontological status" is not the term used):[7]

A NP is virtualized[8] if the idea of the action exists, through desire or obligation (for instance, the idea of stealing something);
A NP is actualized if the action is under way (for instance, the robbery in progress);
A NP is realized if the action has been completed (for instance, the robbery has been carried out).[9]

The ontological status of a NP tends to change as a function of time in the story. Different ontological statuses may follow one after another with no overlap. For example, a NP may be:

1 Non-existent, that is, completely irrelevant at T1 (for example, an honest citizen who has never thought of stealing until T2);
2 Virtualized at T2;
3 Actualized at T3;
4 Realized at T4.

Or they may be collapsed into a single moment (e.g., a malicious glance).

Obviously, not all virtualized NPs are actualized, and not all actualized NPs are realized. The description is generally formulated from the perspective of the last time segment of the story, thus emphasizing NPs that have been realized. However, in some cases it becomes important to account for unrealized NPs, whether virtualized or actualized.

Real/possible narrative programs

Drawing from Rastier's dialogics (1997) (see Chapter 12), we propose the following distinctions in ontological status:

A NP is real (a status indicating what is) if it has been realized;
A NP is possible (a status indicating what could be or could have been) if it may be realized later in the story (a possible future NP) or if it may have been realized at some later moment, but was not (a possible NP that never came to pass, that never became real).

If we make the connections between the two modal systems presented here, "possible" corresponds roughly to virtualized and actualized actions, and "real" corresponds to realized actions.

True/false narrative programs

A NP is marked either implicitly or explicitly for veridictory status (true/false).

Whether ontological or veridictory, modal status may differ from one viewpoint to another, that is, for each observing subject, e.g., the different characters. Modal status can also change over time, as we have mentioned.

We distinguish the reference categories and observing subjects (which correspond to the truth of the text) from what we call the assumptive categories and observing subjects (which are subject to contradiction by the truth of the text). The narrator is generally the reference observing subject, especially if omniscient, and (s)he defines the reference categories.

For example, during his sleep, a character may mistakenly believe that he has attained the object of his desire; upon awakening, he understands his mistake: the conjunction has not really occurred, and it may never. The NP Dreamer n Object of desire is:

A true and real NP according to the dreamer at time 1 (sleeping);
A false and real NP according to the dreamer at time 2 (awakening);
A false and real NP according to the narrator from time 1 to time 2.

Unless there is some indication to the contrary, the statuses 'true' and 'real' are assigned by default to a NP, from the perspective of the reference observing subject. For example, this is the case with the NP: Fox n Cheese (if no other details are given). This is, in fact, the case with most of the NPs we present in this chapter.

An example of a more complex array of narrative programs

Consider the following story:

John is rich and happy. Luke asks Peter to rob John for him. Peter trains in preparation for the robbery. The night of the robbery, Peter opens John's safe. Then, like a dentist pulling a healthy tooth, he robs John; at the same time, Luke is eating a piece of cake. Peter could keep the loot, but he gives it to Luke. Luke checks the loot, keeps it and congratulates Peter. The moral of the story? John is no longer rich, but despite what you might expect, he is still happy.

We propose the following representation for the array of narrative programs contained in this narrative:

Table 7.5 An example of a more complex array of narrative programs

	T1 – NP1	*T2 – NP2*	*T3 – NP3*	*T4 – NP4*	*T5 – NP5*
A	L → P n ask	P → P n training	P → P n open safe	P → P n money	P → P u money
B	[P → L n money]	[P → L n money]	[P → L n money]	[P → L n money]	P → L n money
C				P → J u money	
D				L → L n cake	
E				(P → J u happiness)	
F				Dentist → patient u healthy tooth	

	T6 (NP6)	*T7 (NP7)*	*T8 (NP8)*	*T9 (NP9)*	*T10 (NP10)*
A	L → L n check loot	L → P n congratulations			
B		(L → P n remuneration)			
C					
D					
E					
F					

Legend: L: Luke, P: Peter, J: John. No brackets or parentheses: a real NP (realized). Parentheses: a possible NP that did not come to pass (a NP that was not realized, although it could have been). Square brackets: a possible NP (an action under way that is not yet real, not yet realized).

NOTES:

Other NPs could be added: For instance, J → J n discovers he has been robbed; this NP is presupposed by the affirmation that John remains happy in spite of it all.

It may be relevant to formulate other objects (for example, P → P n money = P → P n robbery). The names of the elements need not be identical to those used in the text (for instance, the text may not mention money by name).

Listed here are only a few of the NPs whose ontological status is "possible".

The ontological status of the NP about the dentist is difficult to define, given that it is a comparing action. But since the compared action is realized, one might say that the same applies to the comparing action.

Applications

Application I: Antoine Tonny's toffee *by Magritte*

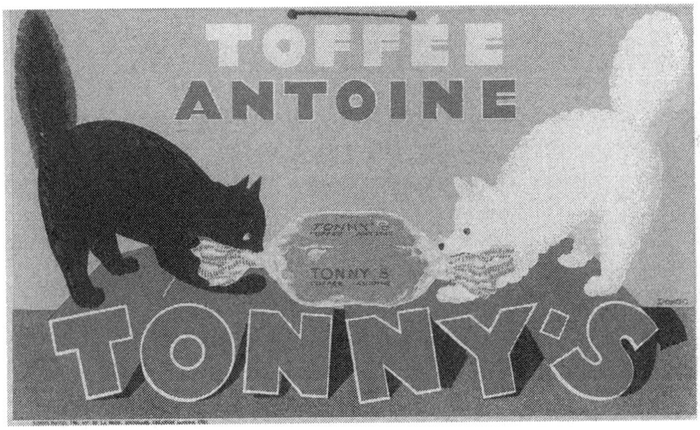

Figure 7.1 Antoine Tonny's toffee

Source: Magritte (1931)

The poster *Antoine Tonny's toffee* by Magritte portrays a polemical situation: the number of coveted objects (a toffee candy) is less than the number of subjects coveting it (a cat and a dog). In all probability, the protagonists are operating under categorial logic (the all-or-nothing kind) as opposed to incremental logic (a logic of compromise, in which it would be possible to share the object in order to resolve the conflict irenically (from the Greek *eirênê*, "peace"; thus, in a manner that reestablishes or promotes peace). The overall effect of selecting this kind of logic is a sort of hyperbole glorifying the advertised product: everyone will fight tooth and nail over toffee this delicious. Rather than using the bone-of-contention topos (where an object's value is such that it disrupts alliances, such as friendship), Magritte uses the topos of consensus between enemies: dogs and cats, no matter how dissimilar they are, go crazy over the same toffee. The general opposition between the dog and the cat is reinforced by a series of visual oppositions: white fur/black fur, kinky fur/smooth fur (even with its hackles up), rounded/pointed ears and tail, and round/almond-shaped eyes. Using two strongly polarized subjects, Magritte somehow manages to cover the spectrum of subjects who like toffee: everyone loves it, even creatures as radically dissimilar as dogs and cats. Since the product is intended for humans, the advertisement establishes a comparison between them and animals. This comparison may underlie the topos in which a subject regresses under the influence of his desire: adults become children; reasoning human beings become instinctive animals. Moreover, the candy is oversized, which is a symbolic indication of its force of attraction.

The primary states involved in the story of this poster are: Cat n Toffee, Cat u Toffee, Dog n Toffee and Dog u Toffee. The scene depicted is located at that moment in time when the pendulum could swing from one state to another. However, there is no indication to tell us whether the cat or the dog will win, in order to determine the final state. Likewise, there is nothing to indicate if one of the protagonists had the toffee in his possession initially, or if both of them snatched the object of desire simultaneously.

The NPs representing the four states of this story are as follows:

A) COMPARING NPS

1 NP of appropriation: Cat → Cat n Toffee
2 NP of dispossession: Cat → Dog u Toffee
3 NP of appropriation: Dog → Dog n Toffee
4 NP of dispossession: Dog → Cat u Toffee

B) COMPARED NPS

5 NP of appropriation: Human 1 → Human 1 n Toffee
6 NP of dispossession: Human 1 → Human 2 u Toffee
7 NP of appropriation: Human 2 → Human 2 n Toffee
8 NP of dispossession: Human 2 → Human 1 u Toffee

A relation of reciprocal presupposition exists between NPs 1 and 2, NPs 3 and 4, NPs 5 and 6, and NPs 7 and 8: in this story, any instance of appropriation by either of the protagonists has as its corollary dispossession for the other protagonist.

A relation of mutual exclusion is established between NPs 1 and 3, NPs 2 and 4, NPs 5 and 7, and NPs 6 and 8: only one of each pair can actually come to pass.

There is also a relation of mutual exclusion between NPs 1 and 4, NPs 2 and 3, NPs 5 and 8, and NPs 6 and 7.

There is a relation of comparison between the NPs of group A and the corresponding NPs of group B.

The following table summarizes these relations.

Table 7.6 Relations between NPs

	NP 1	*NP 2*	*NP 3*	*NP 4*	*NP 5*	*NP 6*	*NP 7*	*NP 8*
NP 1	-	r. presupp.	m. exclusion	m. exclusion	comparison			
NP 2	r. presupp.	-	m. exclusion	m. exclusion		comparison		
NP 3	m. exclusion	m. exclusion	-	r. presupp.			comparison	
NP 4	m. exclusion	m. exclusion	r. presupp.	-				comparison
NP 5	comparison				-	r. presupp.	m. exclusion	m. exclusion
NP 6		comparison			r. presupp.	-	m. exclusion	m. exclusion
NP 7			comparison		m. exclusion	m. exclusion	-	r. presupp.
NP 8				comparison	m. exclusion	m. exclusion	r. presupp.	-

Application II: "The dog and the perfume bottle" by Charles Baudelaire

* * *

"The dog and the perfume bottle"
Baudelaire, *Paris spleen*

"– My good dog, my handsome dog, my dear poochie-woochie, come sit by me. Come here and breathe this excellent perfume purchased of the best parfumeur in town".

And the dog, wagging its tail, a sign, I believe, among those poor creatures corresponding with the laugh or the smile, he steps up and lays his damp nose curiously beside the open bottle of perfume; then, shrinking suddenly with fright, he bays at me. This is a reproach.

"– Ah! miserable dog, if I had offered you a sack of dung you would have sniffed it with delight, and probably eaten it. Thus, you, unworthy companion of my sorry life, in this you resemble the public, to whom one must never offer delicate perfumes – these will just exasperate them. For them, only the most meticulously selected rubbish".

(Adapted from K. Dixon's translation, 6/98)

* * *

Time as represented in the story

T1: *I* purchases the perfume.

T2: *I* calls the dog, flatters him, and offers him an action to do.

T3: The dog approaches, wagging its tail (an iterative action). (The present participle indicates simultaneity, or at least prompts us to think of simultaneity.)

T4: The dog lays his nose on the bottle and inhales.

T5: The dog shrinks back and barks (due to the symmetry between these actions and the actions at T3, one can include both actions in the same time interval). The existence of this time interval is indicated by *then*.

T6: The master rails at the dog. This ranting suggests various actions, the first of which is a possible action whose temporal location is fuzzy: the dog would enjoy excrement. It can be located at T4 (as a substitute task for enjoying the perfume), T7 (as a subsequent activity of verification), or All Time (as a truth that remains valid all of the time). Next there are at least four series of evaluations (thymic evaluations) that are complementary to the dog's evaluation of the perfume: The public's reaction to "rubbish" and its reaction to great works of poetry, and the narrator's reaction to the same objects. These evaluations, unlike the dog's evaluation of dung, do not seem to call for subsequent verification; at least they are not presented in this way. They seem more like truths that were established even before T1. Whatever the case, because of their symmetry with the NP in which the dog evaluates the perfume, we have placed these temporally problematic actions in the same column as this NP.

NOTES:

In order to highlight the symmetries between NPs, we have chosen not to superpose some NPs that are simultaneous (which means that we have columns NP3 and NP3', and also NP4 and NP4').

We could have a NP: I → D n commands, if we distinguish the salutations "my good dog, . . ." from what is being asked of the dog ("come . . ."). This narrative program would be broken down into three consecutive

Table 7.7 A narrative array in "The dog and the perfume bottle"

	T1 (NP1)	*T2 (NP2)*	*T3 (NP3)*	*T3 (NP3')*	*T4 (NP4)*	*T4 (NP4')*	*T5 (NP5)*	*T6 (NP6)*
a	I → I n perfume	I → D n call	C → I n sign of enjoyment {wagging}	D → D n approaches bottle	D → D n sniff	D → D n evaluate perfume	D→ D u approach	I → D n reproach
b		I → D n sign of enjoyment	*Person x → Person y n smile*			OTHER TIMES D → n evaluates dung	D → I n reproach {bark}	(I → D n sign of enjoyment)
c		(I → D n reproach)				*Public → Public n evaluate poetry*	(D → I n sign of enjoyment)	
d						*Public → Public n evaluate Poetry*		
e						*I → I n evaluate poetry*		
f						*I → I n evaluate Poetry*		

Legend: (): possible NP that did not come to pass (did not become real, unrealized), italics: NP of comparison, {}: alternative, more specific NP. The upper and lowercase letters in *poetry* indicate great poetry and mediocre poetry, respectively.

sub-programs that the dog must carry out: D n near the bottle, D n sniff, D n evaluate (or more accurately, evaluate positively).

The narrative program I → I n perfume summarizes the action of obtaining the perfume. If this action were broken down, we would find the narrative program: Parfumeur → I n Perfume. This program has comparative companion programs: Author → Public n poetry and Author → Public n Poetry (insofar as there is no distinction between the perfume's producer and distributor, or if they are mixed up).

The last two NPs are symmetrical: the dog and I insult each other, each in his own language (there is a homology between the oppositions bark/wag and criticize/flatter).

Sniffing and evaluating can be seen as simultaneous.

For additional analysis, read the study on the same text in the chapter on thymic analysis.

Notes

1 According to the principle that action requires only a change in junction, there is no action, strictly speaking, with respect to the object involved in the following "stories" (which does not mean that other actions do not occur with respect to other objects and subjects in the same story): Paul n Illness → Paul n Illness (an identical junction); Paul u Money → Paul n Illness (a different object); Paul n Illness → Andy u Illness (a different subject). Also, note that in the actantial model, the subject, the object and their junction correspond to the second state of the NP.

2 In Greimasian theory, junction relates only to states; therefore, there is no junction of doing. A conjunction of doing might correspond to the actualization or realization of an action, and a disjunction of doing to the virtualization of an action, understood as its non-actualization or non-realization.

3 An incremental junction is conceivable. For example, by combining an intensity with a thymic evaluation of the junction, Zilberberg distinguishes between an insufficient junction, a junction (a correct one, we might say) and an excessive junction (2000, p. 20).

4 We use the term "narrative array" rather than *narrative trajectory*, since the notion of the narrative trajectory is linked with certain Greimasian conceptions that we have not adopted. A narrative trajectory is essentially a series of narrative programs that are consecutive in time and related by simple presupposition. In addition, when we establish temporal relations, we will not use Greimasian theory's reverse-chronological numbering system, in which the presupposing narrative program comes numerically before the presupposed program. Consider the following sequence (where the arrow indicates that a NP presupposes the one preceding it): NP1: John n job ← NP2: John n wage ← NP3: John n money. In Greimas's notation, our third NP would be number one, and so on.

5 In Greimasian semiotics, a distinction is made between paradigmatic relations (*one element or another element*, that is, this NP or that NP) and syntagmatic relations (*one element and another element*, that is, this NP and that NP). These relations do not correspond exactly to the ones we have presented. For example, although syntagmatic parataxis is mentioned in Greimasian semiotics, what we will call "paradigmatic" parataxis apparently is not. It would seem that since the paradigmatic relation, strictly speaking, entails a relation of substitutional equivalence for any one temporal position, it overrides the parataxic relation in simultaneity. In syntagmatic relations, Courtés gives special treatment to comprehensive NPs. A comprehensive NP seems to be nothing more than a more complex narrative trajectory than the usual presuppositional "uni-linear" sequences found in Greimasian theory. For instance, a recipe can be broken down into sub-programs (and some of these into sub-programs as well, and so on), some of which are simultaneous or partially overlapping.

6 When examining successions, we must be wary of the maxim *post hoc ergo propter hoc*, that is, of jumping to the conclusion that whatever occurs after an event is a consequence of it, or in other words, presupposes it.

7 Greimas and Courtés (1982, p. 111) give the following operational definition for semiotic existence: "the

semiotic existence of any entity is determined by the transitive relation which binds this entity to the cognitive subject, and at the same time posits it as an object of knowledge." In semiotics, states of existence, reflected in what we call ontological status (Rastier's term), are not simply categorized as (1) non-existent / (2) existent. The second term of this opposition is broken down into sub-terms that vary in number and kind from one theory to another. (Even when the names are identical, the terms may mean different things.) Greimas and Courtés (1982, pp. 111–112) identify three sub-terms for describing actions: an action may be (2a) virtualized / (2b) actualized / (2c) realized. The ontological statuses in this triad correspond to potential action, action in process and completed action, respectively. Actualization and realization are equivalent to the manifestation of the action. The dynamic processes corresponding to this triad are: virtualization (getting from 1 to 2a), actualization (getting from 2a to 2b) and realization (getting from 2b to 2c). Fontanille mentions that "just as Guillaume proposed inserting "effectuation" between "force" and "effect", Greimas introduced actualization between virtualization and realization (1995, p. 19). The opposition existent/non-existent is homologous to the opposition presence/absence, insofar as non-existence is a radical absence. The triad virtual / actual / realized is closely related to the triad inchoative / progressive (or durative) / terminative, which reflects the beginning, middle and end of an action, respectively (and is manifested in the verbal triad, begin / continue / finish, for example). We can conceive of at least two ways – not mutually exclusive – of interpreting these relations. In the first case, the two triads intersect, and virtualization is an actual beginning to action (in the sense that it sets up wanting-to and/or having-to-do a certain action); in the second case, the triad inchoative / progressive / terminative applies to the portion of the action extending from actualization to realization (the manifestation portion of the action); the terminative may be distinguished from realization in that the latter assumes a completely finished action, whereas the terminative can describe the ending as it is under way. Greimas and Fontanille later proposed adding a fourth mode of semiotic existence, the potential, which would come before the virtual and would correspond to the preconditions for signification, part of the hypothesis of the generative trajectory of signification (1991, pp. 10, 56–59, 145–147, 151–153). Notice that changing the triad into a tetrad adds consistency – which is neither good nor bad in itself – to a theoretical system where dyads and tetrads are clearly dominant.

8 The terms "virtualization" and "actualization" do not have the same meaning in NP analysis that they have in isotopic analysis, such as in Rastier's interpretive semantics (see the chapter on structural relations).

9 Ontological status can be correlated with thymic values: In general, our societies evaluate crimes negatively, or dysphorically, with increasing intensity from the virtualized to the realized crime.

8 The canonical narrative schema

Summary

The canonical narrative schema (CNS), a tool used in Greimasian semiotics, can be used to describe an action as a structure consisting of five components. (1) The action component can be broken down into two components itself: (2) competence, which includes the conditions that are necessary in order to accomplish the action (wanting-to-do, having-to-do, knowing-how-to-do, and being-able-to-do) and (3) performance, the actual accomplishment of the action, made possible by the acquisition of competence. (4) Manipulation is the component that deals specifically with wanting-to-do and having-to-do. (5) The last component, sanction, has to do with evaluating whether the action was in fact accomplished, and the corresponding retribution (reward or punishment) that the performing subject has incurred. Here is an example of an action based on the CNS: The King asks (manipulation: having-to-do) the Prince to rescue the Princess (action). The Prince trains for combat (competence: knowing-how-to-do and being-able-to-do) and then rescues the Princess (performance). The King then grants him half of his kingdom and the hand of the Princess (sanction: positive retribution (reward)).

Theory

Overview

In order to study the canonical narrative schema in detail, we must first present it in summary.[1] The canonical narrative schema (CNS) uses logical, temporal and semantic criteria to arrange the elements of an action (which may or may not be represented as narrative programs (NPs)) into a structure consisting of five components: (1) The action, which is broken down into two components itself: (2) competence (which includes the necessary prerequisites of the action: wanting-to-do, having-to-do, knowing-how-to-do, and being-able-to-do) and (3) performance (which is the actual realization of the action); (4) manipulation (the component concerned specifically with wanting-to-do and having-to-do); and (5) sanction (which includes evaluating the action and assigning the retribution it entails (reward or punishment). As a group, the components of the CNS constitute what might be called a comprehensive action; however, each individual component can itself be seen as an action (or an array of actions) and is amenable as such to description using the CNS. The CNS is "canonical" in that it adequately accounts for the general organization of action of a large number and variety of semiotic acts on various scales (as far as texts go, anything from a paragraph to a monumental work).

Above we mentioned logical, temporal and semantic organization. A few details are in order. The components are linked together by presuppositional relations. For example, the sanction (the presupposing term) presupposes the action (the presupposed term). (Later we will address these relations in more detail.) These presuppositions generally form the basis for relations of temporal succession (with the presupposed term being temporally anterior to the presupposing term).[2] Finally, each component is an actional phase, and so each of its elements is assigned a specific semantic label (an element of manipulation, an element of sanction, etc.).

NOTE: TYPOLOGIZING SEMIOTIC ACTS WITH THE CNS

As is the case with other analytical tools (such as the actantial model and Jakobson's model of the functions of language), it is possible to produce typologies using the CNS, by distinguishing classes of semiotic units (texts, for example) either in terms of which element of the model is emphasized, or in terms of the particular hierarchical configuration between the constituent elements. Courtés (1991, pp. 101–102) proposes a typology based on the component of the CNS that is emphasized: "We should point out that all the components of the CNS are not necessarily used in a given discourse. On a broader level, moreover, this model could provide the basis for a typology of discourse: for example, one can see that while legal discourse in criminal cases is clearly focused on sanction, theological discourse would appear to lean in the opposite direction, toward manipulation; and adventure stories deal primarily with performance. To be sure, in these cases, one or another of the model's constituent elements is emphasized, but the other components are at least implicit. Thus, the penal code, which deals with sanction, can only operate in light of the actions that may be considered as evidence; and similarly, although theological discourse on redemption [. . .] emphasizes divine manipulation (particularly through the mechanism of "grace"), it is also partly oriented toward the Christian subject's action (his "conversion", in this case), and his sanction (as illustrated in [St. Thomas Aquinas'] treatise on "the last end", for example)". We would add that the bildungsroman is a genre that employs the component of competence to great advantage.

Since we will often refer to NPs, we will quickly summarize what they are. (See the corresponding chapter for more details). The narrative program is an abstract formula used to represent an action. The short formula of the conjunctive narrative program is: NP = F {S1 → (S2 n O)} and that of the disjunctive narrative program is: NP = F {S1 → (S2 u O)}. S1 is the subject of doing; S2 is the subject of state; O is the object; n is the conjunction (with the object) and u the disjunction (lacking the object) between the subject of state and the object. For example, in the fable "The crow and the fox", we have the following (conjunctive) narrative program: NP = F {Fox → (Fox n Cheese)}. In its simplest notation, the narrative program is written as follows: S1 → S2 n O, for example Fox → Fox n Cheese.

NOTE: DIFFERENCES BETWEEN THE CNS AND THE ACTANTIAL MODEL

The canonical narrative schema, proposed by Greimas, takes the theoretical place of the actantial model, also developed by Greimas. Let us look at the primary differences between them.

1 The actantial model revolves around a subject and an object. If we place this pair in a NP, we observe firstly, that the subject and the object are implicitly linked by a junction (with a slightly suspect predilection for conjunction: most analyses do in fact describe a subject that wants to be conjoined to an object, rather than one that wants to be disjoined);[3] and secondly, that this triad corresponds to the second state of a NP. As for the CNS, it centers explicitly on a NP.

2 As compared with the actantial model, a pair of actants has been dropped: the helper/opponent pair. The helping and hindering elements are integrated within competence, and if they are considered explicitly as actants, it would only be in the context of a NP, which is composed solely of subject and object actants. Thus, the object of a NP of competence is an element of the competence: for instance, the acquisition of knowing-how-to-do. A helper is therefore a subject of doing in a narrative program of maintenance or acquisition of competence (for example, when the magician enables the Prince to take possession of the magic sword, he grants him being-able-to-do); an opponent is a subject of doing in a narrative program dealing with loss or non-acquisition of competence.

3 Two kinds of senders are distinguished in the CNS: the sender-manipulator (of the manipulation component) and the sender-judge (of the sanction component). The receiver, known as the receiver-subject, corresponds to the subject of doing (S1) of the model's central NP, where it is depicted in its relationship with one of the two senders.

Some methodological considerations: As is the case with other analytical tools (e.g., the actantial model, a narrative array, or the functions of language), one can give equal attention to each constituent element of the model, or one can choose one or more elements as the focus. In the latter case, secondary constituent elements should usually be analyzed at least briefly. As with the actantial model, one must first situate the central element (the action) by careful selection, since all of the other elements depend on this central element. Once the action has been selected, one should make sure that the manipulation, sanction and competence being described actually do apply to this NP, and not some other NP in the same story. Consider the narrative sequence : NP1: Thief n Stethoscope, NP2: Thief n Contents of Safe, NP3: Thief n Prison. If one situates NP1 at the center of the schema, one cannot have NP3 as the sanction, since the latter is the sanction for NP2, and not NP1.

Visual representations

As with all analytical tools that have a specific visual representation (the actantial model, the semiotic square, etc.), one must distinguish between the CNS as a conceptual structure and the CNS as a visual representation of the structure. The following diagram is a possible visual representation of the CNS (a slight modification of the representation in Courtés, 1991, p. 100). The arrows indicate presuppositional relations between components; thus, the sanction presupposes the action, but the action does not presuppose the sanction. For instance, a reward presupposes the accomplishment of some deserving deed, but a deserving deed might not ever be rewarded (even if there was an explicit agreement that it would be).

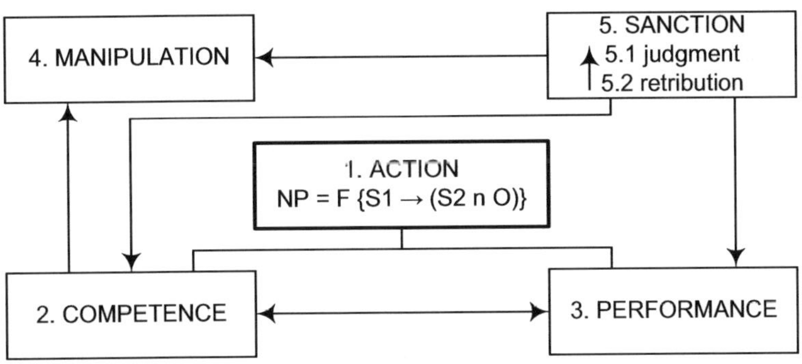

Figure 8.1 Representation of the canonical narrative schema

NOTE: TIME AND THE CNS

We will specify the various presuppositional relations between components as we proceed, but at this point, let us review a few logical (presential, to be specific) and temporal principles. As one would expect, a presupposing element is optional relative to its presupposed element(s). This is the case, for example, with the sanction (presupposing) as opposed to the action (presupposed). A presupposed element, which is logically anterior, is usually temporally anterior, but not always.

We must interject some remarks about time. First of all, there is a distinction between real time (that of reality) and thematized time (which is a representation of real time in a semiotic act, such as a text); secondly, note that succession and simultaneity are relative to the duration of the standard time unit. For example, wanting to blink one's eyes and doing it are successive in real time and from a neurological standpoint (in that the electrical signal takes a certain amount of time to go from the brain to the muscles, and it takes a certain amount of time to perform the blinking). However, they are usually considered as simultaneous in the reality of everyday life, and in time as represented in semiotic acts (unless, for instance, a novel has a neurologist in it who keeps track of fractions of seconds); time is rarely represented in semiotic productions as it is in science.

To return to temporal relations between components, we have an example of temporal simultaneity between components related by presupposition: in the case of a character blinking his eyes, wanting-to (competence) and doing are perfectly simultaneous (with some exceptions). The following is an example of inversion between temporal arrangement and logical (presential) arrangement: if full compensation for a service is payable in advance, then the retribution phase of the sanction precedes the action at least partially. (This does not exclude the possibility of cognitive retribution (recognition) or pragmatic retribution in the form of an unanticipated bonus (a tip) could follow the action.)

The duration of represented time associated with a component can vary from zero to infinity. The duration would theoretically be infinite in some stories, for instance, where an action waiting to be accomplished depends on competence whose acquisition keeps being delayed. It would be counted as zero in a case of immediate performance, as in pushing a detonator to make a bomb explode or blinking one's eyes. It would also be zero in a case where wanting-to-do is already present as soon as the particular action presents itself to be accomplished, if the other elements of competence are "always already there", as in raising one's arm.

Manipulation

Positive and negative manipulation

Manipulation (a term that has no pejorative connotation in semiotics) is the component of the CNS that has to do with changes in wanting-to-do and/or having-to-do. Positive manipulation (a term with no meliorative (ameliorative) connotations) aims to produce or increase these elements, or to maintain them if they are already at adequate levels; negative manipulation (a term with no pejorative connotations) aims to eliminate or decrease them, or to maintain them at inadequate levels. The purpose of positive manipulation is causing-to-do; the purpose of negative manipulation is causing-not-to-do. Manipulation (positive) is equivalent to causing-to-do (written as D → D).[4]

The sender-manipulator and receiver-subject

The sender-manipulator directs his/her manipulation towards the receiver-subject, that is, the subject who is supposed to accomplish or not accomplish the action. In the NP representing this action, the receiver-subject corresponds to the subject of doing, abbreviated as S1. Positive manipulation is represented thusly in a NP: NP = F1 [S1 → F2 {S2 ◊ (S3 n O)}]; This formula differs from that of the standard narrative program (there is an additional subject, and S1 and S2 have become S2 and S3, respectively); here S1 represents the sender-manipulator, and S2 the receiver-subject.

Manipulation and the contract

By means of the explicit or implicit contract it establishes between the sender-manipulator and the receiver-subject, manipulation draws the action to be accomplished or not accomplished into the realm of possibility, along with the positive or negative retribution that will ensue if the contract is fulfilled or not fulfilled.

NOTE: MANIPULATION AND ANTI-MANIPULATION

We propose a typology of manipulation based on the kind of retribution the contract entails, using the following criteria: (1) whether the object of retribution is pragmatic/cognitive (that is, concrete/abstract, a matter of perception/understanding) and (2) whether it is negative/positive; (3) whether the relationship between this object and the receiver-subject is conjunctive/disjunctive. One must take care to distinguish between positive/negative retribution and a positive/negative object of retribution; for instance, a negative object may well be part of a positive retribution: removing (disjunction) a thorn (a negative pragmatic object) from someone's foot may be a reward (positive pragmatic retribution). For more details, see the section in this chapter on sanction. Courtés proposes the following typology (1991, p. 111): In the pragmatic domain, manipulation plays on temptation and/or intimidation (such as promising a money reward and/or threatening to beat someone). In the cognitive domain, manipulation plays on seduction or (and/or?) provocation (e.g., words of encouragement, like "I'm sure you can do it" or a challenge such as "You certainly aren't capable of doing that").

From the standpoint of manipulation, a polemical structure sets a sender-manipulator in opposition with an anti-sender-manipulator, both directed toward a receiver-subject alone, or a receiver-subject and an anti-receiver-subject. Take the case of two opposing armies, each one commanded by a general. The general of the first army (the sender-manipulator) uses positive manipulation (encouragement, the prospect of earning medals, threats, etc.) to induce his soldiers (the receiver-subjects) to advance (or at least not retreat) and he uses negative manipulation (threats, explosions, etc.) to induce the enemy not to advance (or even to retreat). The general of the second army (the anti-sender-manipulator) directs positive manipulation toward his soldiers (the anti-receiver-subjects or receiver-anti-subjects) aimed at the same action (to advance or at least not retreat).

By applying logical negation (represented by the logical negation symbol (¬)), we obtain four kinds of manipulation: (1) cd (causing-to-do: inducing), (2) c¬d (causing-not-to-do: preventing), (3) ¬cd (not-causing-to-do: not-inducing), (3) ¬c¬d (not-causing-not-to-do: leaving be).[5]

Action

The action is the central component (conceptually and visually) of the CNS. This action is generally represented by a narrative program. The action component is broken down into two components itself: competence and performance. Action (or more accurately, performance) presupposes manipulation. If there is action, then there had to be manipulation, but manipulation, even when successful, does not necessarily lead to action; for instance, being-able-to-do could be insufficient. Action corresponds to causing-to-be (written as D → B, where doing governs being).

NOTE: THE CNS AND NARRATIVE PROGRAMS

The theory states that in order to include a NP in the canonical narrative schema, the NP must be one of performance, that is, a reflexive action, where S1 = S2 (for instance, washing oneself), as opposed to a transitive action, where S1 ≠ S2 (for instance, washing someone else). In analytical practice, we are not sure that this principle is necessary. Actantial syncretism (where two actants reside in the same actor) is found not just in action; there are also cases of self-manipulation, self-sanction, and self-qualification (competence).

The other components of the CNS may each be described using a NP. We will use the following action: a knight rescues the princess from the witch who has her imprisoned. The following are some narrative programs illustrating the five components of the CNS: NP1: King → Knight n Mission (manipulation); NP2: Fairy → Knight n Magic Sword (the modality of being-able-to-do, part of competence); NP3: Knight → Knight n Death of witch (being-able-to-do); NP4: Knight → Princess n Freedom (the action at the center of the CNS); NP5: King → Knight n Reward (sanction). And we shall add some additional flexibility: the action component does not necessarily have to be represented by a narrative program.

Competence

Competence (a term with no meliorative (ameliorative) connotation in semiotics) is the component of the CNS that has to do with changes (creation, maintenance, increase, decrease, loss) in the prerequisite elements needed for performance (accomplishing the action). There are four different modalities involved in competence: two that are also factors of manipulation – wanting-to-do (abbreviated as *wd*) and having-to-do (abbreviated *hd*) – and two others – knowing-how-to-do[6] (*kd*) and being-able-to-do (*ad*).[7] Competence is the being-of-doing, the being necessary for doing (notated B → D).

When discussing competence or one of its modalities, we say it is positive (with no meliorative connotation) when it is sufficient to lead to performance; otherwise we call it negative (with no pejorative connotation); or we can speak in terms of competence (in the absolute sense) and anti-competence. Negative competence or a negative modality of competence has a minus sign in its notation (e.g., -*wd* signifies negative wanting-to-do). In order to have performance, competence must be positive, that is: (1) knowing-how-to-do and being-able-to-do must both be positive, and (2) wanting-to-do and/or having-to-do must be positive (positive wanting-to-do can compensate for negative having-to-do and vice versa).[8]

NOTE: NEGATION AND THE MODALITIES

By applying logical negation (indicated by a logical negation symbol (¬)), we obtain four combinations between doing (abbreviated *d*) and the modalities of wanting, having-to, knowing-how, and being-able (abbreviated *w, h, k* and *a*, respectively).[9] Combinations like *x*¬d are expressed as: *x* not-to-do (such as w¬d, wanting not-to-do) and combinations like ¬*x*¬d are expressed as: not-*x* not-to-do (such as ¬w¬d, not-wanting not-to-do). In parentheses we have identified some possible lexical labels (possible names) for the logical categories.

1 wd, w¬d, ¬wd, ¬w¬d
2 hd (required), h¬d (prohibited), ¬hd (optional), ¬h¬d (allowed)
3 kd, k¬d, ¬kd, ¬k¬d
4 ad (freedom), a¬d (independence), ¬ad (powerlessness), ¬a¬d (obedience)

The shift from negative competence to positive competence is a movement from the nonexistence of an action to its potentiality (ontological status: "possible"), whereas performance entails moving from the possibility of an action to its realization (ontological status: "real").

NOTE: VIRTUALIZATION/ACTUALIZATION/REALIZATION

In actual Greimasian terminology, when wanting-to-do and/or having-to-do are positive, it is termed "virtualization" (in the sense of the possibility of an action); when knowing-how-to-do and being-able-to-do are positive, it is known as "actualization"; when performance occurs, it is called "realization". This helps to explain the notion that, even in the competence phase, action presupposes manipulation: virtualization is the first of the three successive phases. The following table (Courtés, 1991, p. 106) shows the relations between the components and the modalities involved in virtualization, actualization and realization (the arrows indicate the presuppositional relations that exist between the modalities).

Table 8.1 Modalities of virtualization, actualization and realization in canonical narrative schema

competence		*competence*		*performance*
modalities of virtualization wanting-to-do having-to-do (inauguration of the subject)	←	modalities of actualization knowing-how-to-do being-able-to-do (qualification of the subject)	←	modalities of realization being doing (realization of the subject)

For our purposes, the essential point, especially from the standpoint of application, lies in the distinction between realized and unrealized. Since we are assigning other meanings to the terms "actualization" and "virtualization" than those used in Greimasian semiotics (cf. our discussion of actualized and virtualized semes), we will opt for the term "possible" (or "possibility") to describe an action in the competence phase. For more details on the way Greimasian semiotics defines virtualization, actualization and realization, see the chapter on narrative programs.

Despite what Courtés claims, it appears that all positive competence leads without fail to performance; if not, then competence was not completely or truly positive. For instance, someone starts to lift his arm, but a meteorite kills him. By appearances, he had competence, as in the general competence required to raise his arm, but it was not true competence suitable for that specific action in those specific circumstances. Considered in this light, it follows that the relation between competence and performance is more accurately a relation of reciprocal presupposition: If there is (positive) competence, there will necessarily be performance; if there is performance, then there was necessarily (positive) competence.

Performance

Performance is the component of the CNS that concerns the action's realization (in the strict sense), made possible by positive competence. Performance presupposes competence (and manipulation, naturally, since it involves wanting-to-do and having-to-do, just as competence does): If there is performance, then competence was necessarily positive. As we have seen, in this context presupposition can be considered reciprocal: when competence is truly and fully positive, realization of the action necessarily follows. Performance corresponds to causing-to-be (written as D→ B, where doing governs being).

Performance – and consequently competence – can be categorial and/or incremental. For example, going off a cliff is generally seen as a categorial action: one either succeeds or one doesn't. (A half-success or near-success is still a failure, and painful). An election is an example of performance that is both categorial and incremental: victory is realized first by obtaining at least 50 percent of the ballots cast plus one; but the incremental dimension should not be ignored: The intensity of the victory increases the closer one comes to obtaining 100 percent of the votes cast (some dictators have understood this quite well).

Sanction

As the final component of the CNS, sanction includes the epistemic judgment (evaluation) of performance and the accompanying retribution that the performing subject has incurred. The sender-judge directs his sanction toward the receiver-subject, that is, the subject who was supposed to accomplish or not accomplish the action (the subject of doing, S1 in the NP). Epistemic judgment determines whether performance conforms to the implicit or explicit contract that was made during the manipulation stage. One must answer questions like the following: Was the action realized, and properly so? Is the presumed receiver-subject the right one, an impostor, or a case of mistaken identity? Retribution is the next stage. It can be categorial or incremental, positive (reward) or negative (punishment), and pragmatic (a gift of gold, for instance) or cognitive (recognition, for example). Retribution presupposes epistemic judgment (but not the reverse, since the sender-judge could die before giving the promised reward, for instance). Sanction presupposes action (or more accurately, performance that took place or should have taken place), but the action does not necessarily presuppose a sanction (as would be the case if the sender-judge died before passing his epistemic judgment, to take our previous example). Sanction corresponds to the being-of-being (written as B → B).[10]

NOTE: PRAGMATIC AND COGNITIVE SANCTIONS

Courtés talks about pragmatic and cognitive sanctions in cases where the epistemic judgment addresses the action and the subject who realized the action, respectively. Pragmatic and cognitive sanctions should not be confused with pragmatic and cognitive retribution.

NOTE: VERIDICTORY STATUS

There are various ways in which veridictory status is factored into Greimasian narrative analysis (in the actantial model, the narrative program, the canonical narrative schema, etc.). In the CNS, it is especially relevant in the sanction component (in evaluating the reality and quality of performance, and the reality of the subject involved in the performance), but it can also apply to the manipulation component (e.g., the manipulator offers a false contract), and the competence component (e.g., the subject mistakenly believes that he has the necessary competence).

If we map out positive retribution (PR)/negative retribution (NR) onto a semiotic square (see the chapter on this subject), we obtain four simple terms (PR/NR ¬PR/¬NR, where ¬ indicates logical negation).[11] Each of these terms can be marked with a thymic value (euphoria/dysphoria – see the chapter on this subject) attributed to the object of retribution and the possible modes of junction between the receiver-subject and the object of retribution. For example, if we combine two thymic values (euphoria/dysphoria in this case) and four junctions (conjunction/disjunction and non-conjunction/non-disjunction), we obtain eight kinds of retribution (or sixteen, if we add in the distinction between pragmatic/cognitive objects of retribution). In the typology we are outlining, S is the receiver-subject, who receives the retribution; n is the conjunction (with the object); u is the disjunction (without the object); ¬n is non-conjunction (not with the object); ¬u is non-disjunction (not without the object); O+ is a euphoric object of retribution (the carrot); O- is a dysphoric object of retribution (the stick, or beating). Each of these possibilities can be illustrated with a short sentence of manipulation.

Types of positive retribution (reward):

1 Type 1 PR: S n O+: If you do X, I will give you a carrot.
2 Type 1 ¬NR: S u O-: If you do X, I will stop beating you.
3 Type 2 ¬NR: S ¬n O-: If you do X, I won't beat you.
4 Type 2 PR: S ¬u O+: If you do X, I won't take away your carrot.

Types of negative retribution (punishment):

5 Type 1 NR: S n O-: If you do X, I will beat you.
6 Type 1 ¬PR : S u O+: If you do X, I will take away your carrot.
7 Type 2 ¬PR: S ¬n O+: If you do X, I won't give you a carrot.
8 Type 2 NR: S ¬u O-: If you do X, I won't stop beating you.

Application: "The crow and the fox" by Jean de La Fontaine

* * *

The crow and the fox

Jean de La Fontaine (1988, pp. 5, 7)

At the top of a tree perched Master Crow;
In his beak he was holding a cheese.
Drawn by the smell, Master Fox spoke, below.
The words, more or less, were these:
Hey, now, Sir Crow! Good day, good day!
How very handsome you do look, how grandly distingué!
No lie, if those songs you sing
Match the plumage of your wing,
You're the phoenix of these woods, our choice".
Hearing this, the Crow was all rapture and wonder.
To show off his handsome voice,
He opened beak wide and let go of his plunder.
The Fox snapped it up and then said, "My Good Sir,
Learn that each flatterer
Lives at the cost of those who heed.
This lesson is well worth the cheese, indeed".

The Crow, ashamed and sick,
Swore, a bit late, not to fall again for that trick.

* * *

In La Fontaine's (1621–1695) "The crow and the fox", we will discuss the action wherein the crow (C) sings at the fox's (F) urging. Here is a simplified CNS that describes this action.

A few explanatory details are in order.

Table 8.2 A canonical narrative schema in "The crow and the fox"

MANIPULATION	*ACTION*	*SANCTION*
• F → (C → C n Sing) This NP corresponds to: • F → C n wanting-to-do This NP presupposes: • F → C n Possibility of positive retribution (Cognitive) retribution of false contract • F → C n Glory	C → C n Sing	Epistemic judgment • F → Action n Positive judgment (The action is judged as being properly realized.) Retribution The true contract's pragmatic retribution • F → C u Cheese (dispossession) The true contract's cognitive retribution • F → C n Humiliation • F → C n Lesson (ironic retribution)
COMPETENCE • F → C n Wanting-to-do • C → C n Knowing-how-to-do (action already realized) • C → C n Being-able-to-do (action already realized)		*PERFORMANCE* • C → C n Sing (action realized)

During the manipulation stage, the fox, in the role of sender-manipulator, chooses seduction over intimidation for the occasion. He implicitly offers two contracts, the real one and the false one. The crow believes that in return for singing, he will receive positive cognitive retribution in the form of glory from showing off his beautiful voice. Keeping the cheese does not even enter into the false contract, since singing and keeping the cheese are not mutually exclusive from the crow's perspective, or at least he forgets their incompatibility momentarily under the influence of the fox's flattery. The real, implicit contract is the following: If he sings, the crow will receive negative retribution, both pragmatic (the loss of his cheese) and cognitive (humiliation).

NOTE: ANTI-MANIPULATION

The Fox is also an anti-manipulator in some ways. The fox has laid a trap, and if the crow does not fall into it, his retribution will be to keep the cheese and receive what we call glory in this model – the glory of outsmarting the fox and making a show of clairvoyance. This hypothesis is no more than the symmetrical counterpart of what happens in reality, which gives it substance: the fox obtains glory as the cognitive retribution for carrying off his action (whether the action is strictly his manipulation or his obtaining the cheese). Besides glory, the fox receives the cheese as retribution, and no doubt a sort of sadistic pleasure at the poor crow's expense (a bit like the cruel ant at the expense of the ill-fated cicada).

The fox concedes that the crow is beautiful at the outset, but says he wants to hear a voice that he assumes is beautiful ("No lie, if those songs you sing/Match the plumage of your wing . . ."). The fox's intellectual superiority is emphasized by the hyperbole of his flattery, which reveals the crow's gullibility and vanity – a crow is neither a peacock nor a nightingale. However, we should point out that the stupidity attributed to the crow is undeserved, for in reality, the crows are very intelligent animals (for example, it has been demonstrated that they can count to four).

During the sanction stage, the fox becomes the judge-manipulator. The epistemic judgment does not present any problems: The action was indeed realized according to the contract (the real one as well as the false one). However, for the retribution, the fox dispenses with pretense and grants the retribution provided by the real contract, to which the crow was an unwitting and unconscious party. He cynically idealizes the crow's loss as an exchange: After all, didn't the crow receive a lesson for his cheese? It is a very unequal exchange, in which a pragmatic object that is a basic necessity is exchanged for a cognitive object that is supposedly unique and not to be shared, although the fox does not deprive himself in giving it – he retains the lesson and, more importantly, the intelligence and the ruse of which the lesson is simply a manifestation.

NOTE: CLOSED VALUE SYSTEMS AND PARTICIPATIVE COMMUNICATION

Technically, we use the term "closed value system" to describe the kind of situation in which one loses what one gives, and "participative communication" for cases in which one keeps the object, despite giving it away. According to Greimas and Fontanille (1993, p. 134): "If we now consider the status of objects, we see that nothing is solved by our calling them "participative" or "non-participative". We have already noted that it is not appropriate to speak of a participative character for objects of value as such. On the one hand, land can be parceled off or it can be held in common; on the other, knowledge can be jealously kept to oneself. The participative character of objects is nothing other than the meaning effect of the consensus reached by subjects in their regard with a view to the constitution of a participative totality. All you need is for one of these subjects to refuse to agree (refuse to share) and his object will become considered "non-participative" and he will be seen as "exclusive". Individuals can assign status in this matter. One can be jealous of one's wife, of one's prestige or discoveries, but cultures also can show this jealousy – they decree that goods or women are to be held in common, or that knowledge is the exclusive right of clerks and sorcerers". In our opinion, we must first disassociate problems concerning the participative/non-participative status of an object from its actual status as shared/not-shared; secondly, we must take into account the assumptive and reference veridictory perspectives (e.g., a certain character may mistakenly believe that an object is non-participative).

One of La Fontaine's consistent oppositions has cropped up here: the opposition between what is useful or essential and what is futile. In this poem it is manifested in the oppositions intelligence/beauty or voice, intellectual superiority/physical superiority (the crow can fly, and he is perched at the top of a tree), and eating/singing. In "The cicada and the ant", we find the opposition work/pleasure, with pleasure manifested as singing again, but also as dancing, in the ant's famous cynical reply. In "The stag seeing himself in a spring" (La Fontaine, 1988, p. 259), we find the following lines: "We make much of beauty, it's the useful we do mistreat/Yet beauty often leads us to our loss".

Notes

1 For this chapter, we shall draw liberally, but not strictly, from an excellent summary of Greimasian semiotics by Courtés (1991, pp. 98–136).
2 For a more in-depth analysis of the interactions between temporal relations and presential relations, including presupposition, see the chapters on structural relations and the narrative program.

3 As Fontanille observes (2003, p. 124), "the model of the quest [the actantial model] neglects narrative situations that place subjects in the presence of objects of negative value, or repulsive or horrifying objects."

4 In this symbolic notation, and in the other notations associated with each component, the arrow indicates that the relation is not symmetrical (D → B is not the same thing as B → D); it indicates the direction of the relation, with the first term governing or determining the second. We shall give a meaningful example: chocolate (C) milk (M) would be written as M → C, and milk chocolate would be C → M; the first term dominates the second; the second one only modulates the first. For more on the subject of direction, or governance, see Bertrand (2000, p. 152).

5 These are the four metaterms of a Klein 4-group (see the chapter on the veridictory square). We have modified three of the four lexical labels proposed by Courtés (1991) for these metaterms, which are: (1) intervention, (2) hindrance, (3) non-intervention, (4) leaving be. The lexical items used to represent logical categories are often approximate, and one should not interpret the lexical item as an exact description of the category.

6 Courtés (1991, p. 104) invites us to distinguish between semantic competence and knowing-how-to-do, which includes semantic competence, but goes beyond it. It is one thing to know the recipe for mayonnaise (semantic competence); it is quite another to be able to make it (knowing-how-to-do).

7 As Courtés notes (1991, p. 104), it is possible to have modalities of competence formed from elements other than wanting, having-to, being-able and knowing-how. We should also note that just as doing can be governed by wanting, having-to, being-able and knowing-how, so can being (see Courtés, 1991, pp. 107–109). Furthermore, it may be possible to define competence as the component that concerns changes in knowing-how-to-do and being-able-to-do, which would effectively eliminate the overlap between competence and manipulation. In this case, we would have to redefine the competence component, since it would no longer involve all of the prerequisite conditions for performance.

8 Some modalities of competence may be linked by converse (direct) or inverse correlation, as seen in utterances like "if you really want to, you can do it" or "the harder I try, the worse I do" or the typical modal formula of "inhibition through interaction" (Fontanille, 2003, p. 228): "the more you push me, the more incompetent I get."

9 By doing this, we are producing Klein 4-groups (see the chapter on the veridictory square).

10 Here we can see that there are limits to the combinatorial antics of which semiotics is so fond. The equivalence between sanction and the being-of-being appears to be quite partial. It seems to relate only to the epistemic judgment, where the being of being is evaluated (the second "being" is understood as the action's being (was it realized and properly so?) and the subject of the action's being (is the subject who he claims to be?), thereby pushing the retribution part of the sanction into the shadows.

11 Metaterms or compound terms are possible too, of course (see the chapter on the semiotic square): for instance, the positive deixis (PR + ¬NR), if interpreted in terms of reinforcement, would be manifested as 1 + 2 in our typology of retribution.

9 Figurative, thematic and axiological analysis

Summary

Figurative/thematic/axiological analysis is based on a semantic typology formulated by Greimas. An element of content (a seme or an isotopy) may be figurative, thematic or axiological. Figurative elements include anything that evokes perception, whereas thematic ones are characterized by their strictly conceptual nature. For example, love is a theme, and its various concrete manifestations (flowers, kisses, etc.) are figures. The figures and themes of a text derive from an axiology: that is, they are correlated with a value in the category euphoria/dysphoria (in non-technical terms, pleasure/displeasure or positive/negative). For instance, the themes love/hate are generally associated with euphoria and dysphoria, respectively.

Theory

Greimas's semantic theory (his linguistic semantics, at least) is based on the seme, which is an element of a signified. The repetition of a seme creates an isotopy. On the textual level (or discursive level, as opposed to the word and sentence levels), a seme – like the isotopy it defines – may be figurative, thematic or axiological.[1]

Figure and theme

In figurative, thematic and axiological analysis[2] the theme is opposed to the figure. "In a given universe of discourse (verbal or non-verbal)", figurative elements include "anything that can be directly registered by one of the five senses: sight, hearing, smell, taste and touch; that is, anything that relates to *perception* of the external world". Conversely, thematic elements are "characterized by their strictly conceptual nature" [3] (Courtés, 1991, p. 163). For instance, love is a theme whose various perceptible manifestations are figures: flowers, kisses, etc.

Axiology

Axiology is based on what is known as the thymic category, that is, the opposition euphoria/dysphoria (or in less technical terms, positive/negative or attractive/repulsive). From this initial opposition, the inventory of axiological values may be created. The primary values are euphoria, dysphoria, phoria (euphoria and dysphoria simultaneously, that is, ambivalence) and aphoria (neither euphoria nor dysphoria, that is, indifference). For other values, and an elaboration of axiological analysis, refer to the chapter on thymic analysis.

NOTE: ICONIC/ABSTRACT AND SPECIFIC/GENERIC SUB-CATEGORIES

Figurative elements are classified as iconic/abstract, while thematic and axiological elements are classified as specific/generic.[4] The first term of each opposition is the more specific (e.g., iconic figurative); the second term is the more general (e.g., abstract figurative). The classification of an element as iconic/abstract or specific/generic depends on the relations involved. Thus, /movement/ is an abstract figure relative to /dance/, which is an iconic figure; but /dance/ becomes an abstract figure in relation to /waltz/, which is an iconic figure. The thematic opposition virtue/vice is generic relative to generosity/selfishness, as generosity is only one of many possible virtues. According to Courtés (1991, p. 243), the axiological category euphoria/dysphoria is generic relative to joy/sorrow or calm/rage.

NOTE: PARALLELS BETWEEN FIGURATIVE/THEMATIC SIGNIFIEDS AND SIGNIFIER/SIGNIFIED

There is a distinction to be made concerning signifier/signified and figure/theme. The signifier is the "perceptible"[5] part of a sign (for example, the letters *v-e-l-v-e-t* of the word "velvet" can be perceived visually.) The signified is the content, the understandable part of the sign (e.g., the signified for "velvet" refers to the idea of a fabric and softness). The figure is an element of content that evokes sensory perception (in the content of the word "velvet", we have the idea of touch, for instance). The theme is an element of content that does not suggest sensory perception (the content of the word "glory" does not suggest sensory perception, at least not directly). In other words, despite being quite distinct, figure and signifier are similar in that they are matters of perception, whereas thematic content is in some ways the quintessence of content, because, like the signified, it belongs to the realm of understanding, rather than perception. In short, there is a homology: the signifier is to the figure as the signified is to the theme.

Courtés (1991, pp. 161–176) observes the homology between signifier/signified and figurative/thematic signifieds, although he qualifies it. The relation of reciprocal presupposition that is said to underlie the sign – homonymy and polysemy apart, any change to the signifier must produce a change in the signified and vice versa (compare "moose" and "noose", for instance) – does not exist between figure and theme. For example, the figure /tears/ may be related to a theme of either joy or sorrow. There are also figures not attached to any theme and themes with no figures. However, recursivity (the repetition of the signifier/signified structure) does not stop there. As we have just seen, the figure and theme categories of the signified are in turn divided into the iconic/abstract and specific/generic sublevels, respectively. According to Courtés, the iconic figurative element is the signifier's homologue, since it is the figure that yields the best referential illusion (illusion of reality) and elicits the greater sensory response. The same would apply, although to a lesser degree, to the thematic and axiological levels. In summary, the various levels and sublevels would be ordered in the following way on a scale from most perceptible to most conceptual: iconic figure, abstract figure, specific theme, generic theme, specific axiology, generic axiology.

The relations between figures, themes and axiology

It is generally helpful to try and group the figures into oppositions, and the themes as well.[6] In this way, the figure /day/ implies /night/, and the theme /love/ implies /hate/. As for axiological values, although the opposition euphoria/dysphoria is readily accepted, other combinations of axiological values, such as phoria/aphoria are not so easily set in opposition, and are subject to debate.

As follows are some of the relations between the different types of content. Various relations may arise between figurative, thematic and axiological content. We shall focus on the figure-theme relation, although the same principles are valid for figure-axiology and theme-axiology relations. We have the following:

(1) One figure may relate to one theme (especially in the case of stereotypical symbols, as in a horseshoe for luck).
(2) One figure may relate to several themes, which may or may not be grouped into opposition(s) (as in the color green representing hope and "Irish-ness").
(3) Several figures, which may or may not be grouped into opposition(s), may relate to a single theme (to take the same example, a horseshoe and a four-leaf clover for luck);[7]
(4) One or more figurative oppositions may relate to one or more thematic oppositions. These oppositions would be homologous with each other (for example, the figurative opposition high/low with the thematic opposition ideal/reality).

NOTE: AXIOLOGY AND HOMOLOGATION

The thymic category is often homologized with a figurative and/or thematic category; for example, in the thematic category love/hate and the figurative category caressing/beating, one of the two terms will be euphoric (usually love and caressing) and the other two will be dysphoric.[8] But many other kinds of relations are possible. There are two reasons for this: (1) figures and themes are not necessarily grouped into oppositions (for example, the figure "boat" may well be present in a given text without any opposite); (2) even when they are, they may not necessarily be homologous with the axiological opposition (for example, the figurative opposition day/night may be associated solely with euphoria, or one of its terms may be associated with euphoria and the other with aphoria).

Symbolic, semi-symbolic and semiotic relations

When a figurative opposition is tied in with a thematic opposition, such as day/night (figures) with virtue/crime (themes), the relation is known as a semi-symbolic one in Greimasian semiotics.[9] It is tempting to extend the semi-symbolic relation to figure-axiology relations (e.g., day/night and euphoria/dysphoria) and theme-axiology relations (hope/despair and euphoria/dysphoria).[10] The common factor in semi-symbolic relations of any kind would then be to establish a homology between two oppositions, one of which is more sensory (perception) and the other of which is more conceptual (understanding). However, the differentia between perception and understanding emerge most clearly in the figure-theme relation. Let us conclude by mentioning that a semi-symbolic relation is always a homologous relation, but that the reverse is not true (see our chapter on homologation).

When a one-on-one relation is established, we call it a symbolic relation: for example, /boat/ as a figure and /journey/ as a theme, in a case where the boat is the only figure associated with the journey in that particular semiotic act. In all other cases, we use the term "semiotic relation", for example, a relation that ties an element to an opposition (in the same text, tears as a figure may go with euphoria in one case (tears of joy), and dysphoria in another).

Relational dynamics

The inventory of figures, themes and axiological values, as well as the relations between these three kinds of content, can and do vary according to the culture, the discourse, the genre, the specific semiotic act, the observing subjects (author, narrator, character, etc.), and the particular moment in a given temporality (whether it involves real time (for example, historical time) or thematized time (time as presented in a text or a painting) or some other type of time).

Application: "I miss the land" by Georges Bouchard

* * *

"I miss the land".
Georges Bouchard (1917, pp. 70–71, translated)

To His Honour Judge Pouliot

Thirteen-year-old René, face haggard with consumption. He shields his chest with an emaciated hand as if to keep life from pouring out in the fits of coughing. Faintly, these barely spoken words slip out:

"I miss the land".

Poor little flower of the fields, all withered in the city! His father left the farm five years ago to come and work in the factories of Victoriaville.

You are not the only one who feels this way, my little tad . . .

He stares at me, his big eyes languid from suffering, the lights of eternity already flickering there.

"I miss the land".

This is the unspoken cry, smothered by pride, rising out of the depths of wretched souls in the destitution of the city. The war adds even more poignancy to their grief, creating distress of an intensity never seen in the countryside.

"I miss the land".

This is the innocent confession of the children suffocating in the tiny courtyards of urban dwellings, starving for air and light. For these youngsters, the wide-open fields, the verdant hillsides and the snowbanks where they first cavorted are a memory that calls out incessantly.

"I miss the land".

This is the deep scar that cuts to the heart when the factory worker in the city recalls the freedom of being in the fields. Gaiety, tenderness, intimacy, domestic peace – these are rural products that often perish when exported.

"I miss the land".

This is the truth that emanates from the works of many famous writers who have made their homes out in the fields and woods, like Botrel, Mercier, Bazin, . . .

"I miss the land".

This is the cry of longing that shrouds the gentle soul, full of dignity and ideals . . . without ever being voiced.

– My boy, you miss the land, but soon you will go live in the gardens of Paradise . . .
You miss the land . . . So do I.

* * *

Let us present a brief application of figurative, thematic and axiological analysis for "I miss the land", a narrative from French-Canadian rural legend (for further analysis, see Hébert, 2000). We will identify just a few of the figurative, thematic and axiological elements present in this text and see how they are organized.

We consider the central figurative opposition to be a spatial one: country/city. Another important figurative opposition corresponds to this one, which is heaven/hell.[11] The figure /heaven/ is explicit: "soon you will go live in the gardens of Paradise". (p. 71). The figure /hell/ is implicit; it crops up in expressions like "wretched souls" (p. 70) and "calls out incessantly" (p. 71). These two oppositions are associated with a third figurative opposition: life/death.[12] The land would have brought life to René, the dying hero of the short story; and as for heaven, isn't it generally considered to be the abode of those who have "eternal life"? Yet another important figurative opposition is the one between nature and culture. In the anthropological sense of the term, any typically human production belongs to culture (a chair, agriculture, war, theatre, etc.). The dominant theme appears to be the opposition between spiritual and temporal. Let us examine the axiology of the figures and themes we have identified. We have formulated our oppositions so that the first term is the one viewed as euphoric in this text. The euphoric elements are: country, heaven, life and nature; conversely, the dysphoric elements are: city, hell, death and culture. These oppositions all appear to be homologized with each other (meaning that the terms on the left are all interrelated and the terms on the right are all interrelated). Even life, in the biological sense of the term, is associated with the spiritual realm, since the countryside, an earthly paradise, promotes health.

Table 9.1 Thematic, figurative and axiological structure in "I miss the land"

Axiology	*Euphoria*	*Dysphoria*
Themes	spiritual	material
Figures	nature	culture
	life	death
	heaven	hell
	country	city

The main ideological concern of the text is René's position in one of the four spaces (temporal death, of course, allows him to go from temporal spaces to spiritual ones). The move from a positive space to a negative space is represented here as an exile. The opposition stay/leave, which is applicable in the first space, turns into stay/return in the second space (returning from exile). Spatial change is not dysphoric in itself (although nomadism, which is associated with the figure of the trapper, among others, is generally dysphoric in French-Canadian rural legend); staying, leaving and returning are euphoric or dysphoric depending on the starting and ending points we have in mind. The temporal exile cannot help but evoke a spiritual exile. No one needs to be reminded that the earthly paradise from which Adam and Eve were banished is described as a garden. Thus, there is a double exile: the farmer from the countryside, and man from paradise. René, who has been exiled for five years from his land, will be definitively cut off from it by his death. However, he will attain a homologous object of higher value: "the gardens of Paradise". A preference for nature under man's dominion shows through in the higher value attributed to the land and the "gardens of Paradise": we are a long way from the forest, and for good reason! In the ideology of rural legend, the forest (a place for trapping and logging) is perceived as a breeding ground for moral straying and perdition. (For example, in *Maria Chapdelaine*, a famous work of French literature, the seductive trapper-logger François Paradis is presented as morally inferior to the dull farmer, Eutrope Gagnon).[13] The story and its genre (and the ideology underlying them) exalt nature, but it is nature as ordered by man, a sort of nature-culture. Notice that René will turn from a "flower of the fields" (that is, a wildflower) into a flower in the "gardens of Paradise", in other words, a cultivated flower (in the anthropological sense as well). The land (and also the garden) is simultaneously in the position of culture relative to the forest, and nature relative to the city. These two dyads can be merged in a semiotic square (see the corresponding chapter): the land and the garden are not just simple contrary terms relative to the forest, but complex terms, simultaneously representing nature and culture. The absolute opposite of the city is the forest. The ancient and classical topos ("common-place" motif) of the happy medium seems to play on this spatial triad.

Notes

1 While it is theoretically possible to classify any seme or any isotopy univocally as figurative, thematic or axiological, this is not true for groups of semes (signifieds and molecules). For example, the signified 'red' is admittedly figurative in nature, but if it contains an axiological evaluation (e.g., dysphoria, as in Rimbaud's "Sleeper in the valley"), then it also derives from axiology.

2 This is what is known as thematic analysis in Greimasian semiotics, and is Courtés's particular area of expertise. However, because there are other kinds of thematic analysis used in other theoretical frameworks, we prefer not to use this term in order to avoid ambiguity. Elsewhere, Greimas and Courtés use the terms "axiological" and "axiology", but in order to avoid confusion with the philosophical acceptations of these terms (axiology being a field of study in philosophy), we advocate using the terms "thymic" and "thymic evaluation." In the chapter on thymic analysis, we have elaborated to some degree on axiological analysis, especially in light of contributions from Rastier's dialogics.

3 For a theoretical critique of the figurative/thematic opposition and of dual semantic typologies in general, see Rastier, 1987, pp. 167–174; Hébert, 1999. What matters to us is the functional value of this kind of analysis, and this we cannot contest.

4 The names "specific" and "generic" have no direct relation to the terms of the same name in interpretive semantics (see the chapter on semic analysis).

5 In actuality, the signifier and the signified are both mental constructs, but one must concede that signifiers (e.g., phonemes, the subject of phonology) have direct correlates in the physical world (e.g., when phonemes take form as particular sounds, which is the subject of phonetics), and as such, are part of perception.

6 Greimasian semiotics distinguishes two possible ways in which an opposition can be manifested: by contrast (where both terms of the opposition are present) or not (where only one of the two terms is present). For example, in a given text, the opposition between black and white can take form as a contrast (if both colors are mentioned) or not (if only black or only white is present).

7 Courtés writes (1991, p. 176): "Of course – and this is unarguably the most important point – any thematic categorization seems to lead invariably to the establishment of an axiology: while each of us is free to mark this

or that value as either positive or negative, we are not free to leave them unmarked. Even the most objectivized discourse, such as scientific discourse, cannot seem to avoid a minimum of axiology. We observed earlier that very often the figurative demands to be thematized, and in addition [. . .], to be axiologized. This seems to be valid primarily for the iconic figure, whereas it is quite possible that the abstract figure does not require thematization – in which case it almost certainly calls for a well-defined axiology at the very least. This is why so many narratives are amenable to categorization at the deep level by the abstract figure "life"/"death", with absolutely no reference to any corresponding intermediate theme: the opposition euphoria/dysphoria thus allows us to mark the two terms (life/death) in a different way." Moreover, in contrast with the figurative, "the thematic level can have a completely autonomous existence, but only under certain conditions and in certain cases. Thus, natural languages are capable of explaining the thematic level with absolutely no reference to any figurative representation; this is in fact characteristic of mathematical or logical discourse, and of philosophy as well, even though it occasionally uses concrete, figurative examples" (Courtés, 1991, pp. 164–165). It seems to go without saying that for Courtés, an axiological value cannot exist in isolation, that is, outside of its application to a figure and/or a theme.

8 "Axiology", says Courtés, "is in fact nothing more than a spontaneous preference, shall we say, when faced with a thematic (or figurative) category, for one term over the other" (Courtés, 1991, p. 173). The preferred term will produce euphoria, and the other, dysphoria. We are persuaded that homologation between a figurative or thematic opposition and the opposition euphoria/dysphoria is actually only one of many possible axiological relations.

9 The principle of the semi-symbolic system was formulated by Lévi-Strauss in his analysis of the myth as an opposition between two figures associated with an opposition between two functions. Greimas has defined the semi-symbolic system as one of the three possible semiotic systems, whereas Jean-Marie Floch uses it as the primary instrument for image analysis (Fontanille, 2003, p. 137). We have borrowed the term *semi-symbolic relation* from Courtés (1995). The advantage of this term is to bypass the theoretical problems associated with the expressions *semi-symbolic system* (a system characterized according to the type of relation between the plane of signifiers and the plane of signifieds) and *semi-symbolic coding* (which, strictly speaking, operates between the thematic level and the figurative level on the plane signifieds). Although there is no relation of reciprocal presupposition between figurative and thematic, this does not prevent Courtés (1991, p. 168), like Floch, from extending the application of the semi-symbolic system to the internal rapports on the plane of signifieds (between figure and theme). Technically speaking, a system is semi-symbolic only when a category of the signified is associated with a category of the signifier. To take a pictorial example, we have a semi-symbolic system if the category (the opposition) white/black (signifier) corresponds to the category life/death (or any other category of content).

10 We do this by applying a principle that is explicit in Greimasian semiotics (as exemplified in the theory of the generative trajectory of meaning – the interpretive trajectory being its mirror image): the progression on a scale from concrete (perceptible, thus analogous to the signifier) to abstract (conceptual, thus analogous to the signified). This takes us from figurative to thematic to axiological elements (progressing through iconic or specific levels toward abstract or generic ones).

11 We must distinguish "real" from "perceptible." Unreal elements like heaven and hell are nonetheless traditionally depicted as places of sensory delight and torture, respectively.

12 One postulate of standard Greimasian semiotics is that the oppositions life/death (an individual opposition) and nature/culture (a social opposition) are found in any semiotic act. For Courtés, life/death and nature/culture are not themes, but abstract figures (1991, p. 232) that he classifies as existential figurative (1991, p. 237). We can quibble at length over this classification, especially for nature/culture, but in any case, we have classified both of these oppositions as figures. Moreover, the dual semantic figure/theme typology, which is debatable from a theoretical standpoint (why would there be two kinds of meaning a priori?), is very nicely wedded to the religious background of the text, in that it forms a hypostasis of the oppositions body/soul and literal/figurative meaning, which come from biblical exegesis (see Hébert, 1999).

13 The text speaks highly of writers who live out in the "woods." But it is always as though the term were being used in the "literary" sense to mean a wooded area of smaller size than the forest (see the *Petit Robert*), not in its French-Canadian meaning, where "woods" is a synonym of "forest" (as in "*coureur des bois*" [trapper, literally "woods runner"]). Being smaller in area, the woods are more cultural than the forest, and closer to man. One thing is certain: that the text mentions "dwellings" in the woods, not a nomadic way of life in the forest. A retreat from active life in this case is not the least bit harmful, since its purpose is simply to pursue contemplation and to transmit the fruit of this contemplation in writing. This is the aesthetic counterpart of a monastic retreat.

10 Thymic analysis

Summary

Thymic analysis, an elaboration by this author on Greimas's and Courtés's axiological analysis, is concerned with evaluations made within the category euphoria/dysphoria, or in less technical terms, positive/negative or pleasure/displeasure. The main elements involved in this sort of analysis are: (1) the evaluating subject, (2) the object being evaluated, (3) the thymic value attributed to the object (euphoria, dysphoria, etc.), (4) the intensity of the value (low, medium, high), (5) the time of the evaluation, and (6) the transformations that may affect thymic elements (a transformation of the subject or object may or may not lead to a change in the value and/or its intensity). For example, in the fable "The grasshopper and the ant", the ant (subject) evaluates work (object) positively (value) and pleasure (object) negatively (value) from the beginning of the story to the end.

Theory

Thymic evaluation defined

Thymic analysis, an elaboration by this author on Greimas's and Courtés's axiological analysis (see the chapter on figurative, thematic and axiological analysis), is concerned with evaluations made within the category euphoria/dysphoria, or in less technical terms, positive/negative or pleasure/displeasure.

The main elements involved in thymic analysis are: (1) the evaluating subject, (2) the object[1] being evaluated, (3) the thymic value attributed to the object (euphoria, dysphoria, etc.), (4) the intensity of the value (low, medium, high, etc.), (5) the time of the evaluation, and (6) the transformations that may affect thymic elements. For example, in the fable "the grasshopper and the ant", the ant (subject) evaluates work (object) positively (value) and leisure (object) negatively (value) from the beginning of the story to the end (time).

NOTE: THYMIC ANALYSIS, AXIOLOGICAL ANALYSIS AND THYMIC DIALOGICS

Greimas and Courtés (1982, p. 21) distinguish between two acceptations for "axiology": The traditional meaning is "the theory and/or the description of value systems – moral, logical, or aesthetic"; in semiotics, it is the micro-system created by the homologation of any opposition with the opposition euphoria/dysphoria, known as the thymic category. ("Thymic" is a term taken from psychology that has to do with mood in general.) For instance, life is to death as euphoria is to dysphoria. The semiotic definition proposed by Greimas and Courtés seems unnecessarily restrictive: A homology between any opposition and the thymic category is only one specific scenario in axiology, and the theory needs to account for semiotic acts in which life and death, for example, are both associated solely with dysphoria, or both with euphoria. For our part, we will speak in terms of thymic analysis rather than axiological analysis, firstly, to avoid possible confusion with axiology as a branch of philosophy, and secondly, to indicate clearly that it is based on the thymic category.

This chapter can be considered an expansion of Greimasian axiological analysis or a simplification of thymic dialogics (see the chapter on dialogics, and Hébert, 2001, pp. 140–166, 2003, 2007a, 2020). The evaluating and evaluated actors in dialogics are referred to here as the subject and object, whereas the concepts of universe, world, image, replica, and others are avoided. Formulated in this way, thymic analysis incorporates elements of Greimasian terminology and theory, and it also presents some important additions to axiological analysis as formulated by Greimas and Courtés, which we have presented in the chapter on figurative, thematic and axiological analysis.

Ontological classification of subjects and objects

The ontological classes into which thymic subjects and objects may fall are not restricted a priori. From the perspective of "natural ontology" (which defines what kinds of entities make up "natural reality"), an object may correspond to: a perceptible element (like the wind), an object (in the restrictive sense, such as a carrot), an action (lying), a state, a situation, an anthropomorphic being (a talking sword, a human being), a collective (society), a class (perfumes in general), an element of a class (a certain perfume), a whole (the rose), a part of a whole (the thorns of the rose), and so on. The same logic applies for the evaluating subject, with one difference: subjects must be equipped with an "awareness" that allows them to make an evaluation (even if it is only awareness bestowed on a machine by men). The subject may be: a member of the animal or plant kingdom (an animal, insect or plant), an anthropomorphic being, a machine (a computer), an abstract entity (morality), a class (women in general), a part of a whole (the id, the superego, and the ego as parts of the human psyche), etc. Later we will come back to classes and their elements, and wholes and their parts.

The thymic values

Modal values or statuses are highly general characteristics that are limited in number and grouped by category (such as thymic values), attributed by an observing subject to an object being observed (for an examination of the ontological and veridictory categories, see the chapters on dialogics and the veridictory square).

When we map out the opposition euphoria/dysphoria, known as the thymic category, onto a semiotic square (see the chapter on the semiotic square), we obtain several thymic values, the main ones being: euphoria (positive), dysphoria (negative), phoria (positive and negative – ambivalence) and aphoria (neither positive nor negative – indifference) (Courtés, 1991, p. 160).

NOTE: THE SEMIOTIC SQUARE AND THYMIC VALUES

Besides the four basic categories (positions 1, 2, 5 and 6), the traditional semiotic square predicts some other possibilities (positions 3, 4, 7 and 8 on the square). We have also added the metaterms in between the contradictory elements (positions 9 and 10) on the semiotic square. However, these six values seem to be less useful than the first four.

Phoria and aphoria are compound values (the "metaterms" of the semiotic square) made up of two simple values, and require some explanation. If we manipulate our conception of time and how we identify the object being evaluated, a simple value can turn into a compound value.

For example, if you like spinach one day, hate it the next day, and like it again the following day, one might consider this as:

(1) a transition from euphoria to dysphoria back to euphoria

if the reference time is a day, or

(2) phoria,
(3) phoria, but with euphoria being dominant,
(4) euphoria, by ignoring the minority judgment,
(5) attenuated euphoria, if the dysphoria is figured into the intensity of the euphoria, and so on

if the reference time is the overall three-day period.

Now we will change how the object is defined: If you like apple pie, and at the same time you hate cream pie, one can consider this as (1) two units, each with a value assigned to it, or (2) a single unit, pie in general (a type), with a compound valued (complex term) assigned to it. To take another example from the Christian philosophies, death is either (1) positive overall, or (2) negative in one aspect (such as the ending, often in suffering, of temporal life) and positive in another (the beginning of spiritual existence, which is positive for the righteous).

Thymic intensity

Unlike other evaluations, such as veridictory ones (true/false), thymic evaluations are often quantified. Then they no longer belong to categorial logic (where something is either euphoric or not), but to incremental logic (where something is a little bit euphoric).[2] We will represent intensity by words or expressions (or even numbers, like *40 percent*, etc.). These may be: descriptive (*low, normal, high*, for instance) or prescriptive (*not enough, enough, too much*, for instance); comparative or relative (*less than, as much as, more than*); or superlative (*least, most*). Within one text, there is nothing to prevent a single subject making use of categorial values at times, and incremental values at other times: all the more so if two subjects are involved.

To give an example of intensity applied to a thymic value, consider the following quotation: "And I had no such defense as Parapine's total indifference" (Céline, 1983, p. 371). Note that a very high intensity is attributed to indifference or aphoria ("total indifference") in the context of "defense", which is not the same as an indifference to everything.

Interactions between value, intensity and quantity

With our example of spinach, we pointed out that a succession of different values (euphoria, dysphoria, and euphoria in the example) can be equivalent to a single value marked with the appropriate intensity (attenuated euphoria in our example). This is how a change of perspective can be applied to one thymic evaluation. There are cases where a variation in intensity may bring about a change in value: If the intensity associated with a value is "excessive", it can turn into another value, especially an opposite value. An example of this phenomenon can be found in this verse by Alain Grandbois (in Mailhot and Nepveu, 1986, p. 180), where too much of a theoretically euphoric element causes a decidedly intense dysphoria: "There were those women who were too beautiful, their foreheads too embellished with rubies". This example helps us to address the issue of the possible impact of quantity – and not just intensity, strictly speaking – on the thymic values. "Too embellished with rubies" can be interpreted in quantitative terms: a few rubies are nice; but you can have too much of a good thing, as the popular wisdom goes.

The following diagram shows a scale of intensity/quantity divided into three sectors. As one moves to the right, the evaluated object's intensity/quantity increases from low to medium to high. This increase has two possible effects: either it does not change the value (cases 1 and 5) or it changes the value (the other cases). We will give some examples of the second possibility. Case 4 can be used to illustrate the law of the happy medium, which has been adopted by ancient scholars, the Buddha, the classicists (of every age), and the middle class: a little bit is good; too little or too much is not good. Case 8 is the opposite of this: what is good is excess, and moderation is dysphoric. One can no doubt find an illustration in Romanticism (considering how very torn it is between ascetic deprivation and debauchery).

intensity / quantity of evaluated object →

	low	medium	high
Case 1	+	+	+
Case 2	-	+	+
Case 3	+	+	-
Case 4	-	+	-
Case 5	-	-	-
Case 6	+	-	-
Case 7	-	-	+
Case 8	+	-	+

Figure 10.1 Values and the scale of intensity/quantity

NOTE: OTHER INTERACTIONS BETWEEN VALUE AND INTENSITY

Thymic intensities are often used to create a hierarchical structure out of what would otherwise be just a straight inventory of evaluated objects, where, for instance, there would be no distinction between the euphoria experienced from a delicious food and the euphoria in the presence of a beloved being. When dealing with an ideology (in the more general sense of the word, not the meaning in Greimasian semiotics), the most strongly evaluated elements will correspond to the fundamental "values". Competing ideologies often evaluate the same objects, but with different values and/or intensities. For example, in a fairy tale, if the ogre and the knight both covet the Princess as their bride, the first one brutally kidnaps the maiden to make her his wife by force, whereas the second one will earn her hand (and the rest). The ogre overvalues the marriage, thymically speaking, at the expense of morality. Moreover, contrastive evaluation of a general opposition seems to apply to the specific oppositions included within the general opposition, through the use of the intensities. Consider the following three oppositions, which are very common in French-Canadian rural legend, in which the first term is euphoric and the second is dysphoric: spiritual world/temporal world, heaven/hell, countryside/city. Since the spiritual has primacy over the temporal in this textual genre, the four specific spaces are sequenced in the following way, from most euphoric to most dysphoric: /heaven/, /countryside/, /city/, /hell/ (for the complete analysis, see Hébert, 2000).

Decidable/undecidable values and intensities

Thymic values and their intensities may be decidable (if they can be determined: for a certain subject, a certain object is euphoric), undecidable (if they cannot be determined, as in a subject who tries to evaluate an object thymically, but cannot manage to give it a value) or undecided (namely, an object that has not (yet) been evaluated or is no longer being evaluated, such as a book that a literary critic has not yet read).

NOTE: THE SEMIOTIC SQUARE AND UNDECIDABLE/UNDECIDED ELEMENTS

With respect to the thymic square's basic opposition (euphoria/dysphoria), undecidable elements might appear to represent aphoria. But in fact, undecidability resides in a *marked* universal non-position: the object cannot be conclusively assigned to any position on the square. The undecided realm is an *unmarked* universal non position: the subject has not (yet) attempted to assign the object to a position on the square. This logic also applies to undecidable and undecided intensities.

Thymic evaluations and time

Sequences of evaluations and changes in evaluations

Sequences of different or repeated thymic evaluations occur in correlation with changes in temporal position, as do changes in the value or intensity of a single object (or a transformed object) as evaluated by a single subject (or a transformed subject). Modal values and intensities attributed to an object can appear (change from undecided to decided), be transformed (e.g., change from euphoric to dysphoric), or even disappear (e.g., go from decided to undecidable or even undecided). In other words, any evaluation (thymic or otherwise) and any element of this evaluation are associated with a temporal interval within which they are valid. We will give an example involving object and subject transformations: As a character ages (a transformed subject), he becomes indifferent (a change in value) to what pleased him when he was young; a status-seeking character may no longer want to marry a woman who has fallen into disgrace (a transformed object), whereas another character who is pure of heart will only want to marry her more (a change of intensity).

Time in the story and tactical time

Thymic analysis, like our other analytical tools, can handle two fundamental kinds of time, and it is useful to distinguish between them: (1) the fictional time of the story, which is how the states and events of the story are sequenced; (2) what we call tactical time (from the Greek "*taktikhê*", "the art of ordering or arranging"), which is created by the sequencing of the "real" units of the semiotic act (words, syntagms, sentences, groups of sentences, etc.). These two kinds of time may or may not coincide (for instance, the second event in the story may be presented in the first sentence and the first event in the second sentence). Consider an example that shows the distinction between the two kinds of time: "When I was young, I liked the pink candies and hated the blue ones". Time as represented in the story consists of only one temporal position in which two evaluations occur, but tactical time puts them in succession.

Temporal segmentation

Temporal segmentation may be based on various criteria. In thymic analysis, the most pertinent criterion for demarcating temporal intervals is a change in one or more key thymic values (for instance, time interval T1 would last until a change in the thymic value initiates interval T2). Naturally, one can establish relations between this temporal segmentation and some other segmentation based on some other criterion, such as time in the usual sense (thymic interval T1 might last from Monday to Wednesday; T2 from Wednesday noon to Thursday evening), or actions (T1 might last from action 1 to the beginning of action 3; T2 from the middle of action 3 to action 7) or the scenes in a play, and so forth.

Thymic rhythm

Any kind of the element may be used rhythmically. Rhythm is traditionally understood as the effect of an element's recurrence in a different temporal position. In the broad sense, thymic rhythm is defined by the recurrence of some thymic element: a value, an intensity, a subject, an object, etc. For example, the four nouns "Writer or hack, Thoroughbred or Percheron?" (Julien Gracq) create an alternating thymic rhythm (A, B, A, B): euphoric, dysphoric, euphoric, dysphoric.

Temporal representation

As a way to represent variations in thymic intensity over time, we can use the curves of aesthetic euphoria presented in the chapter on the tensive model. If we place one of the intensities (low, medium or high) in each of the temporal positions (initial, intermediate and final) we obtain a typology of 27 curves. For example, the first curve of our typology, shown opposite, strings together a low intensity (beginning), a high intensity (middle) and another low intensity (end).

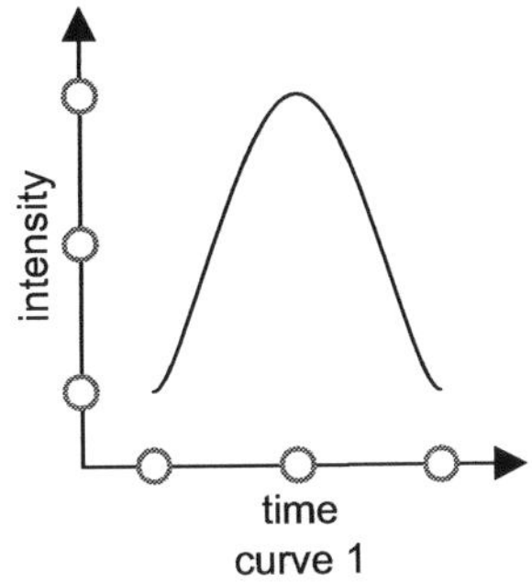

Figure 10.2 A curve with time and intensity

By splitting up the axis of intensity, we can describe the transition from euphoria to dysphoria as a function of time, as well as the variations in their respective intensities. The middle of the axis represents aphoria, or indifference, which is not quantified in this representation. Above that, we have euphoria, which increases in intensity as we go up the graph. Below that, we have dysphoria, which increases in intensity as we go down the graph. For instance, the curve below shows strong dysphoria (beginning) followed by strong euphoria, followed again by strong dysphoria.

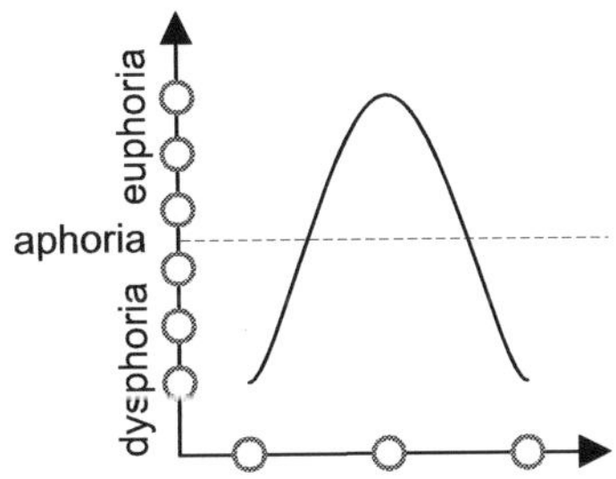

Figure 10.3 A cuvre with main thymic values, time and intensity

We should point out that aphoria can vary in intensity. In *The red and the black*, Madame de Renal believes that Julien Sorel feels "passionate indifference" toward her (Stendhal, 1952, p. 344). Although this is not the only possible interpretation, one could see this as indifference of a strong intensity. In order to represent this intensity, we can transform the zone of aphoria from a straight line to a two-dimensional surface, as for euphoria and dysphoria. The closer we get to the center of the zone, the stronger the indifference would be.

Thymic evaluation and veridictory evaluation

Assumptive evaluations and reference evaluations

Whether stated explicitly or not, thymic evaluations are always marked for veridiction, that is, a status within the category true/false (see the chapters on dialogics and the veridictory square). For example, the thymic evaluation "Wolves like blood" is true, at least for its enunciator.

Note the difference between the veridictory status attributed to the thymic evaluation and the veridictory status that may be attributed to the object being evaluated. In the evaluation "Art appraisers love genuine Picassos", the object is marked for veridiction ("genuine"). A change in the veridictory status is often accompanied by a change in thymic value (and/or a change in its intensity): and in fact, art appraisers do not like counterfeit Picassos (especially when they appear in the inventory due to an error).

To return to the veridictory status attributed to the overall thymic evaluation, a reference evaluation is one that the text deems to be accurate, that is, its veridictory status agrees with what is. An assumptive evaluation is one that is subject to contradiction by the reference evaluation. For example, Paul thinks that Mary is great (assumptive evaluation), whereas Andy thinks she is obnoxious (assumptive evaluation); the narrator settles the question: she really is nice (reference evaluation). Paul is right (technically, because his assumptive evaluation corresponds to the reference evaluation) and Andy is wrong.

NOTE: THYMIC EVALUATION AND ONTOLOGICAL EVALUATION

Whether explicitly stated or not, thymic evaluations are always marked for ontology, that is, a status with respect to the actual (real)/counterfactual (unreal or impossible)/possible realms. Unless otherwise stated, the ontological status is "real". To use a previous example, as a thymic evaluation, "Wolves like blood" is true and real. An ontological status may also apply to the object being evaluated. *One in the hand is worth two in the bush*, goes the saying, to illustrate that it is better to have one object in actuality than two of the same object, but only as a possibility. The sentence for an attempted murder is less harsh than that for a successful, real murder. For more details on ontological status, see the chapter on dialogics. These modal categories play an important role in describing actions. Indeed, often an action is undertaken from weighing up the possible desirable and undesirable consequences of accomplishing or not accomplishing it. The possible consequences may or may not turn into real ones. For an explanation of the semiotic concepts of manipulation (the actional component in which the possible consequences are evaluated) and retribution (where the consequences are manifested, theoretically as foreseen during the manipulation stage), refer to the chapter on the canonical narrative schema.

Evaluative conflict and consensus

Whether or not the protagonists or the observers are aware of them, conflict and consensus over thymic and/or veridictory evaluations tend to follow three phases: appearance, maintenance and resolution. The possibility of an evaluative conflict arises only when there is a logic of mutual exclusion rather than a logic of complementarity between different evaluations. Exclusive logic derives from absolutism: it chooses one and only one evaluation as the right one. Complementary logic derives from relativism: it gives equal credence to several evaluations, or even all of them (absolute relativism).

The little story that we gave as an example is based on exclusive logic, in that the two contradictory opinions cannot be true at the same time. In some other case, the contradictory thymic evaluations might be true simultaneously, in which case Mary could be really great with Paul and really obnoxious with Andy, for instance. In another example of contradictory evaluations coexisting, one character thinks that apple pie is euphoric, while another thinks it is dysphoric, without any reference evaluation to settle the issue. This situation illustrates the popular saying that we all have our likes and dislikes – we would say our thymic evaluations. ("There is no accounting for taste", as they say.)

For each subject involved, an evaluative conflict moves toward consensus only if there is a total or partial conversion, which may be unilateral or reciprocal (or ironically, total and reciprocal on occasion, when both parties change their minds) or if there is a movement toward complementary logic. A "conversion" may or may not be preceded by doubt, introducing the ontological category of possibility, during which the evaluation and the counter-evaluation are set in opposition, or by verification, whose purpose is to select one evaluation according to specific tests and criteria.

The subject of veridictory evaluation and the subject of thymic evaluation

In some cases the subject of the veridictory evaluation and the subject of the thymic evaluation are not the same. For example: If Paul (the subject of the veridictory evaluation) says that Mary (the subject of the thymic evaluation) loves chocolate, then "Mary loves chocolate" is a proposition that Paul considers to be true, although he could be right or wrong.

Set relations and mereological relations

Set relations, that is, relations established within a class (defined by a type, or model) and the elements that they include (the tokens or manifestations of the type) may have an impact on thymic description. The same goes for mereological relations, that is, relations that exist between a whole and its parts.

For example: "He usually prefers blondes, but he really likes that brunette". The first evaluation applies to blonde women as a class (and to the type it defines, the generic blonde woman). The second one applies to an element in the class of brunette women, one specific brunette (who is a token of the type, the generic brunette). In "Americans prefer blondes", the evaluating subject is itself a class (which defines a type: the generic or typical American). To take another kind of example, in *The Little Prince* by Saint-Exupéry, the Prince's rose gets an overall evaluation as a whole and individual evaluations for its parts. As a whole, the rose is evaluated positively by the Little Prince, even though he evaluates some of its physical parts (the thorns) and its psychological parts (its character) negatively.

The overall judgment is made by taking the individual judgments into account, but this is not necessarily a matter of simply "adding up"; there may be a hierarchy assigning different weights to different evaluations. In a case where different values are attributed to the parts, the overall value can be compound (such as phoria) or be resolved into a simple value, possibly by weighting the intensities (the object would be judged as slightly positive, for instance, if there were one dysphoric part that attenuated the positive value of another part without entirely overwhelming it).

Subjects and agents of communication

In a text, and *mutatis mutandis* in other kinds of semiotic acts, we will single out the following agents of production and reception:

(1) the empirical author (the real author),
(2) the invented or implied author (the impression that the empirical or implied reader receives of the empirical or implied author from the text),

(3) the narrator (on various levels, if there are embedded narratives),
(4) the narratee (on various levels, if there are embedded narratives),
(5) the invented or implied reader (the image that the empirical or implied author and/or the text conveys of its average, marginal or model (ideal) reader, as he/she takes form in the text), and
(6) the empirical reader (the real reader).

These agents correspond to semiotic roles that are combinable in various ways: For instance, an empirical author is also his own first (and sometimes most critical) empirical reader.

NOTE: THEMATIZED AND NON-THEMATIZED AGENTS

Any of these agents may be given a thematized, fictive status. In a text, one might find an invented, thematized image of the thematized reader to whom a thematized text is addressed. For example, in *The red and the black*, by the content and the style of Madame Renal's letter to the jury in the trial of Julien Sorel, one can discern the image that she (as a textual function, not as a pseudo-person) has constructed of them.

Thymic disagreements may emerge between evaluations originating from different agents. For example, in *A modest proposal concerning the children of poor people in Ireland . . .* by Jonathan Swift, although the narrator proposes eating the babies of indigent people as a way of fighting poverty and famine, as long as one grasps the caustic irony of this text, one understands that the real author does not find this idea euphoric. Advertising, unfortunately, also provides some excellent examples of discord in promotional texts, where the narrator raves about the advantages of a product that the empirical author knows is mediocre. Conversely, evaluations originating from different agents can be congruent. When Roquentin, the narrator-character in Sartre's *Nausea* exclaims: "I am going to read *Eugénie Grandet*. It isn't that I get any great pleasure out of it: but I have to do something" (1964, p. 47), the direct reference to pleasure (or rather, the lack thereof) is to a thematized pleasure, a pleasure on paper, belonging to Roquentin, but one can also attribute this thymic judgment to the implied author, and, unless we are mistaken, to Sartre himself, who sought in Balzac a foil for the modern novel, and whose displeasure upon reading this particular work may have been real.

Source and relay subjects, dialect/sociolect/idiolect

To enhance our analysis of the agreement/lack of agreement between the thymic evaluations of various agents of communication, it can be helpful to distinguish between the subject to whom the thymic evaluation is ascribed and the subject from which the evaluation actually originates. The first is the relay subject; the second is the source subject.

The importance of this distinction becomes clear when we add the following subjects to our typology of agents of communication. According to Rastier (1997, pp. 27–29), the subjects associated implicitly with the three general systems governing any text are: the dialect (the language system), the sociolect (the particular usage of a dialect specific to a differentiated social practice with its own discourse organized through genres), and the idiolect (a given author's distinct usage of a language and a sociolect). For example, the dysphoric evaluations of Baudelaire's narrators concerning *spleen*, women (real ones, at least) and nature actually come from the dialect, the sociolect and the idiolect, respectively. *Spleen* is a pejorative word by definition in French; the disparagement of real women (as distinguished from ideal, or idealized women) was quite common at the time, especially in literary discourse; and the devaluing of nature is more unique. In the first two evaluations, the narrator is a relay evaluator for the source evaluators implicitly associated with the dialect and the sociolect. However, there is a theoretical question concerning the idiolectal subject: is it the same as the implied author? We do not think so. The implied author, at least by our definition, is developed within a single text, whereas the subject of the idiolect can be, and generally is, developed through a group of texts by the same author. Moreover, the idiolect deals solely with patterns of writing (themes, clichés, etc.), whereas the implied author incorporates inferences about the physical appearance and the psychology of the text's author.

Let us conclude by mentioning that one can integrate other kinds of source subjects, such as those associated with a specific social group or a specific culture. In the statement "I like hamburgers", professed by someone from North America, one can detect the presence of a source subject tied to a specific culture: mainstream North America.

Common thymic configurations

A thymic configuration includes at least two related thymic evaluations, which may or may not fall within the same temporal interval. For example, a minimal thymic conflict or consensus is triangular, and it entails two subjects with a single evaluated object at a single position in time.

The following table presents some of the more common thymic configurations. Below it is a legend giving the thymic elements involved.[3] The examples in the table are of many kinds: phrases, quotations and references to literary texts. The table makes it easy to show dialogic configurations that are attested, or simply foreseeable.

Table 10.1 Common thymic configurations

		EVALUATION 1			*EVALUATION 2*		
ABSTRACT FORMULATION	*TEXTUAL EXAMPLE*	*SUBJECT*	*VALUE*	*OBJECT*	*OBJECT*	*VALUE*	*SUBJECT*
1 For a single evaluated object, the subject changes his evaluation (here the subject has been changed)	Swann, who no longer loves Odette (Proust)	S	+	O	O	¬± or −	S'
2 The same object evaluated differently depending on a variable of the context, in this case, the place	*No man is a prophet in his own land*	S1	+	O	O	− or ¬±	S2

(Continued)

Table 10.1 (Continued)

ABSTRACT FORMULATION	*TEXTUAL EXAMPLE*	*EVALUATION 1*			*EVALUATION 2*		
		SUBJECT	*VALUE*	*OBJECT*	*OBJECT*	*VALUE*	*SUBJECT*
3 The classic conflict between two subjects	*One person's misfortune is another's gain*, "a bad good deed" (Balzac, *Cousin Bette*)	S1	+	O	O	–	S2
4 The classic agreement	The cheese, for the fox and the crow (La Fontaine)	S1	+	O	O	+	S2
5 Identical intensities for opposite evaluations, creating consensus about the significance of the evaluated object	Laertes hates Hamlet – before his final repentance – for causing the death of his father and sister as much as Ophelia loves him (Shakespeare)	S1	+↑	O	O	–↑	S2
6 The object changes, but not its value	Colin still loves Chloé, even in her most wretched state (Vian, *L'écume des jours*)	S	+	O	O'	+	S
7 The object changes, and is evaluated differently	"You're letting yourself go" (Charles Aznavour)	S	+	O	O'	–	S
8 The object takes a different form due to a change in ontological-veridictory status, and the thymic value changes as a result	The falsely pious Tartuffe, unmasked (Molière)	S	+	O	O'	–	S
9 Ambivalence: opposing values attributed simultaneously by a single subject	"For his one source of happiness on this Earth/ He found in his tears" (Le Gascon, anonymous French-Canadian patriot). "In this world we spend our time killing or adoring, or both together. "I hate you! I adore you!" " (Céline	S	±	O			
10 The objects are evaluated identically (as slightly euphoric), and are therefore completely interchangeable in this respect	*Trade a dollar for four quarters* (Québec) or *It's six of one and half a dozen of the other*	S	+↓	O1	O2	+↓	S
11 The value of the whole does not match the value of a specific part	The rose and its thorns in *The Little Prince* (Saint-Exupéry)	S	+	WO	pO	–	S
12 A type (subject) evaluates another type (object) (here, according to the enunciator)	Men prefer blonds	St	+↑	Ot			

Table 10.1 (Continued)

		EVALUATION 1			EVALUATION 2		
ABSTRACT FORMULATION	TEXTUAL EXAMPLE	SUBJECT	VALUE	OBJECT	OBJECT	VALUE	SUBJECT
13 A class is devalued, but an element of the class is valued	The kind parish priest finds favor with the "fanatical anticlerics" in "*La messe au pendu* [Mass for a hanged man]" (songwriter Georges Brassens)	S	–	Ot	Oo	+	S
14 Neutral value (ontological status in this example: possible)	"I'll take to the open sea neither sad nor happy, like an animal, with no idea of what I might have lost" (trans. from *Tit-Coq* by playwright Gratien Gélinas)	S	¬±	O			

Legend:

AGENTS
S: evaluating subject
O: object being evaluated

THYMIC VALUES

+: euphoria (positive)
−: dysphoria (negative)
±: phoria (positive and negative)
+−: phoria, with the positive dominant
−+: phoria, with the negative dominant
¬±: aphoria (neither positive nor negative)
#: undecidable
ø: undecided (not evaluated)

VALUE INTENSITIES
↓: low intensity (for example: O+↓)
↑: high intensity (for example: O- ↑)
[The Below Content Treated as LH1]

MEREOLOGICAL AND SET RELATIONS
W: whole (for example: WO or WS) (such as the rose as a whole)
p: part (ex: O2p1 = object 2 part 1) (such as the thorns as a part of the rose)
t: type or class (ex: Ot or St) (such as perfumes in general, men in general)
o: token or occurrence within a class (ex: Ot1o2 = type 1 token 2) (for instance, this specific perfume, this specific man)

THYMIC PROCESSES

→transformation (ex : O1 → O1')
': transformed element (ex: O' or S')

Application: "The dog and the perfume bottle" by Charles Baudelaire

* * *

"The dog and the perfume bottle"
Baudelaire, *The parisian prowler*

"– My good dog, my handsome dog, my dear poochie-woochie, come sit by me. Come here and breathe this excellent perfume purchased of the best parfumeur in town".

And the dog, wagging its tail, a sign, I believe, among those poor creatures corresponding with the laugh or the smile, he steps up and lays his damp nose curiously beside the open bottle of perfume; then, shrinking suddenly with fright, he bays at me. This is a reproach.

"– Ah! miserable dog, if I had offered you a sack of dung you would have sniffed it with delight, and probably eaten it. Thus, you, unworthy companion of my sorry life, in this you resemble the public, to whom one must never offer delicate perfumes – these will just exasperate them. For them, only the most meticulously selected rubbish".

(Adapted from K. Dixon's translation, 6/98)

* * *

In this text by Baudelaire, the narrator, *I*, seeks to have his taste confirmed by that member of the animal kingdom who, like himself, has the ability to exercise great olfactory skill. Indeed, the best scent goes with the best perfume in town, meaning the perfume that can give the most pleasure. The wagging tail – associated with the human smile[4] – indicates that the dog evaluates the compliments, his master's call and/or the prospect before him positively. So the dog is "happy". The cognitive gratification and the compliments made to the dog are aimed at inducing him to evaluate the perfume positively. When the dog perceives that he has been completely misled by his master, his anticipated pleasure is transformed into displeasure and he communicates his anger to the master, which is a form of punishment. Disappointed, the master admonishes the dog in return, and brings up a hypothetical scenario in which the dog would evaluate dung positively – which is only too likely. The "rubbish" also takes on a metaphorical sense by suggesting aldulterated art (art with a small *a*), which the general public favors (cf. the society that "revels in excrement" in *Mon cœur mis à nu* (Baudelaire, 1975, p. 698)). The narrator is associated by homology (Art is to art as the narrator is to the public) with those who appreciate fine perfumes and true poetry. Since Baudelaire's narrators often correspond to an implied author (as distinguished from the historical Baudelaire), we will narrow down art in this context to literature or even poetry. *I* represents (in a sort of synesthesia) the counterpart of the great poet Baudelaire in the matter of odors, or the best parfumeur.

The following table shows the primary thymic evaluations in Baudelaire's text, whether directly expressed or inferable (deducible). An evaluated object that is capitalized (except for *I*) represents the element most highly valued by the narrator within a given class of elements, whereas the word *standard* designates a type associated with a class. For example, we distinguish between *perfume* (good or appalling), *Perfume* (excellent) and *standard perfume* (perfumes in general).

The reference thymic evaluations are the assumptive evaluations made by *I*. One can ascertain the adequacy of evaluations by other subjects by comparing them with the reference evaluations. (For example, in this case, the dog is wrong to dislike the perfume and *I* assumes – and no one contradicts him – that the dog likes excrement.) To avoid cluttering up the table, we chose to use the opposition euphoria/dysphoria (+/-) rather than showing differences in intensity or aphoria. For additional analysis, read the study on the same text in the chapter on narrative programs.

Table 10.2 Thymic analysis of "The dog and the perfume bottle"

No	*SUBJECT*	*OBJECT*	*THYMIC VALUE*	*THYMIC VALUE time 2 (if different)*	*JUSTIFICATION, COMMENT*
1	dog	Perfume	+	–	The object held out to the dog has a positive value for him initially, since he approaches with his tail wagging and lays his curious nose on the bottle.
2	dog	standard perfume	+	–	*I* is disappointed. The new belief is founded on a paragon (*excellent*) perfume, and can be extended to include all perfumes.
3	dog	dung	+		hypothesis of *I* is unconfirmed, but plausible and uncontested. *I* seems to advance two hypotheses on the intensity of the evaluation, the second one being less certain: the dog likes the dung so much, he "would probably have eaten" it. Since he likes dung, the dog is inferior, even to the masses.
4	dog	*I*	+	–	The dog barks at his master.
5	*I*	standard perfume	+		As the opposite of dung, the perfume is valued. However, mediocre perfumes are devalued relative to excellent perfumes (Perfumes).
6	*I*	dung	–		
7	*I*	Poetry	+		
8	*I*	poetry	–		*Rubbish* in the figurative meaning.
9	*I*	poet	–		
10	*I*	Poet	+		
11	*I*	dog	+	–	First compliments, then reproaches. The initial evaluation may be qualified, since *I* describes dogs as "poor creatures", unless this is a retrospective evaluation made by the narrator from the final temporal perspective telling of his disappointment.
12	*I*	standard dog	–		"poor creatures"
13	*I*	standard parfumeur	+		Same reasoning as for standard perfume.
14	*I*	populace (*public*)	–		
15	*I*	parfumeur	–		Relative to Parfumeur.
16	*I*	Parfumeur	+		
17	*I*	his life	–		"my sorry life"
18	populace	dung	–		*Rubbish* in the literal sense.
19	populace	poetry	+		Rubbish in the figurative sense. *Meticulously selected* indicates a ranking by modal intensity.
20	populace	Poetry	–		The counterpart of excellent perfumes.

(Continued)

Table 10.2 (Continued)

No	*SUBJECT*	*OBJECT*	*THYMIC VALUE*	*THYMIC VALUE time 2 (if different)*	*JUSTIFICATION, COMMENT*
21	populace	Poet (*I*)	–		The topos (common place) of the misunderstood poet, by assimilation of narrator with author. Worse yet, the narrator is even betrayed by his companion.
22	populace	poet	+		
23	populace	Parfumeur	–		Implicitly, an excellent parfumeur could not be valued according to his true worth. The mediocre parfumeur is more highly valued.
24	populace	parfumeur	+		

Notes

1 As with all of the analytical tools that Greimas created (the actantial model, the narrative program, the veridictory square, etc.), the term "object" is used in the philosophical and didactic sense: it is the focus of the subject's awareness. Thus, the object can be a thing (an object in the usual sense of the word), but it can also be a person or concept, etc.

2 Although "a little bit euphoric" seems paradoxical in everyday language (by definition, euphoria is a feeling of great intensity), this does not apply to its usage in semiotics, which is how we are using the term.

3 Some useful thymic factors appear in the legend, although they are not included in the table. We can make endless lists of possible thymic configurations if we so desire. Gaudreault (1996, p. 367), for instance, proposes the following configurations of values: "an example of paired values, where one value exists only because of the other; an example of a string of increasing values, where an initial low value leaves room for larger and larger successive values; and finally, some examples of indirect values, where certain beings take on a value for a specific being only through the intervention of one or more beings."

4 This may be a topos, see Hugo: "A dog's smile is in its tail" (Gagnière, 1996).

11 Semic analysis

Summary

Semic analysis was developed within the field of semantics (the study of meaning in linguistic units). This chapter presents Rastier's interpretive semantics, and semic analysis as formulated therein. Semic analysis is performed on a semiotic act – a text, for example – by identifying the semes, that is, the elements of meaning (parts of the signified), defining clusters of semes (isotopies and molecules) and determining the relations between the clusters (relations of presupposition, comparison, etc., between the isotopies). The repetition of a seme creates an isotopy. For example, in "There was a fine ship, carved from solid gold/With azure reaching masts, on seas unknown" (Émile Nelligan, "The golden ship"), the words "ship", "masts" and "seas" all contain the seme /navigation/ (as well as others). The repetition of this seme creates the isotopy /navigation/. A semic molecule is a cluster of at least two semes appearing together more than once in a single semantic unit (a single word, for instance). For instance, in the poem just quoted, there is a semic molecule formed by the semes /precious/ + /dispersion/. It appears in the "streaming hair" ("*cheveux épars*") of the beautiful Goddess of Love (Venus) who was "spread-eagled" ("*s'étalait*") at the ship's prow, and also in the sinking of the ship's treasure, which the sailors "disputed amongst themselves" ("*entre eux ont disputés*").

Theory

Semic analysis is performed on a semiotic act – such as a text – by identifying the semes (the elements of meaning), finding clusters of semes (isotopies and molecules) and determining the relations between the clusters (relations of presupposition, comparison, etc., between the isotopies). Semic analysis was developed in the field of semantics (the study of meaning in linguistic units). This chapter presents Rastier's interpretive semantics, and semic analysis as formulated within this theory.

Interpretive semantics was founded by François Rastier, a student of Greimas and Pottier (see Rastier, 1996 [1987], 1991, 1997 [1989], 2001; Hébert, 2001, 2007a, 2020). It is a "second-generation" synthesis of European structural semantics, developed in the wake of Bréal and Saussure, then Hjelmslev, Greimas, Coseriu and Pottier.

First we will present the basic concepts of interpretive semantics; then we will discuss the methodology of semic analysis.

Concepts of interpretive semantics

The sign and its constituents

An appropriate way to begin is by reviewing the definition of the sign and giving a brief overview of semes and isotopies. The sign is composed of a signifier, which is the "perceptible"[1] part of the sign (e.g., the letters *s-h-i-p*) and a signified, which is the understandable part of the sign, or the semantic content associated with the signifier (e.g., the meaning of the word "ship"). The signified may be broken down into semes. For example, the signified 'ship' contains semes such as /navigation/, / concrete/, and others. An isotopy is formed by repeating one seme. In "There was a fine ship, carved from solid gold/With azure reaching masts, on seas unknown" (Émile Nelligan, "The golden ship"), the words "ship", "masts" and "seas" all contain the seme /navigation/ (as well as others), thereby creating the isotopy /navigation/.

Symbols used

The standard symbols given in the table below are used to distinguish between (1) the sign (the word or lexia): "concrete"; (2) the signified that it conveys: 'concrete'; (3) the signifier associated with this sign: *concrete*, which is composed of the phonemes *k-o-n-k-r-E-t* and the letters *c-o-n-c-r-e-t-e*; (4) the seme: /concrete/ (in 'knife', for example) or (5) the isotopy: /concrete/ (in "steel knife", for example); and (7) the semantic class: //concrete// (which contains the signifieds 'house', 'cat', and 'wind', for instance). Explanations will be given later concerning symbols 6 and 8.

Table 11.1 Symbols used

	ELEMENT	*SYMBOL*	*EXAMPLE*
01	sign	"sign"	"water"
02	signifier	*signifier*	*water*
03	signified	'signified'	'water'
04	seme and isotopy	/seme/ and /isotopy/	/light/
05	case	(CASE)	(ERG)
06	semic molecule (when the relations between semes are not specified by cases)	/seme/ + /seme/	/dark/ + /negative/
07	class (semantic class, to be specific)	//class//	//times of day// (day and night)
08	interpretive rewriting	|rewriting| or source element → |rewriting|	*rite* → |*right*| "draft" (current of air) → |"draft"| (military conscription) 'eagle' → |United States of America|

Semantic components

In interpretive semantics, four **components** make up the semantic plane of texts (the plane of content, or signifieds, as opposed to the plane of expression, or signifiers): **thematics** (the invested content), **dialectics** (states and processes and the actors they involve), **dialogics** (modal evaluations, such as veridictory (true/false) and thymic (positive/negative) evaluations; see the chapter on dialogics) and **tactics** (the linear sequencing of content).

NOTE: MICROSEMANTICS, MESOSEMANTICS AND MACROSEMANTICS

Microsemantics is associated with the lower levels of the text (from the morpheme to the lexia), **mesosemantics** with the intermediate levels (from the functional syntagm to the period; this level can go beyond the sentence) and **macrosemantics** with the higher levels of the text (beyond the period and up to the text level). To simplify, we will associate the three levels with the word, the sentence and the text, respectively.

Type/token, morpheme/lexia, sememe/semia

Semantic units operate on two levels. The **type** is a unit that is manifested to varying degrees through its **tokens**. For example, the content of the morphemes "water" and "love", independent of context, are types, and their actual content can vary depending on their tokens, or occurrences, in different expressions and sentences.

The minimal linguistic sign is called the **morpheme**. The **lexia** is a functional unit that includes more than one morpheme. Sometimes morphemes overlap in a single linear position; for example, in the French lexia "*eau*", units known as "zero morphemes" that indicate grammatical gender and number are "superposed" onto the morpheme containing the defining semes /concrete/, /liquid/, and so on. A lexia may correspond to one word or more than one word ("water", "Brussel-s sprout-s", "walk-ing"). The word is a unit that is quite easily definable by its graphic signifiers – it is preceded and followed by a space – and for this reason, we favor it over the lexia. A **sememe** is the signified of a morpheme and a **semia** is the signified of a lexia.

NOTE: THE SEMEME AND THE WORD

In order to simplify representations of sememe analyses, a sememe is generally designated by the word in which it occurs (for example, "fuse" and "spirit" stand for the sememes "fus-" (cf. "fusion") and "spir" (cf. "inspire")). The generic term *signified* includes the *sememe* (the signified of a morpheme) and the *semia* (the signified of a lexia), but also encompasses other semic groups that act on the same level as the morpheme and the lexia or on higher levels: the syntagm, the period (a group of sentences, more or less), the section (a chapter, for instance), and the text. Semic molecules, for example, are found at all levels of analysis.

Semes and semantic classes

The signified of any semantic unit can be broken down into **semes**, or features of content. A **generic seme** indicates that the sememe belongs to a **semantic class** (a semantic paradigm, made up of sememes). A **specific seme** distinguishes a sememe from all other sememes of the same class. The specific semes of a sememe constitute its **semanteme**; the generic semes make up its **classeme**. There are three kinds of generic semes: **microgeneric**, **mesogeneric** and **macrogeneric**. These correspond to three kinds of semantic classes: **taxemes** (the minimal classes by which sememes are interdefined), **domains** (which are linked to the social context and correspond to spheres of human activity; dictionary field labels exemplify this, as in *chem.*, *phys.*) and **dimensions** (the most general of classes, grouped by oppositions, such as //animate// *vs.* //inanimate//, //concrete// *vs.* //abstract//, //human// *vs.* //animal//, //animal// *vs.* //plant//, etc.).

To give an example, the taxeme //tableware// (eating utensils) includes three sememes. Each one contains the microgeneric seme /tableware/ and is distinguished from the other sememes of the same taxeme by a specific seme: /for piercing/ in 'fork', /for cutting/ in 'knife' and /for containing/ in 'spoon'. Since this taxeme comes under the domain //food//, the three sememes also contain the mesogeneric seme /food/. And finally, the three sememes are also members of the common dimensions that define macrogeneric semes, like /inanimate/. (The term "inanimate" is not used to designate things that are dead or do not move, but things that cannot be alive, such as a rock or freedom.)

Inherent/afferent and actualized/virtualized semes

A seme belonging to a sememe's type is called an **inherent seme**, and in context it is **actualized** (that is, activated) by default, unless there is some instruction to **virtualize** it (neutralize it). **Afferent semes** are semes that are present only in the sememe's token, that is, only by contextual indication. To simplify, we will say that if a seme is present in context, it is actualized; if it should normally have been present but is not, it is virtualized.

For example, in "albino crow", the inherent seme /black/ found in the type for the sememe 'crow' is virtualized in the context of this sememe's token, because this crow is said to be albino. On the other hand, the afferent sememe /white/ is actualized in this token. As we can see, the concepts of actualization and virtualization come in very handy in describing rhetorical figures such as the oxymoron (as in "black sun", from Nerval's poem).

NOTE: DEGREES OF ACTUALIZATION

Actualization occurs by degrees (as does virtualization, no doubt). Because of this, a seme can be salient or not salient (normal). In "the black crow is flying", /black/ is salient in 'crow'; in "the crow is flying" it is not salient in 'crow'. Theoretically, one could have a scale with three degrees: salient/normal/attenuated (or minimized, subdued), but it remains to be seen how one would distinguish between normal and attenuated.

NOTE: DIALECT, SOCIOLECT AND IDIOLECT

A text's meaning arises from the interaction of three systems: (1) the **dialect**, or functional language (as opposed to the historical language), (2) the **sociolect**, which is the usage of a dialect specific to a genre or a discourse (not a social group), and (3) the **idiolect**, which is a specific enunciator's usage of a language and other social norms. For example, in Baudelaire's texts, the seme /negative/, which is associated with *spleen*, women and nature, can be traced to the dialect, the sociolect and the idiolect, respectively. *Spleen* is a pejorative word by definition in French; the disparagement of women was quite common at the time, especially in literary discourse; and the devaluing of nature is more individual. The status of the seme /negative/ is different in each case: it is inherent in the first, sociolectally afferent in the second, and idiolectally afferent in the third case. Note that not all semes are necessarily sociolectal or idiolectal. For example, in "the blue wall", the seme /blue/, which is afferent in 'wall', is neither sociolectal nor idiolectal; it is said to be contextually afferent.

Metaphorical/symbolic connections

There are two possible kinds of connections between sememes (or groups of sememes). A **metaphorical connection** links two sememes that are present in a linguistic chain (as in a comparison). A **symbolic connection** (for example, the *in absentia* metaphor, where the compared term is absent) links two sememes, one of which is present in the chain, the other of which is present in the reading: In the political utterance "The Eagle overcame the Bear", |'United States'| and |'USSR'| are rewritings that are present only in the reading. The two connected sememes have at least one incompatible (generic) seme and at least one identical (specific) seme. For instance, in the expression "this woman is a flower", the metaphorical connection involves the incompatible semes /human/ and /plant/, while a seme like /beauty/ is present in both sememes.

Isotopy

The iteration of a single seme (either inherent or afferent) in context forms an **isotopy**. Isotopies are distinguished not only by the name of the seme on which they are based (for instance, /inanimate/, /religion/), but also by the type of seme involved (specific/micro-, meso-, or macrogeneric). For example, the sentence "I only use a knife for picking up peas" contains the (mesogeneric) isotopy /food/, which indexes the sememes 'knife' and 'peas'. In addition, it virtualizes the inherent specific seme /for cutting/ in 'knife' and actualizes the afferent seme /for picking up/.

Isotopy creates an equivalence between the signifieds containing the seme that defines the particular isotopy. Allotopy is the oppositional relation that arises between two sememes (or groups of sememes, such as a lexia) containing incompatible semes (as in 'black snow').

Meaning/signification and reading

All of the semes actualized in a context, whether inherent or afferent, define the **meaning** of that particular unit. The **signification** is the set of (inherent) semes of a given unit defined out of context. For instance, in "albino crow", the afferent seme /white/ is part of the meaning of 'crow' in this context; however, the seme /white/ is not part of the signification (decontextualized) of 'crow', whereas the seme /black/ is.

Interpretation is the process of assigning meaning to a linguistic chain. Interpretation produces a **reading**. **Intrinsic interpretation** reveals the semes present in a linguistic chain and yields either a **descriptive reading** or a **methodologically reductive reading** (that is, a purposely restricted one). **Extrinsic interpretation** adds semes, whether intentionally or not (a **productive reading**) or mistakenly leaves semes out (a **reductive reading**).

Interpretant, topos and rewriting

An **interpretant** is an element of a text or its surroundings (non-linguistic context) that allows one to establish a semic relation, that is, to definitively actualize or virtualize at least one seme. In "albino crow", the interpretant that justifies virtualizing the seme /black/ and actualizing the seme /white/ in 'crow' is the presence of the signified 'albino'. For example, when the phonic signifiers are identical (homophonic), as in Hamlet's response to King Claudius: "Not so, my lord: I am too much in the sun [→ |son|]", then the mesogeneric semes /weather/ and /filiation/ can be realized simultaneously. A **topos** is a socially normed interpretant (one defined by a sociolect) that can often be expressed as an axiom (e.g., *the countryside is preferable to the city* in rural legend).

A **rewriting** is an interpretive operation of the type X → |Y|, by which one or more signs, signifiers, or signifieds are rewritten as one or more different signs, signifiers, or signifieds. The source unit (X) is part of the object-text, and the target unit (Y) is part of its reading (although it can have correspondences in the source text). From a practical standpoint, rewriting allows one to clearly designate the element being analyzed, particularly in cases of symbolic connection and homonymy (e.g., it allows one to distinguish draft |'current of air'| from draft |'military conscription'|).

Semic molecules and isotopic bundles

A semic **molecule** is a cluster of at least two co-recurrent (appearing together) semes (especially specific semes).[2] In Nelligan's poem "The golden ship", there is a semic molecule made up of the semes /precious/ + /dispersion/. It appears at least three times: (1) the "streaming hair" ("*cheveux épars*") of the beautiful Goddess of Love who was (2) "spread-eagled" ("*s'étalait*") at the ship's prow, and (3) the sinking of the ship's treasure, which the sailors "disputed amongst themselves" ("*entre eux ont disputés*"). This molecule is in opposition to another, with which it overlaps partially, composed of /precious/ + /concentration/, and which is found in the "solid gold" ("*or massif*") of the ship, and even the "blazing sun" ("*soleil excessif*").

It is essential to distinguish between the molecule in the abstract (the type) and its manifestations (the tokens).[3] The tokens do not all necessarily possess the same number of semes as the molecule's type. For example, we consider the molecule /body/ + /precious/ + /dispersion/ to be valid for the three manifestations given above, although the third manifestation is less representative of the molecule's type, since the treasure bears no relation to the human body (possible metaphorical meanings aside). The variations in typicality of the tokens can be interpreted as variations in the salience of the molecule (the intensity of its presence or degree of actualization). One can study the formation, maintenance (full or partial) and eventual dissolution of a semic molecule by following the thread of its tokens.[4]

An **isotopic bundle** is a group of isotopies that index more or less the same units (the same sememes, in the most exacting analysis). A molecule engenders or produces an isotopic bundle (usually made of specific isotopies).

NOTE: RELATIONS BETWEEN SEMES AND BETWEEN ISOTOPIES

There are several kinds of possible relations between semes and between the isotopies they form, such as: opposition, homologation, simple presupposition (where the presence of one seme implies the presence of another), reciprocal presupposition (where the presence of one seme implies the presence of another and vice versa), mutual exclusion (where two semes cannot appear at the same time), and comparison (where one isotopy is comparing and the other compared, as in /bird/ and /poet/ in Baudelaire's "Albatross"). Isotopies can often be grouped as oppositions (as in /animal/ *vs.* /human/). These oppositions may arise through homologation (for example, if /life/ is to /death/ as /human/ is to /animal/ in a text). The elements on the same "side" of a homology (in this case, /life/ and /human/ on the one side and /death/ and /animal/ on the other) constitute a group of semes and isotopies that presuppose each other reciprocally (/life/ and /human/ form one molecule, whereas /death/ and /animal/ form another).[5] When there is a semic molecule present, it is because the isotopies corresponding to the constituent semes of the molecule form a group of isotopies, known as an isotopic bundle; these isotopies tend to index, or include, the same signifieds at the same time, thereby producing the molecule.

Semantic case

Semes and cases are the two **constituent** elements of signifieds (not to be confused with the four semantic *components*). **Semantic cases**, which are limited in number, are semantic primitives or universals of method (they are not de facto).[6] By integrating semantic cases into the typology of the parts of the signified, we can arrange the semes of a single signified into a structure, which is a step further than simply making an inventory of them. Then the semes become elements interconnected by cases (see the chapter on semantic graphs). If a semic structure is repeated, then we have a semic molecule.

Interpretive semantics uses primarily (although not exclusively) the following semantic cases: (1) ACC (accusative): a patient of an action; (2) ATT (attributive): a characteristic; (3) BEN (benefactive): an entity benefiting from something; (4) CLAS (classitive): an element of a class; (5) COMP (comparative): a comparison; (6) DAT (dative): an entity receiving a transmission; (7) ERG (ergative): the agent of an action; (8) FIN (final): a goal; (9) INST (instrumental): a means used; LOC (locative): (10) spatial location (LOC S) or (11) temporal location (LOC T); (12) MAL (malefactive): an entity affected negatively by something; (13) WHOL (wholitive): a part of a whole; (14) RES (the resultative): result, consequence.

For example, if we say that a woman is beautiful, we have the following semantic structure: the semes /woman/ and /beautiful/ linked by the attributive case (ATT). In our example of a molecule, the semes /precious/ + /dispersion/ are connected by an attributive link to what they describe: /hair/, /Goddess/, and /treasure/. To give another example, the type for the sememe 'kill' admittedly covers a process involving the semes /inanimate/ and /animate/, but these semes vary in the ergative (the thing doing the killing can be animate or inanimate), whereas only the second seme is found in the accusative (whatever is killed is, by definition, animate; although /animate/ could be virtualized in the context and replaced by /inanimate/, as in the expressions "killing time" and "Kill your television", for example).

NOTE: ISOTOPIES INVOLVING SEMES AND CASES

Theoretically, one could distinguish between isotopies formed by semes and isotopies formed by cases. But establishing an isotopy means that one is in fact dealing with cases, knowingly or unknowingly, explicitly or not. We are actually looking for not just a specific seme, but a specific seme marked with a specific case, that is, a hybrid molecule made up of a seme and a case. Consider the macrogeneric isotopies /animate/ (living being) and/inanimate/. We would spontaneously index the signified 'glass' in the second isotopy. However, the glass is intended for a human being, which is animate. In other words, we are actually looking for a hybrid molecule made up of the seme /animate/ or /inanimate/ and the attributive case (ATT), and not the seme /animate/ or /inanimate/ with the final case (FIN), which represents the proposed goal. In the first case, 'glass' is excluded from the isotopy; in the second case it is included. Our example may be a bit extreme: the seme /animate/ may not be in the final case in our word; however, we simply want to show that matters of case are never absent in an isotopic and molecular analysis. This being the case, there are two possible methods of analysis: 1. One must have identical cases as well as identical semes in order to establish a semic recurrence that may be used for an isotopy or a molecule. 2. Identical semes alone can be used to establish a valid semic recurrence. In our analysis of Magritte's painting, we will occasionally describe what the effect is on the indexation of signifieds when we include the case associated with the seme that forms the isotopy

The semantic graph

Semantic graphs (based on Sowa, 1984; see the chapter on semantic graphs) are a convention used to visually represent semantic structures (semes and the cases that link them together). Cases are the **links** between the semes (actors, for example), which are structured as **nodes**. Two formats are used for semantic graphs: the proposition and the straight graph. The proposition is a textual format, with the links shown in brackets and the nodes in parentheses. For example, the structure mentioned previously could be represented thusly: [animate] or [inanimate] ← (ERG) ← [KILL] → (ACC) → [animate]. In the strictly graphic format, we generally use ellipses and rectangles, respectively. In both formats of a semantic graph, the arrows indicate the direction of the relations between nodes.

Example: analyzing the title of a novel: Black snow

It would be impossible to give a complete presentation of the possible applications of interpretive semantics in the assigned space. More applications using dialogics and semantic graphs may be found in other chapters.

In this section we will give a brief semic analysis of the title of a novel: *Black snow*, by the prominent French-Canadian author, Hubert Aquin (1978).

Table 11.2 Semic analysis of the title of a novel by Hubert Aquin

'Sememe' / *Seme*	*'Snow'*	*'Black'*	*/Isotopy/*	*Molecule (Isotopic Bundle)*
/precipitation/	actualized seme microgeneric inherent	Ø	Ø	
/color/	Ø	actualized seme microgeneric inherent	Ø	

(Continued)

Table 11.2 (Continued)

'Sememe' / *Seme*	*'Snow'*	*'Black'*	*/Isotopy/*	*Molecule (Isotopic Bundle)*
/whiteness/	virtualized seme specific inherent	Ø	Ø	
/blackness/	actualized seme specific afferent (qualifier)	actualized seme specific inherent	specific isotopy /blackness/	molecule /blackness/
/dysphoric/	actualized seme (salient) macrogeneric afferent	actualized seme macrogeneric afferent	macrogeneric isotopy /dysphoric/	+ /dysphoric/

A few details are in order:

Independent of context (at the level of *langue*), the sememe 'Snow' contains the inherent microgeneric seme /precipitation/ (which refers to the taxeme //precipitation//, which includes the sememes 'snow', 'rain', etc.) and the specific inherent seme /whiteness/ (which distinguishes between 'snow' and 'rain', for example, within the taxeme). In context, the second seme is virtualized by the effect of the qualifier: the snow is described as black, and by correlation, the afferent seme / blackness/ is actualized for the same reason.

Independent of context, the sememe 'Black' contains the microgeneric inherent seme /color/ (which refers to the taxeme of //colors//, which includes sememes like 'black', 'white', etc.) and the inherent specific seme /blackness/ (which distinguishes between 'black' and 'white', for example, within the taxeme). Both of the semes are actualized in context. Since the seme /blackness/ is actualized in two different signifieds, 'snow' and 'black', the isotopy /blackness/ is created.

The title refers to a topos, or literary (and non-literary) common place that renders black as a dysphoric, harmful element (for instance, one finds it in Nerval: "black sun", "black spot"). For this reason, the macrogeneric afferent seme /dysphoric/ is actualized in 'black' (and since it is actualized through a topos, it can be considered as sociolectally afferent).

Since the snow is said to be black, the same seme is actualized in 'snow'; but the sememe 'snow' is itself a potential carrier of the afferent seme /dysphoric/, also by virtue of a topos. Therefore, both semes reinforce each other mutually and become salient as a result; the two sememes serve as interpretants for each other. However, the effect of salience, or prominence, is achieved primarily to the noun's advantage, due to the direction in which qualifiers operate (actualizations generally go from the adjective to the noun). As the seme /dysphoric/ is actualized in two different signifieds, the isotopy /dysphoric/ is formed. This macrogeneric seme refers to the dimension //dysphoria//, which is in opposition to the dimension //euphoria//. (These semes can also be viewed as modal values: see the chapter on dialogics).

Moreover, since the semes /blackness/ and /dysphoric/ are co-recurrent in two different signifieds, the title thus contains the semic molecule /blackness/ + /dysphoric/.

NOTE: OTHER SEMES PRESENT IN THE TITLE

Obviously, other semes are featured in the title, specifically, /woman/ (see Aquin's diary (cited in Aquin, 1995, XXXIV: "*la nuit féminoïde*", "*la femme obscure*", "*la femme est noire*", etc.) and /literature/ (cf. the "*roman noir*", which, like *Black snow*, is characterized by eroticism and religious references). We do not claim to have exhausted the meaning of this title, but let us finish with a very probable symbolic connection. The sign "snow", as we know, can refer to "cocaine powder" (*Le petit Robert* and *The american heritage dictionary*). If this homonymic wordplay were recognized, the symbolic connection would be based on the opposition between the mesogeneric inherent semes /weather/ and /addiction/ (and/or the microgeneric inherent semes /precipitation/ and /drugs in powder form/) of "snow" and |"cocaine"| on the one hand, and their identical specific inherent semes /whiteness/ on the other. (There are undoubtedly other identical specific semes).

According to some who were close to him, "Aquin was addicted to medications (particularly amphetamines), which he had used liberally since his youth [. . .] to maintain his 'dynamism'" (Aquin, 1995, p. 175). In 1963 he went through a detox program during the three months of hospitalization following a suicide attempt (Aquin, 1995, p. 202). There is a significant isotopy /medication-drugs/ in several of his works (for example, *Next episode* and "*De retour le 11 avril*"), and in *Black snow* (1978, p. 262), Linda says: "*C'est comme si j'étais intoxiquée par un divin poison . . .*" ["I felt like I had been drugged with a divine poison".]

An analytical methodology: semic tables

We recommend using three kinds of semic tables.

1 In the heuristic, or exploratory phase of analysis, one begins by briefly picking out the semes or isotopies present in the text, or by formulating hypotheses based on genres, eras and authors (for example, the isotopies /countryside/, /city/, etc. in a text from rural legend). The heuristic table is for recording these preliminary findings.

Table 11.3 An example of a heuristic semic table

Signified no.	*Reference no. (word, verse, line, page, etc.)*	*SIGNIFIED*	*SEME*	*JUSTIFICATION*
1	v1	'signified 1'	/X/, /Y/	
2	v1	'signified 2'	/Y/	
3	v1	'signified 3'	/X/	

NOTE: NAMING THE SEME AND THE ISOTOPY

It is particularly important to select an appropriate name for the seme and the isotopy based on it. The idea is to choose the name that will yield the richest analysis in quantitative and qualitative terms, namely by adjusting the degree of generality/specificity (e.g., from /action/ to /movement/ to /dance/ to /waltz/ or the reverse). Since any signified contains several semes, one signified may be present in several of the isotopies selected for analysis, perhaps even in two incompatible isotopies.

2 In the strictly analytical stage of the analysis, one selects a few semes or isotopies that are of interest either intrinsically (e.g., the isotopy /aerospace/ in a love story) or because of the relations they maintain with other semes or isotopies. The analytical table can be used to record

actualizations of a given seme in the text. One would create as many analytical tables as there are isotopies one wants to detail (+ indicates an actualized seme, no plus sign a non-actualized seme, and the minus sign a virtualized seme).

Table 11.4 An example of an analytical semic table

SIGNIFIED	*SEME /X/*	*JUSTIFICATION*
'signified 1'	inherent	
'signified 2'		
'signified 3'	afferent	

NOTE: LIMITING CRITERIA

In order to streamline the tables and the analysis, one can use limiting criteria in one's methodology, for instance, by excluding all or some of the free grammemes, as they are called (prepositions, pronouns, conjunctions, adverbs, articles, non-qualifying adjectives). In addition, rather than including all of the signifieds of the text in our table, one can select only the signifieds that are indexed by one of the isotopies selected for the analysis (but still include any signifieds whose non-indexation calls for comment). This approach is useful in analyzing longer texts.

3 Table 11.5 compares the indexations of signifieds in the various isotopies selected in order to distinguish the presence of molecules (in our table, a molecule /X/ + /Y/ appears in signifieds 1 and 2).

Table 11.5 An example of a comprehensive semic table

SIGNIFIED	*SEME /X/, mesogeneric*	*SEME /Y/, mesogeneric*	*JUSTIFICATION*
'signified 1'	inherent	afferent	
'signified 2'	inherent	inherent	
'signified 3'	afferent	(virtualized)	

The comprehensive table makes it easy to identify the logical relations between isotopies and between semes, and is especially helpful in identifying semic molecules.[7]

NOTE: JUSTIFICATIONS

Where appropriate, justifications are given in the last column of the table or in the footnotes for: (1) a seme's actualization (especially for afferent semes, which are theoretically more questionable than inherent semes); (2) a seme's virtualization (e.g., in "black snow", the inherent seme /whiteness/ is virtualized; in this context, 'snow' cannot be part of a hypothetical isotopy /whiteness/). Sometimes one needs to give evidence for (3) non-actualization or (4) non-virtualization, in cases where the reader might misjudge a specific seme's status as actualized or virtualized. In every case, the reasons cited will be interpretants. One must also give evidence for the type of seme involved: why is it inherent/afferent or specific/micro-, meso-, macrogeneric, and so forth?

Applications

Application I: Amazon's logo

The aim of semic analysis is to identify (1) potential and plausible meanings of the semiotic product being analyzed (2) at the moment of its creation, (3) whether or not its creator was conscious of such meanings. On one hand, the analysis does not have to be limited to the (conscious) intentions of creators, if only because they may be mistaken about the actual marking of their intentions in the product (they may fail to achieve their communication and creation objectives). On the other hand, it need not necessarily be limited to a "naive", surface analysis, that of the average or hurried receiver; it may instead be a more in-depth analysis that accounts for effects that are less obvious. This does not mean that these more obscure effects cannot affect "naive" or hurried receivers without them being (fully) conscious of such effects. Naturally, the plausibility of the interpretations is both gradual (varying in intensity) and relative (varying, for example, based on the observers). To prevent (excessive) subjectivity, interpretations must be supported by arguments that are presented in an explicit manner and that are as objective as possible.

We will be presenting our analysis of only some elements of the Amazon logo. Like many logos, Amazon's logo is a combination of written linguistic signs (letter-based, or more specifically, grapheme-based) and pictorial signs. Written signs are also, of course, mentally pronounced, which adds another level of analysis. We will later be describing the principles of polysemiotic analysis (for example, of a text with an image, as is the case in this logo). This is a simple application of such an analysis.

The logo consists of the word "amazon" in black (with a lowercase "a"). A yellow – or more specifically, red ochre – curved arrow begins under the first "a", with the arrowhead ending under the "z", creating a slight indentation.

We will begin with the written and oral linguistic signs. Several linguistic signifieds overlap in the "amazon" sign (we can also consider that there is in fact overlap between several signs). The first signified is of course 'Amazon' – the company. Note that in the logo, the capital "A" has been replaced by a lowercase "a"; we will later see a visual reason that gives meaning to this substitution. There is also an emotional reason: the lowercase letter gives the company a more friendly, less formal image. The second signified is 'Amazons' – the legendary warriors of antiquity. In relation to the function of the company, this signified contains semes such as /energy/ and /important/ (through the legendary hyperbole), even /woman/ or, going further, /feminist/ (we will go even further at the end of the analysis). The written signifier *amazon* is, in relation to *Amazons*, produced through apocope, because the *s* at the end of the word is lost (unless referring to only one Amazon warrior, in which case there is no need for the plural); the capital letter has also been replaced by a lowercase letter. In speech, the final phoneme of *Amazons* is also lost when pronouncing the word in the logo.

The third signified is 'Amazon' – the river; it contains semes such as /energy/ and /important/ as well, but also, without a doubt, in the commercial context, at least one other seme: /provider/. The river has the highest discharge rate on the planet, with massive, steady flow upstream; we will come back to this. In this case, the written signifier *amazon* is produced simply through the substitution of the capital letter with a lowercase letter.

A fourth signified is 'Amazon' – rainforest; it contains the semes of /energy/, /important/, /variety/, and /quantity/ (due to the luxuriance of this forest). Some signifieds of the logo contain the seme of /green/; this is particularly clear and strong in this signified, since the Amazon Rainforest is often described as the lungs of the planet and as an extraordinary source of animal and plant biodiversity. The same operation as that for the previous signifier is needed to achieve the text in the logo.

A fifth signified is 'amazing'. It supports the hyperbolic reading we have already identified. It also contains the seme /satisfaction/: what surprises us, in the good sense of the word – the only one that should be attributed here – is more than satisfactory.

A sixth signified, 'zone', can be read together with the previous signified: the company is presented as a "place" that will "surprise" us. Moreover, the combination of (*to*) *amaze* and *on* – associated with a seventh signified – indicates that the amazement is active; at the very least, a seme of energy is associated with *on* its own. It refers to a place, as had been mentioned, but one that is rather metaphorical, as it is dematerialized; however, the Internet is often represented by spatial metaphors. The past three signifieds we examined were produced by stronger manipulations of the signifier *amazon*. However, for the fifth signified, the first lowercase "a", in contrast with certain other past signifiers, is maintained (while the capital letter would have created a hyperbole).

We will now move on to the pictorial analysis. Naturally, the yellow shape below the word could or even must be interpreted as an arrow, which is the first main iconic signified. The signified associated with this arrow contains the seme /Amazons/, since the Amazons were considered to be excellent archers. It is even said that they would cut off or burn one of their breasts to make it easier to shoot arrows; we will come back to this. This legendary rumour, while undoubtedly having no historical basis, is well known, which makes it relevant to the analysis. The relationship between the arrow and the Amazons therefore, from a rhetorical perspective, falls into the category of metonymy (an action to represent the agent) or synecdoche (a part to represent the whole). The signified, 'arrow' contains, among others, the semes of /energy/, /speed/ (that of purchasing and of delivery), and /satisfaction/ (since the arrow reaches its target, which, for the consumer, is a satisfying, or even euphoric, purchase). The arrow may have been curved due to the intensity of being fired, again activating the semes of /energy/ and /speed/, which thus become even more salient. The arrow is that of the consumer, that of the Amazons, but also perhaps that of the numerous Indigenous peoples living in the Amazon Rainforest. The arrowhead could, as a second signified, evoke the image of a boomerang – a throwing weapon with an overall meaning that is the same as that of the arrow; in this case, based on standard visual conventions (used, for example, in comics), the shaft or stem of the arrow would represent the boomerang's trajectory or at least its movement. The boomerang interpretation is even more relevant since this weapon used by the Aboriginal people of Australia also speaks to the notion of Indigenous peoples present, as mentioned, in the "Amazon" – Indigenous peoples associated, in the popular mindset, with bows and arrows.

Here, the arrow is also an indexical sign that points to the written part of the logo, and therefore to what the logo definitely represents – the company Amazon. In this sense, it is like a finger that points to the moon and tells us, "Look!" Naturally, things are pointed out when they deserve to be on display (for good or bad reasons; here, for good reasons), which once again hyperbolizes the value of the company. This third signified is separate from the first signified: the first represents an arrow – projectile, while this signified represents an arrow – pointer. Finally, the curved arrow takes the shape of a bow, which is a rhetorical slip that is metonymic or synecdochic in nature (the propelled for the one propelling or one part for another of the same whole) and forms a fourth signified.

However, the fact that the arrow is curvilinear instead of straight moves us toward another reading of the shape – if one had not already seen this sign – the recognition of a fifth iconic signified: a smile. This reading is supported in certain animated versions of the logo, for example, in films or television series made by the company, where the "arrow" is seen to progressively take shape, like a smile appears progressively on the face of a person. The arrowhead also thus represents a dimple at the corner of the mouth, near the lips. It is clearly a sign of the company's high level of consumer satisfaction and the friendly nature of the company – a company that makes us smile. This anthropomorphic reading – underpinned by the phenomenon of pareidolia, which tends to make known shapes, especially those that are anthropomorphic in nature, visible in abstract or vague shapes – transforms the two "a's" into eyes and the "m" into a nose (with, why not, two nostrils formed by the legs of the "m") of the smiling face. If the first "a" were a capital letter, as it would normally be for a trademark, the resemblance to eyes would have been less strong; this no doubt explains, at least in part, why a lowercase letter was used. We noted that, on the part of the consumer, it is a smile of satisfaction, and more generally of happiness, since the advertisements by and large hyperbolize its product as being the (unique) source of (ultimate) happiness. It could also be a smile that is sly, mischievous, or clever in nature, one of consumers who are efficient and informed because they use Amazon.

The arrow, by indenting the base of the "z" due to its impact, further conveys the seme of /energy/. The fact that the arrow impacts the word has the effect of making the word, as an object, inhabit the same world as the arrow; it is therefore no longer an intangible element. This word-object is flexible, as indicated by the indentation of the "z", when it could have instead been breakable or pierceable. The fact that the beginning of the arrow is continuous with the leg of the first "a" and that the arrowhead forms an identical curve to that of the base of the impacted "z", creates an effect of organic harmony and evident naturalization for the scriptovisual whole. In some logos, the text and visual components do not directly interact, but that is not the case here. Moreover, the arrow is located so that it connects the letter at the beginning of the alphabet, "a", to that at the end, "z". This shows that the company meets all needs through the variety of products and services it offers. Meanwhile, a boomerang, by definition, completes not only an initial trajectory, but also a returning trajectory, which metaphorizes the process of online shopping (from the consumer to Amazon – order, and from Amazon to the consumer – delivery).

The trajectory of the arrow – from start to finish (the arrowhead) and from its point of origin "a" to its target "z" – goes from left to right, which is also the order in which the word above it is to be read. This idea of a complete journey across an area can also be found in another possible reading of the iconic shape, that of the Amazon River, which clearly flows from its most upstream point (the start of the arrow) downstream (the arrowhead). This is the sixth iconic signified of the arrow. At the very least, the arrowhead represents the massive mouth of the river; however, it is inverted, which reduces the relevance of the interpretation, even if spatial inversion is common in logos and more generally in images. Instead of continuing to look at the textual content of the word, we will now look at the iconic potentialities of the word in the logo. The loops of the "a's" produce a shape that is very similar to a drop of water, which supports the idea of the Amazon River. The dips in these two drops – and other dips in the word's letters, for example, the inverted dips, or peaks, in "m" and "n" and the dips at the bottom of the "a's" – echo the arrowhead, which harmoniously brings together the text and the arrow. The dips of the "a's" also resemble waves – another link to water, and thus the river. A wave, like a river, clearly conveys the idea of energy, flow, and vitality. Presumably, to the extent that it is possible for this degree of accuracy, the waves in the logo travel from left to right like the arrow. More generally, several curves from the top and bottom of the letters evoke the idea of waves. The whole word thus becomes a subtle visual representation of a river – the Amazon River no doubt.

There is no need to have a twisted or – what is, for some, the same thing! – psychoanalytic mind to see a seventh signified, an erect male symbol in the arrow's shape. Presumably, this interpretation was not lost on the advertisers who created the logo and whose job it is to analyze the various meanings – both evident and subtle, desired and undesired – of logos. No need to stress that energy – a traditionally male characteristic – is once again present. The penis is curved. Through this curve, it in a way becomes feminine: traditionally, straight lines are viewed as more masculine in nature, while curved lines are considered to be more feminine. However, in the natural sense, an erect penis is curved, generally upwards – exactly as it is in the logo. Clearly, the many curves that make up the arrow refer back to the curvatures in the letters of the word above it. Nevertheless, some letters also have straight lines, and the word itself, in general, is defined by two straight lines: the (imaginary) line that the word is sitting on and the (imaginary) line that sits atop the letters.

The stylized phallus is consistent, as another sexualized body part, with the breast mentioned earlier. As such, the same shape, the arrow, brings together the two traditional genders: women, in the allusion to the Amazons and the breast, and men, through an allusion to men in general (again by means of synecdoche, a given erection representing the entire gender). As a result, several body parts are found in the logo: breast, head (and its subparts: eyes, nose, mouth, lips, dimples), and penis. The Amazons, seen in the context of this logo, are lacking two things: a breast and – again without having to resort to psychoanalysis – a penis. If that is indeed the case, from this fact, a contradiction can be seen between the "feminism" easily discerned from the word "Amazon" (due to the matriarchal society of the warriors) and non-feminism, or even machismo, in the visual interpretation that is more subtle – and no doubt not (officially) accepted by the creators of the logo, due to its controversial nature – the phallus. Another way of looking at things is to consider that just as the logo brings together the feminine and the masculine, so did the Amazons as women who adopted traditionally male values and behaviour. To continue with more obscure interpretations, the arrowhead could also represent a breast, an eighth signified. Within the arrow, there would thus be a visual union between women and men, the two traditional genders, and even of a non-traditional gender (one that may be a synecdoche for all non-traditional genders and sexual identities) – since the Amazons are often used as a lesbian symbol.

Application II: "The golden ship" by Émile Nelligan

* * *

The golden ship
Émile Nelligan (1960)

There was a fine ship, carved from solid gold
With azure reaching masts, on seas unknown.
Spread-eagled Venus, naked, hair back thrown,
Stood at the prow. The sun blazed uncontrolled.

But on the treacherous ocean in the gloom
She struck the great reef where the Sirens chant.
Appalling shipwreck plunged her keel aslant
To the Gulf's depths, that unrelenting tomb.

She was a Golden Ship: but there showed through
Translucent sides treasures the blasphemous crew,
Hatred, Disgust and Madness, fought to share.

How much survives after the storm's brief race?
Where is my heart, that empty ship, oh where?
Alas, in Dream's abyss sunk without trace.

* * *

We will present an isotopic analysis of Nelligan's "The golden ship" (1879–1941), the best-known poem of the greatest French-Canadian poet of the 19th century (he was institutionalized from 1899 on).[8]

Our isotopic analysis will be simplified in two ways. Firstly, we will address only one isotopy here – the one relating to the domain /navigation/. Secondly, we will not examine every possible signified that could be indexed by this isotopy, but retain only those signifieds represented by nouns, verbs and qualifying adjectives (this eliminates all of the pronouns that refer to a word containing the seme /navigation/, such as "she" for "ship" and "where" for "reef"). In this way we can steer clear of some of the most problematic indexations, especially those relating to possible plays on words (in French, we have "*il*" and "*île*", "*aux*" and "*eau*", for example).

Limited space prohibits us from delving into another extremely interesting isotopy that also relates to a domain: /sexuality/. While the first isotopy is especially obvious, the second is no less evident: It has a solid foundation in words and syntagms like "naked" ("*chairs nues*"), "Sirens" and obviously, "Venus" ("*la Cyprine d'amour*"), which we will examine next. The main difficulty concerning this second isotopy is in knowing where to draw the line between an adequate interpretation and an overinterpretation (for instance, should one interpret "storm" ("*tempête brève*") as a metaphor for coitus, and "masts" as a phallic symbol?). We will advance the hypothesis that our two isotopies are joined in a comparative relation, with navigation as the comparing and sexuality as the compared isotopy (which does not mean that only signifieds indexed by /navigation/ can be indexed by /sexuality/).[9]

NOTE: OUR TREATMENT OF METAPHORICAL COMPARISONS AND METAPHORS

We have adopted interpretive semantics' principles for addressing metaphorical comparisons. We have two examples taken from the text we are analyzing. In the metaphorical comparison "gulf" – "tomb", each of the two elements remains within its respective domain and within the isotopy associated with it, that is, /navigation/ and /funeral rite/ (the same applies to "the crew" on the one hand, and "Hatred", "Disgust" and "Madness" on the other). By contrast, in the metaphor "storm" – "coitus" (a word not present in the text) – a metaphor that is subject to debate – "storm" belongs simultaneously to the isotopy /navigation/ and the isotopy /sexuality/, insofar as it serves to manifest "coitus". There do not seem to be any words that index the isotopy /navigation/ by means of a metaphor; this is why we have given an example from the isotopy /sexuality/.

The table below shows the main signifieds indexing the isotopy /navigation/ (actualized seme: +; inherent seme: *i*; afferent seme: *a*; doubt about actualization or inherent/afferent status: ?).

Table 11.6 The isotopy /navigation/ in "The golden ship"

WORDS AND SIGNIFIEDS	*THE SEME AND ISOTOPY /NAVIGATION/*		
ship	+	i	type of boat
masts	+	i	
azure	+?	a	"Her[aldry]. The color blue. The blue sky". (*The american heritage dictionary*)
seas	+	i	
Cyprine	+	a	[Found in the original French version.] "From the Latin *Cypris*, from the Greek *Kupris*, Aphrodite's surname" (*Le petit Robert*), a goddess worshipped on the island of Cyprus. As we know, Aphrodite (Venus) was born of the water. In the context, she is a benevolent feminine "aquatic" figure in opposition to the Sirens, who appear later. As a possible metaphor for a figurehead, the word is also indexed by /navigation/. Since these interpretants are combined, we conclude that the seme is especially salient. In addition, this word is undoubtedly also indexed by the isotopy /sexuality/. Being derived from Aphrodite's surname, it automatically relates to love, particularly in its sensual meaning. Moreover, the only meaning reported in *Le petit Robert* is "*Sécrétion vaginale, signe physique du désir sexuel*" ["Vaginal secretion, a physical sign of sexual desire"], a meaning attested in the *Petit Robert* around 1970. And in fact, it appeared well before that, as Gervais (1994, pp. 38–39) proves in this letter from Apollinaire to Louise de Coligny (13 January 1915): "*le vagin royal où bouillonne la cyprine voluptueuse que tu me prodigues ô chérie et d'où s'épanche l'or en fusion de ton pipi mignon*" (quoted from Gervais, 1994, p. 39, no translation available). And lastly, as a possible metaphor to designate a figurehead, the word is also indexed by / sexuality/, as figureheads are often bare-breasted.
prow	+	i	The forward part of a ship's hull, the bow.
vint	+?	a	[Found in the original French version.] Assumes navigation: a voyage on water
reef	+	i	"A strip or ridge of rocks, sand, or coral that rises to or near the surface of a body of water". (*The american heritage dictionary*)
ocean	+	i	
siren	+	i?	"One of a group of sea nymphs whose sweet singing lured mariners to destruction on the rocks around their island". (*The american heritage dictionary*)
shipwreck	+	i	
keel	+	i	The submerged part of the hull of a boat
depths	+	a	In this context, the depths referred to are the ocean's.
Gulf	+	a	This type of gulf is not marine by definition, making the seme afferent: "A deep wide chasm; an abyss". Note the following meaning, although it does not seem to apply directly here: "Something, such as a whirlpool, that draws down or engulfs" (*The american heritage dictionary*).
Ship	+	i	
flancs	+	i	"*Partie latérale de certaines choses. Flanc d'un vaisseau.* [The lateral part of certain things. The side of a boat".] (*Le petit Robert*) The word in the English translation, "sides", contains no inherent or afferent seme.

(*Continued*)

Table 11.6 (Continued)

WORDS AND SIGNIFIEDS	*THE SEME AND ISOTOPY /NAVIGATION/*		
treasures	+	a	A treasure is not necessarily from a ship, although it often is in literary texts, for example.
sailors	+	i	
tempête	+	i?	The word "*tempête*" in the original may contain an inherent seme, based on the *Petit Robert*: "*Violente perturbation atmosphérique [. . .] Spécial[emen]t Ce temps sur mer, qui provoque l'agitation des eaux et met les navires en péril*". ["Violent atmospheric disturbance [. . .] esp. weather at sea of the kind that produces high waves, endangering ships".] The word "storm" in the translation contains no inherent seme.
ship	+	i	
sunk	+	i	"To descend to the bottom; submerge" (*The american heritage dictionary*)
abyss			"An immeasurably profound depth or void" (*The american heritage dictionary*).

***Application III:* The key to dreams**

It is not the intent of this book on applied semiotics to present the theory of visual semiotics. We will steer clear of certain problems that are as challenging as they are crucial from a theoretical standpoint, and focus on a few methodological questions. We want to show how we can apply some of the principles and concepts of textual semic analysis and interpretive semantics (e.g., the oppositions specific/generic and actualized/virtualized seme), with some adjustments, to the analysis of images, with or without text.

The seme

Our point of departure, which calls for some fine-tuning from a theoretical perspective, is that textual and pictorial signifieds are identical and that they may be broken down into semes. A seme by any name is identical to another seme of the same name, whether they are part of the same semiotic system (text, images) or not.

Segmentation

In the semiotics of images, the units seem to lend themselves to alternative segmentations using signifieds of differing magnitudes. Switching from one segmentation to another can cause multiple signifieds to be differentiated in one signified and possibly generate new semic iterations and/or reinforce existing ones. Our analysis features one position per compartment for the textual signified (thereby merging the two words of the legend for each compartment into one signified). It also features one position per compartment for the pictorial signified. For example, although the seme /solid/ is found in the whole signified of the hammer image in the painting, and also in the signifieds corresponding to its two parts, the handle and the head, we list the seme /solid/ only once, for the whole image of the hammer.

Iteration and semic molecules

Iteration, recurrence and semic repetition are the terms we use for inter-semiotic repetition (e.g., in a text and an image) and intra-semiotic repetition (e.g., in a text) of a single seme in one object (e.g., a specific painting by Magritte). We prefer to avoid the term "isotopy", whose original meaning implies the successive repetition of one unit over time (more accurately, in different positions that can be sequenced relative to each other), which is problematic in still images.

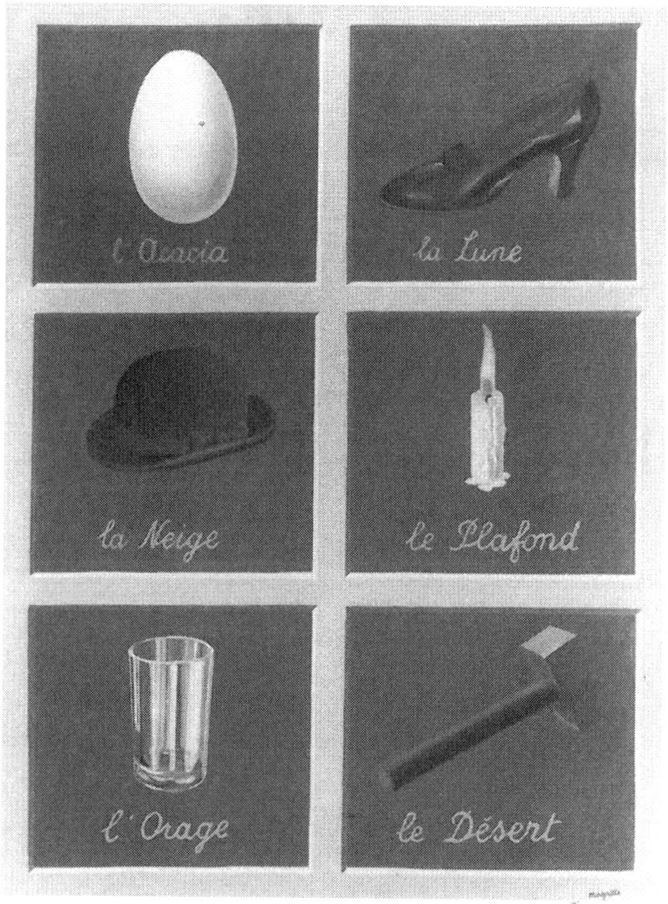

Figure 11.1 *The key to dreams*

Source: Magritte (1930)

To give an example of a semic molecule in Magritte's painting, /white/ + /small/ is a molecule occurring in 'egg' and 'candle'; we say that this molecule is intra-semiotic, since it is exclusively pictorial. The molecule /white/ + /curvature/ has occurrences in 'egg' and 'moon', and by this token, it is inter-semiotic. Just as for semic iterations, the way in which semic molecules are identified in an image depends on what sort of segmentation system is worked out, an issue mentioned earlier.

Categorization

There is a distinction to be made between categorizing what is represented in an image and categorizing its lexical label. Categorization is an operation by which a unit becomes part of an ontological class, that is, a class of beings.

It is not immaterial that the hammer represented in the painting is the kind used for forging metal. In the *Larousse du XX*^e^ *siècle* (1928–1933), Magritte's hammer corresponds to number 9 on the "Hammers" plate, that is, the "forging hammer". There are semic impacts due to the fact that this hammer is used for forging. For example, it provides an iteration of the semes /melting/ and /fire/, found in 'candle'. In addition, the seme /melting/ in 'snow' has a stronger presence than it would just in the context of 'candle'. Recognizing the frame and/or window depicted by the six-compartment grid will have semic implications as well. The window categorization is supported by the history of art in general: the notion of the painting as a window goes back at least to Alberti ("*fenestra aperta per donde io miri quello que quivi sara dipinto*", 1436) and Leonardo ("*pariete di vetro*") (see Clair, 1977); but it also appears in several other paintings by Magritte.[10] Recognizing the presence of a window allows us to establish an iteration /glass/ that indexes 'window' and 'glass', as well as an iteration /dwelling/ that indexes 'window', 'ceiling' and perhaps 'key'.

Lexical selection

Lexical selection is the process of naming a category or a representative of the category.

In themselves, lexical labels for images have no influence on the semic content of the images. However, like several other modern painters, Magritte often uses homonymic shifts and transformations of set expressions in his titles and legends. Lexical labels are crucial in setting up these actual or potential "games". These hypothetical "word plays" on the textual signifier are of interest here only insofar as they can be used as interpretants for textual or pictorial semes. Let us take a case of homonymy: The presence of a sponge* in one of the versions of this painting, the chalky, handwritten letters, and the classroom parody of associating a simple image with a simple lexical item (supposedly to deliver meaning in a package) all point to the notion that the background of *The key to dreams* may be lexicalized in French as "*tableau*" ["blackboard"] //education//, with a shift to the homonym |"*tableau*"| [painting] //painting//. Homonymy, then, serves as a partial, but decisive interpretant to actualize at least one seme: /painting/. To give another example, it seems plausible to rewrite "*plafond*" ["ceiling"] as |"*fond*"| ["melts"], in correlation with the signified 'snow', the seme /water/ and of course, the image of a candle that is "melting" in the same compartment as the word in question.

In our analysis, we have chosen one lexical item for each of the six images. The lexical labels we have selected are as follows, with alternative lexical choices in parentheses: "egg" ("chicken egg"), "shoe" ("high-heeled shoe", "footwear"), "hat" ("cloche", "derby hat", "derby"), "candle", "glass" ("water glass", "drinking glass"?), "hammer" ("sledge hammer", "mallet", "forging hammer"). It is easy to see that this list has been methodologically restricted to iconic signifieds (signifieds that form recognizable, nameable images), by excluding malleable signifieds, and that the signifieds represented by the following lexical labels were not selected: "*tableau*" ["painting" or "blackboard"], "frame" or "window", "word" and "signature". In addition, we have also excluded from the textual part of our analysis the word "Magritte" (which appears as the signature depicted) and the title *The key to dreams* (*La clef des songes*).

NOTE: THE HAMMER

The hammer is of special interest: Did Magritte know the specific function of the forging hammer, did he know its precise name, or did he know its function without knowing its name? One can ask the same questions concerning reception, for the model viewer and the empirical viewer. In our analysis, we have opted for the lexical label "hammer", but we have taken its categorization as a forging hammer into account in order to determine the presence of certain semes.

Semic analysis table of The key to dreams

Opposite is the semic analysis table for Magritte's painting. The legend for the symbols used appears at the end of the table.[11]

Table 11.7 Semic analysis table of *The key to dreams* by Magritte

	/seme/ /a/, /b/, /c/ . . . — *signified*	*Type of seme*	*Word 1 Acacia*[1]	*Word 2 Moon*	*Word 3 Snow*	*Word 4 Ceiling*	*Word 5 Storm*	*Word 6 Desert*	*Image 1 [egg]*	*Image 2 [shoe]*	*Image 3 [hat]*	*Image 4 [candle]*	*Image 5 [glass]*	*Image 6 [hammer]*
01	a concrete, b conceptual[2]	mag	a	a	a	a	a	a	a	a	a	a	a	a
02	a animate (living being), b inanimate[3]	mag	a	b4	b	b	b	b[4]	a	b	b	b	b	b
03	a nature, b culture	mag	a	a	a	b	a	a	a	b	b	b	b	b
04	a feminine, b masculine	mag ?	a ?[5]	a?[6]					a ?[7]	a[8]	b[9]			b[10]
05	a food, b botany, c clothing, d weather, e ornithology[11]	meg	b	d?[12]	a?[13] d		a? d	d	a e[14]	c	a ? c		a	
06	a edible, b inedible, c not applicable[15]	spe	b	c	a	c	c[16]	c	a	b	a?[17] b	b	a?[18] b	b
07	a hot, b cold[19]	spe		b?[20]	b	a?[24]	b?[21]	a b?[22]	a?[23]	a?[24]	a?[24]	a	b?[25]	a?[26]
08	a brightness, b darkness	spe	a ?[27]	a b[28]	a	b ?[29]	a b[30]	a[31]	b ?[32]		a ?[33]	a	a ?[34]	a ?[35]
09	a white, b black, c gray d other[36]	spe	d[37]	a[38]	a	?	?[39]	?[40]	a	b	b	a d	d[36]	c d[41]
10	a straight, b curved[42]	spe	a?[43]	b	a?[44]	a	a?[44]	a[45]	b	a b[46]	b[47]	a b[48]	a b[49]	a b[50]
11	a low, b high[51]	spe?	a	b	b	a	b	a[52]	a[53]	a[54]	a	a	a[55]	a[56]
12	a container, b contents	spe?			b?[57]	a[58]	b?[57]	a[59]	a b[60]	a[61]	a[62]		a	
13	a solid, b liquid	spe ?	a	a[63]	a b[64]	a	b	a[63]	a b[65]	a b[66]	a b[66]	a b[67]	a b[68]	a[69]
14	a water, b absence of water, c protection from water, d fire[70]	spe		a b?[71]	a	c	a d ?[72]	b d[73]	[74]	c	c	d[75]	b[76]	d[77]
15	a damaging, b damageable, c damaged, d not damaging, e undamageable, f protective[78]	spe	b ?	e	a b	f	a	a	b f	a f	f	a b c	a ? b	a e
16	a familiar, b exotic	spe?	a b[79]	a	a	a	a	b	a[80]	a	a[81]	a	a	a[82]

1 The acacia is a tree with yellow flowers, certain species of which produce acacia gum, also known as arabic gum or Senegal gum. The mimosa is a type of acacia. In the usual meaning, "acacia" means "locust tree" or "false acacia" (*Le petit Robert*). The context 'desert' tends to validate the first meaning; the context /ordinary object/ validates the second meaning.

2 We are using the term "conceptual" rather than "abstract" in order to avoid confusion with the meaning of the term "abstract" in art ("conceptual art" is a recognized term, too, of course, but is far less common).

3 Inanimate elements can be qualified depending on the initial state of the materials from which they are made. For instance, the hat and the handle of the hammer are made of animate things, of living products that have been "de-animated" (leather, wool and wood).

4 The desert in itself is inanimate and not very hospitable for animate beings. In our discussion, we mentioned the possibility of including the interaction between semantic cases and semes to create a "hybrid molecule." The desert is an example of this: on the one hand, it is in the ergative case if one considers it as acting aggressively toward some element marked as /animate/ in the accusative, and on the other hand it is in a spatial locative case for this same element. The moon is an example of a space that is even more inhospitable to animate beings.

(*Continued*)

Table 11.7 (Continued)

5 Should we associate the acacia with femininity because of its flowers and its aesthetic function?

6 The moon is traditionally associated with femininity, if for no other reason than it is said to govern the menstrual cycle, especially in context with fertility (the egg).

7 The egg undoubtedly conveys the semes /fertility/, /maternity/ and thus, /femininity/.

8 The shoe in this image (the token of a shoe) is feminine.

9 The hat in this image (the token of a hat) is masculine.

10 Tools of this kind are traditionally associated with men, especially since this is a forging hammer, not a household hammer (one "aggravating" factor is that this painting dates from the late thirties, an era when women were more confined to traditional roles).

11 Indexing by domains is a complex process. As relevant as they appear to be, some domains cover only one signified; should one then increase the degree of generality in order to increase one's chances of including other signifieds in the domain? The domain //construction// would index 'hammer' (//tools// would work just as well) and possibly 'ceiling' (//dwelling// is more appropriate, and has the advantage of including //lighting// and possibly //construction//); acacia wood is apparently not used in construction or cabinet making. The moon is in the domain //astronomy// and the desert in the domain //geography//. The domain //lighting//, if it is indeed a domain, would be suitable for 'candle'.

12 In context with 'storm', 'snow' and 'desert', one could no doubt index 'moon' in the domain //weather//, since it is associated with the tides and the seasons.

13 Especially in context with 'glass', the aqueous nature of snow and storms activates a possible seme: /food/.

14 The domain //ornithology// will be even more appropriate if this is not a "lowly" chicken egg, but due to its elongation, the egg of some other bird.

15 With this semic series, we are introducing a class called "not applicable", and its applicability should be investigated, both here and in other series.

16 Although the storm, like snow, implies the presence of water, the storm itself is not edible.

17 This indexation is valid in French (but not in English) by homonymic rewriting, from '*chapeau melon*' ['melon hat'] (//clothing//) → |'melon'| (//food//).

18 'Glass' contains an application-oriented seme /for an edible element/, but is not edible itself. In other words, /edible/ is not governed here by the attributive case (ATT), only by the final case (FIN).

19 If we have a heat-producing function, we will indicate only the final seme intended (/hot/ or /warm/), and the same applies for a cooling function.

20 Should the moon be seen as a reflective celestial body, with no light or heat of its own, a nocturnal presence in opposition with the sun, and thus associated with cold (especially in context with 'snow')?

21 Should the storm be seen as a cooling climatic event?

22 The typical desert is hot, but in context with 'snow', the seme /cold/ may have some relevance.

23 The egg is intrinsically neutral, but implies a seme /to be warmed/ (by brooding) or even /to be cooked/.

24 The hat, the shoe and the ceiling are intrinsically neutral (that is, in the attributive), but they imply a seme /for keeping warm/ or /for keeping the cold out/ (or the seme /warm/ in the final).

25 A glass typically contains a cooling liquid. The cooling function – not just the thirst-quenching function – is no doubt made salient in context with the 'desert'.

26 Known as a "forging hammer", this kind of hammer is neutral in itself (that is, in the attributive), but implies a seme /for heated metals/ (or a seme /hot/ in the final case).

27 As an exotic tree, the acacia could be associated with the brightness attributed to a contextual element: the desert.

28 The moon itself appears to be bright, but it shines in darkness.

29 Since it is a covering, and opaque, thereby preventing light from coming in (usually from above), the ceiling would relate to darkness.

30 In our mental images, the storm and its "black" clouds darken the sky by intercepting rays of light from above, like the ceiling, but the storm also produces lightning.

31 The hot desert is associated with powerful, excessive brightness.

32 Since it hides its contents inside an opaque shell, the egg may be associated with darkness; it is in opposition with the obliging transparency of the glass, which lets us see whatever it holds.

33 By the fact that it affords protection from the sun, the hat could relate to brightness and heat. However, this kind of hat is used for "keeping warm", not for "cooling off."

34 Unlike the egg, the glass reveals its contents by its transparency, thus associating it with light.

35 The hammer is used to pound on heated (and thus bright) metals. The credibility of this interpretation is reinforced in context with the candle, another bright, melting object.

36 We are talking about colors that are thematized, colors as signifieds. As far as the images go, the thematized colors are a priori independent from the pigmentary colors used to generate the thematic representation. The glass obliges us to distinguish clearly between thematized color and the color of the signifier. The "color" being represented is transparency, whereas the color that is used to render transparency in the signifier is a blend of white, black and gray.

37 The color could be "other", in that the yellow acacia flowers are vivid in our mental images.

38 The moon is traditionally considered to be white.

39 Perhaps we should have gray and black for the storm, in reference to the darkening of the sky and the color of the storm clouds.

40 The desert's /bright/ feature would seem to evoke brilliant color series.

41 On this particular reproduction, the handle of the hammer is brownish, whereas the head is gray.

42 This relates to semes, of course, and therefore elements of content, or thematized elements.

43 We will ascribe straightness to the tree, if not for its general appearance, then certainly for the powerful force impelling it upward.

44 We traditionally view precipitation as forming straight, more or less continuous lines, slanted to some degree by the wind (as in Appollinaire's calligrams). Shifting from snow to snowflakes, straight lines predominate: under a microscope, the snowflake is replete with straight lines.

45 We generally think of deserts as rather flat expanses, relating them to surfaces dominated by straight lines.

46 The front part of the heel is a straight line, but curves seem to predominate overall.

47 Curves are clearly predominant, especially since this is a derby hat, and therefore rounded.

48 The tapered shape of the candle predisposes it toward straightness, but a few curves are present in the (ovoid) shape of the flame, the cylindrical shape of the candle and the pool of melted wax.

49 The longish shape of the glass has an element of straightness, but it appears less straight than the candle, because the shape is less elongated.

50 Although the predominant shape of the hammer is straight, the cylindrical shape of the head gives it some curvature as well.

51 Since high and low are relative, we should give a few more details. There is a large spatial amplitude evoked by the presence of celestial objects (the moon) or at least aerial objects (snow and the storm), along with elements located more or less at ground level (the shoe, the egg, precipitation). To take the example of the hat, it is among the terrestrial objects, and of these, it is lower than the ceiling or the acacia. Being located at the top of the human body, it is higher than the shoe. Moreover, some elements go from high to low or low to high at

(*Continued*)

Table 11.7 (Continued)

different speeds and with different amplitudes; in other words, the locative cases are different for the starting point and the destination: this is true of precipitation, the candle (driven upward by the flame and downward by melting), and the acacia (whose destination point is above the hat, since it grows three to six meters high). In this semic series, /high/ and /low/ are considered as synonyms of /celestial/ and /terrestrial/, but we will note other spatial details in passing.

52 The desert is usually thought of as a low-altitude expanse with very little relief.

53 The egg is a terrestrial product that comes from a creature of the air, theoretically, but since chickens and are not proficient at flying, they are associated with the ground, and in French, with the appropriately named "*basse-cour*" ["low-yard", which is the chicken yard].

54 The seme /high/ can be distinguished in 'shoe', since this shoe is "high-heeled", but this particular /high/ would not have the same value as the /high/ in our semic series. However, we should note that there is some upward movement from very low to slightly less low.

55 The glass can be linked to upward movement, since one raises it to one's mouth.

56 One moves a hammer from high to low to use it. The absence of shadows results in a kinesthetic interpretation of the image, and the head appears in a higher position, ready to come crashing down from gravitational force. This is the downward movement of a hammer in use. However, we should point out that this hammer is shown "upside down", with the crown upward and the peen downward.

57 In context with /water/ and 'glass', snow can be seen as a contained element, as can the storm, due to the water that it brings down.

58 Since it is part of a house, the ceiling participates in containing of a sort.

59 As a spatial substrate, the desert is somewhat like a container, or at least a supporting structure.

60 The eggshell is a container for what is inside.

61 The shoe is used to contain a foot.

62 The hat has a head as its contents, naturally.

63 The moon, the desert and the candle are similar in that they are not only solid, but clearly lacking in water (especially the first two).

64 Snow evokes the process of converting liquid to solid and vice versa, especially in context with 'candle'.

65 The shell and its contents are related to solid and liquid, respectively.

66 The shoe and the hat are used for protection from liquids.

67 The process of converting solid to liquid is depicted here in the durative phase (that is, in the middle of the action). The modal category of (strong) possibility allows us to anticipate the terminative phase (the end of the action). Note that the object melting ["*fond*"] in this image is labelled "*plafond*" ["ceiling"], that another signified, 'snow', refers directly to melting, and that another one, the forging hammer, indirectly suggests partial melting of metals. The effect of this rather plausible homonymic game is clearly to add salience to the seme /melt/ in 'candle' and in the other signifieds where it is already found. One has to wonder if the wordplay actualizes the same seme in '*plafond*' [ceiling].

68 The glass, which is solid, is by definition intended for liquids, and it is produced by going through a melting state, which is no doubt relevant in the context of what is suggested by the forging hammer and the candle, with the candle being a direct illustration of the melting process.

69 Although the hammer is solid, the elements being hammered are heated metals, that is, they are in an intermediate state between liquid and solid.

70 We have added /fire/ to this semic series because of the traditional opposition between this element and water, an opposition which seems to be recaptured in this painting, where water, flame and the desert are dramatically juxtaposed.

71 The aridity of the moon is emphasized in context with 'desert'. The contexts /water/ and /fertility/ bring out the (proven) function of regulating tides and (supposed) regulation of uterine fluid (which is not exactly water, though).

72 If lightning is involved, then we have fire.

73 It is clear that the fire involved here, a hyperbolic image for heat, is not the same kind of fire as in the candle or the lightning.

74 Strictly speaking, the seme /liquid/ is more applicable to the contents of the egg than the seme /water/.

75 The candle generates a liquid substance, but it is not water, strictly speaking.

76 The absence of water depicted in the glass is made salient by the label, "storm", which contains an overabundance of water.

77 Again, note that this is a hammer used for forging.

78 These semes must be seen as illustrating the interplay between modal variations (possible, impossible, real) and semantic cases (ergative, accusative). The search for these particular semes is motivated by the conspicuous presence of groups of terms that entertain destructive relations: 'snow'/'candle' and 'desert', 'hammer'/'egg' and 'glass'. Because of the childlike quality of the painting, with its A-B-C classroom style, it is tempting to view the collection of elements in this painting as a sort of "rock-scissors-paper" game. If there is a game, it is not as systematized as "rock-scissors-paper" (there is not just one destroying and destroyed element for each element of the combinatorial game). Some of the possible combinations are as follows: The glass can be broken by the hammer or even the shoe. The eggshell can be smashed by the shoe, the hammer or the glass. The desert (and less realistically, the moon) is fairly harmful to the egg. The fire and the candle (and less realistically, the desert) can damage the snow. The candle can be extinguished by precipitation and wind (or even by the glass, turned over). The candle damages itself by consuming itself. Over and above its aesthetic (or even seductive) function, the purpose of the shoe is to cover and protect the foot. The acacia is subject to the violence of the storm and the destructive force of the desert. The hat protects one from precipitation and cold (the word "snow" is used for its label), but it also protects from the sun, especially in context with 'desert' and, by opposition, with 'moon'. The eggshell protects the embryo. "Damage" is meant as a transformation deemed to be negative, which does not appear to be the case with the abstract forging of metal suggested by the sledge hammer. The moon plays the role of the most un-damageable element, along with the hammer, to a lesser degree; it is in opposition with the egg, snow and the glass, which are clearly the most fragile elements.

79 The acacia is both familiar and exotic: it produces a well-known flower and it comes from "Arabia" (which is where we get the name "Arabia gum" for the gum it produces). In this respect, it is connected with the desert, possibly serving to locate it.

80 By itself, an egg is familiar, especially if it is a chicken egg.

81 It was much more common for men to wear hats during the era when the painting was produced than it is now; the hat is not a particularly unusual accessory. However, we should check on the status of the derby hat in European men's headwear during that period.

82 This hammer is in fact more specialized than a household hammer; it is a "forging hammer."

(*Continued*)

Table 11.7 (Continued)

Others semes: animal/plant/mineral, aesthetic/utilitarian, durable/fragile, full/empty, dynamic/static, heavy/light, single/compound, precipitation, etc.

Legend:

Basic symbols

"sign"
'signified'
signifier

Semic symbols

/seme/ or /semic repetition/
/a/, /b/, /c/, /d/, /e/ . . . : actualized seme, identified by letter according to its position in a series of semes
mag: macrogeneric seme (indicates that it belongs to a dimension)
meg: mesogeneric seme (indicates that it belongs to a domain)
mig: microgeneric seme (indicates that it belongs to a taxeme)
spe: specific seme (distinguishes a signified from the other signifieds belonging to the same taxeme)

Case symbols (links between semes)

(ACC): accusative, the patient of an action; the entity affected by the action
(ASS): assumptive, point of view
(ATT): attributive, a characteristic
(BEN): benefactive, the entity for whose benefit the action is performed
(COMP): comparative, compared elements
(DAT): dative, the receiver, entity that receives a transmission
(ERG): ergative, the agent of a process or an action
(FIN): final, goal (result or effect sought)
(INST): instrumental, the means used
(MAL): malefactive, the entity to whose disadvantage the action is performed
(LOC): locative, position as represented in time (LOC T) or space (LOC S)
(RES): resultative, result, consequence.

Other symbols

//semantic class// (a group of interdefined signifieds)
→ |interpretive rewriting|
[lexical label]

Notes

1 In actuality, the signifier and the signified are both mental constructs, and in this respect, they derive from understanding and not perception (and this is why we have placed "perceptible" in quotation marks). Unlike the signified, the signifier (e.g., a phoneme, as in phonology) does have correlates in the physical world (e.g., a phoneme taking form as a particular sound, which is the subject of phonetics).

2 One can broaden the usual meaning of "molecule" (a cluster of specific semes) to include generic and/or specific semes. In addition, we propose the notion of a hybrid molecule for a semic cluster that contains at least one semantic case.

3 In order to distinguish between types and tokens of semic molecules, one can use the terms "semic molecule" (a term with a restricted sense) and "**semic complex**."

4 As an element of macrosemantic dialectics, an actor is a semic molecule lexicalized by its tokens at the mesosemantic level, which are called **actants** (which have no direct relation to Greimas's concept of the same name). For example, the actor 'cicada' in "The cicada and the ant" is manifested by the following tokens, in order of tactical appearance: 'Cicada', 'her', 'herself", 'she', 'she', 'she', 'I', 'my', 'mendicant', 'I', 'I', 'You'. An actor is not limited a priori to any particular class of natural ontology (it can be human, an object, a concept, etc.).

5 Each "side" of the homology thus defines a semic molecule and an isotopic bundle that are in opposition with the molecule and the bundle on the other side. However, not every molecule or every bundle has to be part of a homology.

6 Like semes, cases will be inherent/afferent and actualized/virtualized.

7 The significance of each molecule one identifies is proportional to the significance of each of its semic actualizations; this is why isotopic analysis must be conscientiously done before identifying the molecules, or at least before "visually" identifying them with a table.

8 This sonnet, which was written sometime between May 26 and August 9, 1899, is strongly reminiscent of Rimbaud: "A great golden ship, above me, flutters many-colored pennants in the morning breeze." ("Farewell", from *A season in hell*, a collection that came out in October 1873).

9 In addition, the isotopy /navigation/ is also the comparing term for an isotopy that we will call /existential/; this comparative relation is "revealed" in the line "Where is my heart, that empty ship, or where?"

10 In literature, Stendhal comes to mind; the novel is a mirror that we hold up as we travel down a road.

11 We would like to acknowledge Judith Langevin for her help with the preliminary version of this analysis.

12 Dialogics

Summary

In François Rastier's interpretive semantics, dialogics is the component based on the modalization of semantic units, and includes evaluations of ontological status (real/unreal (or impossible)/possible), veridictory status (true/false), thymic value (positive/negative (or euphoric/dysphoric)), and any other modal evaluation. In this chapter we will cover only the ontological and veridictory aspects of dialogics. In ontological and veridictory dialogics, each semantic unit is assigned a veridictory status and an ontological status (corresponding to a specific world), and is situated in a universe associated with an evaluative focus (a specific character, for example). In the universe of reference, the units are modalized in accordance with the absolute truth of the text; the other universes, which may be contradicted by the universe of reference, are called universes of assumption. Consider the following story: *On Monday, Lucy and Paul buy a lottery ticket. On Tuesday, Lucy finds out that they have won, but Paul – the idiot – doesn't believe it, leaves her on the spot, and dies without giving in.* On Monday, the semantic unit *they win* is marked as 'possible' and 'true' in the universe of assumption of each of the two characters. On Tuesday, it becomes real and true in Lucy's universe, but real and false in Paul's. The universe of reference, which corresponds to the narrator's universe of assumption, is identical to Lucy's universe and different from Paul's. (Paul is wrong – the narrator describes him as an idiot.)

Theory

Dialogics defined

In François Rastier's interpretive semantics, four components make up the semantic plane of texts (the plane of content, or signifieds, as opposed to the plane of expression, or signifiers): (1) thematics (the invested content), (2) dialectics (states and processes and the actors involved in them), (3) tactics (the linear sequencing of content) and (4) dialogics. Dialogics is the semantic component that relates to modalization, which includes evaluations of ontological status (real/unreal (or impossible)/possible), veridictory status (true/false), thymic value (positive/negative (or euphoric/dysphoric)), and other modal evaluations. In this section we will focus on the ontological and veridictory aspects of dialogics[1] (for further analysis, see Rastier, 1997; Hébert, 2001, 2003, 2007a, 2020).

Elements of ontological and veridictory analysis

In ontological and veridictory dialogics, each belief is analyzed by means of the following elements:

(1) A semantic unit (modalized unit), formulated as a logical proposition (for instance: *the Earth is round*).

(2) The proposition is assigned a truth value, that is to say, a veridictory status (true or false) (for example: *the Earth is round*: true). Furthermore, this proposition is situated in one of the three worlds into which a universe may be subdivided: the actual world (what is), the counterfactual world (what is not, or cannot be), or the possible world (what could be).

NOTE: UNDECIDABLE AND UNDECIDED UNITS

A unit is said to be *decidable* with respect to a given modal category (e.g., veridiction) if it is assigned at least one status in that category (such as true); otherwise, it is said to be *undecidable* (notated # or UND). In addition, the concept *undecided* will no doubt be of some use to describe units that have not (yet) been modalized. A unit is said to be undecided (notated as ø) with respect to a given modal category if it is present in a universe and it has not (yet) been evaluated in terms of that particular modal category. For example, the unit *this wine is excellent*, marked as real and true by one enologist, maybe undecided for another enologist who completely withholds judgment as long as he has not personally tasted it (this would exclude the category of possibility). The concepts decidable, undecidable and undecided can be applied, in fact, to any classification, whether modal or not.

(3) To each world there corresponds a specific ontological status, that is, its status relative to ontology, or existence. The status is assigned to a semantic unit situated in that world. Ontological status is assigned as follows: for the actual world: real (or assertoric) (for example: *the Earth is round*: true, real); for the counterfactual world: unreal or impossible (for example: the Earth is flat: true, unreal); for the possible world: possible (for example: *I will win the lottery with my ticket*: possible).

(4) A universe is associated with a specific focus (an evaluating subject), which provides the propositions and modalizes them (for instance, a character or even several characters, if they share exactly the same beliefs, or at least those selected for the analysis). A universe, then, is made up of a set of evaluated units and their respective ontological and veridictory statuses, which are associated with a specific focus, or "point of view" (such as a certain character, the narrator, or an evaluator that is implicit in the lexicon of the language (in pejorative or meliorative (ameliorative) words and expressions)).

NOTE: FOCUS AND RELAY FOCUS

There is a distinction to be made between focus and relay focus. A relay focus conveys a unit and an accompanying evaluation that actually originates from another, hierarchically superior focus. For example, the proposition "Women are weak creatures", marked as real and true, which one finds in many texts, especially prior to the 20th century, is a cliché, a common place or topos, and because of this, it belongs to a system (a sociolect) that goes beyond the author or the character that conveys it. As a point of methodology, one can choose not to distinguish the focus from the relay focus.

(5) Over time, a proposition may appear in or disappear from a universe, shift to another world and thereby change its ontological status, its veridictory status, or even its formulation (*Mary is beautiful* could become *Mary is very beautiful*). In addition, a single unit can be situated simultaneously in several worlds. There are several kinds of time, and each type can form the basis for a temporal structure in the semiotic act being analyzed: time as represented in the story being told, the narrative time of the story (which can even be the reverse of the story's time), and tactical time (based on the sequencing of elements such as words, sentences and chapters). For further details on temporal segmentation, consult the chapter on the veridictory square.

The origin of units

Any unit may be an original, an image or a replica. An image is a unit that happens to be duplicated, either within one universe (usually in another world of that universe) or in another, but is modalized in a different manner. Replicas are units that are modalized in the same manner as the units they are "copied" from in another universe. It does not seem to be an essential part of descriptive practice to specify a unit's origin. We should simply point out that any modalized unit relayed by a relay focus (see above) is a replica of the unit from the original focus.

Possible worlds and the veridictory category

We consider semantic units situated in the possible world as having no veridictory status (true or false). (For example: It will rain tomorrow: possible). Obviously, when a proposition is possible, the reverse proposition is also possible; in order to simplify, we use only the proposition that is being emphasized. (For instance, saying that it is possible I will win also implies that it is possible I will not win; so we can simply use the first proposition by itself.) When a possible proposition is validated or invalidated, it then moves to the actual world (and/or the counterfactual world). If on Monday the weather forecaster says that it will rain Tuesday, for instance, this proposition is situated in the possible world on Monday; on Tuesday it moves to the actual world and is assigned a status of either 'true' (if it rained) or 'false' (if it didn't rain).

The counterfactual world, lies and conflicts of belief

In descriptive practice, the counterfactual world essentially serves to account for the most common forms of lies and "conflicts of belief" (other kinds do exist, involving the possible world). In a conflict of belief (the reverse being a consensus of belief), the contradictor's semantic unit and its veridictory status are found in the counterfactual world.

The classic change of belief that can often follow a conflict of belief and resolve it is represented by the movement of one semantic unit and its veridictory status from the actual world to the counterfactual world. Conversely, the unit previously situated in the counterfactual world "changes residence" along with its veridictory status to the actual world. For instance, for a Christian who converts to Buddhism, the true proposition *reincarnation does not exist* moves to the counterfactual world, while the true proposition *reincarnation exists* moves to the actual world. A "conversion" may or may not be preceded by doubt, during which the belief and the counter-belief confront each other in the possible world, or by verification, whose purpose is to select one belief according to specific tests and criteria.

In the classic lie, the evaluating actor (a character, for instance) presents his counterfactual world as actual and vice-versa. For example, in Molière's *Don Juan*, the true proposition *I want to marry you* is part of Don Juan's counterfactual world, but he presents it as residing in his actual world; the false proposition *I want to marry you* is part of Don Juan's actual world, but he presents it as residing in his counterfactual world.

Let us distinguish the different phases of a consensus or conflict of belief: appearance, maintenance and resolution. The possibility of a conflict of belief arises only when there is a restrictive standard of validity, judged to be erroneous by some other agent. (A relativist will regard as equally valid all of the beliefs set in opposition by an absolutist, who will select a particular belief as *the* right one.)

A conflict of beliefs has an internal and/or external dimension, and it operates in active or passive mode. The external dimension appears only if the conflict involves more than one evaluating actor (which excludes internal conflicts within one actor). The internal dimension is always present. In its internal dimension, the presence of an active conflict is indicated by the appearance of (or emphasis on, considering that the propositions are already implicitly there) opposing propositions and their veridictory status in the counterfactual world of the actor or actors involved.

For each actor involved, a conflict moves toward consensus only if there is a total or partial conversion, which may be unilateral or reciprocal (or ironically, total and reciprocal on occasion) or if there is a movement toward a mutually nonexclusive system. If the conflict is not resolved, this means that it is integral to maintain the beliefs or the exclusive system.

There are different degrees of conflict (a disagreement on modal status or values is often more "serious" than a disagreement on the intensity of those values, if the perspective is incremental), which may be experienced by all of the involved parties, some of them, only one, or none of them. For example, Paul knows that Mary and Andrew (who do not know each other) do not have the same values, or Paul discovers that Mary is wrong, but he does not tell her.

For convenience, the analysis may leave out the counterfactual world and use only the actual and possible worlds. The distinction between these two worlds can even become optional, if we establish a modal triad with equal weight given to the ontological status "possible" and the veridictory statuses "true" and "false"; For instance, the proposition *it is raining Monday* would simply be marked as possible on Sunday, and as true or false come Tuesday. At that point, if the counterfactual world is left out, the distinction between worlds and universes becomes useless.

Up until now, we have only implicitly addressed the relations between dialogic units. We will add some details. Any two units, whether identical, similar or different, can be connected dialogically. For instance, if p is true, then q is false (if $2 + 2 = 4$ is true, then $2 + 2 = 5$ is false); if p is true in the actual world, then it is false if it is located in the counterfactual world (for example: if $2 + 2 = 4$ is true and real, then it is false if it is located in the counterfactual world). The rules of association (presupposition, implication, exclusion, compatibility, etc.) have no a priori validity; they depend on the genre and the text being analyzed.

Universes of assumption and universes of reference

There are two kinds of universes: universes of assumption and universes of reference. A text's universe of reference is the universe containing the units that are accurately modalized according to the text. The universe of reference may or may not be reflected in one or more universes of assumption (the character-narrator's universe, for instance, or the omniscient narrator's). The universe of reference is what allows us to find out the "actual truth" in a text.

To give an example, in simple terms, one can say that the proposition *The Big Bad Wolf wants to devour Little Red Riding Hood* is true and real in the BBW's universe and in the story's universe of reference, from the time he meets RRH to the end of the story. Conversely, it is false and real in RRH's universe (we could also say that it is absent from her universe, since the idea never even occurs to her) until the cruel moment of awakening when the BBW reveals who he really is, a BBW.

NOTE: UNIVERSES AND AGENTS OF COMMUNICATION

It is helpful, and sometimes necessary when there is disagreement between universes, to set up separate universes for each agent of communication (an example is given in the next section). We shall distinguish in textual terms (although most distinctions are valid for other kinds of semiotic acts) between the empirical author (the "real" flesh-and-blood author), the invented or implied author (the impression that the text gives of its author), the narrator, the narratee, the invented or implied reader (a model reader, for instance, supplied by the text), and the empirical reader.

A simple ontological-veridictory analysis

Consider the following story:

Mary says that the sun rises in the West. Paul does not believe it. Andy maintains that it's possible. They decide to stay awake that night to wait for the sunrise . . . The victims of a collective illusion, they observe that . . . the sun rises in the East.

This is an analytical table describing the story about Mary and Paul (possibility is included on the same level as true/false):

Table 12.1 A simple ontological-veridictory analysis

	TIME	*UNIVERSE AND FOCUS*	*STATUS*	*SEMANTIC UNIT*
1	T1	Mary's U.	true	Proposition 1: The sun rises in the West
2	T1	Paul's U.	false	P1
3	T1	Andy's U.	possible	P1
4	T2	Mary's, Paul's and Andy's U.	false	P1
5	T1-T2	U. of reference	true	P1
6	T1-T2	Reader's (invented and empirical) U.	false	P1

"The victims of a collective illusion" indicates that P1 is true in the universe of reference, which is identical to the narrator's. However, in the reader's reality (implied or empirical), the sun rises in the East.

Applications

Application I: does the earth revolve around the sun?

Confronted with the inadequacies of Ptolemy's cosmological system, Nicholas Copernicus (1473–1543) initiated the shift from geocentrism to heliocentrism (the recognition of the planets' individual rotation coupled with their movement around the Sun). The proofs that were lacking in Copernicus's system were developed by Kepler (1571–1630) and Galileo (1564–1642). In 1616, Pope Paul V condemned Copernicus's ideas as being contrary to Scripture.

Proposition 1: The Earth is motionless and is located at the center of the universe.
Proposition 2: The Earth rotates and it revolves around the Sun.

A At Time 1: The Vatican's dialogic universe, before its confrontation with Copernicus, Kepler and Galileo, is as follows:

Actual world: P1 true, P2 irrelevant (P1 is a given).

B At Time 2: Galileo's dialogic universe is configured in the following way:

Actual world: P1 false, P2 true.
Counterfactual world (which reflects the actual universe of the contradictors, the universe of the popes and the church): P1 true, P2 false.

C At Time 3: Condemned, Galileo recants his theory. After his retraction, however, he is supposed to have muttered: "*Eppur', si muove!*" ("And yet, it does move!"). In other words, he presented his counterfactual world as actual (one of the "lie" scenarios) to the Inquisition. The structure of his dialogic worlds did not actually change, then, compared with time 2 (see point B).

D At Times 2 and 3: The official position[2] of the Vatican – and therefore of the Church – during and after Copernicus, Kepler and Galileo, up until John-Paul II, was as follows:

Actual world: P1: true, P2 false.
Counterfactual world (reflects the actual universe of the heliocentric contradictors): P1: false, P2: true.

E At Time 4: Pope John-Paul II (and his successors, we presume!) officially accepts Copernicus's and Galileo's position. His dialogic universe, and that of the Church, was configured thusly:

Actual world: P1 false, P2 true.
Counterfactual world: P1 true, P2 false.

There were and are other possible positions, such as:

F At Time 2: Contemporary thinkers whose views were shaken by Galileo's arguments, but who were not totally convinced or those who were influenced by the skeptics would have a dialogic universe structured in this way:

Possible world: P2 (or P1 possibly false and P2 possibly true).

Our complete analysis is summarized in the following table.

Table 12.2 An ontological-veridictory analysis

	TIME	*UNIVERSE AND FOCUS*	*WORLD*	*VERIDICTORY STATUS*	*SEMANTIC UNIT*
1	T2-T3	Galileo's U.	actual	true	P2: The Earth rotates and revolves around the Sun.
2				false	P1: The Earth is motionless and is located at the center of the universe
3			counterfactual	false	P2
4				true	P1
5	T3	Galileo's U. (he is lying)	actual	false	P2
6				true	P1
7			counterfactual	true	P2
8				false	P1
9	T1	The popes' U.	actual	true	P1
10					(P2 is absent from this universe)
11	T2-T3	The popes' U.	actual	false	P2
12				true	P1
13			counterfactual	true	P2
14				false	P1
15	T4	U. of John-Paul II	actual	true	P2
16				false	P1
17			counterfactual	false	P2
18				true	P1
19	T2	U. of open-minded people	possible		P2 (or P1 false, P2 true)

The analysis in the table below is a simplified one. It lists only proposition 1 (since the veridictory statuses of the two propositions are always opposite, anyway) and it does not include the distinction between the worlds (it is understood that anything marked as true or false is part of the actual world, and anything marked as possible resides in the possible world). If we want to leave out proposition 2, we are obliged to put a veridictory status (false, in this instance) for the proposition that is in the possible world.

Table 12.3 A simplified ontological-veridictory analysis

	TIME	*UNIVERSE AND FOCUS*	*STATUS*	*SEMANTIC UNIT*
1	T2-T3	Galileo's U.	false	P1: The Earth is motionless and is located at the center of the universe
2	T3	Galileo's U. (he is lying)	true	P1
3	T1-T3	The popes' U.	true	P1
4	T4	U. of John-Paul II	false	P1
5	T2	U. of open-minded people	false (possible)	P1

Application II: "Which is the true one?" by Charles Baudelaire

* * *

"Which is the true one?"
Baudelaire, *The parisian prowler*

I met a certain Benedicta, who filled the atmosphere with the ideal, and whose eyes spread the desire for grandeur, beauty, fame, and everything which makes us believe in immortality.

But that miraculous girl was too beautiful to live a long time. So she died a few days after I had made her acquaintance, and it is I myself who buried her, one day when spring was shaking its censer even into the cemeteries. It is I who buried her, tightly sealed into a coffin made of aromatic and rot-proof wood like Indian chests.

And since my eyes were fastened on the place where my treasure was buried, all of a sudden I saw a little person who amazingly resembled the deceased, and who, stamping the fresh soil with a hysterical and weird violence, was saying with bursts of laughter, "It is I, the true Benedicta! It is I, a first-class riffraff! And to punish your madness and your blindness, you will love me as I am!"

But I was furious, and answered, "No! No! No!" And to emphasize my refusal more, I stamped the ground so violently that my leg sank up to the knee in the recent burial place and so, like a trapped wolf, I remain fettered, perhaps forever, to the grave of the ideal.

* * *

The two dialogic units that we have selected from this prose poem by Baudelaire are the following:

P1: *B1 is Benedicta*;
P2: *B2 is Benedicta*;

If one presumes the text's mimetic mode to be realistic, then there is a relation of mutual exclusion between the two propositions: they cannot both be true or false at the same time.[3]

NOTE: FORMULATING THE PROPOSITIONS

Our central proposition is formulated in terms of existence rather than in terms of truth. This allows us to keep the same kind of proposition for all of the text's time intervals. A proposition like *B1 is the real Benedicta* actually has no relevance, strictly speaking, before time T6. Until then, it is not part of the characters' universes (although one can include it in hindsight). Even formulated as they are, our propositions are not always completely relevant, except in hindsight, since there is an assumption when we speak of *B1* that we know about the existence of *B2*.

We have four universes that relate to the propositions we have selected:

U *I*: The universe of *I*;
UN *I*: The universe of the narrator *I*;

The narrative's past tense is what justifies separating *I* into two characters, each one associated with a universe. As a general rule, narrating in the first person and the past tense allows for dialogic discord between the narrator and the narrator as he presents himself in the past.[4]

U B2: The universe of B2 (the living Benedicta);
UR: The text's universe of reference.

We will make use of two of the three kinds of worlds, and the ontological categories defining them:

AW: The actual world; status: assertoric (real);
CFW: The counterfactual world, status: unreal or impossible.

We have identified eight textual time intervals:

T1 = *I* has not yet met Benedicta 1;
T2 = *I* meets Benedicta 1;
T3 = *I* keeps company briefly with Benedicta 1;
T4 = Benedicta 1 dies;
T5 = *I* buries Benedicta 1;
T6 = Benedicta 2 accosts *I* and states her propositions;
T7 = *I* replies and is caught in the grave;
T8 = *I* "remains" (changing to the present indicative) in that state, "perhaps forever".

At the beginning of the text, *I* believes that *B1 is Benedicta* is true. The absence of a conflict of belief is signaled by the absence of opposing propositions in his counterfactual world; or at least they are not salient. The irruption of the second Benedict tests the firmness of his belief. The counterfactual propositions and their veridictory statuses correspond to the propositions located in the actual world of the other character. Thus, we have two conflicting hypotheses: *B1 is Benedicta* is evaluated as a true hypothesis by *I*, and *B2 is Benedicta* is submitted and held as a true proposition by B2 (and there is nothing to indicate that she is employing deception to present her counterfactual world as actual).

Who is right? Is someone right or wrong? In other words, what does the universe of reference contain? Two likely answers are directly opposed: the first leans toward the undecidable; the other posits the second Benedicta as the real one, and sets us in pursuit of another question: Does *I* change his mind, and if so, to undecidability or to the opposing hypothesis? The second solution, which requires a more demanding interpretive trajectory, is of particular interest, and we will attempt to substantiate it.[5]

In order to demonstrate the plausibility of the second hypothesis, it may help to review some of the elements of Baudelaire's idiolect.[6] We know that one of the features of Baudelairean aesthetics is to *pervert* the Platonic triad of truth, goodness and beauty by elevating falseness, evil, and sometimes ugliness (in the ordinary meaning of the word: for instance, a carcass) by correlating them, or by subjugating the first two to the primacy of beauty (in the highest meaning of the word). In this version of Pancalism, beauty generally originates from falseness and evil; it is the main escape route from *spleen* and somehow leads to a higher truth. In the text we are analyzing, the narrator, confronted with two apparently identical women, wonders which one is the real one: the ideal one, who is dead, or the one who is still alive and full of faults? Baudelaire's habit of glorifying falseness and his disparagement of the real woman, the natural one, support the second hypothesis. The false one is the perfect woman, the ephemeral, dazzling one, who is dead precisely because, like the poet (the albatross in Baudelaire's poem), she was a misfit in this too-real, prosaic, pernicious world (a Christian, and no doubt symbolist, topos). Although it is always possible to find tokens that contradict Baudelaire's type, and although some features of his idiolect point in a different direction ("Baudelairean doubt", for instance), we must conclude that the idiolect supports the second hypothesis.

We will now address the corollary issue. There are a few elements pointing to the plausibility of *I*'s conversion to the second hypothesis. First, the veridictory status of the first hypothesis in *I*'s universe is of low intensity.[7] *I* has only a limited acquaintance with Benedicta, whom he knew for just a few days. He speaks about a *certain* Benedicta – a way of speaking doubtfully, but by using a term that also is a marker for certainty. Then, at the end of the text, the narrator manifests values of the Baudelairean idiolect by taking them on, supporting the second interpretation, as we have just described: *I remain fettered, perhaps forever, to the grave of the ideal* [*la fosse de l'idéal*]. Moreover, a homonymic relation seemingly delivers a reply: Benedicta 1 is the *fausse de l'idéal* [the false of the ideal].[8] If this is actually the case, does the conversion occur before the character *I* "merges" with the narrator *I* (time 8); in other words, does it apply just to the narrator *I*? In our opinion, the conversion involves both *I*'s, meaning that it occurs before the narrative fusion, probably during *I*'s fit of rage. His anger, in this case, would indicate not so much his certainty about being right as his vexation over beliefs that are not so. However, there is nothing to indicate that B2 notices *I*'s conversion. In conclusion, *I* moves from error to truth, relative to the (final) reference universe. The effect of this conversion is to exchange propositions between the actual world and the counterfactual world (or to exchange veridictory statuses, if you prefer). Other than the origin of the units, then, the universe of reference is identical to the assumptive universes of B2, the narrator *I*, and the actor *I* after his conversion.

The following table illustrates the (simplified) dialogic configuration of the two propositions in "Which is the true one?" In it, we show only the interpretation that we have analyzed (*B2 is the true one;* both *I*'s are in agreement). And even for this interpretation, we have not indexed every occurrence of each proposition or the potential propositions in the possible worlds.

Table 12.4 Two propositions in "Which is the true one?"

	TIME	*UNIVERSE*	*WORLD*	*VERIDICTORY STATUS*	*PROPOSITION*
1	T2-T5	U *I*	AW	T	B1 is Benedicta
2	T6-T8	U *I*	AW	T	B2 is Benedicta
3	T6-T8	U *I*	AW	F	B1 is Benedicta
4	T6-T8	U *I*	CFW	T	B1 is Benedicta
5	T6-T8	U *I*	CFW	F	B2 is Benedicta
6	T6-T8	U B2	AW	T	B2 is Benedicta
7	T6-T8	U B2	AW	F	B1 is Benedicta
8	T6-T8	U B2	CFW	T	B1 is Benedicta
9	T6-T8	U B2	CFW	F	B2 is Benedicta
10		UR	AW	T	B2 is Benedicta
11		UR	AW	F	B1 is Benedicta
12		UR	CFW	T	B1 is Benedicta
13		UR	CFW	F	B2 is Benedicta

Notes

1 In the chapter on thymic analysis, we present a simplified version of Rastier's thymic dialogics, to which we have added some details (Hébert, 2001, pp. 140–166, 2003, 2007a, 2020); one could also consider it as a further development of Greimasian axiological analysis (presented in the chapter on figurative, thematic and axiological analysis). To compare thymic analysis with thymic dialogics, the opposition between the evaluator (focus) and the unit being evaluated (the unit) has been replaced with the opposition between subject and object, and the concepts of universe, world, image and replica are avoided. For an example of an analysis using thymic dialogics, refer to the chapter on thymic analysis and replace the terms *subject* and *object* with *focus* (or *evaluating actor*) and *unit being evaluated* (or *actor being evaluated*), respectively.

2 One would hope that there were disagreements about this matter between the "official" universe of several popes and their "unofficial" universe. The process of reversing the two worlds (presenting the actual world as counterfactual and vice versa) entails a false participation in the contradictors' universe, since the falsified universe becomes identical to that of the contradictors, at least with regard to the propositions at issue. The example under discussion allows us to discern other elements for a typology of universes and focuses, since in calling forth a sort of model believer whom the "empirical", "real" believers must imitate, it establishes an opposition between empirical focuses (or evaluators) and model focuses, between empirical universes and model universes.

3 In fact, the presence of an isotopy, "miraculous", discloses a mimetic mode that is not realistic. So the opposing propositions are not mutually exclusive: the two people can both be Benedicta. The second Benedicta could also be some form in which the first survived: Did they not resemble each other "*singulièrement*" [amazingly]? – a word full of associations, occurring as it does in a text on duality. The character seems to be predesigned to elude death: This "miraculous" girl who created the desire for "everything which makes us believe in immortality" is buried in a coffin of "rot-proof" wood, which no doubt "explains" why the narrator is trapped, "perhaps forever."

4 In the main interpretation that we have worked out, B2 exists before her encounter with *I*, and her universe contains the proposition *B2 is Benedicta*, which is uncontested at that point. In the "miraculous" interpretation that we touch upon, as the continuance of B1, B2 cannot inhabit a temporal space prior to the death or burial of B1.

5 An interpretation that incorporates undecidability poses more difficulties than one would think: If, for instance, the universe of reference is concerned with undecidability, then does the same apply to the assumptive universes of the actor *I* and the narrator *I*?

6 An idiolect may be identified by doing a comparative analysis of other works by the same author and the sociolects from which the idiolect separated (see the chapter on semic analysis). We can only briefly sketch out a comparative analysis of the author's works. Another prose poem by Baudelaire deals with the same theme: "The counterfeit coin." The narrator tells how his friend, after carefully sorting through his change, gives a counterfeit coin to a beggar in an appearance of generosity. After his friend sets him straight, the narrator begins to imagine the extraordinary possibilities opened up by this gesture: the beggar could receive real coins in exchange for the counterfeit one, or end up in jail . . . The narrator would have forgiven his friend for wanting to add some spice to the beggar's life, but he finally realizes that his small-minded friend was trying to scrimp on a good deed. Veridiction is strongly thematized in both of these texts through their emphasis on falseness, and in both cases the narrator believes in an object valued as euphoric, which is then revealed to be false. But the title of the first poem is a question and its veridictory status is disputable; the title of the second one is affirmative, and its veridictory status is clear. In the first case the valued object is false; in the second it is valued because it is false. In the prose poem "Windows", the veridictory status is considered to be negligible, but notice that the exhilarating "legend" constructed by the narrator is very likely false: "Perhaps you will ask, "Are you sure that legend is the true one?" Does it matter what the reality located outside of me might be, if it has helped me to live, to feel that I am and *what* I am?" Some other elements in the same collection of poems

deserve closer attention than space allows: the title "The double room", the cortège of men, each carrying a chimera ("To each his chimera"), the "little savage [. . .] so perfectly resembling the first that you could take him for his twin brother" (in "The cake"), "the false goddess" (in "The temptations"), the reflections on illusion in "The rope", and others still.

7 We could incorporate the attenuation of veridictory status in our analysis by assigning an incremental veridictory status (± T) to the proposition *B1 is Benedicta*, or a more far-reaching approach would be to mark it as very true in a possible world, or even as slightly undecidable in the actual world. The attenuation of veridictory status does not necessarily come from *I*; we could also consider it as a part of the universe of narration: The narrator lets a hint of suspicion creep through in hindsight, and in keeping with the standards for plausibility, the time intervals prior to the conversion are peppered with indices (for example, the expression "a certain Benedicta").

8 In placing the homonymic wordplay in final position tactically, the poem follows a general standard: a text usually delivers the answer to the question under debate (which in this case appears in the title) somewhere near the end. In the first edition of the text (*Le boulevard*, June 14, 1863), "fosse" was replaced with "folie" ["madness"], but Pichois (Baudelaire, 1975, p. 1344) wonders if this was a typographical error.

13 The semantic graph

Summary

A tool introduced by Rastier (and based on Sowa, 1984), the semantic graph can be used to represent any semantic structure in terms of semes and the relations between them. The semes are the nodes of the semantic graph (shown in boxes or brackets) and the relations are the links (shown in ellipses or parentheses). The arrows indicate the direction of the relation between nodes. Most semantic structures can be described using fifteen or so different links – like ERG (ergative) for the agent of an action and ACC (accusative) for the patient of an action. This is an example of a simple graph: [Prince] ← (ERG) ← [RESCUE] → (ACC) → [Princess].

Theory

Function

Rastier's semantic graphs (see Rastier, 1997 [1989]; Hébert, 2001, 2007a, 2020), which are based on Sowa's conceptual graphs (1984), can be used to make a formal, rigorous, comprehensive and elegant representation of any semantic structure: a word, an entire text, a topos (an argumentative or narrative cliché), a character, an action, an image, or what have you.[1] A structure is an entity composed of at least two terms (the linked elements) joined by at least one relation.

Elements

Nodes, links and the direction of the link

The elements that make up this structure are the nodes (the terms), the links (the relations) and the direction of the links.[2] A node is generally labelled with one or more semes (semantic features, or parts of a signified) and a link is labelled with a semantic case (or case, for short).[3] At the center of the graph one generally places a node corresponding to a process (filled in with either a verb or a noun, such as *transmit* or *transmission*), written in uppercase letters.

NOTE: NODES, LINKS AND LABELS

The particular semes and cases that invest the nodes and links on a given graph are known as the labels for these nodes and links. Where necessary, we will distinguish the node or link per se (as a sort of empty slot) from its label. Otherwise, when we speak of nodes and links, we are including their labels.

Here is a simple graph shown in text format (later we will give the strictly graphical format), where (ERG) corresponds to the ergative case (the agent of an action) and (ACC) to the accusative case (the patient of an action, the one affected by it):

[dog] ← (ERG) ← [BITE] → (ACC) → [mailman]

The following table summarizes the constituent elements of a semantic graph and the symbols used to represent them:

Table 13.1 The elements and symbols of a graph

	ELEMENTS OF A GRAPH	*TYPE OF LABEL*	*SYMBOL USABLE IN TEXT FORMAT*	*SYMBOL USABLE IN GRAPH FORMAT*
1	node	seme	brackets: [seme]	rectangular box
2	link	case	uppercase abbreviation in parentheses: (CAS)	uppercase abbreviation inside an ellipse (Rastier) or on the link (Hébert)
3	direction of a link between nodes		arrow: → or ←	arrow

NOTE: ALTERNATIVE FORMATS

To make the graphs more immediately understandable, the links may be written out as complete words rather than abbreviations. And to distinguish nodes from links, one can simply use the opposition between upper and lowercase by itself, or use parentheses or circles for the links, with no symbol for the nodes.

Case

The inventory of possible labels for nodes is open-ended; the inventory of labels for the links (that is, the cases) is limited methodologically, depending on the discourse, the genre, the author, or even the particular semiotic act one is analyzing.[4] The semantic cases shown in the following table can adequately account for most textual semantic structures.[5]

Table 13.2 The primary semantic cases

	CASE	*DEFINITION*	*POSSIBLE NAME FOR TEACHING PURPOSES*
(ACC)	accusative	the patient of an action; the entity affected by the action	PATient
(ASS)	assumptive	point of view	PERspective
(ATT)	attributive	property, characteristic	CHARacteristic
(BEN)	benefactive	the entity for whose benefit the action is performed	BENeficiary
(CLAS)	classitive	an element of a class	CLASsitive
(COMP)	comparative	elements joined by a metaphorical comparison	COMParison
(DAT)	dative	receiver, entity that receives a transmission	RECeiver
(ERG)	ergative	the agent of a process or an action	AGEnt
(FIN)	final	goal (result or effect sought)	GOAL
(INST)	instrumental	means used	MEAns
(LOC S)	spatial locative	position in the space represented (LOC S)	SPAce
(LOC T)	temporal locative	position in the time represented (LOC T)	TIME
(MAL)	malefactive	the entity to whose disadvantage the action is performed	MALeficiary
(WHOL)	wholitive	part of a whole	WHOLitive
(RES)	resultative	result, effect, consequence	EFFect (or CAUse)

NOTE: CHANGES TO RASTIER'S LIST OF THE PRIMARY CASES

We have modified the inventory of primary cases established by Rastier (the essentials can be found in Rastier, 1997, p. xv). We are distinguishing the temporal locative from the spatial locative by using different abbreviations (both of which were labelled (LOC) by Rastier). We are adding the assumptive, the malefactive, the classitive (for set relations, as in [dog] → (CLAS) → [mammal]) and the wholitive (for mereological relations, as in [word] ← (WHOL) ← [sentence]). Note that the typology of cases developed for textual analysis, which is primarily focused on narrative functions, is inadequate for analyzing images. In particular, we will need to have cases relating to color (blue, white, red, etc.), texture (smooth, rough, sticky, etc.), and materials (wood, glass, metal, stone, etc.), and the specific spatial locative cases (in front, behind, above, next to, on, etc.). Since we are describing the semantic plane, we must be careful in image analysis not to confuse signifiers with semes that evoke perception. The colors we are talking about are thematized colors, not the colors of the signifier. For example, the color seme /transparent/, which is in the signified 'drinking glass' in a painting by Magritte, is produced using a complex, organized blend of signifiers: white, gray and black brush strokes.

Arrows

The nodes and links are connected by arrows indicating the direction of the relation. The table opposite shows the direction of the arrows in the simplest graphs and is based on the directions Sowa used (1984).

For the sake of uniformity, horizontal arrows pointing to the left were used in the above table, which dictated the relative positions of the nodes. As we will see in our examples, in practice, the

Table 13.3 The direction of the arrows in the graphs

[element to which the action applies]	←	(ACC)	←	[process]
[focus of a point of view]	←	(ASS)	←	[element to which a point of view applies]
[specific characteristic]	←	(ATT)	←	[element to which the attribute is given]
[beneficiary element]	←	(BEN)	←	[element given to the beneficiary]
[element of class]	←	(CLAS)	←	[element being classified]
[comparing element]	←	(COMP)	←	[compared element]
[element that receives the transmission]	←	(DAT)	←	[element being transmitted]
[acting element]	←	(ERG)	←	[process]
[element of desired effect]	←	(FIN)	←	[element of cause]
[element being used]	←	(INST)	←	[element to which the means is applied]
[place associated with the element]	←	(LOC S)	←	[spatially located element]
[time associated with the element]	←	(LOC T)	←	[temporally located element]
[maleficiary element]	←	(MAL)	←	[element given to the maleficiary]
[the whole]	←	(PART)	←	[the part]
[element of effect]	←	(RES)	←	[element of cause]

arrows in a given graph can also point to the right (for instance, [process] → (ACC) → [element to which the action applies]) or vertically (up or down). Rather than following Sowa's rules, one can orient the arrows "intuitively" (for example: [man] → (ERG) → [LOVE] → (ACC) → [woman] ← [brilliant]), or even replace them with lines minus the arrows if there is no possible ambiguity in the direction of the link. It is also permissible to draw a link with only one arrow on its trajectory rather than two, as we have done in our strictly graphical-format examples).

NOTE: ENDOCENTRIC/EXOCENTRIC ARROWS

An arrow may point toward a link or node, or it may originate from a link or node. Each node is joined to at least one arrow, which is either endocentric (→ [node]) or exocentric to it ([node] →). Each link is joined to at least two arrows, of which one is endocentric and the other exocentric (→ (LINK) →). However, as we have already mentioned, in contrast with Sowa and Rastier, we use only one (exocentric) arrow per link in our strictly graphical format. The opposition endocentric/exocentric should be kept separate from the oppositions right/left and high/low since its only function is to stipulate that the arrow goes either toward the node or link (endocentric) or away from it (exocentric). Thus, despite the fact that they point in both directions, the following arrows are endocentric: → [node] ←, whereas these are exocentric: ← [node] →.

Temporal relations between graphs

The primary temporal relations between any terms – graphs in this case (and narrative programs or actantial models elsewhere) – are simultaneity (complete or partial) and succession (complete (immediate or delayed) or partial).

These relations are based on the temporal segmentation of the semiotic act (which establishes the beginnings and ends of the elements that constitute the act) and on assigning segments to positions in a given temporality (time as represented in the story, narrative time, or the tactical sequencing of units such as sentences and paragraphs). Besides these relations, one should include comparative relations that involve recurrence and thereby produce rhythms (cyclical or non-cyclical).

Non-temporal relations between graphs

Of the possible non-temporal relations between elements, we should mention identity, alterity, opposition, similarity, homologation, transformation, presupposition, mutual exclusion, and type-token relations. We will take a look at two of these, inclusion or embedding and the type-token relation (refer to the chapter on structural relations for the others).

Embedding

A graph or group of nodes may be condensed or expanded. A node can in fact be expanded into a graph, or a graph condensed into a node (embedding). In this case, the node "summarizes" a graph (for example, [man] summarizes [human] → (ATT) → [male sex]) and/or refers to it (for example: (RES) → [graph 5]).[6] Moreover, instead of being joined to another node (which may or may not be the result of condensation), a node maybe joined to a group within the same graph, made up of one or more links and/or nodes. The group can be demarcated using any sort of closed shape, such as a dashed-line rectangle enclosing the group, with at least one arrow either originating or ending at its boundary; any arrow going through this boundary would then apply only to the element indicated, and not to the group (see our analysis of "Playing bones").

Relations of typicality between graphs

There are five basic transformational operations by which two entities may be related when one of them "originates" from the other.

1 Preservation: both entities remain identical;
2 Deletion: an element is deleted in the transformed entity;
3 Insertion (addition): an element is added in the transformed entity;
4 Deletion-insertion
5 Permutation: the order of the elements changes in the transformed entity.

In terms of graphing, these operations affect: (1) the number of nodes and links, (2) the labeling of nodes and links, (3) the specific configuration of the nodes and links. A common deletion-insertion in graphs consists of replacing an element by making it more general (e.g., human instead of woman) or more specific (e.g., man instead of human). As for permutation, in the simplest of cases, the permuted configurations have the same number of elements and positions that may be occupied. For example, one can invert the relative position of two nodes: [human] ← (ERG) ← [KILL] → (ACC) → [animal] becomes [animal] ← (ERG) ← [KILL] → (ACC) → [human].

These five operations describe the transformational relations between a graph's type (a model graph) and its tokens, or between one graph's type and another's. We shall identify four kinds of typicality in the relations between a graph type and its corresponding tokens, based on whether or not the token preserves the form of the graph and the labels for its links and nodes.[7] The number of tokens covered by the type varies depending on the kind of typicality selected and its tolerance for variation.

Table 13.4 Typicality in graphs

TYPICALITY	*ELEMENTS PRESERVED (+)*			*EXAMPLES OF GRAPH TYPES*	*EXAMPLES OF GRAPH TOKENS*
	Graph form	Labels for the links	Labels for the nodes		
1	+	–	–	[] ← () ← [] → () → []	1. [garden] ← (LOC S) ← [flower] → (LOC T) → [spring] 2. [rich] ← (ERG) ← [GIFT] → (ATT) → [inadequate] 3. [wolf] ← (ERG) ← [KILL] → (ACC) → [human] etc.
2	+	+	–	[] ← (ERG) ← [] → (ACC) → []	3. [wolf] ← (ERG) ← [KILL] → (ACC) → [human] 4. [flea] ← (ERG) ← [BITE] → (ACC) → [John] 5. [Mary] ← (ERG) ← [LOVE] → (ACC) → [freedom] etc.
3	+	–	+	[animal] ← () ← [KILL] → () → [human]	3. [wolf] ← (ERG) ← [KILL] → (ACC) → [human] 6. [animal] ← (ERG) ← [KILL] → (ACC) → [human] 7. [animal] ← (ACC) ← [KILL] → (ERG) → [human] etc.
4	+	+	+	[animal] ← (ERG) ← [KILL] → (ACC) → [human]	3. [wolf] ← (ERG) ← [KILL] → (ACC) → [human] 6. [animal] ← (ERG) ← [KILL] → (ACC) → [human] 8. [bull] ← (ERG) ← [KILL] → (ACC) → [toreador] etc.

Graphs and modal evaluations

Some elements may be implicit in a graph, such as the time of the story in which the graph occurs and the modal evaluations applied to it. Modal evaluations and the observing subjects involved in them may be integrated directly into the graph by using attributive and assumptive links, respectively, or they may be included in the labels for the nodes or links. Modal status may also be indicated by using an element internal to the graph, which is neither a node nor a link (such as the designation true/false in our graph illustrating the fundamental cases (below) or the use of a symbol, such as ◊, to indicate possibility). One can also specify modal evaluations and observing subjects (and other elements, like the time of the story) "outside" of the graph, by setting it in context (for example: "This graph represents the character's thoughts and beliefs at this moment".) In principle, in the absence of any explicit assumptive case in the graph or outside of it, the ontological and veridictory status of the graph is implicitly ("by default") real and true, and this evaluation is the "reference" one: that is, it corresponds to the absolute truth of the text.

NOTE: GRAPHS AND NEGATION

In this section, we will consider logical negation as a modal category. The logical negation of a graph or one of its parts is represented in various ways within the graph: by using a negation operator (such as ¬), a veridictory status (such as false) or indicating it in the formulation of the label (e.g., the process [GIVE] *vs.* [NOT GIVE] or [KEEP]).

Examples of graphs

This is how Rastier represents the content of the French word (lexia) "agriculturist" (section 1 of the graph represents the signified (sememe) 'agri-', section 2 the signified '-cultur-', and section 3 the signified '-ist'; the overlap between sections is due to the semes that recur in each of the signifieds):

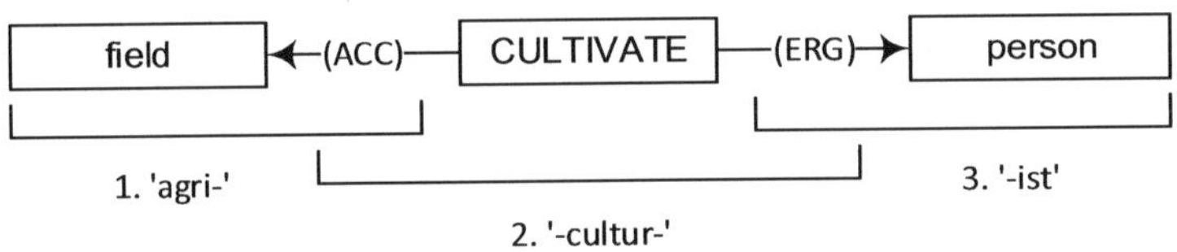

Figure 13.1 Graph of the word "agriculturist"

This is how one would represent the group of semes (the semic molecule) /tangible/ + /hot/ + /yellow/ + /viscous/ + /harmful/ present in Zola's *L'assommoir [The drunkard]* (see Rastier, 1997, pp. 129–131):

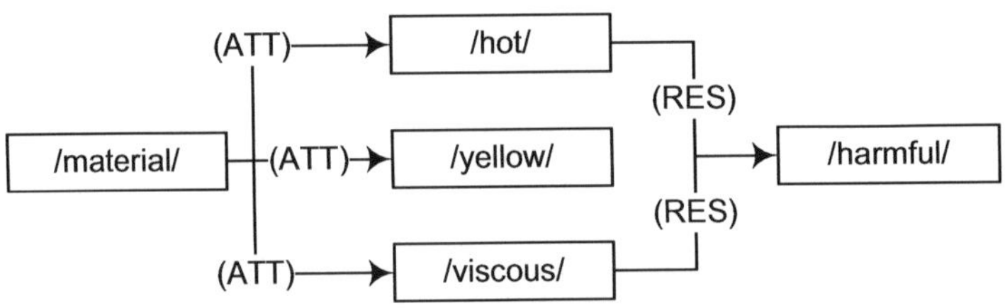

Figure 13.2 Graph of a semic molecule

The typical act (dialectical function)[8] of "giving", in which someone (actor 1) gives something (actor 2) for the benefit of someone (actor 3), can be represented as follows:

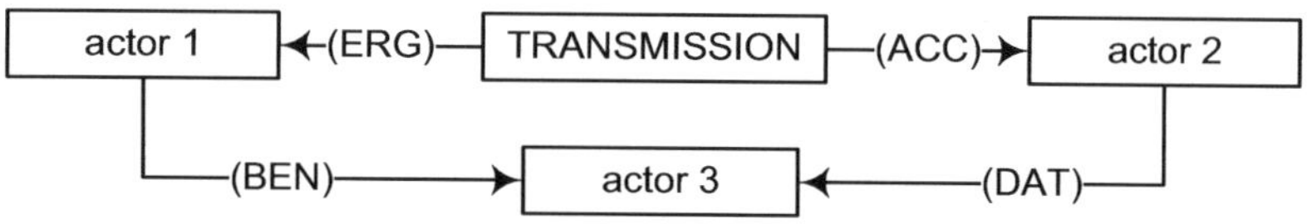

Figure 13.3 Graph of the dialectical function "giving"

Graph illustrating the primary cases

The following is an example illustrating the primary cases, in which both the analysis and its representation are simplified: "According to John, yesterday, right here, Peter – a generous sort – gave Mary a doll and a cup-and-ball game so that she would have fun with these presents; but instead she cried like a geyser". We are using the opposition true/false to show the distance separating the intention (Mary as beneficiary) from the result (Mary as maleficiary).[9]

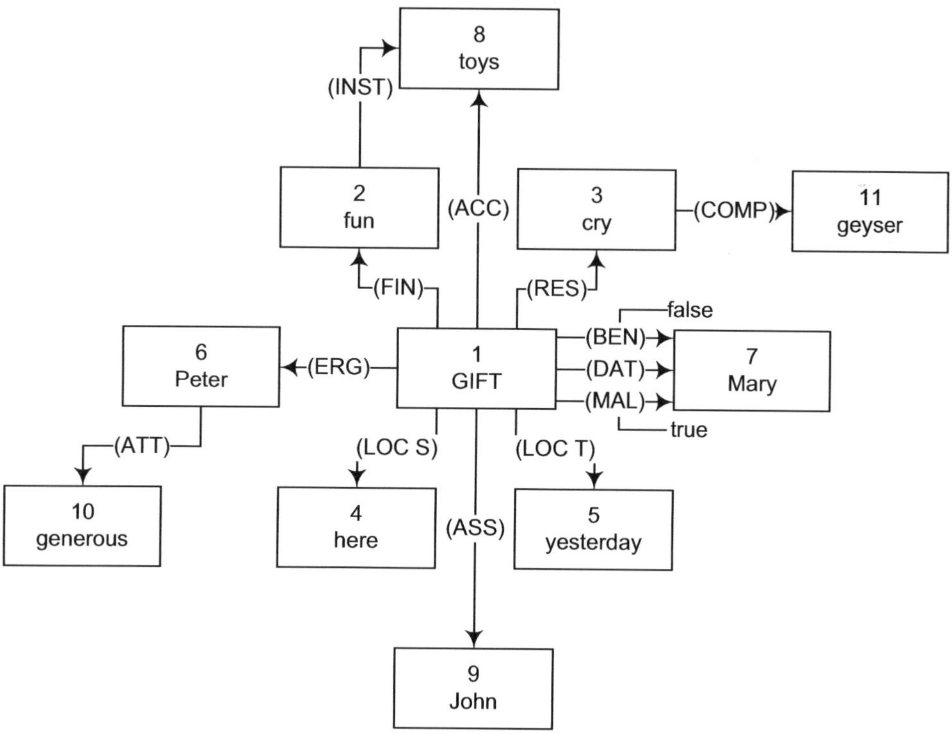

Figure 13.4 A graph illustrating the primary cases

Applications

Application I: "The cicada and the ant" by La Fontaine

* * *

"The cicada and the ant"
Jean de La Fontaine (1988, p. 5)

Cicada, having sung her song
All summer long,
Found herself without a crumb
When winter winds did come.
Not a scrap was there to find
Of fly or earthworm, any kind.
Hungry she ran off to cry
To neighbor Ant, and specify:
Asking for a loan of grist,
A seed or two so she'd subsist
Just until the coming spring.
She said, "I'll pay you everything
Before fall, my word as animal,
Interest and principal".
Well, no hasty lender is the Ant;
It's her finest virtue by a lot.
"And what did you do when it was hot?"
She then asked this mendicant.
"To all comers, night and day,
I sang. I hope you don't mind".
"You sang? Why, my joy is unconfined.
Now dance the winter away".

* * *

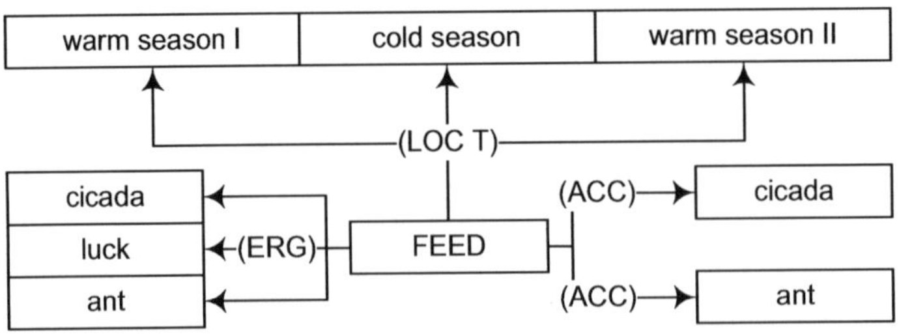

Figure 13.5 Graph type of "The cicada and the ant"

Table 13.5 The main graph tokens derived from the graph type

GRAPH N°	*(ERG)*	*[PROCESS]*	*(ACC)*	*(LOC)*	*ACTUAL STATUS*	*POSSIBLE STATUS*
1	The cicada	feed	the cicada	warm season I	false	possible true (it could have been true)
2	The cicada	feed	the cicada	cold season	false	possible true (it could have been true)
3	The ant	feed	the ant	warm season I	true	possible false (it could have been false)
4	The ant	feed	the ant	cold season	true	possible true (it could have been true)
5	The ant	feed	the cicada	cold season	false	possible true (it could have been true)
6	Luck	feed	the cicada	warm season I	true	possible false (it could have been false)
7	Luck	feed	the cicada	cold season	false	impossible true (it could not have been true)
8	Luck	feed	the ant	warm season I	false	possible true (it could have been true)
9	Luck	feed	the ant	cold season	false	impossible true (it could not have been true)

Our graph type is a synthesis of the graphs centered on the process FEED, the preeminent process in the fable "The cicada and the ant", by Jean de La Fontaine (1621–1695). The inventory of links is identical in all of the graphs covered by this graph type. However, the labels for the nodes in ergative, accusative and temporal locative positions are variable. Deductively, it would be possible to produce a very large number of graph tokens from this graph, by exhausting all of the potential combinations of labels for the nodes it contains. But we have selected only the most pertinent graphs (for a detailed analysis, see Hébert, 2001, p. 177 and following).

Each graph corresponds to a logical proposition marked for ontological and veridictory status. Ontological and veridictory dialogics (see the chapter on this subject) is the study of true/false evaluations and their relations with the actual (what is), counterfactual (what is not), possible (what could be or could have been) and impossible (what could not be or could not have been) realms. Each graph does not necessarily correspond to a proposition marked as true and real in the universe of reference (the universe that defines the ultimate truth of the text). For example, the proposition *The ant feeds the cicada during the cold season* (graph 5) is actually false, but possibly true: it could have been actually true (if we put ourselves in the past) or it could be actually true (if we put ourselves in the present at the time when the cicada is making her request, or at the time when the cold season has not yet gone by). Propositions of this kind are actually false by chance; at the other end of the spectrum, one finds propositions that are actually false in their substance, that is, they are impossibly true: for instance, in the logic of the story, *Luck feeds the cicada during the cold season* is actually false and impossibly true.

NOTE: NEGATION OF AN ACTION

We have elected to indicate the negation of an action with ontological and veridictory status alone, rather than introducing an action marked by negation (such as NOT FEED or using a negation operator like ¬ FEED). Thus, the real and false proposition *Luck feeds the cicada during the cold season* (graph 7) is equivalent to the real and true proposition *Luck does not feed the cicada during the cold season.*

Proposition 1: The cicada does not provide for her own needs; she is dependent on good luck, or mother nature, which is evident from her powerlessness during the cold season, when flies and worms are no longer abundant.

Propositions 3 and 8: The strongly contrastive nature of the text no doubt justifies the idea that even during the summer, the ant is self-sufficient and does not rely on her good luck (or Providence, to put it in terms of human faith). But if we do not espouse this reading, we could consider these propositions as partially true and partially false: if we read these propositions restrictively, for instance, it is not completely true to say that the ant alone feeds the ant, since luck also plays a part in it.

Proposition 5: As it happens, this proposition is presented by the cicada, who knows perfectly well that it is possible in the context of proposing an exchange. The ant can lend food (this is possible), but does not want to. As long as the cold season has not gone by, technically, this proposition is still possibly true (after that, it automatically becomes actually false). However, it seems doubtful that the opinionated ant will change her mind, so one can consider this proposition as actually false.

Propositions 1, 2, 3 and 4: The ant implicitly formulates possible propositions that might have become true or false at some hypothetical time that has already gone by. For instance, the cicada's providing for herself during the cold season could have become true if only she had worked (graph 2). Likewise, the ant could have not provided for herself during the summer, and played, like the cicada did (graph 3). This group of propositions illustrates the cicada's and the ant's free will; the cicada could have worked, and the ant could have played instead of the reverse. The ant's moralizing lays out the choice illustrated by the whole text: play or work. Her remarks show that she was clearly aware of this choice. What distinguishes her from the cicada (before its mishap) is her awareness of the relation of absolute presupposition between eating and working.

Application II: the death in Hamlet

The chapter dealing with the actantial model provides a comprehensive analysis of Shakespeare's *Hamlet*. In the chapter "Analysis by classification", we learn that most of the deaths in *Hamlet* (except in the case of Ophelia, who dies an accidental or suicidal death) are homicides, in the ordinary sense of the word.

The central structure of a homicide, whether the killing oneself (suicide) or the killing of another, may be represented graphically as shown opposite. We have not shown the instrument (means of killing) of the request to kill (depicted within the dotted lines), the means being generally contingent on and not included in the request per se.

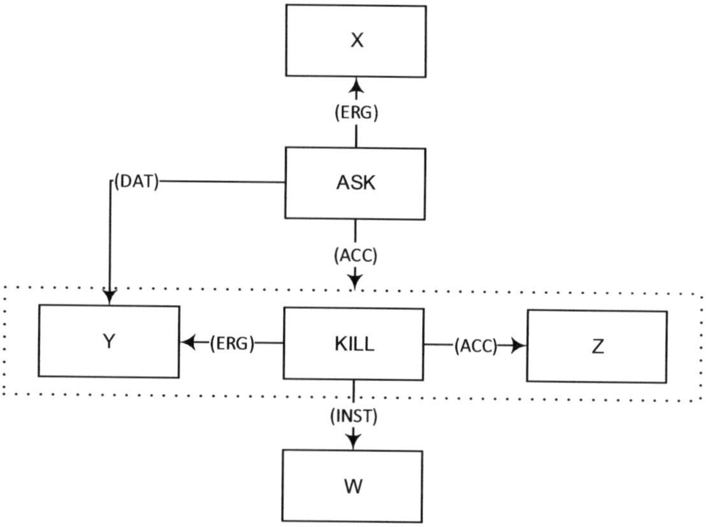

Figure 13.6 Homicide graph

The table below (prepared initially in collaboration with Marie Josée St-Laurent) presents the main elements of the graph, based on the play. Note that "*X* asks", where it appears in the graph, refers to the characters (thus excluding non-character forces: sense of duty, filial love, etc.) who ask – for example, the ghost of Hamlet – Y to kill Z or urge – Hamlet, for example, being urged to kill the queen with his *words, like daggers*, according to the play – Y to kill Z.

Table 13.6 The request to kill in *Hamlet*

*N^os^*	*Act, Sc., P.*	*X asks*	*Y*	*to kill (*= successful)*	*Z*	*with W*
1	I, 1	Hamlet Sr.	Hamlet Sr.	*	Fortinbras Sr.	probably a sword (duel)
2	I, 1	Young Fortinbras	Young Fortinbras		King Claudius	not specified
3	I, 5	The ghost	Hamlet	*	King Claudius	not specified
4	I, 5	Claudius	Claudius	*	Hamlet Sr.	poison (hebenon) poured in the ear
5	I, 5	The ghost	Hamlet	not to kill	The Queen	not specified
6	III, 2, (pantomime in the stage directions)	A man (comedian)	a man	* (fictitious murder: play-within-the-play)	The King (comedian)	poison poured in the ear
7	III, 1	Every man (or woman)	himself	to kill (desire)/not to kill (fear of the afterlife)	himself	sharp object (*bodkin*) (as a symbol of all means)

(*Continued*)

Table 13.6 (Continued)

Nos	Act, Sc., P.	X asks	Y	to kill (*= successful)	Z	with W
8	III, 2	Luciano (Gonzago's nephew)	Luciano	* (fictitious murder: play-within-the-play)	King Gonzago	poison poured in the ear
9	II, 2	Hamlet	Hamlet	with words alone	The Queen	words like daggers (comparison)
10	III, 3	Hamlet	Hamlet	To delay the killing until when there is no chance of redemption	King Claudius (at prayer)	a sword
11	III, 4	Hamlet (in accordance with the Queen)	Hamlet		The Queen	not specified
12	III, 4	Hamlet	Hamlet	* (successful but unintentional: Polonius; unsuccessful: Claudius)	Claudius concealed (in reality, Polonius concealed)	a sword
13	III, 4	Hamlet	Hamlet	with words alone	The Queen	words like daggers (comparison)
14	IV, 3	King Claudius	(King of) England		Hamlet	execution (beheading)
15	IV, 5	King Claudius (it is falsely rumored)	King Claudius or one of his subordinates		Polonius	a sword
16	IV, VII	Laertes	Laertes		Hamlet	a sword?
17	IV, 7	Laertes	Laertes	*	Hamlet	poison-tipped sword
18	VII, 4	King Claudius	King Claudius		Hamlet	poisoned wine
19	VII, 4	Ophelia	Ophelia	*	Ophelia	drowning (possibly suicide)
20	V, 2	King Claudius (writing style mimicked by Hamlet)	England	* (due to Hamlet's deception)	Guildenstern et Rosencrantz	execution
21	V, 2	?	Hamlet	* unintentionally	Laertes	switched poison-tipped sword
22	V, 2	?	King Claudius	* unintentionally	The Queen	poisoned wine meant for Hamlet
23	V, 2	Hamlet	Hamlet	*	King Claudius	poison-tipped sword and poisoned wine
24	V, 2	Horatio	Horatio		Horatio	poisoned wine (a wish that Hamlet asks Horatio to refrain from carrying out)

Application III: the topos of the scorned poet

We will examine a topos (a common-place, or narrative cliché) that is pervasive in French poetry: the misunderstood, scorned poet. Topos analysis entails relating the topos type to the various topos tokens that manifest it.

The graph we propose is a generalized one representing the topos of the scorned poet: In it, the poet becomes an exceptional individual, and his poetry a positive transmission to the collective group. With this generalized representation, one can illustrate the cross-disciplinary nature of the topos, which applies not only to its occurrences in literature, but also in religion (the *Bible*), philosophy (Plato), song lyrics (Charles Aznavour), and so on. As far as literature goes, with a few exceptions, we will limit our analysis to the poet figure (and not generalize him as a writer or an artist) as represented in 19th- and 20th-century French poems (not as represented in novels). Obviously, one could apply the transformational operations (insertion, deletion, insertion-deletion, permutation) to this generalized topos, which would change the number and inventory of tokens related to this type. For example, the number of tokens covered by the topos type will decrease if we change /exceptional individual/ to /exceptional poet/ (deletion-insertion).

The graph may be verbalized as follows: An (3) exceptional individual, who is part of (1) a superior world, effects (5) a positive transmission (an exceptional work of poetry, for instance) to (4) the collective group, which belongs to (2) an inferior world; but in return, the collective group sends a (6) negative transmission (for example, by revealing its scorn for the work of poetry).

NOTE: OTHER POSSIBLE REPRESENTATIONS

Let us briefly discuss the ways we have chosen to represent this topos. In the same node, we have included both the transmission and its positive or negative quality, which we could have identified by using attributive links connected to the transmission nodes. We could also have connected the dative link with a benefactive or malefactive link, depending on the circumstances. In addition, we have not shown the many other thymic evaluations underlying the graph. The two separate evaluators – the individual and the masses – have contradictory evaluations about the two worlds and the two transmitters in our graph, but they agree on the negativity of the scorn directed at the poet (unless the poet adopts an attitude of stoicism). The names superior world/inferior world are meant in the value-related sense, but these thymic evaluations are often homologized with the spatial positions high/low, as we will see, which is why we have chosen these terms.[10] The people's evaluation of the transmission and the transmitter occurs on a scale ranging from not-positive to extremely negative: the transmitter could be viewed as laughable, but inoffensive (see Baudelaire's "The albatross") or as threateningly subversive (Jesus, Socrates, the poet in Plato's city). In summary, the labels we have chosen for the graph type reflect the transmitter's point of view, which corresponds to the truth of the text (we will see some exceptions). Technically speaking, this is the universe of reference, which says that the masses are indeed wrong to discount the transmitter.

Between the masses and the exceptional individual, one can place a third agent, which we will call the enlightened elite (e.g., Socrates' and Jesus' disciples); they will compensate – although poorly in numerical terms – for the scorn of the public. The producer is usually seeking both critical and popular acclaim.

In our graph of the scorned poet, the two transmissions have no temporal location relative to each other, but they seem to occur in succession, with the poet going first and the crowd retorting. (This does not exclude the possibility that some sort of implicit or explicit inducement may have been directed at the poet previously.) The poems in which this topos is strongly thematized are a sort of tit-for-tat, since the poet complains about the scorn in a new positive transmission to the masses: positive in the aesthetic sense, that is, since the poet often responds to scorn by giving it back (see "The dog and the perfume bottle" by Baudelaire). Be that as it may, in dialectical time (the time of the story), the whole graph may be followed by a complementary graph to form a syntagm, or stereotyped sequence of topoi. The second graph is that of later recognition, traditionally posthumous, by the masses (as for the elite, it can either maintain or reverse its evaluation).

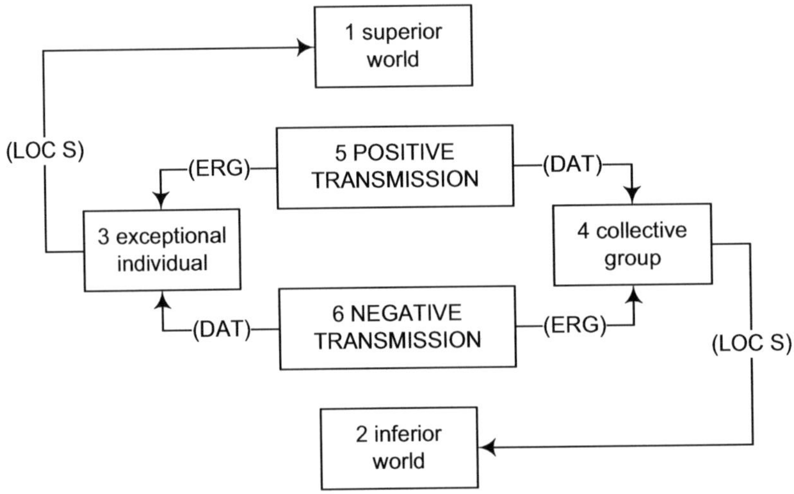

Figure 13.7 Generalized graph representing the topos of the scorned poet

The following are a few tokens that exemplify this topos.[11] Obviously, this list is not exhaustive:

A Plato, the Myth of the Cave (*The republic*). 1. The world of ultimate reality (ideality). 2. The world of illusion. 3. The man who gains access to ultimate reality. 4. Mankind, enslaved to illusion. 5. The exceptional man tries to liberate his fellows, as he liberated himself. 6. Rejection; they don't believe him; they think he is crazy.

B Plato. 1. The world of understanding. 2. The world of ignorance. 3. Socrates. 4. Socrates' accusers. 5. Socratic understanding. 6. The punishment: drinking hemlock. This transmission is object-related (pragmatic, and not solely cognitive, as is often the case).

C *The new testament* 1. The spiritual world. 2. The material world. 3. Jesus. 4. Mankind. 5. Christ gives his life out of love for mankind. 6. Rejection by the majority (for example, Barabbas is preferred over Jesus), with the exception of Palm Sunday, the kindness of the disciples, the "enlightened few" (aside from some denials).

D Victor Hugo, "The poet's function". *Sunbeams and shadows* (March 25–April 1, 1839). 1. The world to come. 2. The world as it is. 3. The poet (lexicalized as "singer", "prophet", etc.). 4. "Brothers", "city". 5. The poet is tempted to escape from the city and merge with nature (the secularization of the spiritual world), and like Christ, tempted to shirk his duty, but "Alas! Duty calls each of us to the others!" and moreover, the poet-prophet has a higher responsibility. 6. The poet fulfills his role, whether he is insulted or praised: However, the rejection may be in appearance only: "many a false prophet at his words/Laughs aloud and reflects silently". (The false prophet introduces the theme of the mediocre poet, as well as the theme of the usurper).

E Baudelaire, "The albatross", *The flowers of evil* (1857). 1. The poetic world (compared element)/ the aerial world (comparing element). 2. The prosaic world/the non-aerial world. 3. The poet/ the albatross. 4. The masses/the sailors. 5. Positive transmission or autonomy, withdrawal of the poet-albatross (a Parnassian position)? Here the metaphor doesn't fly, it seems, since the albatross transmits nothing positive to the sailors, except his beauty in flight. 6. Jeers. In the aerial-poetic world, the albatross-poet can simply launch attacks on the inhabitants of lower worlds: He "haunts the storm and laughs at the archer".

F Baudelaire, "Benediction", *The flowers of evil* (1857). 1. The spiritual and poetic world. 2. The temporal and prosaic world. 3. Poet: "I know that among the uplifted legions/Of saints, a place awaits the Poet's arrival". 4. The masses and even the poet's mother and his wife. 5. Messenger from the spiritual world. 6. Rejection. "Those he would love [. . .] experiment/With various possible methods of exciting derision/By trying out their cruelty [. . .]" This token, like the one from Hugo, is a merging of two subspecies of the topos: the scorned poet and the scorned prophet (as in the *Bible*).

G Baudelaire, "The dog and the perfume bottle", *The parisian prowler* (1869). 1. The world of superior art. 2. The world of inferior art. 3. The great poet and the great parfumeur. 4. The dog, the masses ("the public"). 5. The parfumeur and the poet give superior products to the people, like the master (narrator) to his dog. 6. The people reject them, preferring "rubbish", and even the dog rebuffs his master. Between the lines, we find the motif of the usurper, the charlatan (the bad poet adored by the masses).

H Uderzo and Goscinny, the comic strip *Astérix*. 1. The poetic world. 2. The prosaic world. 3. The bard. 4. The masses. 5. He bestows his art generously. 6. Harassment. In this case, the topos is reversed; the poet has no talent and everyone is right to scorn him. This rejection of poets in general or a poet in particular may also be expressed by a poet, which is exactly what happens in "To an ignorant poet" by Marot. And Cendrars (*Prose of the trans-siberian*) criticizes a poet as well, himself in fact, although perhaps just in days gone by: "Anyway, I was a really bad poet".

I Charles Aznavour, "*Je m'voyais déjà*" ["I could already see myself"] 1. The world of superior art. 2. The world of inferior art. 3. The singer. 4. The public. 5. "I have talent". 6. The singer has had only "cheap victories, night trains and soldiers' whores". He blames "the public, who just didn't get it". Success and recognition are presented by the narrator as being possible, but the universe of reference leads us to believe they are impossible, since the singer has been trying his luck in vain for "30 years". This relates to the topos of absurd perseverance, also found in "Madeleine" by Jacques Brel, to give another example from a songwriter.

Application IV: half-human, half-animal characters

We would like to briefly describe a certain kind of "mythical" half-human, half-animal character commonly found in images and texts. The characters we are interested in have two parts: an upper part and a lower part. These parts are derived from the upper or lower part of a human or an animal, of masculine, feminine or undetermined gender. The following graph represents this combinatorial set.

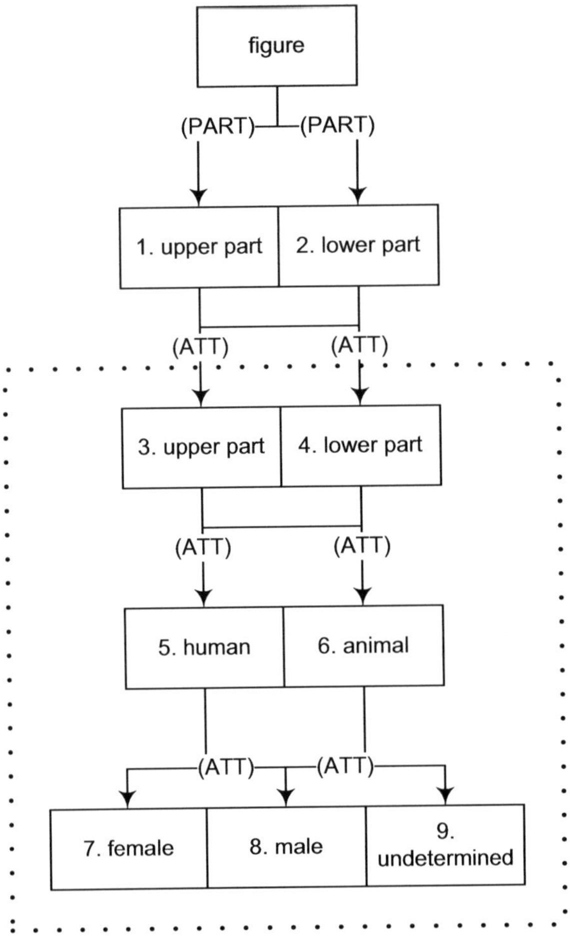

Figure 13.8 Graph of half-human, half-animal characters

In the table opposite, we have examples of the possible combinations between the different elements of the graph.[12] For example, a siren (mermaid) combines the upper part of a woman (1 + 3 + 5 + 7) and the lower part of a fish, which one would presume to be female, more out of coherence than from any external signs of its gender ((2 + 4 + 6 + 7 or 9). The character may be created by permuting the parts of one single source character (e.g., *The rape* by Magritte permutes different parts of what one would assume to be one feminine body) or by combining parts from two source characters (a woman and a fish for the siren). A character produced by permuting or combining parts conjures up what we will call a reciprocal character, made by combining the leftover parts of the source character(s) (such as an anti-siren, made out of the upper part of a fish and the lower part of a woman). This reciprocal character might be represented in the same semiotic act or in another act in a specified corpus. Lastly, we will distinguish the two ways of combining parts in a character: the parts may be merged (as they are in a siren) or simply juxtaposed. In the latter case, the character is formed by juxtaposing two sub-characters (e.g., in Goya's *Tu que no puedes*, one finds two characters that are each made up of two sub-characters: a horseman and a mount).

Table 13.7 Examples of half-human, half-animal characters

	DESCRIPTION	*IMAGE OR TEXT EXAMPLE*	*TOP OF CHARACTER*	*BOTTOM OF CHARACTER*	*NOTE*
A	centaur		1 + 3 + 5 + 8	2 + 4 + 6 + 8	a
B	siren (mermaid)	*The forbidden universe* (Magritte, 1943)	1 + 3 + 5 + 7	2 + 4 + 6 + 7	a
	male siren (merman)	*Merman hanging from a gibbet* (Magritte, 1946)	1 + 3 + 5 + 8	2 + 4 + 6 + 8	
C	pig-man	*A stroke of luck* (Magritte, 1945))	1 + 3 + 6 + 8	2 + 4 + 5 + 8	a
D	female anti-siren	*Collective invention* (Magritte, 1934) *The wonders of nature* (Magritte, 1953)	1 + 3 + 6 + 7	2 + 4 + 5 + 7	a
E	male anti-siren	*The wonders of nature* (Magritte, 1953)	1 + 3 + 6 +8	2 + 4 + 5 + 8	a
F	face-torso	*The rape* (Magritte, 1934)	1 (head) + 4 (torso) + 5 + 7	partially represented	a
G	man carrying animal	*Tu que no puedes* (Goya, 1799)	horseman: 1 + 3–4 + 6 + 8?	mount: 2 + 3–4 + 5 + 8	b
H	man-animal carrying man-animal	*Miren que grabes!* (Goya, 1799)	rider: 1 + 3–4 + 5–6 (merged man-animal) + 8?	mount: 2 + 3–4 + 6 (merged animals) + 8?	b, c, d
I	man carrying chimera, more or less merged	*To each his chimera* (Baudelaire, 1869 [1862])	rider: 1 + 3–4 + 6 (chimera: merging of animals) + 9?	mount: 2 + 3–4 (whole man) + 5 + 8	a-b, c

NOTES:

a: character created by merging upper and lower parts;
b: character created by juxtaposing upper and lower parts of two sub-characters;
c: upper sub-character (rider) created by merging parts;
d: lower sub-character (mount) created by merging parts.

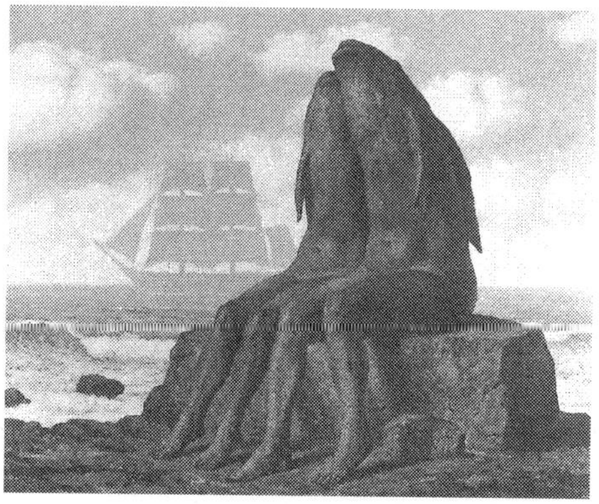

Figure 13.9 The wonders of nature

Source: Magritte (1953)

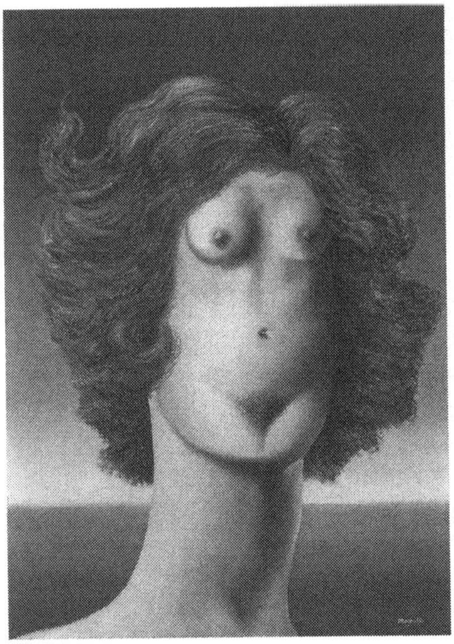

Figure 13.10 The rape

Source: Magritte (1934)

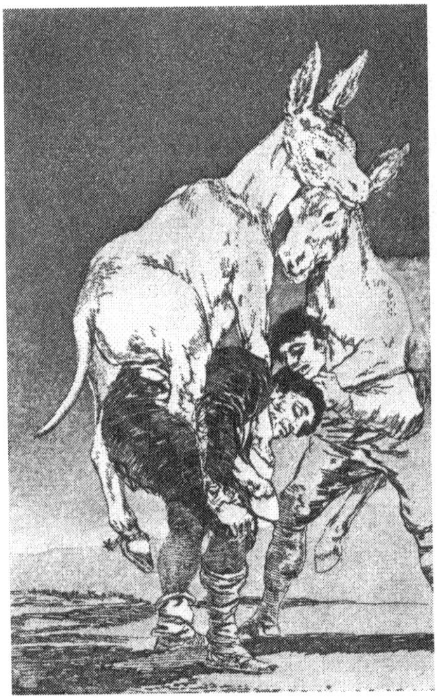

Figure 13.11 Tu que no puedes

Source: Goya (1799)

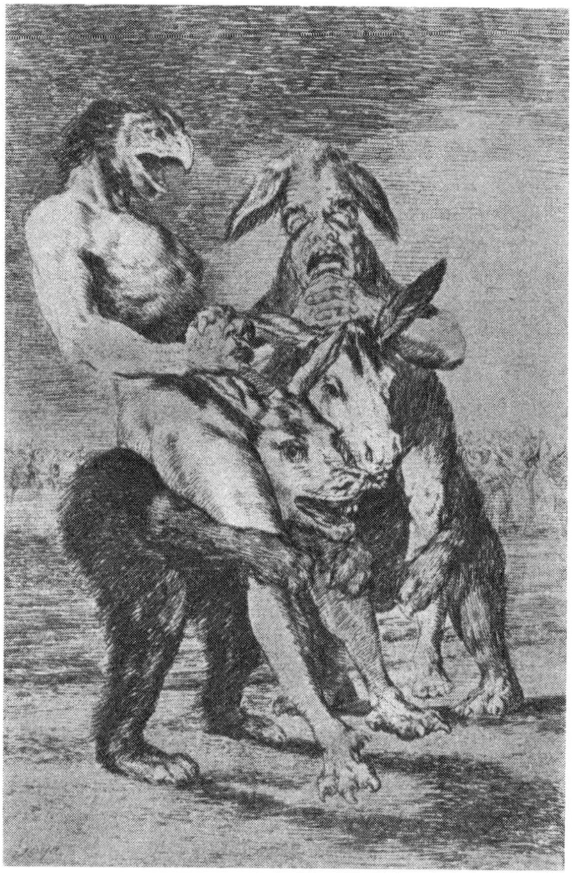

Figure 13.12 Miren que grabes!

Source: Goya (1799)

Notes

1 Using the graphs, content may be conceived of and represented as a complex structure, not just as an inventory of semes (see Pottier) or a simple semic hierarchy (see Greimas).

2 Nodes and links correspond to the logical notions of subject (or argument) (what we are talking about) and predicate (what we say about it). In theory, a link may be joined directly to another link (with no intervening node), and a node may be joined directly to another node (with no intervening link).

3 Nodes and links may be left blank or unlabelled (Ø), especially (or only?) for type-token relations (see the section on typicality).

4 For the sake of descriptive precision, it is helpful to add to the inventory of cases. "The case primitive LOC (locative) can then be particularized with all sorts of values indicating specific positions in the represented space or time". This points to a general principle: links and nodes may vary in generality/specificity.

5 Semantic cases are not to be confused with morphosyntactic functions. To give an example of the distinction between semantic cases and morphosyntactic (surface) cases, in *The crow was outsmarted by the fox*, 'the crow' is in the nominative morphosyntactically, but in the accusative semantically; the fox is in the agentive morphosyntactically, but in the ergative semantically.

6 Hypertext (in the computer science sense of the term) allows one to "hide" a graph under a node, which can be accessed by clicking on the appropriate hyperlink.

7 Rastier says (1994, p. 138): "In representations, the rapport between type and token is basically a rapport between two semantic graphs. Depending on the objectives of the description, different kinds of typicality may be defined: (1) the most abstract type preserves only the form of the graph, and not the labels for the nodes or the links. (2) traditional types preserve the form of the graph and the labels for the links, but they change the labels for the nodes (by replacing the names of the variables with names of particular agents). (3) a third kind of typicality concerns the links and their labels." These three kinds of typicality are found (with the same numbers) in our table. But should we not consider a fourth kind of typicality, in which the form of the graph is preserved as well as the labels for the nodes and links? In fact, typicalities three and four seem irreducible to one another: in number three, labels are absent, and in number four, the labels demarcate the semantic range of the nodes, within which the tokens must remain. We will give an example from literature for the third kind of typicality. In the work of Gérard de Nerval, a graph type with the nodes /sun/ and /black/ is manifested in at least two tokens: in one of them, the link is in the resultative ("The black spot", where the sun causes a black spot in the narrator's vision); and in the other, it is in the attributive (the "*Black sun* of *melancholia*" in "*El desdichado*"). This chapter's analysis of the topos of the scorned poet is based on a literary example of the fourth kind of typicality.

8 For the list of the ten dialectical functions that can be used to describe most narratives, see Rastier, 1997, p. 47; Hébert, 2001, p. 130.

9 In order to simplify our representation, while certain links or nodes should apply to a group or even the whole graph, we have tried to attach them to just one link or node. For example, in the story on which our graph is based, the gift of toys (a group made up of a node and links) is what provokes the tears, not the gift in isolation. Obviously, it is also possible for a node to apply to only one node of the graph (e.g., [generous] applies to [Peter] in this graph).

10 The locative link can take on a metaphorical value, as can other links, no doubt; for instance, "the world of poetry" is not a space a priori, although it can be associated with a celestial world (e.g., in Baudelaire's "The albatross").

11 Using numbers or letters to identify the nodes and/or links makes it easy to present the labels for the graph (or references to explanatory quotations and glosses), especially when the graph tokens are numerous, as they are in this case.

12 All of the characters we present are real in the fictitious universe created by a semiotic act (technically speaking, they belong to the actual world of the universe described in that semiotic act): for example, in the painting, the siren is real. However tokens can simply be comparative, like this one: "I'm conscious of my body all the time as if it were made of lead, or as if I were carrying another man on my back" (Ionesco, 1960, p. 18).

14 Analysis by classification

Summary

A unit belongs to a class – is one of its elements – if it corresponds to the definition of the class, i.e., if it possesses the defining properties (or features) thereof; in this sense, an analysis by classification is always a comparative analysis, since it is a matter of comparing the defining features of the class and the defining features of the potential element. Two main forms of analysis by classification can be performed on a semiotic act (text, image, etc.): (1) classification *of* the act, which consists in classifying the whole of the act into a particular class (for example, into a genre acting as a class) and (2) classification *within* the act, which consists in classifying elements that make up the act, whether they are (2.1) "real" elements (e.g., classifying each sentence of a text as affirmative, negative, interrogative, etc.) or (2.2) thematized elements, represented in the content (in the signifieds). The latter kind of analysis will be the focus here. This type of analysis by classification consists in examining the object under analysis – and interpreting its causes, modalities, and the effects of its presence – to discern a thematized structure of any complexity made up of (1) encompassing classes, (2) encompassed classes, and (3) elements belonging to these classes. To give an example, Mallarmé's sonnet, "Her pure nails" ("*Ses purs ongles très haut dédiant leur onyx*") deals with at least three classes of absence: absence in the ordinary sense (elements: the empty parlor, oblivion, etc.); absence through destruction (elements: the ashes of the funerary urn, the deceased, etc.); absence through unreality (elements: the mythological characters, the dream, etc.). Absence, then, is an encompassing class, and each of the three subclasses of absence is an encompassed class. Once it reaches a certain degree of complexity, a classification is usually represented by some sort of visual diagram, e.g., set-notation graphs or a tree diagram.

Theory

Overview

Four cognitive operations

Consider four major cognitive operations and the forms of complex analysis rooted in them:

1 Comparison: a particular observing subject, in a particular time frame, establishes one or more comparative relations (identity, similarity, opposition, alterity, metaphorical similarity, etc.) between two or more objects.
2 Decomposition: an observing subject, in a particular time frame, identifies the parts of a whole. The reverse operation is composition, which is to envision the whole rather than the parts (to not "see" the sugar and the eggs in the meringue). Decomposition can apply to a physical object: the object "knife" = blade + handle + rivets, or to a conceptual object: the signified 'knife' = the semes /utensil/ + /for cutting/ + /equipped with a blade/, etc. Decomposition can be physical-cognitive, such as taking a knife or a chair apart (then we can call it disassembly or conversely, assembly), or simply cognitive, as in mentally identifying the parts of a knife without actually taking it apart.
3 Typing (or categorization): an observing subject, in a particular time frame, relates a token (this particular animal) to a type (a dog), i.e., a model, of which it is a manifestation, a more or less consistent and complete emanation.
4 Classification: an observing subject, in a particular time frame, relates an element (e.g., a black marble) to a class (black marbles). Classification can be physical-cognitive (sorting the marbles by color) or just cognitive (relating a particular marble to its set). Later we will cover how to distinguish a class from a type and a token from an element.

The last three operations are similar in that they bring together including forms (whole, class, type) and included forms (part, element, token). In addition, classification and typing are forms of comparison. That is, to determine whether a unit belongs to a class (i.e., is one of its elements) one compares the defining properties (or features) of the class (e.g., vertebrate creature) and those of the potential element (this animal is indeed a vertebrate). To determine whether a unit belongs to a particular type, one compares the properties of the type (e.g., a romantic text is written in the first person, expresses emotional intensity, etc.) and the properties of its potential token (this text has the properties of a romantic text, so it is a romantic text). Lastly, the same phenomenon may be seen simultaneously from the standpoint of all three operations: decomposition (this whole-word is made up of these parts-letters), classification (this element-word belongs to the class of nouns), and typing (this token-word is a manifestation of the type-noun).

The meaning of the word "classification"

The word "classification" designates: (1) a cognitive operation; (2) a single product thereof (classifying a particular element in a particular class); (3) the more or less complex structure built from more than one single classification (e.g., a taxonomic typology of the animal species, or a typology of textual forms); and lastly, (4) a form of analysis.

We can distinguish two main forms of analysis by classification to be performed on a semiotic act (text, image, etc.): (1) classification *of* the act, which consists in classifying the whole of the act into a particular class (for example, into a genre acting as a class) and (2) classification *within* the act, a local classification which consists in classifying elements that make up the act, whether they are (2.1) "real" elements (e.g., classifying each sentence of a text as affirmative, negative, interrogative, etc.) or (2.2) thematized elements, represented in the content (in the signifieds), e.g., the forms of friendship present in a novel. A global classification [overall classification] necessarily uses one or more local classifications. For example, to verify whether a poem is a romantic poem, one would check to see whether the main romantic themes are present (the first person, intense emotion, etc.). But a local classification can be autonomous and not target an overall classification of the text. For example, one might classify each sentence in the text as affirmative, negative, interrogative, etc., without necessarily aiming to classify the text overall as an affirmative text, for instance, because the sentences of that type are preponderant.

Next, we will examine the classification of thematized elements. This type of analysis by classification consists in examining the object under analysis – and interpreting its causes, modalities, and the effects of its presence – to discern a thematized structure of any complexity made up of (1) encompassing classes, (2) encompassed classes, and (3) elements belonging to these classes. To give an example, Mallarmé's sonnet, "Her pure nails" ("*Ses purs ongles très haut dédiant leur onyx*") deals with at least three classes of absence: absence in the ordinary sense (elements: the empty parlor, oblivion, etc.); absence through destruction (elements: the ashes of the funerary urn, the deceased, etc.); absence through unreality (elements: the mythological characters, the dream, etc.). Absence, then, is an encompassing class, and each of the three subclasses of absence is an encompassed class.

Encompassing/encompassed is a relational status, and is therefore relative and has no absolute value. So a class B may be encompassing relative to a class C, but encompassed relative to a class A. Not to mention that the roles can be reversed: class B which encompasses class A can become encompassed by it (an example will be given later). The relation between an encompassing class and its encompassed classes is inclusion (e.g., the class of mammals includes the class of canines). The relation between an indexed element and the class(es) in which it is indexed (from most specific to most general) is membership or indexation (e.g., between a particular dog and the class of canines).

The components of a classification

To be precise, here are the components of a classification:

1 A class is a *rational* grouping of units that are counted as elements. In textual representation format (graphic format will be presented later), the classes can be notated as follows: //class//. The word "rational" makes it possible to distinguish a class from any random grouping of units.

2 The definition of the class stipulates (1) which feature(s) the elements must have in order to be part of the class; (2) which value these features must take, and (3) the rules for evaluating and determining membership. The definition is what we traditionally call the comprehension or the intension (with an "s") of the class. The features can have three values: mandatory, alternating mandatory (this feature OR else that feature), or optional (but predictable – there is no point in specifying features in the definition that are not very predictable). In textual representation for-

mat, the features can be notated as follows: /feature/. The rules for evaluating membership may be simple (e.g., the class is defined by a single, mandatory feature) or complex (e.g., to diagnose depression, at least two out of six symptoms must be present).

3 An element is a unit that belongs to a class. In textual representation format, elements can be notated as follows: 'element'. Altogether, the elements of a class form what is traditionally called the extension or enumeration of the class. The features of the included element must match the mandatory features of the class. The element can also have – or not have – one or more non-mandatory features. Since an element has more than one feature (allowing for exceptions), it can belong to more than one class, defined by a single feature or multiple features. A feature may match the name of the class (e.g., the feature /fruit/ for 'apple' in the class //fruit//).

Discussion

The distinction between class and type

What exactly is the difference between a type (e.g., the poetry genre) and a class (e.g., the class of poems)? Strictly speaking, a type is not a class because rather than *containing,* or *bringing together* the token units (the poems) governed by it, it generates them. The distinction between a type and the definition, or intension, of a class may seem vague, but they are indeed two distinct things. Type and definition are necessarily abstract entities; token and element can be concrete (this poem as a representative of the poetry genre; this marble as a member of the class of the marbles in this bag) as well as abstract (this love, which is a manifestation of love; humiliation, a member of the class of negative emotions). The difference, then, lies elsewhere. The type is an abstract "individual" that is the result of an induction made from what will become its tokens, relative to which it subsequently acquires the status of a generative entity (as opposed to genetic).[1] The definition of a class is not an individual entity, but rather an inventory of one or more properties, optionally accompanied by rules for evaluating the membership of the element. This does not keep us from potentially associating a type with a class.

Furthermore, an element may correspond to a token – a particular wolf in the class of wolves in a particular zoo – or to a type – the wolf as a member of the canine class (along with the dog, etc.).

How classifications are represented

A classification – at least if it is simple – may be visually represented in linear textual format, e.g.: wolf < canines < mammals, where the first term is the element (element < included class < including class); animal > werewolf < human, where the element is the term in the middle (class 1 > element < class 2)

Once it reaches a certain degree of complexity, a classification is usually represented by mapping it out in a strictly visual manner, e.g., with set-notation graphs or a tree diagram. An organizational chart is a tree diagram, but it does not exactly correspond to a classification (for instance, the class //CEO//, which includes the element 'Paul Dupont', does not encompass the class //Marketing Director//, which includes the element 'Pierre Durand'). In a vertical tree diagram, the more specific units are placed below the more general units: an encompassed class appears below the class that encompasses it, an element appears below the least general class to which it belongs (it can also be placed inside the geometric shape representing this class, e.g., a rectangle). *Mutatis mutandis* for a horizontal tree diagram. Below is an example of a vertical tree diagram. The classes here are the naive ontological classes (the classes of beings), and the elements are given in parentheses inside the rectangles representing the classes.

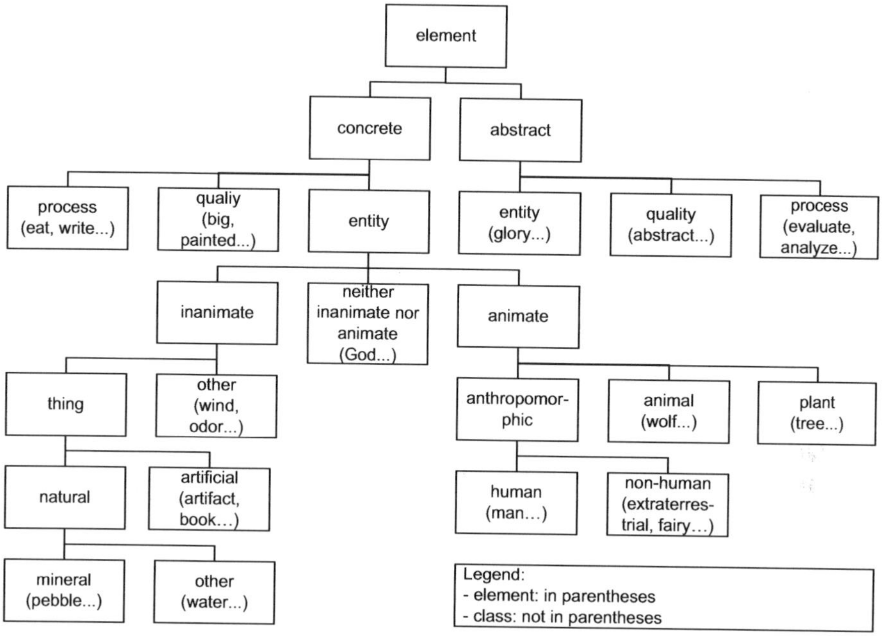

Figure 14.1 The naive ontological classes

The following convention can be used to visually summarize conceptual networks made up of classes/elements (or types/tokens) and wholes/parts: horizontal arrow: classification operation (the relation between class and element); vertical arrow: decomposition operation (the relation between whole and part). The following is an example of a simple conceptual network.

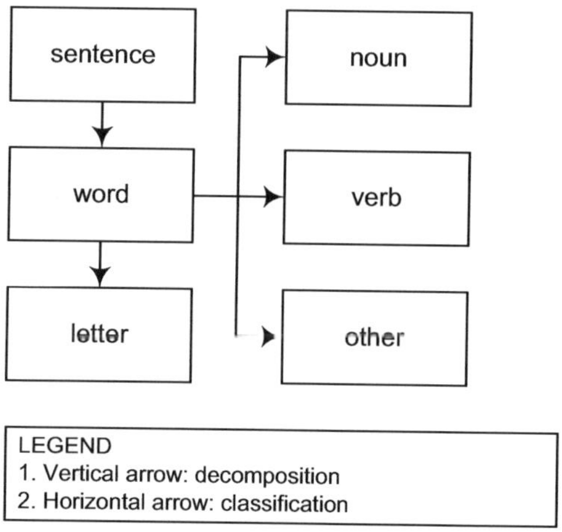

Figure 14.2 Example of a simple conceptual network

In order to have access to the most effective visual representation, one must be able to convert from a table to a diagram or the reverse. A table may be useful for complex structures, particularly the ones that contain numerous horizontal poly-classifications. Below we give the example of the same very simple structure shown both as a table and as a diagram.

Table 14.1 A simple classification represented in a table

Seme → *Signified ↓*	*not edible*	*edible*	*plant*	*animal*
apple		+	+	
fish		+		+

Various relations exist between the units of the table. "Apple" is a whole whose parts are the semes (features of meaning) "edible" and "plant"; the same principle applies for "fish" and its semes. Each seme is also the defining feature of a class by that name; this class indexes the units that have the feature as elements: for example, the feature /edible/ defines the class //edible//, which indexes the elements 'apple' and 'fish'. The table shows two aspects of the analysis rather well: a) the descending mereological aspect: it takes a whole (a signified, in this case) and defines the parts (the semes) that compose it (reading across a line in the table); b) the descending set aspect: it takes a class (defined by a seme, in this case) and identifies the elements (the signifieds) that are part of it (reading down a column in the table).

Below is the same structure in graphical representation (the opposition normal boxes/shaded boxes is used to distinguish a class from an indexed element, respectively). It should be noted that the value more general/more specific is apt to vary for the same classes. For example, in this case, one could easily invert the structure and set up //plant// and //animal// as encompassing classes, and //inedible// and //edible// as encompassed classes (so that each encompassing class would have an //inedible// class and an //edible// class under it).

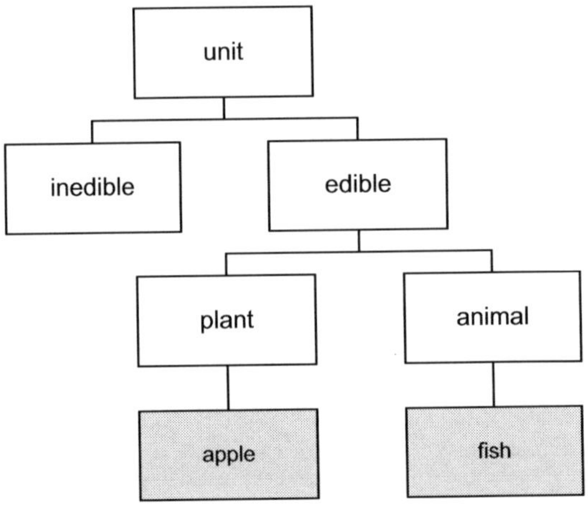

Figure 14.3 A simple classification represented in a diagram

Classes with plus/minus features and monocriteria/polycriteria classes

When a defining feature of the class must be present, it can be called a plus feature (e.g., vertebrates must have a spinal column); in the opposite case, it is called a minus feature (invertebrates). If the classification is based on a dyadic categorial opposition (e.g., vertebrate/invertebrate or true/false), the plus feature (vertebrate, true) is identical to the negation of the minus feature (not-invertebrate, not-false; as a counter example, the feature /not-black/ indexes not only the white elements, but also the red, blue, etc.).

A monocriteria class (or simple class) is a class defined by just one feature (e.g., the French textual genre of "*formes brèves*", in the broadest sense of the term; or the carnivore class). In the opposite case, it will be called a "polycriteria class" (or "complex class"). However, a monocriteria class can presuppose features that come from mono- or polycriteria encompassing classes (for example, the "*formes brèves*" are literary forms, which are in turn textual forms, which are in turn artistic acts, etc.). In a polycriteria class, all of the features can be mandatory; or all of the features can be alternating, with optionally a minimum number of them present (refer back to the example of depression); or some features can be mandatory and others can alternate with one another (in which case not all the features are weighted the same, since a mandatory feature counts more than an alternating feature).

The degree of specificity

In theory, one cannot go beyond the degree of precision – the grain, or pixel – of the semiotic act being analyzed. The classification will end where the act ends (although it is possible to indicate the potential classes that are left empty). That is, a text may or may not specify the class of dogs according to breed (e.g., poodle, German Shepherd, etc.). However, by methodological reduction (which is intentional, relevant, and explicitly stated), the analyst may choose to not go as far as the semiotic act (e.g., by stopping at the class of dogs even though the text distinguishes between a poodle and a Saint Bernard). In short, although a class may not necessarily be the most specific one per se, it can be for the semiotic act being analyzed, or for a particular analysis of this act, through methodological reduction.

A semiotic act may create narrower classes than the ones that are generally used (e.g., the class of 19th-century southern Hungarian waltzes!). A semiotic act may create classes of the same generality as the ones that are generally used (in a song, Jacques Brel adds the four-beat waltz and the thousand-beat waltz to the regular waltz, which has three beats by definition).

Distinct classes and distinct elements

A distinction should be made between the element or class entity and the name(s) given to it. Two forms of names should be distinguished, since they may not match: the analytical name, i.e., the name given to an element or a class by the analyst (who can simply copy the commonly used names for these entities, of course); and the de facto name, i.e., the name given to an element or a class in the object being analyzed. It would be an error to think that elements or classes are different when they are actually the same element or class designated by different names. That being said, one can merge elements or classes as needed by methodological reduction.

An example will serve to illustrate these problems. In a text, "garbage" and "trash": (1) may be synonymous names referring to one element that is mentioned several times (there is a single rebus entity, sometimes called "garbage" and sometimes called "trash"); (2) may be synonymous names, each used to designate a different element, but belonging to the same class (there are two rebus entities; the first one is called "garbage", and the second one "trash"); (3) may each designate a different element, each belonging to a different class (in this text, garbage is distinguished from trash, even if they are both encompassed elsewhere in an inclusive class).

Exhaustive/non-exhaustive and decidable/undecidable classifications

An exhaustive classification uses all of the elements of the set being described; e.g., for a bag in which all the marbles are black or white, the classes //white marbles// and //black marbles// will be used. A non-exhaustive classification does not use all of the elements of the set being described; e.g., the classes //white marbles// and //black marbles// will be used for a bag that also contains red ones. In the latter case, there is also a residual class (//other elements//), even if it is implicit, where the elements that don't correspond to any of the selected classes are indexed.[2] Classifications may have different degrees of precision, depending on the number of potential classes that are left in the residual class. For example, the classification: //human//, //animal//, //plant//, //mineral//, //other// is more precise than the classification: //human//, //animal//, //other//.

NOTE: FURTHER DETAILS ON THE RESIDUAL CLASS

The residual class may not be explicitly stated, but this does not mean that the classification structure does not anticipate its existence; it may just be a more sparing approach to analysis. For example, the classes //red marbles// and //black marbles// may be the only ones mentioned, and not the class //other marbles//. In addition, residual classes can be found at various levels in a single classification. To continue with our example, if it so happens that the marbles – no matter what color they are – can have four diameters, but only two are selected, then there will be two residual classes: one for color and one for diameter. So there will be a class //marbles with diameter *x*// that encompasses //red marbles//, //black marbles//, //marbles of any other color//, a class //marbles with diameter *y*// that encompasses the same three subclasses, and a class //marbles of other diameters// that encompasses the same three subclasses.

Any property is either decidable or undecidable, and membership in a class is no exception. If the observing subject is not in a position to say which of the proposed classes a particular element fits into, then it is undecidable. If the element can be classified in the residual class, then it is not undecidable.

Monoclassification/polyclassification

A single element may belong to more than one series of classes. One can distinguish between a "vertical" polyclassification, which includes one or more encompassing classes (wolf < canines (subclass) < mammal (class)), and a "horizontal" polyclassification, which is made at the same level of generality (human > werewolf < canines). The object being analyzed and/or the type of classification used in the act and/or the analysis of this act may allow for only single classifications of a single unit, or may admit multiple classifications. The scientific typologies (e.g., the animal classifications) tend to create single classifications (e.g., an animal is an invertebrate or a vertebrate; it cannot be both at the same time).

Categorial/incremental classifications

In an incremental classification, membership in a class is subject to quantification, using a number (e.g., a percentage or coefficient) or a mark of intensity ("not very", "medium", etc.). An incremental class has an inverse correlation with another incremental class (even if it is the residual class). That is, if someone is less human, he is necessarily more of something else, such as animal. Consequently, we will say that the incremental classes call for horizontal polyclassifications. In a categorial classification, a unit belongs or does not belong to a class; there is no possible quantification. For example, a text may regard a being as human or not, with no middle ground; a marble as red or not, with no middle ground.

Monadic/polyadic classifications

A classification may also be characterized in terms of the number of classes it includes; it may be monadic (just one class) or polyadic (dyadic: two classes, triadic: three classes, etc.). The residual class will be included in the count only if it is among the accepted possibilities. For example, for a bag containing only black marbles and white marbles, the classification will be dyadic, since the relevant classes are //white// and //black// (//other color// is not relevant).

Isomorphic/allomorphic classifications

A classification may be isomorphic (structured identically throughout) or allomorphic (structured differently from one part to another), relative to the various aspects we have mentioned. For example, the number of defining features may be the same for each class or may vary from one class to another; polyclassifications may be possible throughout, or only in certain places; one classification may be entirely dyadic, and thus any class other than a terminal class may be broken down into two subclasses; another classification may include some parts that are dyadic and others that are triadic; one classification may be entirely categorial, while another may have both categorial and incremental classes.

Time and the observing subject

In analysis by classification – as in any analysis – the relative variables must be taken into account, particularly time and the observing subject (for details, see the chapter on structural relations). As far as time is concerned, it's a matter of seeing whether the classification changes in response to changes in time: in the indexation of the elements, the characteristics of the classes (defining features, incremental vs. categorial, etc.), the structure of the tree diagram, and so on. For example, the history of physics is punctuated by the discovery of new particles that change the particle classification. Thus, the atom was part of the class of undecomposable elements until it was discovered that it could be broken down into electrons, protons, and neutrons.

As for the observing subject, it's a matter of seeing whether the classification changes based on which agent is taken into account. In a literary text, the observers can be the following, among others: the real or empirical author, the implied author (the impression that the text gives of its author), the narrator, the narratee, the character, the implied reader (the impression that the text gives of its expected and unexpected readers), the real or empirical reader. For example, within one text, the explicit or implicit classification made by a particular character (an assumptive observing subject) may or may not match that of another character (also an assumptive observing subject) or those which the text definitively considers as valid, traditionally through the voice of the omniscient narrator (the reference observing subject). This dynamic between points of view can operate from one semiotic act to another, e.g., in a particular text the reference observing subject views the tomato as a fruit, and in another, the reference observing subject views it as a vegetable. For details on the dynamic between observing subjects, see the chapter on dialogics.

Lastly, one can verify whether the observing subject and the classification are related to a system. For example, an observing subject and a classification that proclaim the tomato to be a fruit reflect an observing subject and classification whose stereotypical sociolect is one of scientific discourse. An observing subject and classification that view the tomato as a vegetable (since it is used in vegetable salads rather than fruit salads) reflect an observing subject and classification whose stereotypical sociolect is one of non-scientific, "naive" discourse. An observing subject and classification that view the tomato as an animal in two texts by the same author reflect an idiolectal observing subject and classification specific to an individual. For details on the various system levels (dialect, sociolect, idiolect, textolect, and analect), see the chapter on structural relations.

Application: classifying death in *Hamlet*

In the chapter dealing with the actantial model, we provide a comprehensive analysis of Shakespeare's *Hamlet*. The recurrent structure of the requests to kill occurring throughout the play will be presented in the chapter on semantic graphs. The present chapter demonstrates how to link together a general typology of possible types of death and of actual deaths occurring in the play.

The diagram below shows a general typology of the types of death.

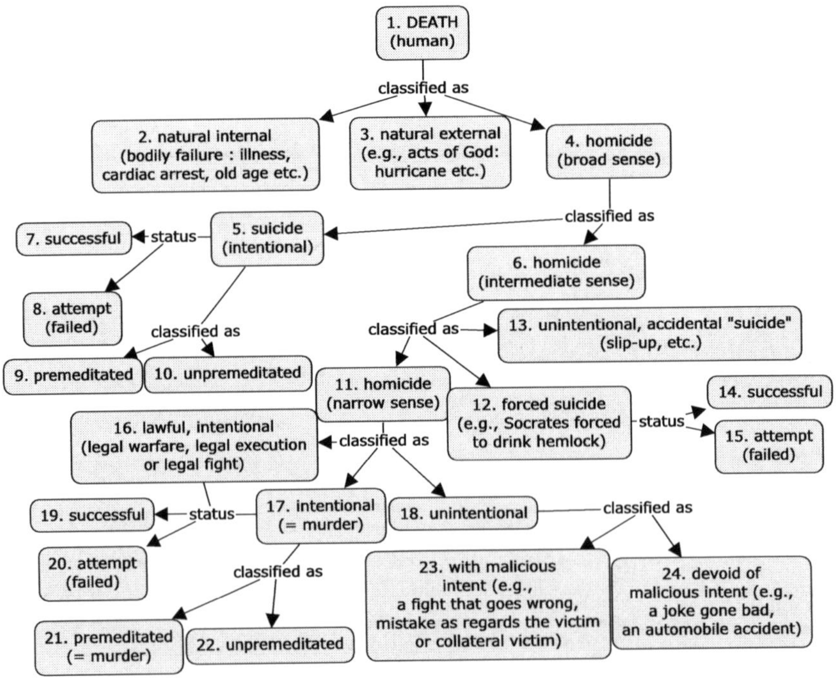

Figure 14.4 Typology of the types of death

This general typology of death can be applied in a twofold manner in analyzing not only Shakespeare's *Hamlet* (but any semiotic work): the deaths occurring in the play are situated within the categories of the general typology which is intended to cover all possible real-life deaths (without going into every last detail, such as the motives for murder); the general typology is described or modified to correspond to the deaths in the play. The latter approach is adopted here.

A distinction must first be made between real death (Hamlet's death in the play, for example) and unreal death, the latter further classified as symbolic death and death as a form of entertainment – such as the death of the loser in the friendly swordplay between Hamlet and Laertes – and fictitious death. In the play, death occurs in the play staged by Hamlet that depicts the murder of the king, initially through a pantomime, then as a dramatic play with speeches. It can also be observed in Pyrrhus's brutal slaughter of Priam (Greek mythology) a passage Hamlet begins to recite himself before calling on one of the Players to take over. This murder is a hyperbolic regicide (for one, it is based on legend and, secondly, Claudius is a dark, pitiful version of Priam) that portends the regicide of Claudius and Hamlet (Hamlet becomes king for the briefest of moments between Claudius's death and his own).

The death of Ophelia, occurring offstage unlike that of all the other main characters save Rosencrantz and Guildenstern, is either a suicide (box 5 in the diagram), an "unintentional suicide" (box 13), or a natural death from external causes (box 3): she falls from the broken branch of a tree into the water below and drowns. The play supports either interpretation: accidental death or suicide. The death of Hamlet's two "friends" who personally and unsuspectingly deliver the letter ordering their execution, can similarly be categorized as "unintentional suicide".

Ophelia's case aside, other instances of suicide are referenced elsewhere in the play. Hamlet, for example, believes that but for the fear of what the afterlife might hold, every man (or woman) would commit suicide. Hamlet, thus, like virtually all mortals, decides, in spite of everything, to continue to live. Yet, notwithstanding a dark foreboding of his demise, he engages in the deadly duel – in essence, nothing short of suicide. In addition, there is evidence of his usual prescience in that prior to the revelation by his father's ghost, Hamlet senses that there was foul play afoot in the death of his father. Yet again, Hamlet's doubt, in this case concerning his premonition, will have fatal consequences for someone – this time, himself. Horatio, witnessing the death of his friend Hamlet, wants to take his own life. But Hamlet orders him to stay alive to tell his tragic story.

Does Claudius die from being stabbed with the sword, coupled with the effect of the poison or does he die from poison only? Struck by Hamlet's poisoned sword, the king cries out for help, saying he is but wounded. From this, we may infer that it is the poison from which he dies. At the same time, Claudius is forced by Hamlet to drink the poisoned wine. Is this, thus, forced suicide? Or is it murder? The play seems to suggest that Hamlet compels Claudius to drink the wine by using physical force. But an alternative explanation may exist: Hamlet forces him to drink by threatening him with his sword (this, however, is hardly convincing since the king, poisoned by the sword is well aware he is all but dead). This second reading is the one adopted in Gregory Doran's 2009 film production of Hamlet. Either way, scholars will likely be reminded of the death of Socrates (who was forced to drink hemlock), a celebrated case of forced suicide. This would be an undesired effect, Claudius, unlike Socrates, being evil, wretched, and genuinely guilty.

The main characters – all with the exception of Ophelia and Horatio, the latter enjoined by Hamlet to not take his own life – are victims of murder. In some instances, the murder is intentional: the two carried out by Claudius, the slaying of Claudius by Hamlet, and the murder of Hamlet's two "friends", sent to their death by Hamlet himself. The play is silent on the type of death suffered by Yorick, King Hamlet's court jester. We can assume, nonetheless, that it is neither homicide nor – since he is buried on holy ground – suicide. This undetermined death thus stands in contrast to the deaths of the main characters.

In several other instances, the murders are unintentional, i.e., lacking in motive and unpremeditated: Hamlet's mistaken killing of Polonius (he thought he was killing Claudius; box 23); Claudius *v* the queen (the poisoned wine was meant for Hamlet, not the queen; box 23); Hamlet *v* Laertes (Hamlet unwittingly poisons Laertes by cutting him with the latter's own poisoned sword; box 24).

The homicides (suicides excluded) all have different motives; winning a war and gaining lands – both lawfully (the combat between Hamlet Sr. and Fortinbras Sr.); usurping power and stealing the queen (Claudius); lawful and honorable vengeance (Hamlet *vis-à-vis* Claudius, who is responsible not only for killing Hamlet but for the murder of both his father and his mother); lawful but dishonorable vengeance (Laertes *vis-à-vis* Hamlet); self-preservation (Claudius *vis-à-vis* Hamlet, who exposes him). Claudius, we believe, genuinely loves the queen as evidenced by his dismay at seeing her drink the poisoned wine; but the question remains: what is his ultimate aim – the throne? The queen? Or the throne *and* the queen? A number of unsuccessful homicides are interspersed throughout the play: Claudius's attempt on Hamlet's life in England; Hamlet's mistaken killing of Polonius for Claudius; Hamlet's last-minute decision not to kill Claudius while the latter is at prayer.

The three lawful forms of homicide are present in the play: war (between Hamlet Sr. and the Fortinbras Sr. as well young Fortinbras's wars; duelling that leads to possible or mandatory death (the wartime duel between Hamlet Sr. and Fortinbras Sr.); execution (the unexpected execution of Hamlet's "friends" Rosencrantz and Guildenstern in his stead). What is meant to be friendly and entertaining swordplay between Laertes and Hamlet turns out to be as deadly as the duel between Hamlet Sr. and Fortinbras Sr. Whereas Hamlet Sr.'s duel with Fortinbras Sr.is the motive for young Fortinbras's revenge, Laertes's duel with Hamlet Jr. cancels the debt: Laertes slays his father's killer. Revenge for death is presented throughout the play as justifiable if not lawful. The eye-for-an-eye, tooth-for-a-tooth principle is an anomaly in this supposedly Christian work – "Thou shalt not kill", goes the sixth Commandment – which, for example, makes much of the spiritual immorality of Ophelia's putative suicide.

Notes

1 We will give a simple example of generative and genetic viewpoints: If we isolated the world view governing the production of a work of literature, we would be isolating a hypothetical, abstract form that generated the work; if we studied the notes and the rough drafts for this work, we would be looking from a genetic viewpoint.

2 Even when one thinks that the classification is exhaustive and that it covers all the units to be described, it may be wise to provide a residual class "just in case" some units were inadvertently neglected. The neutral term of a semiotic square might seem like a residual class for a classification that is both dyadic and oppositional, but the potential residual elements must be checked to ascertain that they actually do represent the negation of the two basic oppositions of the square. For example, in the semiotic square wealth/poverty, "tomato" does not fit under the neutral term (it is simply a unit external to this square), but "middle-class" does. For details, see the chapter on the semiotic square.

15 Analyzing rhythm and arrangement

Summary

Three operations are needed to produce a rhythm: a segmentation into units, and the arrangement and seriation of the units. "Arrangement" also designates the component that concerns the arrangement of the units in a temporal and/or spatial range. Rhythm can be defined as the specific configuration produced by combining at least two units of identical (A, A) or different (A, B) "value" in at least two positions that follow one another in time.

Rhythmic analysis takes the following principal factors into account. **1. The number of successive positions** in the rhythmic sequence. For example, a quatrain is a grouping of four lines, and an alexandrine is a grouping of 12 syllables. **2. The number of simultaneous positions** in the rhythmic sequence. The number of simultaneous positions defines the planarity of sequence. If there is no simultaneous position possible, the rhythm is monoplanar; otherwise it is pluriplanar (or polyplanar). For example, a line and a stanza are monoplanar sequences relative to syllables and lines, respectively: a single syllable or a single line occupies one relevant position in the succession. **3. The number of units per successive position** (including potential superposed units). For example, a quatrain is arranged with one line per position; an alexandrine is arranged with one syllable per position. **4. The number of units that can occupy each position**. This does not mean the number of units per successive or simultaneous position, but the number of different units from which one can select to occupy the successive or simultaneous position. In order to represent a rhythmic pattern, each different kind of unit can be represented with a different letter. For example, A and B could represent the two rhymes of a quatrain in a sonnet. **5. The organization of the pattern**. With respect to what type of succession of units occurs, the major organizational patterns are: (1) immediate succession (e.g., A, B) and (2) mediate succession (e.g., between A and B in: A, X, B, where X = silence; however, there is immediate succession between A and X and between X and B). With respect to how the different kinds of units are ordered, the major organizational patterns are: (1) grouping (e.g., A, A, B, B); (2) interlacing (e.g., A, B, A, B); (3) embedding (e.g., A, B, B, A). **6. The type of units involved**. Rhythms are not restricted to the so-called "temporal" semiotics, like music, film, and literature. Rhythm, then, is not a characteristic solely of poetry, nor solely of versified poetry. In order to have rhythm, all that is needed is at least two units strung together (even if it is the same unit, reapeated) in at least two successives positions. **7. The actual units involved**. The actual units involved are the tokens of the types of units involved, e.g., a particular seme or a particular phoneme used in the rhythmic sequence. For example, in a particular quatrain of a sonnet, the rhymes may be *–our* (A) and *–aine* (B). **8. The duration of the units**. With respect to the length of its lines, a stanza of alexandrines is isometric (and thus monometric): it contains units that always have 12 syllables.

Theory

Rhythm is a complex notion. What we will present here is not a scholarly synthesis on the subject. Our objective is simply to offer some avenues for analyzing rhythm and the arrangement it presupposes.

Arrangement and rhythm

Three operations are needed to produce a rhythm: a segmentation into units, and the arrangement and seriation of the units.

These units can be strictly semiotic:

1 The signifier (or its parts, e.g., the phonological features of the phonemes: vowel, consonant, open, closed, etc.);
2 The signified (or its parts, such as semes and cases, e.g., the semes /liquid/ and /edible/ in the signified 'water', or groupings of these parts: isotopies, semic molecules, etc.);
3 The sign (i.e., the combination of a signifier and a signified, e.g., the word "water").

The units can also be peri-semiotic:

4 The stimulus to which a signifier refers (e.g., a particular phone, i.e., a specific utterance of a phoneme; or a particular phonic feature);
5 The mental image (or multimodal simulacrum (Rastier)) that a signified defines (e.g., the representation of a pet fish created by the syntagm "the canary and the fish"; or a particular representational feature).

Lastly, the units can be mixed, at least in theory (stimulus and signifier, simulacrum and signified, etc.).

Rastier uses the term **distribution** (2001, p. 249) for the textual component relating to the arrangement of the units of the linguistic signifier, and the term **tactics** (1989) for the component relating to the arrangement of the units of the linguistic signified.[1] These names can be extended to non-linguistic signifiers and signifieds. We can have an arrangement of stimuli and an arrangement of representations (or mental images). **Arrangement** can then be viewed as the overall component relating to the arrangement of semiotic and peri-semiotic units in a temporal and/or spatial range. The propositions we advance are in the context of arrangement, and are therefore an indirect contribution to distribution and tactics.

The various specific arrangements (distribution, tactics, etc.) must be distinguished because the way they are segmented does not exactly correspond. We will give just a few instances of non-correspondance. For tactics and distribution, one signified may be distributed over multiple elements of the signifier (e.g., the signified 'water' distributed over five graphemes: *w*, *a*, *t*, *e* and *r*). One signifier may be associated with multiple signifieds, particularly with symbolic connections, which "superpose" a "literal" signified (*flower* with the signified 'rose') and a "figurative" signified (*flower* with the signified 'woman'). Linguistic signifiers have two distributions: one for the phonemic signifiers and one for the graphemic signifiers (whose associated stimuli are the graphs, i.e., the letters indicating the graphemes). These two distributions do not coincide exactly; for example, one phoneme may be associated with more than one grapheme, such as the phoneme [*o*] and the graphemes *e-a-u*).

Succession may occur in time only, or in time and space, such as a succession of elements in a table that is read, say, from left to right. Going beyond the rough distinction between semiotics of space and semiotics of time, we will distinguish semiotics or languages: (1) of constrained time and consecution: e.g., a film screening is generally not interrupted, slowed down, accelerated, run backward, etc.; (2) of unconstrained time with constrained consecution: a text is generally read from one word to the next, but one can take a break between two words, go back, skip ahead, etc.; (3) of unconstrained time and consecution: e.g., one can look at a painting for as long as one chooses, and go from certain figures in it to others at will.

A definition of rhythm

Rhythm can be defined as the specific configuration produced by combining at least two units of identical or different "value" in at least two positions that follow one another in time. With respect to this definition, the **minimal rhythmic configuration** – two units placed in two successive positions – will take one of the following four forms: (1) A, B; (2) B, A; (3) A, A or (4) B, B.[2]

In this minimal rhythmic configuration, the value used, one of the two values used, or both values (in some cases, the silences will be of different kinds) may be a "**semiotic silence**", i.e., the absence of a "full" unit. Considering the four preceding forms again, if we assign a semiotic silence to B, then we will have: (1) A, Ø; (2) Ø, A; (3) A, A or (4) Ø, Ø.

If a moment in a rhythmic sequence can take the form of the fourth configuration, e.g., the two silences between two words separated by a double space (A, Ø, Ø, B), what would it be like to have a semiotic production based entirely on this configuration? First, we have to realize that semiotic silence is never absolute; so our double space between two words is not the vacuum of space or the absolute void between atomic particles, but simply the lack of a letter. Imagine a painting whose white canvas is simply divided in two by a vertical line. From left to right there will be a temporalized succession of two lacks of paint (the line is thought of as a non-stripe and a non-pigment). "Time" elapses, something happens (it's not an absolute semiotic silence), but the expected phenomena (of pigmentation) do not occur.

We are not defining rhythm restrictively as the same elements returning. This way we can be sure we do not exclude from rhythmic analysis **rhythms that are partially repetitive** (e.g., A, B, A, C) and **rhythms that are entirely non-repetitive** (e.g., A, B or A, B, C), alongside the **rhythms that are entirely repetitive** (e.g., A, A or A B, B, A), as far as the inventory of units is concerned.

Factors of rhythm

The inventory of rhythmic patterns – even the general ones – is certainly vast. Rhythmic analysis takes the following principal factors into account, which we will explain in detail afterwards.

1 **The number of successive positions** in the rhythmic sequence. For example, a quatrain is a grouping of four lines, and an alexandrine is a grouping of 12 syllables.
2 **The number of simultaneous positions** in the rhythmic sequence. The number of simultaneous positions defines the planarity of sequence. If there is no simultaneous position possible, the rhythm is monoplanar; otherwise it is pluriplanar (or polyplanar). For example, a line and a stanza are monoplanar sequences relative to syllables and lines, respectively: a single syllable or a single line occupies one relevant position in the succession.
3 **The number of units per successive position** (including possible superposed units). For example, a quatrain is arranged with one line per position; an alexandrine is arranged with one syllable per position.
4 **The number of units that can occupy each position**. This does not mean the number of units per successive or simultaneous position, but the number of different units from which one can select to occupy the position. This number can be a priori open or closed. In order to represent a rhythmic pattern, each different kind of unit can be represented by a different letter. For example, A and B could represent the two rhymes of a quatrain in a sonnet.
5 **The organization of the pattern**. With respect to what type of succession of units occurs, the major organizational patterns are: (1) **immediate succession** (e.g., A, B) and (2) **mediate succession** (e.g., between A and B in: A, X, B, where X = silence; however, there is immediate succession between A and X and X and B). And with respect to how the different kinds of units are ordered, the major organizational patterns are: (1) **grouping** (for example, A, A, B, B); (2) **interlacing** (for example, A, B, A, B); and (3) **embedding** (for example, A, B, B, A). In a tetradic rhythmic pattern (four units) with two values (A and B), like that of the rhymes in a quatrain of a sonnet, these three major organizational patterns correspond respectively to 1) couplet rhymes (A, A, B, B); 2) cross rhymes (A, B, A, B); and 3) envelope rhymes (A, B, B, A).
6 **The type of units involved**. As for the types of semiotic productions in which they occur, rhythms are not restricted to the so-called "temporal" semiotics, like music, film, and literature. Thus rhythm is not solely a characteristic of poetry in particular, nor just of versified poetry. In order to have rhythm, all that is needed is at least two units strung together (or even the same unit repeated) in at least two successive positions. So it makes perfect sense to talk about rhythm in a pictorial work.
7 **The actual units involved**. The actual units involved are the tokens of the types of units involved, e.g., a particular seme or a particular phoneme used in the rhythmic sequence. For example, in a particular quatrain of a French sonnet, the rhymes may be *–our* (A) and *–aine* (B).
8 **The duration of the units**. Times and rhythms can be: (1) **isometric**: all of the units have the same range (*de facto* or by "rounding" to standard values); (2) **allometric**: all the units have different ranges; or (3) **parametric**: some units have the same range and others do not. Isometric times and rhythms are necessarily **monometric**. Allo- or parametric times and rhythms are necessarily **polymetric**. With respect to the length of its lines, a stanza of alexandrines is isometric (and thus monometric): it contains units that always have 12 syllables; a stanza alternating

between dodecasyllabic lines (alexandrines) and octosyllabic lines (eight syllables) would be parametric (and thus polymetric). We can distinguish **major cadence** rhythmic sequences and others in **minor cadences**. The latter use longer and longer units in their succession; the former use shorter and shorter units.

Discussion

The number of successive positions

The structures produced by the succession of positions can be short, medium, or long; dyadic, triadic, etc.; even or odd; and so forth. Each of these structures has its own potential aesthetic effects. For example, odd rhythms create an effect of asymmetry, instability and/or dynamism, at least if they are short enough that the odd rhythm can register. If the sequence is monoplanar, the number of successive positions is also the number of units that form the sequence (including possible silences).

The number of simultaneous positions

A rhythm is **monoplanar** if it uses only one unit in each position: e.g., A, B, C. A rhythm is **pluriplanar** if it uses more than one unit in each position: e.g., A + B, C + D. If it uses two units per position, it will be described more precisely as biplanar; if it uses three, triplanar, etc. Obviously, a rhythm can be partially monoplanar and partially pluriplanar, i.e., monoplanar in one or more parts of the rhythmic sequence and pluriplanar in one or more other parts: e.g., A, B + C.

The term **homoplanar** will be used to describe rhythms whose planarity does not change along the way (e.g., whose rhythm is biplanar from the beginning to the end of the rhythmic sequence). And the term **heteroplanar** will be used to describe rhythms whose number of planes changes along the way (e.g., monoplanar in one place and pluriplanar in another; or biplanar in one place and triplanar in another).

The signifiers of language (except for special phenomena such as simultaneous replies in theater or in Altman's films) always proceed from monoplanar rhythms, since a given signifier position cannot be occupied by more than one unit. For example, you don't find two graphemes in a position allotted to one grapheme, except in special cases.

NOTE: PLANARITY AND INTERPRETIVE PERSPECTIVE

We will distinguish three **interpretive postures**: **presential** (defined by a "window" that is moved from one position to the next), **retrospective** (e.g., at position 2, changing the status of position 1), and **prospective** (anticipatory, e.g., at position 1, anticipating what position 2 will be). Depending on the posture, the planarity may be modified. Take the sequence A, B + C, D. In the "interpretive present", it is initially monoplanar, then biplanar, then monoplanar. But from the second position, through retrospection, the first position becomes biplanar (A+Ø), and through prospection (anticipation) the third position becomes biplanar as well (D+X; X would correspond to a value of some sort or a non-value, i.e., a silence).

NECESSARY AND ACCIDENTAL PLANARITIES

The planarity of a phenomenon with respect to a particular normative system or particular physical constraint will be either accidental or necessary (essential). The planarity is necessary if it cannot

not occur. It is accidental if although it did occur, it could have been otherwise. For example, the monoplanarity of the linguistic signifier is necessary, since this signifier is linear, with no possibility of superposition (at least that is how it is understood and generally used). In contrast, the monoplanarity of the image in a particular film is accidental: the film could have superposed fade-in and fade-out images (during the entire film or just at certain moments).

A voluntarily silent contemporary film (with no soundtrack – no words, music or noise) is accidentally monoplanar with respect to the relation between visual and auditory signs. Monoplanarity is then the result of a specific aesthetic vision (standard). But during the silent film era, this monoplanarity was necessary, since the sound could not be reproduced (a physical constraint).

NOTE: PLANARITY AND SYSTEM

The status accidental/necessary may vary depending on the systems involved. So it can also be said that our contemporary silent film is necessarily monoplanar if viewed in terms not of what was possible (according to film language in general, the system that we will call "lectal"), but in terms of what was done (this film's own system – the textolectal system – to which we will return later): The standard for this film dictated that no sound could be superposed on any images. For a typology of normative systems, see the chapter on structural relations.

TEMPORAL RELATIONS BETWEEN UNITS IN THE SAME SUCCESSIVE POSITION

The temporal relation between the formal units that are copresent in a single successive position can be: (1) strict simultaneity (in the diagram below, A and B); (2) partial simultaneity (C and D; only one of the four possible forms of partial simultaneity is shown in the diagram); (3) immediate succession (E and F, in particular); (4) delayed or mediate succession (which inserts a silence between the units, between G and H). For details on temporal relations, see the chapter on structural relations. All of the cases shown – except strict superposition – yield a different segmentation of units and positions; we will return to this question later, distinguishing the segmentation of rhythmic forms (units) from the segmentation of the rhythmic ground (positions).

The number of units per successive position

If the rhythm is pluriplanar, then the number of units per successive position is greater than one (including potential silences). If the rhythm is monoplanar, then this number is equal to one.

A change in the **grain of segmentation** (in the size of the units produced by the segmentation) may change the planarity and thus the number of units per successive position. For instance, a syllable can combine multiple phonemes in a single syllabic position, of course; from this standpoint, there is pluriplanarity. But the fact remains that there is only one syllable in a single syllabic position and only one phoneme in a single phonemic position; from this standpoint, there is monoplanarity.

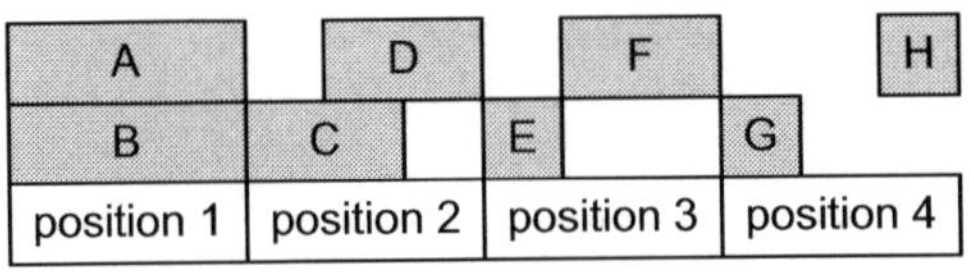

Figure 15.1 Temporal relations between units in a single successive position

Consider this quote by Julien Gracq: "Écrivain ou plumitif, percheron ou pur-sang" ["Writer or pen pusher, draft horse or thoroughbred"], where "plumitif" signifies "hack writer" and "percheron" means "draft horse". If the grain of segmentation is the word, then the rhythm of the semes /positive/ (A) and /negative/ (B) is monoplanar and has four positions: A, B, B, A. Note that a rhythm may discard positions that do not contain the relevant units (in this case, the positions defined by the word "or"), rather than recognizing them as bearing silences. If the grain is the syntagm (whose demarcation is the comma here), the rhythm of these same semes is biplanar and has two positions: A+B, B+A.

Consider this quote by Baudelaire (from the poem "Tout entière"): "Son haleine fait la musique,/ Comme sa voix fait le parfum" [Her breath makes music,/And her voice makes perfume"]. If the grain of segmentation is the word, and one counts only the nouns, the rhythm of the semes /smell/ (A) and /hearing/ (B) is monoplanar and has four positions: A ("breath"), B ("music"), B ("voice"), A ("perfume"). If the grain of segmentation is the line (whose demarcation is the slash here), the rhythm of these same semes is biplanar and has two positions: A + B, B + A. This is not a chiasmus, since it does not matter in which order the As and the Bs appear in each line; each line creates a simultaneity of As and Bs.

This issue of how variations in segmentation affect the analysis is a broad one; it does not apply just to analysis of rhythms, but to any analysis that involves an arrangement, and more generally, to any analysis that involves wholes and parts. For details, see the chapter on thymic analysis.

The number of units that can occupy each position

The number of units from which one can select may be essential (defined a priori, e.g., in classical French poetry, a rhyme is necessarily feminine or masculine), or conversely, it may be accidental (a priori somewhat open, e.g., the color of the vertical stripes of color in a painting, or the choice of a phoneme in a phonic poem). Whether it is an open or closed "paradigm" (the pool of units from which one draws to produce a rhythmic sequence), once the sequence is completed (with the exception of potential infinite rhythmic sequences), it is possible to establish the inventory of the various units that were used (and the various units that were not used). For example, a traditional sonnet will employ only five rhymes (A, B, C, D, E). To give another example, a painter can theoretically choose from thousands of colors, but his striped painting will only use three, and thus in each stripe of the painting, he has in a way chosen from three colors.

When one calculates the number of units or values that can occupy a position, one must define whether one of these values can be a "silence", i.e., the absence of a full value. For example, when counting syllables in lines of poetry, there is no silence possible; there has to be one (and only one) syllable in each position. On the other hand, in a film, the music can appear at the beginning and end of a sequence, for example, but be absent in the middle, creating the rhythm: music, silence, music (A, Ø, A).

VARIATIONS IN THE INVENTORY OF UNITS

At a given point in a rhythmic sequence, the next unit will be either the same as the previous one (A → A; the arrows here separate successive units), or it will be different (A → B). If the units are quantitative, the next unit will be an increase over the previous one (100 → 150; a little → a lot), a decrease (100 → 50; a lot → a little), or a continuance (100 → 100; a little → a little). Whether the units are qualitative or quantitative, if the next unit is different, it will be either a unit already present in an earlier position (A, B → A), or a new unit (A, B, → C). In the first instance, the variety of the inventory is kept the same (two different units in our example, A and B); in the second instance, the variety of the inventory of values has just expanded, and there will be an addition to (or increase in) the variety of the inventory (three different units in our example: A, B, C).

Organization of the pattern

We have presented three main rhythmic patterns – grouping, embedding, and interlacing – and illustrated them with dual-value (A and B) tetradic rhythms, respectively: A, A, B, B; A, B, B, A; and A, B, A, B. But we must remember that these main patterns also apply to non-tetradic rhythms, and rhythms other than those with two values; that they can be combined and can be applied not just to units, but to groups of units, and that a single unit in a sequence can proceed from multiple patterns. Here are some of the many examples of patterns:

1 A, A: grouping (minimal grouping);
2 A, A, A, A, A: grouping;
3 A, B, B: grouping;
4 A, A, B, B, C, C: grouping (of As, Bs, and Cs) and embedding (of the group of Bs);
5 A, B, C, A, B, C: interlacing (with not two, but three values: A, B and C);
6 A, B, A : embedding (minimal embedding, as embedding requires at least one unit surrounded by at least two identical units);
7 A, B, A, B, C, C: interlacing (of As and Bs, minimal in this case, since interlacing requires at least four units, and then two values at most) followed by a grouping (a minimal grouping of Cs);
8 A, B, B, A, A: embedding (of the Bs) and grouping (of the As at the end of the sequence).

OPERATIONS FOR TRANSFORMING PATTERNS

The major operations of transformation are applied to one or more **source elements** in order to obtain one or more **target elements**. Target and source elements can correspond to **types** (models) or **tokens** (more or less complete manifestations of the model). Operations can occur: (1) within a token; (2) within a type; (3) from a type to its token; (4) from the token to its type; (5) from one token to another (of the same type or of a different type); (6) from one type to another.

The major operations of transformation are (the arrow separates the source elements and the target elements):

1 **Addition** (example: A, B → A, B, C);
2 **Deletion** (example: A, B, C → A, B);
3 **Substitution** (example: A, B, A, B → A, B, A, C);
4 **Permutation** (example: A, B, C → C, A, B);
5 **Continuance** (example: A, B → A, B).

It will serve our purpose to provide just a few details on these operations. For further discussion, see the chapter on transformational operations.

We will distinguish **simple addition** (e.g., A, B → A, B, C) and **reduplicative addition** (or repetitive addition). Reduplicative addition adds one or more units that are already present elsewhere. It can be partial (e.g., A, B → A, B, A) or complete (e.g., A, B → A, B, A, B).

We will distinguish **partial deletion** (e.g., A, B → A) and **complete deletion** (e.g., A, B → Ø). Complete deletion produces semiotic silence, and as such, is always relative.

We will distinguish **any permutation** (e.g., A, B, C → C, A, B) and **permutation by inversion** (e.g., A, B, C → C, A, B). If multiple units are permuted, this permutation can be seen as the result of permuting single units, or one or more permutations of blocks of units (e.g., A, B, C, D → C, D, A, B).

Note that by broadening and clarifying a notion of Rastier's (1987, p. 83), we are adding **continuance** to the four operations defined by the Mu Group (1982, pp. 45–49; Klinkenberg, 1996, pp. 259–361). Unmarked continuance occurs when a unit that can be transformed is not. Marked continuance – the kind that interests us – occurs when expected transformations do not occur (since expectations may or may not be based on standards).

Additions/deletions of successive units result in the following correlative operations, respectively:

1 Expansion/condensation (range);
2 Lengthening/shortening (the passage of time);
3 Deceleration/acceleration (speed);
4 Lateness/earliness (expectation).

For example, in the sequence A, B, C, D, A, D, the A, D is a shortened version of the A, B, C, D that precedes it, and the D appears ahead of time due to the deletion of the expected intervening B and C. Note that permutation can produce lateness/earliness.

Rhythmic expectations may or may not be met. For example, an expectation of the chiasmus A, B, B, A is created after A, B, and is met when B, A comes. Conversely, rhythmic expectations are not met when A, C replaces A, B in A, B, A, B, A, C; or when A replaces F in A, B, C, D, E, A. Expectations produce an "image" (with the status 'possible') of the structure that will be realized (with the status 'real') if the prediction is right. An expectation that is met does not necessarily produce aesthetic euphoria: one could be hoping for the prediction to be wrong. An expectation that is not met does not necessarily produce aesthetic euphoria (or dysphoria).

As we have said, operations occur between a source pattern and a target pattern, and these can have the status of type or token. We will give a few examples. The type pattern can simply be kept as is in the token (or from a different point of view, perfectly reduplicated in the token): a particular text might manifest a perfect chiasmus (A, B, B, A). But the type pattern can also be transformed in its token: in A, B, C, B, A, the C can be seen as a delaying element inserted into a chiasmus. The token can be seen as the site of an internal transformation operation: for example, a particular token chiasmus can be seen as the result of a reduplicative addition through reverse permutation (the A, B is followed by the B, A). Clearly, operations can act between a type pattern and another type pattern. For example, groupings (e.g., A, A, B, B) can be seen as the result of a permutation starting from an embedding (the two Bs are simply permuted with the second A in the source pattern A, B, B, A).

CIRCULAR AND LINEAR PATTERNS

A **circular pattern** ends the way it begins (e.g., A, B, A or A, B, A, B). A **linear pattern** does not end the same way it begins (e.g., A, B, C). A pattern can be partially circular, and thus partially linear (e.g., A, B, A, C). The beginning and the end used to determine circularity vs. linearity can each be composed of one unit (e.g., A and F in A, B, C, D, E, F) or a group of units (e.g., A, B, and E, F in A, B,

C, D, E, F). So A, B, A, C is linear if we use a single unit to evaluate its status (A and C are different), and partially circular if we use two units to do this (A, B is approximately repeated by A, C).

The type of units involved

As far as the type of units concerned, rhythms are not restricted to signifiers (e.g., phonemes or graphemes) and the physical stimuli associated with signifiers (e.g., a particular phone (concrete utterance of a phoneme)).

Consequently, purely semantic rhythms, in particular, do exist. For example, as we saw, the four nouns in the utterance "Writer or pen pusher, draft horse or thoroughbred" form an embedded semantic rhythm (A, B, B, A) with the semes /positive/ (A), /negative/ (B), /negative/ (B), /positive/ (A).

The units involved in a rhythm can be qualitative. But they can also be quantitative and establish extensities or intensities of elements. Remember that the quantitative – i.e., the measurable – is divided into two subcategories: firstly, extensity, which is measurable and countable (e.g., 1, 2, 3, etc.); secondly, intensity, which is measurable and not countable (uncountable) (e.g., not any, a little, average, a lot, etc.; none, minimal, low, medium, high, maximal, etc.). For more on this subject, see the chapter on the tensive model. For example, in traditional French versification, one analyzes the arrangement of tonic accents based on intense units. In the chapter on the tensive model, we proposed a typology of curves of euphoric intensity with three levels of intensity and three successive positions, with the curves defining as many rhythmic patterns.

NOTE: QUALITATIVE AND QUANTITATIVE VALUES

If the variety of quantitative values is reduced (at the outset or after rounding), these quantitative values also become qualitative values in some sense, for example, in a rhythm that combines only 500s (A), 1000s (B), 1500s (C) and 2000s (D), and not, let's say, 400 different values that vary between 0 and 2000. It is possible to convert extensity to intensity: for example, the value 50 or the range 50–99 = very low intensity (A); 100 or 100–199 = low intensity (B), etc. It is also possible to convert intensity to extensity: for example, low = 1, medium = 5, high = 10.

The actual units involved

The relations between the different units involved are not restricted to identity (between A and A, for example) and alterity (between A and B, for example). The relation can be opposition, e.g., the alternation between masculine and feminine rhymes in traditional French versification. An oppositional relation can be represented as a sequence of the type A, B, or of the type A, -A (where the minus sign indicates negation). The relation can also be similarity. For example, Baudelaire's poem "L'irréparable" is composed of stanzas in which the first and last lines are either identical or very similar, yielding the sequence: A, A"; B, B'; C, C; D, D"; E, E; F, F"; G, G; H, H'; I, I'; J, J". We are distinguishing two degrees of similarity: the single apostrophe (') indicates a mere difference in punctuation; The double apostrophe (") indicates a lexical, syntactic, or other difference. For details on comparative relations, see the chapter on structural relations.

The duration of the units

INDICATING DURATIONS

Allo- and parametric times and rhythms may be **factometric**: the range of the units is derived by multiplying by one or more given factors (whole numbers, such as 2, 3, non-whole numbers, such as

1.2, 3.5). For example, A might last one second and B two seconds; The factor is then 2 (B = 2 x A) or 0.5 (A = 0.5 x B).

The ranges whose factors are whole numbers can be indicated by cumulating symbols (or by multiplying them by the factor). For example, AA, B, C (or 2A, B, C) indicates not that there are two A units, but that this unit has a double duration. The factors that are not whole numbers can be indicated directly in the rhythmic pattern, e.g., 3A, 2B, ½C.

By methodological reduction (i.e., intentional, made explicit, and justified) an analysis can be restricted to the qualitative data. For example, the pattern: 3A, 2B, ½C would become A, B, C.

The empty set symbol (Ø) can be used to indicate silence. In order to indicate potentially different kinds of silences, one can use the end-of-alphabet variables, like X, Y, Z. To indicate the range of the silences, the conventions we have already presented can be used; for example, A, XX, B, X, C indicates that the interval of silence between A and B is twice as long as the one between B and C.

FOUNDATIONAL AND FORMAL RANGES

We will distinguish between two ranges that are operative in rhythm: (1) the range (temporal duration and/or spatial length) of the units that are strung together to produce the rhythm; (2) the range of the intervals of the temporal or temporalized ground against which the forms constituted by the units stand out.

Foundational time, like formal time, can be isometric, allometric, or parametric. But foundational time is often, even usually, isometric: it founds the regularity upon which formal temporal irregularity stands out when it is present.

In some cases, the range of the formal units can define the segmentation even of the temporal ground, and then there is no need to distinguish the two temporalities. In other cases, the segmentation produced by the range of the sequenced units and that produced in the temporal ground do not fully correspond, and it is helpful to distinguish these two segmentations.

Ultimately, the metric of the units can be established internally, by comparing the relative ranges of the units, or externally, in relation to a different metric whose grain might describe the ranges of the units perfectly (possibly by "rounding") or not so perfectly. This different metric can be temporal, and might be measured in seconds, or it can be spatial and might be measured in centimeters or pixels, for example.

Suppose that the metric ground is integrated into the actual semiotic production.[3] For example, the stripes in the picture we created below are the foundational rhythm. The stripes of paint on the painting by Molinari that we will analyze later are the formal rhythm and the foundational rhythm simultaneously. Or the metric ground may be solely in the "reading", or interpretation, of the sequence (e.g., if one uses a ruler or a chronometer to measure the range of the units).

If the metric ground is found in the actual work and is distinct from the temporality of the forms therein, then the rhythm is biplanar: units overlap one another, and therefore two rhythms are superposed. But not every polyplanar rhythm separates its rhythms into formal rhythms and foundational rhythms.

Suppose we have a rhythmic sequence A, B, C.

Case 1. If the units have the same range, and they are not separated by one or more silences, there is no need to distinguish the range of the units from the range of the positions provided in the temporal ground, as the two articulations – that of the units and that of the ground – are identical. (See, for example, the painting by Molinari that we analyze later).

Case 2. However, if a silence occurs, say between A and B, and we want to take this variable into account, then it becomes necessary to distinguish the time of the forms from that of the ground. Then the pattern becomes: A, X, B, C (X = silence, with the same range as the actual values).
Case 3. Additionally, if one unit lasts longer than another, and we want to take this variable into account, then it becomes necessary to distinguish the time of the forms from that of the ground. Then the pattern becomes: A, BB, C (BB = double duration).
Case 4. Now suppose that the units have the same range, that they are not separated by silences, that we want to relate these ranges to standard seconds, and that the units do not each last exactly a second (e.g., a second and one-half). The grains of the two temporalities are then different; they are allomorphic, and it is helpful to distinguish them.

The following diagram illustrates these cases.

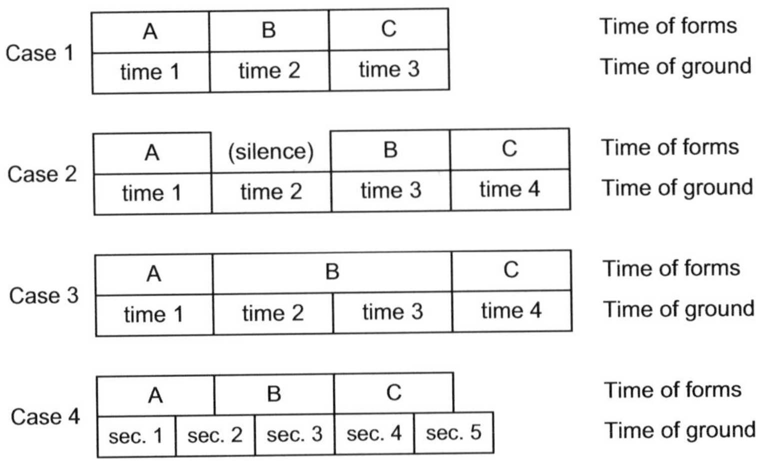

Figure 15.2 Examples of relations between foundational and formal time

Let's take a simple, concrete example. A canvas is separated into 10 vertical stripes of the same width. A rectangle (unit) has been set in each stripe. Each unit has the same height, but not necessarily the same width. Some units (A) are of the same width as the stripe; others (B) are only half as wide; others (C) are only a quarter as wide. The rhythm is then factometric. The stripes of the painting are the foundational time. The rectangles are the formal time. From left to right, the series of rectangles forms this rhythm: A, B, B, A, A, C, B, B, A, A. This sequence is represented in the diagram below (we have alternated the height of the position of the rectangles to aid comprehension, but we do not consider this as a biplanar rhythm).

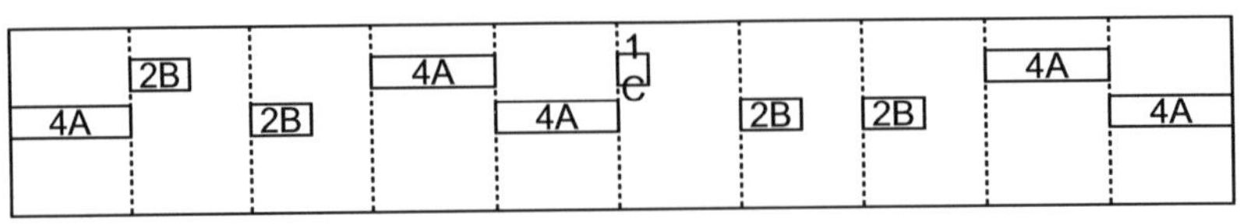

Figure 15.3 Example of a canvas with ten stripes

If we take the duration of the units into account, the rhythm is more precisely: AAAA, BB, BB, AAAA, AAAA, C, BB, BB, AAAA, AAAA or, using a different convention, 4A, 2B, 2B, 4A, 4A, C, 2B, 2B, 4A, 4A. If we now include the silences (X), taking the silence to be the difference between the width of the stripe and the width of the rectangle inside it, we have: 4A, 2B, 2X, 2B, 2X, 4A, 4A, C, 3X, 2B, 2X, 2B, 2X, 4A, 4A. Note that the stripes could have been different sizes, producing an allometric foundational time; and the rectangles could have been identical in size.

Applications

Application I: Green-red serial mutation *by Guido Molinari*

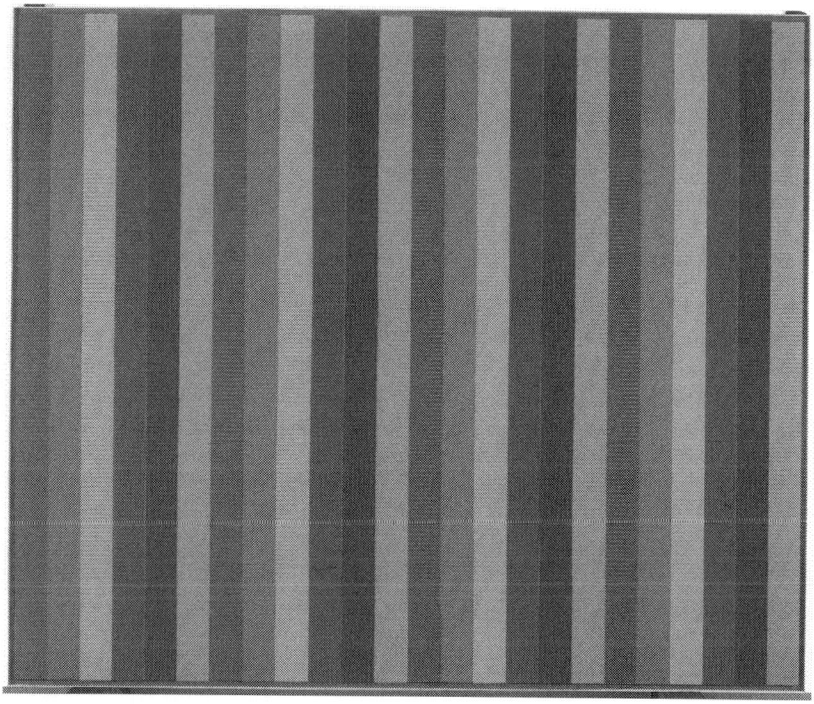

Figure 15.4 Green-red serial mutation

Source: Guido Molinari (1966)

We will present a partial analysis of the rhythmic sequence in the painting *Green-red serial mutation* (1966) by the Québecois painter Guido Molinari (1933–2004).[4] The artist was aware of the possible rhythmic interpretations of his paintings, judging from the titles of others of his works that contain "rhythm", e.g., the similar painting, *Bi-yellow rhythmic mutation* (1965).

The painting has an arrangement of 24 vertical stripes of the same width (despite what the reproduction leads us to believe), which constitute the formal and foundational rhythmic units simultaneously. Note that the structure is fairly uniform on the vertical axis, which makes it so that there is notable rhythm only horizontally, and not vertically, or diagonally, or otherwise.

One can see that the artist chose an even structure, so there is no central unit; the axis of symmetry falls between two stripes. Traditionally, even structures are said to produce an effect of symmetry-stability-statisme, and odd structures an effect of asymmetry-instability-dynamism. Clearly, none of these effects is a priori negative or positive; it is possible they will be given value, but only within a particular aesthetic (e.g., in *Art poétique*, Verlaine explicitly assigns value to long lines of odd-numbers of syllables). One can also see that the artist chose an even number that is particularly important in our culture (with its 24-hour day), rather than 16 or 22, for example.

Each stripe is the site where a choice is made between four colors, which we will call by their common names, green, red, blue, and orange. Notice that as complementary colors, green and red form an opposition; likewise for blue and orange. The painting's title gives preponderance to two of the colors: *Green-red serial mutation*. But it is not certain that this intentional preponderance comes out in the analysis of the painting; at least, it is not certain that it is established at all analytical levels.

The painting is constituted by a fourfold repetition of a six-unit sequence: light green (lg), dark red (dr), orange (or), blue (bl), dark green (dg), light red (lr). The light/dark variation does not show up well on the reproduction of the painting that we have. Blue and orange are of a different stripe, shall we say, relative to green and red, since they do not come in light and dark versions. However, the opposition at work between green and red can be found in some sense, since blue is a darker and more somber color than orange, which is lighter and brighter. If we use color intensity as a rhythmic criterion, we identify the following rhythm: l, d, l, d, d, l.

This rhythm is constructed by reduplicative addition, i.e., adding a second l, d to the first l, d, followed by an inverted reduplicative addition, with l, d becoming d, l. The second l, d and the d, l at the end of the sequence constitute a chiasmus. One can also take the view that the first l, d and the d, l constitute a delayed chiasmus, by virtue of the second l, d inserted in between. In terms of intensity, the series begins and ends "gently", and reserves its moments of intensity for the middle part (which is not entirely intense, since there is an l in it).

Note that the matrix structure alternates the complementaries green and red at the beginning (the first stripe) and the end (the sixth stripe), but these two colors are the same strength (light), which attenuates the opposition and makes them sub-contraries. Actually, in terms of the intensity of the opposition, dark green and dark red can be seen as super-contraries (a strong opposition between tonic elements) and light green and light red can be seen as sub-contraries (a weak opposition between atonic elements) in a device with four positions: dg, lg, lr, dr. The opposition super-contraries/sub-contraries was proposed by Zilberberg (2006). It should be distinguished from the opposition contraries/subcontraries found in the semiotic square (see the chapter on the semiotic square).

Another rhythm occurs in the painting, which is that of the primary (1) and secondary (2) colors: 2, 1, 2, 1, 2, 1. This rhythm is produced by a double reduplicative addition of the sequence 2, 1. This interlaced rhythm is highly repetitive, but it is not circular, since it does not end the way it begins.

From stripes 5 to 8, one observes an alternating structure – g, r, g, r – and an embedded structure – d, l, l, d. This combination is powerful because it plays off the complementaries, and is relatively subtle at the same time, because it varies between two shades of each color. Because of its resonance, it is tempting to see it as the generative structure of the painting; we saw that the title emphasizes red and green, after all. In some ways, this should be the structure that begins the painting, but the painting prefers to start (stripes 1 to 4) and end (stripes 21–24) with a weaker structure, reserving its power for parts in the "center".

The table below shows the main rhythmic structures in Molinari's painting.

Table 15.1 The main rhythmic structures in *Green-red serial mutation*

STRIPE→ *CRITERION↓*	*1*	*2*	*3*	*4*	*5*	*6*	*7*	*8*	*9*	*10*	*11*	*12*	*13*	*14*	*15*	*16*	*17*	*18*	*19*	*20*	*21*	*22*	*23*	*24*
color	g	r	or	bl	g	r	g	r	or	bl	g	r	g	r	or	bl	g	r	g	r	or	bl	g	r
dark/light and color	lg	dr	or	bl	dg	lr	lg	dr	or	bl	dg	lr	lg	dr	or	bl	dg	lr	lg	dr	or	bl	dg	lr
dark/light (except blue and orange)	l	d	nil	nil	d	l	l	d	nil	nil	d	l	l	d	nil	nil	d	l	l	d	nil	nil	d	l
dark/light (orange = light, blue = dark)	l	d	l	d	d	l	l	d	l	d	d	l	l	d	l	d	d	l	l	d	l	d	d	l
primary (1)/ secondary (2)	2	1	2	1	2	1	2	1	2	1	2	1	2	1	2	1	2	1	2	1	2	1	2	1

Application II: an excerpt from Le bourgeois gentilhomme *by Molière*

Consider the following excerpt from *The bourgeois gentleman* by Molière, in which the succession of different speakers produces a rhythm. The context: Monsieur Jourdain's various tutors are each insisting on the superiority of their own discipline, and they come to blows.

"The philosopher flings himself at them, and all three [the fencing master, the dancing master, and the music master] start punching at him and go out fighting".

1 [A] MONSIEUR JOURDAIN – Monsieur Philosopher!
2 [B] PHILOSOPHY MASTER – Rogues! Scoundrels! Insolent dogs!
3 [A] MONSIEUR JOURDAIN – Monsieur Philosopher!
4 [C] FENCING MASTER – A pox on the beast!
5 [A] MONSIEUR JOURDAIN – Gentlemen!
6 [B] PHILOSOPHY MASTER – Impudent rogues!
7 [A] MONSIEUR JOURDAIN – Monsieur Philosopher!
8 [D] DANCING MASTER – The devil take the jackass!
9 [A] MONSIEUR JOURDAIN – Gentlemen!
10 [B] PHILOSOPHY MASTER – Villains!
11 [A] MONSIEUR JOURDAIN – Monsieur Philosopher!
12 [E] MUSIC MASTER – To the devil with the impertinent fellow!
13 [A] MONSIEUR JOURDAIN – Gentlemen!
14 [B] PHILOSOPHY MASTER – Rascals! Beggars! Traitors! Impostors!

They leave.

MONSIEUR JOURDAIN Monsieur Philosopher, Gentlemen! Monsieur Philosopher! Gentlemen! Monsieur Philosopher! Oh! Fight as much as you like. I don't know what to do, and I'll not spoil my robe to separate you. I would be a fool to go among them and receive some damaging blow".

In central portion of the excerpt is a rhythmic structure with respect to who is speaking, a structure whose organization can be revealed by using a letter to designate each speaker: A: Monsieur Jourdain; B: Philosophy Master; C: Fencing Master; D: Dancing Master; E: Music Master.

1 The number of successive positions. The structure contains 14 units (just as a sonnet contains 14 lines, for example). It is even, thus making it possible to have perfect symmetry, whether in the number and kind of units assembled (the kind of unit is shown by the letter), or just in the number of units. Note, however, that odd structures can also be symmetrical if they are organized around an axis of symmetry that is one unit, such as E in the following sequence: A, B, C, E, A, B, C).

2 The number of simultaneous positions. One can observe that in this excerpt, Molière chose a monoplanar rhythm by excluding simultaneities, which would have meant two or more characters speaking at the same time. This preserves the very classical "clarity" in the scene, despite the free-for-all. We should note that it is rare in classical theater to have characters speaking at the same time, especially if they are saying different lines.

3 The number of units per successive position. Each successive position has just one unit, since the rhythm is monoplanar.

4 The number of units that can occupy each position. Five different units are combined: A, B, C, D and E. Consequently, in a completely free combinatorics, each of these units could have in theory occupied each position.

5 The organization of the rhythmic pattern. The rhythmic pattern is obtained by combining three occurrences of the (even) structure A, B, A, Y, followed by half of this structure (A, B), where Y is a variable equal to C first, then D, then E. This yields: A, B, A, C (Y = C) A, B, A, D (Y = D) A, B, A, E (Y = E) A, B.

This organization seems to follow a certain logic: each line spoken by the philosopher is followed by a line from Monsieur Jourdain (the line is "Monsieur philosopher!", to be exact). Each line spoken by the other characters is also followed by a line from Monsieur Jourdain (the line: "Gentlemen!"). Despite appearances, Monsieur Jourdain's first line follows this logic, since it is a response to the last of the philosopher's lines in the preceding scene, a line in which the latter begins insulting his colleagues and then flings himself at them ("What! Rascals that you are . . ."). This arrangement makes it so that Monsieur Jourdain says 7 lines, the philosopher says 4 (excluding the closing line from the preceding scene), and the other characters say one line each.

Monsieur Jourdain's last line, with which he closes the scene, is a sort of condensation of the 14-element structure that precedes it. We actually find Jourdain's lines repeated as they were in the structure that precedes. Since a complete cycle of Jourdain's lines occurs when "Monsieur Philosopher!" is followed by "Gentlemen!", the last line of the scene contains two and a half cycles (the half cycle because it ends with "Monsieur Philosopher!" rather than "Gentlemen!"). Note that it ends with a half cycle, as does the 14-unit structure that precedes; this half cycle is the structure A, B (instead of A, B, A, Y) that ends the exchange with the other characters. Consequently, one could say that the last line is a micro-representation of the preceding structure.

6 The type of units involved. The units that create the rhythm are the speakers. There are other types of units present that create rhythms as well. For example, the content of the lines creates the rhythm: A, B, A, C, D, E, A, F, D, G, A, H, D, I (where A = "Monsieur Philosopher!" and D = "Gentlemen!"). Note that all of the repeated lines are said by the "moderator" of the dispute, Jourdain.

7 The actual units involved. The speakers involved are: (A) Monsieur Jourdain, (B) the philosopher, (C) the fencing master, (D) the dancing master, and (E) the music master.

8 The duration of the units. Since we are not keeping track of the duration of the lines (in words, syllables, phonemes, or otherwise), the units have the same duration. That said, looking at actual duration, we should note that one of Jourdain's lines ("Gentlemen!") is distinctly shorter than the others (particularly in French), which are similar in duration.

Notes

1 Tactics is one of the four components of textual signifieds, along with **thematics**, **dialectics**, and **dialogics**, according to Rastier. Tactics was set out in Rastier, 1989 (1997 in English). For details on these components, see the chapter on semic analysis.

2 The distinction between A, A and B, B is made in connection to the considerations on silence that follow; in reality, A, A and B, B are identical in terms of minimal rhythmic configurations, since they both represent the repetition of a single element.

3 Some works can include foundational socially normed rhythmic elements like time measured in seconds, hours, etc., and space measured in centimeters, pixels, etc. For example, a painting could reproduce a measuring tape.

4 Our thanks go to the Art Gallery of Ontario for authorizing us to reproduce the painting in the book.

16 The functions of language

Summary

Jakobson's model of the functions of language distinguishes six elements, or factors of communication, that are necessary for communication to occur: (1) context, (2) addresser (sender), (3) addressee (receiver), (4) contact, (5) common code and (6) message. Each factor is the focal point of a relation, or function, that operates between the message and the factor. The functions are the following, in order: (1) referential ("The Earth is round"), (2) emotive ("Yuck!"), (3) conative ("Come here"), (4) phatic ("Hello?"), (5) metalingual ("What do you mean by 'krill'?"), and (6) poetic ("Smurf"). When we analyze the functions of language for a given unit (such as a word, a text or an image), we specify to which class or type it belongs (e.g., a textual or pictorial genre), which functions are present/absent, and the characteristics of these functions, including the hierarchical relations and any other relations that may operate between them.

Theory

The well-known model of the functions of language introduced by the Russian-American linguist, Roman Jakobson (1960, pp. 350–377), can be disputed on several grounds from a theoretical standpoint. Our purpose in this chapter is simply to suggest a few ways of exploiting the analytical potential of this device. When we analyze the functions of language for a given unit (such as a word, a text or an image), we specify to which class or type it belongs (e.g., a textual or pictorial genre), which functions are present/absent, and the characteristics of the functions, including the hierarchical relations and any other relations that may operate between them.

NOTE: THE NUMBER OF FACTORS, FUNCTIONS AND SUB-FUNCTIONS

We will mention just one point of controversy here, which is the number of factors (terms) and functions (relations between the terms) the model contains and the possible subtypes of any factor or function. Rastier (1997, p. 25) sees the metalingual function simply as a specific subtype of the referential function. Arcand and Bourbeau (1995, pp. 27–28) believe that there are two forms of the appellative function (conative function): in a "directive-appellative discourse, the sender leads others to act without justifying his will with arguments of any kind. In an argumentative-appellative discourse, the prompting [. . .] takes the form of an argument. The sender can give the pros and cons, defend his ideas and counter other people's ideas".

(trans. of Arcand and Bourbeau, 1995, p. 28)

Factors of communication and functions of language

According to Jakobson, any act of verbal communication is composed of six elements, or factors (the terms of the model): (1) a context (the co-text, that is, the other verbal signs in the same message, and the world in which the message takes place), (2) an addresser (a sender, or enunciator), (3) an addressee (a receiver, or enunciatee), (4) a contact between an addresser and addressee, (5) a common code and (6) a message.

Each factor is the focal point of an oriented relation, or function, that operates between the message and the factor. This yields six functions:

Table 16.1 Factors of communication and functions of language

Target factor and function no.	*TARGET FACTOR*	*SOURCE FACTOR*	*FUNCTION*
1	Context	Message	Referential
2	Addresser	Message	Emotive
3	Addressee	Message	Conative
4	Contact	Message	Phatic
5	Code	Message	Metalingual
6	Message	Message	Poetic

Briefly, these six functions can be described as follows:

(1) the referential function is oriented toward the context (the dominant function in a message like 'Water boils at 100 degrees'); (2) the emotive function is oriented toward the addresser (as in the interjections 'Bah!' and 'Oh!'); (3) the conative function is oriented toward the addressee (imperatives and apostrophes); (4) the phatic function serves to establish, prolong or discontinue communication [or confirm whether the contact is still there] (as in 'Hello?'); (5) the metalingual function is used to establish mutual agreement on the code (for example, a definition); (6) the poetic function (e.g., 'Smurf'), puts 'the focus on the message for its own sake' [(Jakobson, 1960, p. 356)].

(trans. of Tritsmans, 1987, p. 19)

NOTE: OTHER NAMES

Several competing names have been proposed for the "same" factors and functions. (A different name often indicates, insists on, reveals, hides, or even results in an important conceptual difference.) Some other names for the factors are (numbers refer to the table above): 1. referent, 2. sender or enunciator, 3. receiver or enunciatee, 4. channel. Some other names for the functions are: 1. denotative, cognitive, representative, informative, 2. expressive, 3. appellative, imperative, directive, 4. relational or contact, 5. metasemiotic (in order to extend the function to any semiotic act, such as an image), 6. esthetic or rhetorical.

The functions: presence and hierarchy

In a proper analysis, we start by determining whether each of the functions of language is present or absent. Each factor must be present and concordant in order for communication to succeed. Consequently, relations are established between all of the factors, particularly between the message and the other factors. But here, we are interested in particular relations or functions. We will assume that while one or more – or even all – of the functions of language may be absent in short units (such as an isolated sign), lengthy units can activate all of them. Where more than one function is present, we will establish either: (1) a simple hierarchy, by identifying the dominant function and not ranking the other functions, or (2) a complex hierarchy, by specifying the degree of presence of some or all of the functions.

Ranking criteria

Various criteria can be used to establish the functional hierarchy. For example, Arcand and Bourbeau (trans. of 1995, p. 35) use an intention-based criterion: "The dominant function is the one that answers the question, 'With what intention was this message transmitted?' and [. . .] the secondary functions are there to support it". We must distinguish the intention associated with each fragment from the overall intention, which is "a sentence or series of sentences that corresponds to an intention" (1995, p. 27). Since the intention can be hidden, the function that is dominant in terms of overt degree of presence may not be dominant in terms of intention. Arcand and Bourbeau also distinguish between direct and indirect manifestations of intention, which correlate to the opposition between actual and overt functions. The appellative (conative) function is manifested directly in "Go answer the door" and indirectly in "The doorbell rang" (which is equivalent to "Go answer the door"), where the overt function is the referential (or informative) function (1995, pp. 30–33). In addition, we need to distinguish between cause and effect functions, as well as ends and means functions (the ends being the effect that is sought). For example, when the phatic function (cause) is overactivated, it can trigger the poetic function (effect); overactivation can be used for esthetic ends, and in this case the poetic function is an end and the phatic function is a means.

Real functions and thematized functions

The functions of language can be linked to the various possible enunciative agents. In a literary text, for example, these agents are as follows: the empirical (real) author, the implied author (our impression of the author from reading his text), the narrator, the character, the narratee, the implied reader and the empirical (real) reader. (For more details, see the chapter on dialogics.) To take a simple example, in a disconnected interaction between characters, the disintegration of the phatic function (as when dialogue degenerates into parallel monologues) might correspond to a) symbolically, a phatic dysfunction between the empirical author and reader, and b) the poetic function being activated through the dysfunction between characters. In this case the phatic function is thematized, and it is fictional (it is operating between characters), and the poetic function is "real" (it originates from the real author and is meant to be perceived by the real reader). This thematized, fictional phatic function is thus a way of activating the poetic function in reality.

Functions and genres

The presence/absence of the functions and their hierarchical structure can be used not only to describe units, but also classes or types of units (e.g., textual or pictorial genres). For Jakobson, what characterizes poetry and distinguishes it from other genres (literary and textual in general) is not so much the presence of the poetic function as its dominance. By identifying the functional configuration (e.g., by specifying the secondary dominant function) we can create a typology. Jakobson recognizes that epic poetry – focused on the third person, as opposed to lyric poetry (first-person) or poetry of the second person – "strongly involves the referential function of language" (Jakobson, 1960, p. 357)

Functions and thrust

Without going into all of the details, let us posit an "energy-based model" to describe the dynamics (in the literal sense) of the functions of language. (Dynamics is defined as "the set of interacting and opposing forces in a phenomenon or structure" [trans. from *Le petit Robert*].) The strength of a function in a particular configuration (the target configuration) may be interpreted dynamically (and metaphorically) as resulting from an upward or downward "thrust" applied to the function as it appeared in a configuration (the source configuration) considered as the source of this particular configuration.

If we are going to analyze changes in the functional balance, this implies a comparison between two models, a source and a target. For example, in epic poetry (or narrative poetry) the referential function is intensified as compared to lyric poetry, while the emotive function is diminished.

This dynamic model seems useful from a descriptive standpoint. Certain works and certain genres appear to be based on emphasizing and/or deemphasizing (or even neutralizing) one or more functions. For example, hyper-realism in painting is an exaggeration of the referential function; pictorial abstraction, and in literature, the "destruction" of the Balzacian universe by Robbe-Grillet and Kafka are attempts to neutralize the referential function.

Relations between functions

When relations between functions are studied, most analyses are limited to establishing a hierarchy. We would like to go a step beyond that. Let us posit that two kinds of correlations can be shown to exist between two functions. The correlation is said to be converse, or direct, if (1) an intensification of one of the two functions is accompanied by an intensification of the other and (2) a decline in one function causes a decline in the other. The correlation is said to be inverse if an intensification of one of the two functions is accompanied by a decline in the other, and vice versa.

We will sketch out a brief analysis of this type in the next section. Generally speaking, when one function is accentuated, it tends to diminish the importance of all the others, and the opposite happens when the function is deemphasized. But we will also postulate that some functions are generally paired in an even more definite inverse relation. The most obvious pairings are the expressive and conative functions and the referential and poetic functions.

NOTE: OTHER INTERACTIONS BETWEEN FUNCTIONS

It is difficult to draw the line between interaction and merging of functions. Klinkenberg asks the question directly (trans. of 1996, p. 61): "Are functions actually distinct from one another?" It remains to be determined just how much is interaction and how much is commingling in each possible pairing of functions. Klinkenberg describes some of these pairings (1996, pp. 61–62). Let's look at one of them: the referential and conative functions. "Any information – the referential function – changes the receiver's knowledge stock; we can thus say that it acts on the receiver: that is the conative function. Moreover, a lot of so-called information leads to a behaviour as its final result. The sign 'falling rock' is meant not just to convey information, but most of all to elicit a certain attitude in the driver" (trans. of Klinkenberg, 1996, p. 61). The second interaction Klinkenberg mentions, as we will show, involves the opposition actual vs. overt function – in this case, the conative and referential functions, respectively.

The correlation between the expressive and conative functions

The perfect addresser-message equivalence would have to be the spontaneous cry of pain. Even though the cry may be "addressed" to a receiver, it is associated almost consubstantially with the addresser, thereby leaving the conative function empty, so to speak. Conversely, an educational message is intended for the addressee, and generally entails an attenuation of the emotive function (when the emotive and conative functions are incompatible, at any rate).

The correlation between the poetic and referential functions

Jakobson appears to recognize the relation between the poetic and the referential functions, since he places them in a sort of battle for supremacy (1960, pp. 370–371):

> "Ambiguity is an intrinsic, inalienable character of any self-focused message, briefly a corollary feature of poetry. [. . .] The supremacy of poetic function over referential function does not obliterate the reference but makes it ambiguous. The double-sensed message finds correspondence in a split addresser, in a split addressee, and besides in a split reference, as it is cogently exposed in the preambles to fairy tales of various peoples, for instance, in the usual exordium of the Majorca storytellers: 'Axio era y no era' (It was and it was not)".

We will call this relation an inverse correlation. The more the message "talks" about itself and refers to itself (the poetic function), the less it talks about the context and refers to it (the referential function) and vice versa.

The poetic function and the changing functional balance

The functions (and the factors) do not necessarily all operate on the same analytical level. The poetic function in particular can operate at least partially on a second level, as the beneficiary of certain transformations in the functional balance, especially if they are marked (Klinkenberg, 1996, p. 58). In this case, the poetic function is linked to the other functions by a non-symmetrical relation. We will call it the ascending correlation: The poetic function is intensified as a result of a significant and selective strengthening or weakening of any other language function, but the reverse is not necessarily true (e.g., the emotive function is not necessarily strengthened by intensifying the poetic function). It is hard to imagine that a marked emphasis or attenuation in one function would not draw attention to the message itself, at least in some cases. This is what happens when the phatic function breaks down in Ionesco's *The bald soprano*, developing into parallel monologues as opposed to real dialogues. This contributes to the poetic effect of the play. It remains to be seen whether all variations in the poetic function necessarily result from a change, either qualitative or quantitative, in one or more other functions. Moreover, the poetic function is not necessarily the only one affected in cause-and-effect relations with one or more other functions. For example, when the poetic function is suddenly accentuated, the result and/or effect may be to keep the addressee's attention at a time when it was beginning to wander (the phatic function).

A closer look at some functions

The emotive or expressive function

Let us incorporate Klinkenberg's suggestion to extend the range of the emotive function (1996, p. 53): "The expression of 'emotive function' (which could more aptly be called the '*expressive* function') should not be understood in the usual sense, as referring to human affect. It actually has nothing to do with emotion. Any message, including the most neutral, reveals the condition of its sender". Even the crackling of a defective electrical part on a stereo system reflects this function, since it indicates the stereo's poor condition.

NOTE: THE EXPRESSIVE FUNCTION AND INDICES

Rather than using the term "expressive function", we could approach this function in terms of symptoms and indices. As Rastier points out,

> The main contemporary representations of linguistic functions are based on the sign model presented by Karl Bühler. The sign functions as such through its relations with the sender, the receiver (*Empfänger*), and the referent (*Gegenständen und Sachverhalten*). Relative to each of these three poles, the sign pertains to a different semiotic type: it is a symptom [an *index*] in relation to the sender, a signal in relation to the receiver, and a symbol in relation to the referent.
>
> (Rastier, 1997, pp. 24–25)

Any semiotic act, then, is indexical in relation to its producer (the expressive function) and a means of signalling to its receiver (the conative function). We could add that it is also an index of the state of the other factors and of the mental image that the message's producer makes, rightly or wrongly, consciously or unconsciously. For example, a written message containing the word "loose" instead of "lose" (as in "Did you loose your keys again?") – a common lexical error – results from a warped image of the language code. We will add that while the relation between the sign and the referent is indeed symbolic in nature, at least from Bühler's perspective, this symbol can function as an index (someone – the sender – gives us a garment belonging to the loved one), an icon (someone gives us a photo of the loved one), or a symbol (someone gives us a text describing the loved one). (See the chapter on Peirce's semiotics.)

The referential function

Jakobson remarks that the context is what is known as the "'referent' in another, somewhat ambiguous, nomenclature" (1960, p. 353). Amazingly, this does not stop him from using the term "referential" for the function whose target factor is the context. Moreover, the term "context" is no less ambiguous, both in general and in this particular case. Jakobson says that the context is "either verbal or capable of being verbalized". As for the referential function, Jakobson gives the synonyms "denotative" and "cognitive" (1960, p. 353), but unlike all the other functions, this one is not presented in detail, and seems to be taken for granted. We believe that there are two main ways of interpreting this function in the work of Jakobson and those who use his model.

1 The referential function relates to the thing "spoken of" (Jakobson, 1960, p. 355).
2 The second way of viewing the referential function seems more useful and operative than the first. The referential function is associated with an element whose truth value (true or false status) is being affirmed (or questioned), particularly when this truth value is identical in the real universe and in the assumptive or reference universe that is taking it on.

This calls for some explanation (for more details, see the chapter on dialogics). A universe of assumption (such as the universe of a character in a literary work) may be reinforced or contradicted by the universe of reference (as defined by the omniscient narrator, for example), which stipulates what is ultimately true or false (or undecidable) in the more or less "realistic" universe constructed by the semiotic act. So the statement "the sun rises in the East" – which is true in reality and in a realistic text – would be more of a referential assertion than "the sun rises in the West", which would be perceived as somewhat poetic, in that the incongruity draws attention to the message (even if the utterance is true in the universe of reference, say, of a science-fiction novel).

NOTE: THE REFERENTIAL FUNCTION AND TRUTH VALUES

Jakobson says that unlike declarative sentences, imperatives (linked to the conative function) cannot be tested for their truth value. The imperative "Drink!" "cannot be challenged by the question 'is it true or not?' which may be, however, perfectly well asked after such sentences as 'one drank', 'one will drink', 'one would drink'". (Jakobson, 1960, p. 355) Considering that declarative sentences clearly activate the referential function, then the "truth value test" becomes a test we can use to identify the referential function.

The metalingual function

Firstly, we propose making the metalingual function into a more general "metacode" (or "metasystem") function. This will allow us to apply it to non-linguistic "messages". Secondly, we propose recognizing any normed and norming system as a code, and not restricting ourselves to the language code where text is concerned. Rastier takes the view that a text is the result of three systems interacting (1994, pp. 222 and 224, 1997, pp. 27–29): (1) the dialect (the language system), (2) the sociolect (the particular usage of a dialect specific to a differentiated social practice with its own discourse organized through genres), and the idolect (a given author's individual usage of a language and a sociolect). In this case, utterances like "A Sonnet has 14 lines" (which deals with a genre, or sociolectal phenomenon) and "Baudelaire liked antitheses" (which deals with an individual's style, or idiolectal phenomenon) are as much about a code as "How do you spell 'surreptitiously'?" (which deals with the language system).

The examples given use a thematized metacode function, embedded in the signified, or content. However, we should expect that non-thematized metacode functions may also exist. When the code norm is transgressed, attention is directed indexically, but clearly, to the code, as in: "The wind, he blow". Or if a given sonnet simply deviates from the norm, doesn't this evoke the model sonnet by contrast, and thus the system that defines it?

Application: *[If you drink, then drive, you're a bloody idiot]*

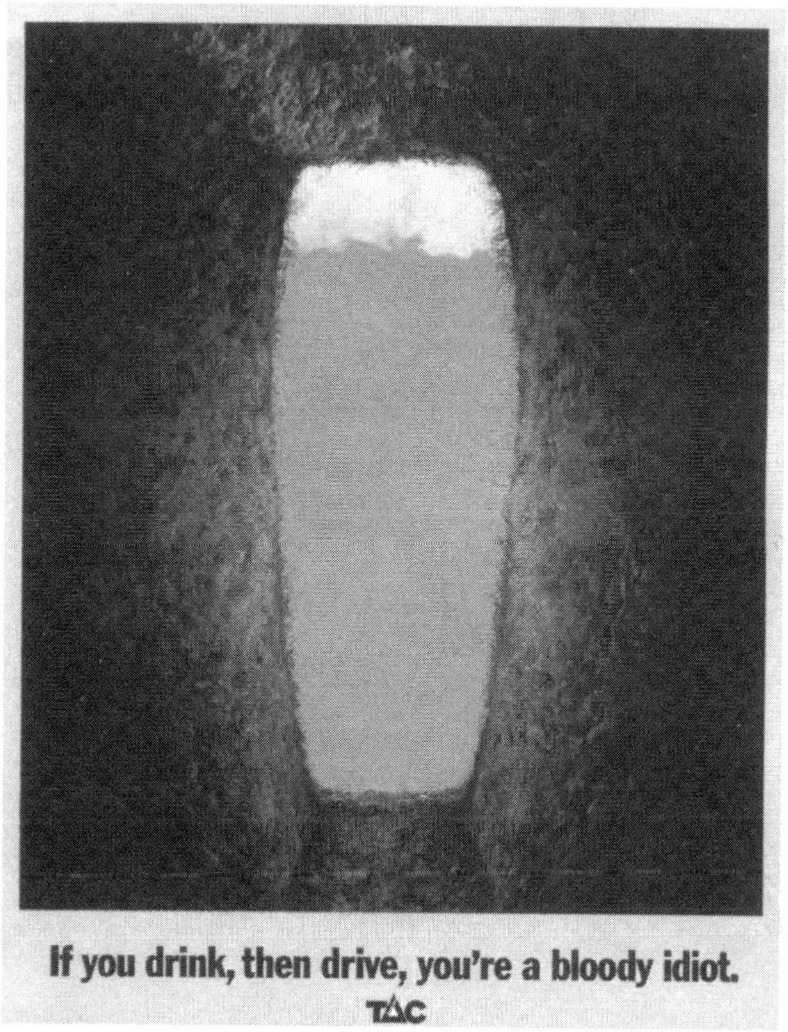

Figure 16.1 [*If you drink, then drive, you're a bloody idiot*]

The poster advertisement *[If you drink, then drive, you're a bloody idiot]* is part of a series of advertising campaigns based on the same slogan and launched in 1989 by the Australian Transport Accident Commission (TAC). The image was reproduced in *Touring* (2002), Laval (Québec), 80, 2, summer, p. 33.

Generally speaking, the advertising message has to accomplish the following, in three successive stages: (1) attract attention (the phatic function), (2) convince (the conative function), by appealing to reason (the referential function) or emotion (the emotive function), and (3) get people to act (the conative and referential functions). The third objective is clearly the most important, and the others are subordinate.

Two actions – drinking and driving – are combined into sequences: this is an attack, not on drinking-and-driving, but on the act of drinking-then-driving, which is more commonplace. Three possible sequences (the referential function) are open to the addressee (the conative function): (1) not drinking, then driving, (2) drinking, then not driving, (3) drinking, then driving. While neither action is good or bad in itself (with a possible nuance for excessive consumption of alcohol), all of their possible sequencings are given a moral value: the first two scenarios fall under good behaviour, and the third comes under bad behaviour. The advertising message clearly takes aim at the third scenario. It does this by showing the possible dire consequences – the addressee's death – in a very striking way (the emotive and poetic functions). This is not the death of some other person, be they a stranger or a loved one (these two scenarios, which appeal to the drunk driver's sense of guilt, appear in other messages by the same organization); this is the worst possible death: yours (the conative function). In other words, this is not a referential third-person death, but a conative second-person death. This death is the concrete (pragmatic, in Greimas's terms) punishment for – or at least the consequence of – not toeing the mark, not keeping the contract contained in this ad. Likewise, the symbolic (cognitive, in Greimas's terms) punishment is being called an "idiot".

This death is presented as being highly avoidable, since it is reserved for the "bloody idiots" with whom no addressee with any glimmer of intelligence would want to associate. The word "bloody" indicates the level of idiocy within the class of idiots, and at the same time it demonstrates the intensity of the addresser's emotion (the emotive function); note that there is no exclamation point, which would have emphasized the expressive function. Perhaps the addresser is highly concerned about what could happen to us (the conative function), or perhaps his utterance merely expresses a coldly objective truth (the referential function) along with an unsympathetic "too-bad-for-you" attitude. In addition to the standard meaning, indicating intensity (the expressive function), possible concern (the expressive function) and familiarity (the conative function), "bloody" happens to be a polysemic word, and thereby draws attention to itself (the poetic function). It alludes to blood – the blood we will shed, but also the blood that shows our blood alcohol level. Speakers of English no longer make the connection to blood when they say "bloody", just as speakers of French (in France) no longer make the connection to a hooker when they use "*putain*" as an interjection. By re-actualizing the original content, the slogan de-automates the use of this word, drawing our attention to an otherwise innocuous, transparent word. Moreover, "bloody" is a term used in the names of drinks like "bloody Mary" and "bloody Caesar". It stands in opposition to "virgin" (virgin Mary, virgin Cesar). "Bloody" indicates an alcoholic drink; "virgin" indicates a non-alcoholic drink. So "bloody idiot" roguishly suggests a new kind of alcoholic drink.

17 Peirce's semiotics

Nicole Everaert-Desmedt

Summary

We will present Charles Sanders Peirce's three philosophical categories, and then explain how these categories operate at various levels in the process of semiosis, or sign functioning. The process of semiosis is a triadic relationship between a sign or representamen (a first), an object (a second) and an interpretant (a third). Each of these three terms is in turn broken down following the three categories. From this structure, by observing the hierarchy of categories, ten mechanisms of signification may be identified.

Theory

Three general principles

Peirce developed a semiotic theory that is general, triadic and pragmatic.[1]

It is **general**:

in that it takes into consideration emotional, practical and intellectual experience;
it includes all of the components of semiotics;
it broadens the concept of the sign.

It is **triadic**:

in that it is founded upon three philosophical categories: firstness, secondness and thirdness;
it brings three terms into relation: the sign or representamen, the object and the interpretant.

It is **pragmatic**:

in that it takes into consideration the context in which signs are produced and interpreted;
it defines the sign by its effect on the interpreter.

The foundational categories of semiotics

According to Peirce, three categories are necessary and sufficient to account for all of human experience. These categories correspond to the numbers first, second and third. They have been designated as "firstness", "secondness", and "thirdness".

Firstness

Firstness is a conception of being that is independent of anything else. For example, this would be the mode of being of a "redness" before anything in the universe was yet red, or of a general sensation of hurt, before one starts to wonder whether the sensation comes from a headache, a burn or some emotional pain. We must be clear that in firstness, there is only ONENESS. Thus, it is a conception of being in its wholeness or completeness, with no boundaries or parts, and no cause or effect. A quality is a pure, latent potentiality. Firstness belongs to the realm of possibility; it is experienced within a kind of timelessness. Firstness corresponds to emotional experience.

Secondness

Secondness is the mode of being that is in relation to something else. This is the category that includes the individual, experience, fact, existence, and action-reaction. For example, the stone that we drop falls to the ground; the weathervane turns to point in the direction of the wind; and now you feel pain because of a toothache. Secondness operates within discontinuous time, where the dimension of past time enters in: a certain event occurred at a certain moment, before some other event, which was its consequence. Secondness corresponds to practical experience.

Thirdness

Thirdness is the mediator through which a first and a second are brought into relation. Thirdness belongs to the domain of rules and laws; however, a law can only be manifested through the occurrences of its application, that is, by secondness; and these occurrences themselves actualize qualities, and therefore, firstness. Whereas secondness is a category of individuality, thirdness and firstness are categories of generality; but the generality of firstness is on the level of possibility, and the generality of thirdness is on the level of necessity, and therefore, prediction. The law of gravity, for example, allows us to predict that each time we drop a stone, it will fall to the ground. Thirdness is the category of thought, language, representation, and the process of semiosis; it makes social communication possible. Thirdness corresponds to intellectual experience.

The process of semiosis: triadic and unlimited

According to Peirce, a **sign** may be simple or complex. Unlike Saussure, Peirce does not define the sign as the smallest unit of signification. Any thing or phenomenon, no matter how complex, may be considered as a sign from the moment it enters into a process of semiosis.

The **process of semiosis** involves a triadic relationship between a sign or representamen (a first), an object (a second) and an interpretant (a third).

The **representamen** is a thing that represents another thing: its object. Before it is interpreted, the representamen is a pure potentiality: a first.

The **object** is what the sign represents. The sign can only represent the object; it cannot furnish acquaintance with it. The sign can express something about the object, providing that it is an object with which the interpreter is already familiar from collateral observation (experience created from other signs, which are always from previous history). For example, a piece of red paper that is used as a sample (= representamen) for a can of paint (= object) indicates only the red color of the object, since it is assumed that one already knows all of its other characteristics (packaging, content, usage, etc.). The piece of paper shows that the paint in the can is red in color, but it says nothing about the other characteristics of the object. Furthermore, if the interpreter knows that it refers to a can of paint, then, and only then, does the sample give him the information that this particular can of paint must be red. To put it more succinctly, Peirce distinguishes the **dynamical object** (the object as it is in reality) from the **immediate object** (the object as it is represented by the sign). In our example, the can of paint is the dynamical object, and the color red (of the can of paint) is the immediate object.

Upon being interpreted, the representamen has the ability to trigger an **interpretant**, which in turn becomes a representamen by triggering another interpretant referring to the same object as the first representamen, and thereby allowing the first one to refer to the object. And so on, ad infinitum. For example, the definition of a word in the dictionary is an interpretant of the word, because the definition refers to the object (= what the word represents) and thereby allows the representamen (= the word) to refer to this object. But in order to be understood, the definition itself requires a series, or more accurately, a bundle of other interpretants (other definitions) . . . Thus, the process of semiosis is theoretically unlimited. We are engaged in a thought process that is always incomplete, that has always begun previously.

NOTE: THE FINAL INTERPRETANT: HABIT

The process of semiosis is theoretically unlimited. However, it is limited in practice, being short-circuited by force of habit, which Peirce calls the final logical interpretant – our habit of attributing a certain signification to a certain sign in a certain context with which we are familiar. Force of habit temporarily freezes the infinite recursivity of one sign to other signs, which allows interlocutors to quickly reach consensus on reality in a given communication context. But habit is formed by the effect of previous signs. Signs are the catalysts that cause habits to be reinforced or changed.

Peirce's view of semiosis integrates all the components of semiotics: pragmatics (the domain of the interpretant) is inseparable from semantics (the domain of the object) and from syntax (the domain of the representamen).

The three trichotomies

Each of the three terms of semiosis is further subdivided following the three categories: thus, we distinguish firstness, secondness and thirdness in the representamen, in representamen-object relations, and in the way the interpretant implements the relationship between representamen and object.

The first trichotomy: the representamen

The **representamen** can be (1) a **qualisign** (firstness), meaning a quality that functions like a sign; (2) a **sinsign** (secondness), meaning a specific spatiotemporal thing or event that functions like a sign; or (3) a **legisign** (thirdness), meaning a conventional sign.

Examples of legisigns are passwords, insignias, tickets for a show, traffic signals, and the words of a language. However, legisigns cannot act until embodied as sinsigns, which are "replicas". For instance, the article "the" is a legisign in the English language system. But it can only be used within the medium of the voice or the text that embodies it. It is embodied in sinsigns (its occurrences, occupying different spatiotemporal positions), but also includes qualisigns, such as the intonation of the oral replica, or the shape of the letters of the written replica.

The second trichotomy: the object

A representamen can refer to its **object** by virtue of firstness, secondness or thirdness, that is, through relationships of similarity, contextual contiguity or law. Following this trichotomy, the sign is called (1) an **icon**, (2) an **index** or (3) a **symbol**, respectively.

The reference between a sign and its object is **iconic** if the sign resembles the object. An icon may have as its representamen a qualisign, a sinsign or legisign. For example, the feeling (qualisign) produced by playing a piece of music is the icon of that piece of music. Someone's portrait (sinsign) is the icon of that person, and a model (sinsign) is the icon of a building. A drawing of a glass (sinsign) is the icon of a glass, but if it is placed on a crate, then it belongs to the pictogram code and becomes a replica of the legisign signifying 'fragile' through iconic portrayal of a species (a glass) that is part of a genera (fragile objects).

The reference between a sign and its object is **indexical** if the sign really is affected by the object. For example, the position of a weathervane is caused by the direction of the wind; it is the index of the wind direction. A knock on the door is the index of a visit. The symptom of an illness is the index of that illness. An index cannot have a qualisign as its representamen, because there is only "sameness" in firstness, and no contextual contiguity; therefore, a qualisign is always iconic (refer to the hierarchy of categories below). An index may have as its representamen a sinsign, as in the examples given, or a legisign, as in certain words known as "indexical" words ("this", "that", "I", "here").

A sign is a **symbol** when it refers to its object by virtue of a law. Passwords, tickets to a show, banknotes, and the words of a language are symbols. The symbolic rule may have been formulated a priori by convention, or a posteriori by cultural habit. A symbol's representamen is necessarily a legisign, but the legisign cannot really act until it is embodied in a replica, and from that point on, the symbol implies an index. For example, in the traffic code, the red light in the abstract is a symbolic legisign, but each one of its replicas is an indexical sinsign.

The third trichotomy: the interpretant

In the sign trichotomy of the **interpretant**, the sign is called (1) a **rheme** (firstness), (2) a **dicisign** or dicent sign (secondness) or (3) an **argument** or reasoning (thirdness).

The **rhematic** interpretant has a firstness structure: thus in implementing the relationship between the representamen and object, it does not refer to anything "else" but the qualities of the representamen, which are also the qualities of a whole class of possible objects. The rheme is neither true nor false; it is equivalent to a variable in a functional proposition. It functions like a form with blanks to be filled in or a space on a questionnaire: "... is red". For instance, a person's portrait, with no other indications, represents a whole class of possible objects: the people who look like the portrait. This is a rhematic iconic sinsign. But if the portrait is considered in a context where it is accompanied by something indicating the person's name, for example on a passport, then the level of interpretation changes: now we are dealing with secondness (a dicent indexical sinsign). The hierarchy of categories (see Table 17.1) produces six classes of rhematic signs.

The **dicisign** is a sign interpreted at the level of secondness; it functions like a logical proposition, which establishes a relationship between constants (a subject (what we are talking about) and a predicate (what we say about it)) and it is either true or false. For example, a person's portrait with an indication of his/her name is a dicent indexical sinsign. The interpretant of this sign would be the proposition that "the person shown in this picture is Mr. So-and-So". Later we will see that by virtue of the hierarchy of categories, there are three classes of dicent signs. As we have said, a dicisign is true or false, in contrast to a rheme, which represents a possibility and has no truth value. But a dicisign does not furnish reasons for being true or false, in contrast to an argument, which arrives at a conclusion by following a rational process.

The **argument** is a sign interpreted at the level of thirdness; it formulates the rule joining the representamen to its object. An argument always has a legisign as its representamen and a symbol as its object. However, three kinds of arguments may be distinguished depending on the nature of the rule that binds the representamen to its object. The rule may be (1) imposed on the facts (**deduction**: "Every time there is a red light, there is an order to stop"; (2) a result of the facts (**induction**: "Wherever there is smoke, there is fire"); or (3) the argument may consist of formulating a rule in the form of a hypothesis that would explain a fact (abduction). Peirce gives this example of abduction: Imagine that upon entering a room, I see a table with a handful of white beans on it, and next to it, a bag of beans. I observe that this bag contains only white beans. I then formulate the hypothesis that the beans on the table came from this bag. Abduction is an argument that appeals to firstness in order to formulate the rule (it is a hypothesis, and therefore a possible rule), whereas induction is based on secondness (the rule follows from repeated observation of actual, contingent facts), and deduction falls exclusively under thirdness (as a rule, it justifies itself).

NOTE: ABDUCTION

Deduction and induction were studied in depth by the classical philosophers, but no logician before Peirce had recognized the importance or the specific character of this third form of reasoning, which Peirce called abduction. Nonetheless, it is a form of reasoning that happens to be used in the most mundane circumstances as well as in scientific research, and on this point, Peirce anticipates Karl Popper's epistemology.

The interpretive process of abduction (or process of deductive hypothesis) can be described in four stages:

1. We encounter a curious fact that is unexplainable according to our previous knowledge; in other words, this fact startles us in our daily habits and prejudices. In the case of scientific research, the fact is not accounted for by any existing theory.
2. We formulate a hypothesis that may explain the fact. Our reasoning is grounded in firstness, in that the hypothesis, which springs to mind with instinctive force, is suggested by the fact. Indeed, there is an analogy between the fact and the possible consequences of applying the hypothesis.
3. Next we apply the hypothesis deductively, and we infer the consequences that follow from it. We adopt an attitude in life that matches the hypothesis. In scientific research, this is a matter of rigorously determining which tests might allow us to disprove the hypothesis if need be (to prove it is false or does not match the facts). While a single experiment can invalidate a hypothesis, it would take an infinite series of experiments to confirm it.

4 By using a kind of induction, or making generalizations based on a number of positive test results, we conclude that the results verify the hypothesis, at least provisionally, until there is proof to the contrary.

Take an example of abduction from everyday conversation:

1 The startling event: Someone says, "It's cold in here", when the conversation had nothing to do with air temperatures. Let us say that we are in a room with an open window, that I am the listener, and am near the open window.
2 The explanatory hypothesis: I refer to a rule that is part of the commonly shared store of knowledge about things cultural and practical. It is less cold in a room when the window is closed. I have already been in similar situations, and when a room is judged to be cold, one closes the window. Immediately I establish a connection between my previous knowledge and what the speaker actually said, and come up with the hypothesis that the speaker would like me to close the window.
3 Deduction: I take the consequence of the hypothesis as a prediction, and I act accordingly: I close the window.
4 Induction: The speaker makes no objection when I close the window; in fact he thanks me. This result confirms my hypothesis.

The hierarchy of categories

Firstness includes nothing other than itself, whereas secondness includes firstness, and thirdness includes both secondness and firstness. For this reason, in semiosis there exists a principle of hierarchy among the categories, and by this principle a representamen (a first) cannot refer to an object (a second) from a higher category; as for the interpretant (a third), it cannot belong to a category higher than its object's. For example, a sinsign (the category 2 representamen) cannot be a symbol (the category 3 object), but it can be considered as an icon (the category 1 object) or an index (the category 2 object). By adhering to the hierarchy of categories, we can construct **ten mechanisms of signification**, shown below, with an example for each case. (R, O and I indicate the representamen, the object and the interpretant, respectively):

Table 17.1 The ten classes of signs

	R O I	
1)	1 1 1	rhematic iconic qualisign: a general sensation of hurt.
2)	2 1 1	rhematic iconic sinsign: a model.
3)	2 2 1	rhematic indexical sinsign: an involuntary shout.
4)	2 2 2	dicent indexical sinsign: a weathervane.
5)	3 1 1	rhematic iconic legisign: onomatopoeia: "cock-a-doodle-doo".
6)	3 2 1	rhematic indexical legisign: an indexical word: "that".
7)	3 2 2	dicent indexical legisign: a red light in context.[2]
8)	3 3 1	rhematic symbolic legisign: a common noun: "apple".
9)	3 3 2	dicent symbolic legisign: a proposition: "it's cold in here".
10)	3 3 3	argument symbolic legisign: (1) abduction: "It's cold in here" interpreted as a request to close the window. (2) induction: "Where there is smoke there is fire". (3) deduction: the red light of the traffic code in the abstract.

The list opposite does not represent classes of signs to which we can assign phenomena by labelling them, but rather different levels of interpretation to which we can submit a single phenomenon, as we will show in the following application.

The following diagram shows the distribution of categories in semiosis.

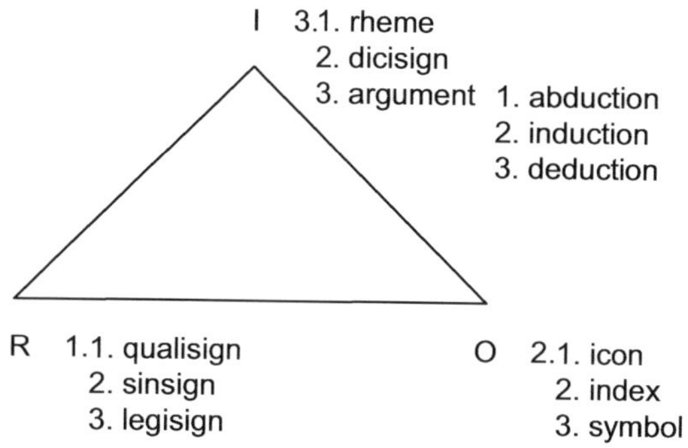

Figure 17.1 The distribution of categories

Application: a footprint in the sand

Consider the following phenomenon: a footprint in the sand.

1 This is a phenomenon located in space (a sinsign) whose shape resembles a foot (icon). In it we recognize the pertinent qualities and features of any foot (rheme). This sort of interpretation is situated in the present moment.

2 We could possibly become absorbed in the timeless contemplation of this shape pressed into matter (rhematic iconic qualisign), and perhaps we could capture its emotional depth in a photograph.

3 It is more likely that we will consider the past, along with the context in which the phenomenon occurred: This print was actually caused by someone who came by here (index). Our interpretation relates to concrete facts: this footprint and a specific foot that made it (dicisign).

4 But now suppose a detective is on the trail of a killer: He recognizes this print as a replica of a model (legisign) that he obtained previously. What interests him is to find out the actual whereabouts of the person he is looking for, not just to observe that the person came by here. Therefore, the object to which the print refers is situated in the future. So for the detective, the print becomes a symbol showing what direction to take; because of the footprint, he can predict the direction he needs to go to continue his investigation. In order for the sign to function as a symbol, its iconic and indexical features must be perceived first, and then it must be seen as a replica of a model, which must appeal to an argument for interpretation. We have abduction: "This is a sign that the killer was here; we can postulate that whoever it was continued in this direction". Then the detective acts according to this hypothesis: He goes in the same direction.

Note that the detective's situation is different from that of a treasure hunt, where arrows are used as so many replicas of a legisign, which functions as a symbol of the direction to go according to a pre-established code. The arrows are interpreted by deduction, since the replicas were put there intentionally to show the way.

Nicole Everaert-Desmedt

How to use Peirce's semiotics

Peirce's semiotics can be used in multiple ways. We will present some such ways. It is important to remember that, for a given interpretation, a given sign is a link in a chain – a point in a semiosic path. It is a result of the transformation or recovery of the preceding sign and transforms or is recovered in the following sign. Simply put, it is through methodological (i.e., intentional, made explicit and relevant) reduction that we can take a "snapshot" of a given "point" of this path.

For the sign, we can specify the representamen, interpretant, and object, and, potentially, characterize them.

Another possibility is to specify the different chains of signs that constitute a semiosic path of such a product and specify the various commutations from part of one sign to part of another sign (for example, when an interpretant of a sign becomes the representamen of a sign that follows).

Membership class can be determined specifically for a given sign of a semiotic product (for example, an index) or on the whole for said semiotic product (for example, an image).

The typologies of semiotic products can be set out based on the quantitative and/or qualitative predominance of a given type of sign, for example, the icon in (pictorial, photographic, or even literary) portraits, the index in enigma narratives (for example, detective novels), or the symbol in symbolist or hermetic poetry.

The semiotic status of the type and of its token can be compared: for example, a finger that points is normally (as a type) an index that there is something relevant to look at. However, if the wise man points at the moon and the fool looks at the finger, the index becomes (as a token) a sort of vague, mysterious symbol.

The possibilities presented can also be examined without the parts of the sign or the typologies of signs, and instead through the semiotic categories of firstness, secondness, and thirdness.

Obviously, as is the case for all types of analysis in general, we can and must take into account relativity factors, which may change the status of the analyzed element. Examples of such factors are the subject-observer, the observed element, observation time, and the inventory of interdefined elements. One can either change perspectives (e.g., from that of one subject-observer to another) or go from one condition of a factor to another condition of the same factor (e.g., the same subject-observer could be transformed, and the way the subject-observer classifies signs could potentially change as a result).

Obviously, once again, as is the case for all types of analysis, once the descriptive phase is complete, the interpretive phase can commence. In short, the interpretation can be based on (1) causal relations (cause and intention, as well as effect); (2) comparative relations (identity, similarity, opposition, otherness, etc.); or (3) presential relations (a given element presupposes another given element or given elements mutually exclude one another). The interpretation may also (4) involve a second approach to interpret the data produced by the first approach (e.g., psychoanalysis would be used to give meaning to the findings of a thematic or actantial analysis). Finally, the interpretation could be based not on the subject of the analysis, but on the approach used: (5) do the results (or non-results, mixed results, or insufficient results) of the analysis require the validation, invalidation, addition, deletion, clarification, etc. of one or several concepts of the approach (or even the entire approach) or of one or more elements of its methodology? The interpretation can be internal – linking elements of the analyzed product – or external – linking elements of the analyzed product with other products. Essentially, description and interpretation relate to the presence/absence of features, the conditions related to the presence/absence of such features, as well as the causes and effects of such features (e.g., on the meaning of the analyzed product). For more information, see Hébert (2014).

Louis Hébert

Notes

1 Theoretical development and analysis examples can be found in Everaert-Desmedt (1990, 2006).

2 More exactly, we shall distinguish two levels: the red light in context is a replica (a dicent indexical sinsign) of the type 'red light' of the traffic code (a deductive symbolic legisign).

18 Narratology

Lucie Guillemette and Cynthia Lévesque

Summary

In order to understand narratology's contribution to semiotics, it is important to grasp the distinction between its three fundamental entities: story, narrative and narration. The story generally corresponds to a series of events and actions that are told by someone (the narrator), and represented in some final form, producing a narrative. As a field of study, narratology looks at the internal mechanisms of narrative, the form taken by a narrated story.

In the field of narrative discourse, we endeavour to identify the common, near-universal principles of text composition. Thus, we attempt to discern what relations are possible between the elements of the narrative/story/narration triad. These relations operate within four analytical categories: mood, the narrative instance, level and time.

Theory

Origins and function

Gérard Genette's work (1972, 1983) fits into the German and Anglo-Saxon academic tradition, and is intended to serve as both a culmination and a renewal of this school of narratological criticism. We should point out that internal analysis, like any semiotic analysis, exhibits two characteristics. Firstly, it is concerned with narratives as independent linguistic objects, detached from their context of production and reception. Secondly, it aims to reveal an underlying structure that can be identified in many different narratives.

Using a rigorous typology, Genette has developed a theory of narratological poetics that may be used to address the entire inventory of narrative processes in use. According to Genette, every text discloses traces of narration, which can be studied in order to understand exactly how the narrative is organized. The approach advocated here clearly addresses a level that lies below the threshold of interpretation, and as such, it constitutes a solid foundation, complementing other research being done in the social sciences, e.g., in sociology, literary history, ethnology and psychoanalysis.

NOTE: NARRATOLOGY: BETWEEN TEXTUALISM AND PRAGMATICS

As a typology of narrative, Gérard Genette's theory of narratology is regarded by many specialists in the field as a reading method that marks an important milestone in the development of literary theory and discourse analysis. By using narrative voice as a concept through which all the other categories are articulated, Genette engages the context of production as a fundamental element.

Narrative mood

When a text is written, technical choices must be made in view of producing a particular result in the story's verbal representation. In this way, the narrative employs distancing and other effects to create a particular narrative mood that governs "the regulation of narrative information" provided to the reader (1980, p. 41). According to Genette, all narrative is necessarily *diegesis* (telling), in that it can attain no more than an illusion of *mimesis* (showing) by making the story real and alive. Thus, every narrative implies a narrator.

For Genette, then, a narrative cannot in fact imitate reality, no matter how realistic; it is intended to be a fictional act of language arising from a *narrative instance*. "Narrative does not 'represent' a (real or fictive) story, it recounts it – that is, it signifies it by means of language [. . .]. There is no place for imitation in narrative [. . .]" (1988, p. 43). Thus, in place of the two main traditional narrative moods, *diegesis* and *mimesis*, Genette contends that there are simply varying degrees of *diegesis*, with the narrator either more involved or less involved in the narrative, and leaving less room or more room for the narrative act. However, Genette insists that in no case is the narrator completely absent.

Distance

Any study of narrative mood requires that we assess the distance between the narrator and the story. Distance helps us to determine the degree of precision in a narrative and the accuracy of the information conveyed. Whether the text is a narrative of events (tells what the character is doing) or a narrative of words (tells what the character is saying or thinking), there are four types of discourse, each demonstrating progressively greater distance taken by the narrator with respect to the text (1980, pp. 171–172):

1 *Narratized speech*: The character's words and actions are integrated into the narration and are treated like any other event (+ + distant).
Example: *He confided in his friend, telling him about his mother's death.*

2 *Transposed speech, indirect style*: The character's words or actions are reported by the narrator, who presents them with his interpretation (+ distant).
Example: *He confided to his friend that his mother had passed away.*

3 *Transposed speech, free indirect style*: The character's words or actions are reported by the narrator, but without using a subordinating conjunction (– distant).
Example: *He confided to his friend: his mother had passed away.*

4 *Reported speech*: The character's words are cited verbatim by the narrator (– – distant).
Example: *He confided to his friend: "My mother passed away".*

The functions of the narrator

Using the notion of narrative distance as a starting point, Genette presents the functions of the narrator as such (1980, pp. 255–256). He lists five functions that also reveal the degree to which the narrator intervenes in his narrative, based on the desired degree of detachment or involvement.

1. *The narrative function*: The narrative function is a fundamental one. Any time we have a narrative, this role (detachment) is assumed by the narrator, whether present in the text or not.
2. *The directing function*: The narrator performs a directing function when he interrupts the story to comment on the organization or articulation of his text (involvement).
3. *The communication function*: The narrator addresses the narratee directly (that is, the text's potential reader) in order to establish or maintain contact with him or her (involvement).
4. *The testimonial function*: The narrator affirms the truth of his story, the degree of precision in his narration, his certainty regarding the events, his sources of information, and the like. This function also comes into play when the narrator expresses his emotions about the story, that is, the affective relation he has with it (involvement).
5. *The ideological function*: The narrator interrupts his story to introduce instructive comments or general wisdom concerning his narrative (involvement).

The *diegetic* narrative mood, then, is expressed to varying degrees, depending on the degree to which the narrator is effaced from or represented in his narrative. This distancing between the narration and the story helps the narratee to evaluate the narrative information being presented, "as the view I have of a picture depends for precision on the distance separating me from it [. . .]" (1980, p. 162).

The narrative instance

The narrative instance is said to be the conjunction between (1) narrative voice (*who is speaking?*), (2) time of the narration (*when does the telling occur, relative to the story?*) and (3) narrative perspective (*through whom are we perceiving?*). As with narrative mood, by examining the narrative instance we can gain a better understanding of the relations between the narrator and the story in a given narrative.

The narrative voice

If the narrator lets signs of his presence appear in the narrative he is recounting, he may acquire a particular status, depending on the way the story is rendered. "We will therefore distinguish here two types of narrative: one with the narrator absent from the story he tells [. . .], the other with the narrator present as a character in the story he tells [. . .]. I call the first type, for obvious reasons, *heterodiegetic*, and the second type *homodiegetic*" (1980, pp. 244–245).

In addition, if the homodiegetic narrator is the hero of the story, he/she is called *autodiegetic*.

The time of the narration

The narrator is always in a specific temporal position relative to the story he/she is telling. Genette describes four kinds of narration:

1. *Subsequent narration*: This is the most common temporal position. The narrator tells what happened in some past time.
2. *Prior narration*: The narrator tells what is going to happen at some future time. This kind of narration often takes the form of a dream or prophecy.

3 *Simultaneous narration*: The narrator tells his/her story at the very moment it occurs.
4 *Interpolated narration*: This complex type of narration combines subsequent and simultaneous narration. For example, a narrator tells what he experienced during the day (after the fact), and also includes his current impressions about these events.

Narrative perspective

A distinction should be made between narrative voice and narrative perspective; the latter is the point of view adopted by the narrator, which Genette calls focalization. "So by focalization I certainly mean a restriction of 'field' – actually, that is, a selection of narrative information with respect to what was traditionally called *omniscience*" (1988, p. 74). These are matters of perception: the one who perceives is not necessarily the one who tells, and vice versa.

Genette distinguishes three kinds of focalization:

1 *Zero focalization*: The narrator knows more than the characters. He may know the facts about all of the protagonists, as well as their thoughts and gestures. This is the traditional "omniscient narrator".
2 *Internal focalization*: The narrator knows as much as the focal character. This character filters the information provided to the reader. He cannot report the thoughts of other characters.
3 *External focalization*: The narrator knows less than the characters. He acts a bit like a camera lens, following the protagonists' actions and gestures from the outside; he is unable to guess their thoughts.

By examining the characteristics of a narrative instance and the particulars of the narrative mood, we can clarify the mechanisms used in the narrative act and identify exactly what methodological choices the author made in order to render his/her story. The use of different narratological processes creates different effects for the reader. For example, one could have a hero-narrator (*autodiegetic* narrator) who uses simultaneous narration and internal focalization and whose speech is often in reported form. This would undoubtedly produce a strong illusion of realism and credibility.

Levels

Various reading effects result from shifts in narrative level, traditionally known as embedding. Within the main plot, the author can insert other short embedded narratives, told by other narrators from other narrative perspectives. This is a rather common technique that adds diversity to the narrative act and increases the complexity of the narrative.

Embedded narratives

Narration of the main (first-level) narrative occurs at the *extradiegetic* level. The event-story being narrated on this first level fills a second-level position, known as *intradiegetic*. If a character found in this story takes the floor and tells some other narrative, his narrative act will also be on the same *intradiegetic* level. However, the events being told through the second-level narration are *metadiegetic*.

Example (fictitious): *Today I saw a teacher come up to a group of children at play. After a few minutes, she spoke: "Listen, children, I'm going to tell you an amazing story of courage that happened a few hundred years ago. This is the story of Marguerite Bourgeoys . . ."*

Below is a table shows the narrative levels.

Table 18.1 Narrative levels

OBJECTS	*LEVELS*	*NARRATIVE CONTENT*
main plot	*Extradiegetic*	*Homodiegetic* narration ("I")
Event-story	*Intradiegetic*	Story about the teacher and the children
Second-level narrative act	*Intradiegetic*	The teacher speaks
Embedded narrative	*Metadiegetic*	Story of Marguerite Bourgeoys

Metalepsis

Writers sometimes also use metalepsis, a process in which the boundary between two narrative levels (which is normally impervious) is breached so as to deliberately blur the line between reality and fiction. Metalepsis is a way of playing with variations in narrative level in order to create an effect of displacement or illusion. This would be a case in which a character or narrator from one level appears on the scene at a higher level, whereas plausibility completely excludes this possibility. "All these games, by the intensity of their effects, demonstrate the importance of the boundaries they [the authors] tax their ingenuity to overstep, in defiance of verisimilitude – a boundary *that is precisely the narrating (or the performance) itself*: a shifting but sacred frontier between two worlds, the world in which one tells, the world of which one tells" (1980, p. 236).

To return to our previous example, if the *homodiegetic* narrator from the main story line intervenes in the *metadiegetic* story of Marguerite Bourgeoys, this would be a case of metalepsis. Marguerite Bourgeoys is a 17th-century heroine who founded the Notre-Dame Congregation school for girls in Montreal. So it would be impossible for a contemporary ("current") narrator to appear on the scene, camping out in New France in this embedded story.

Narrative time

We have already seen that the time of narration has to do with the relation between the narration and the story: What is the narrator's temporal position relative to the events being told? Genette also gave some thought to the question of narrative time: How is the story presented with respect to the narrative as a whole, with respect to the final result? Once again, several methodological choices are available to writers. In order to achieve the expected result, they can vary (1) the order of the narrative, (2) the speed of the narrative and (3) the frequency of events. Skillful use of these techniques allows the narratee to identify which narrative elements are being emphasized by the author(s) and what the structure and organization of the text is.

Order

Order is the relation between the sequencing of events in the story and their arrangement in the narrative. A narrator may choose to present the events in the order they occurred, that is, chronologically, or he can recount them out of order. For example, detective novels often begin with a murder that has to be solved. The events preceding the crime, along with the facts leading to the killer, are presented afterwards. The order in which the events actually occurred does not match the order in which they are presented in the narrative. This mixing of temporal order yields a more gripping, complex plot.

The term Genette uses to designate non-chronological order is *anachrony*. There are two types of anachrony:

1. *Analepsis*: The narrator recounts after the fact an event that took place earlier than the present point in the main story.
   Example (fictitious): *I woke up in a good mood this morning. In my mind were memories of my childhood, with Mum singing every morning, her voice ringing out.*
2. *Prolepsis*: The narrator anticipates events that will occur after the main story ends.
   Example (fictitious): *How will my adventure in Europe affect me? I will never be able to look at my family and friends in the same way; surely I will become contentious and distant.*

There are two factors that can enter into analepsis and prolepsis: *reach* and *extent*. "An anachrony can reach into the past or the future, either more or less far from the "present" moment (that is, from the moment in the story when the narrative was interrupted to make room for the anachrony): this temporal distance we will name the anachrony's *reach*. The anachrony itself can also cover a duration of story that is more or less long: we will call this its *extent*" (1980, p. 48).

Anachronies can have several functions in a narrative. While analepses often take on an explanatory role, developing a character's psychology by relating events from his past, prolepses can arouse the reader's curiosity by partially revealing facts that will surface later. These breaks in chronology may also simply fulfill a dissenting role, if the author wishes to disrupt the classical novel's linear representation to some degree.

Narrative speed

Other reading effects may be obtained by varying the narrative speed. Genette uses theatrical performances as his basis, in which the event-story ideally has the same duration as the staged narration. However, in literary texts, the narrator can speed up or slow down the narration with respect to the events being told. For example, we can summarize someone's entire life in a single sentence, or we can take a thousand pages to recount events occurring over a 24-hour period.

Genette lists four narrative movements (1980, p. 94) (NT: narrative time; ST: the story's time):

1. *Pause*: NT = *n*; ST = 0. The event-story is interrupted to make room exclusively for narratorial discourse. Static descriptions fall into this category.
2. *Scene*: NT = ST. Narrative time corresponds to the story's time. Dialogue is a good example of this.

3 *Summary*: NT < ST. Some part of the event-story is summarized in the narrative, creating an acceleration. Summaries can be of variable length.
4 *Ellipsis*: NT = 0; ST = *n*. The narrative says absolutely nothing about some part of the event-story.

Needless to say, these four kinds of narrative speed can be used to varying degrees. They can also be combined: A dialogue scene can contain a summary within it, for example. Variations in speed within a narrative can show the relative importance assigned to different events in the story. If an author passes quickly over a particular fact, lingers over it, or omits it entirely, there is certainly reason to ask why he made these textual choices.

Genette did not overlook the following possibility: NT > ST. Rather, he believes that these scenes that might be designated *slowed-down scenes* "are extended mainly by extranarrative elements or interrupted by descriptive pauses but are not exactly slowed down. And needless to say, pure dialogue cannot be slowed down". (Genette, 1972, p. 130). In sum, in Ginette's view it's neither purely a matter of slowing down nor even about a canonical form in literature (Mauriac's *enlargement* provides a counterexample. He "devotes some two hundred pages to a period of two minutes" (Genette, 1972, p. 30)). In our view, what may be true for textual narrative (literary narrative included) does not hold true for general narratology: slowing down is a feature of film narratology in particular (which clearly utilizes both slowed down action and speech) and indeed theatre narratology (where the performance of action or the recitation of speech can be slowed down). In literature, slowing down can be achieved where, for example, no more than one word is inscribed per page.

This narrative possibility may be termed "development" or "amplification". It occurs, for example, when a few seconds of the time "lived" are developed over many lines. In theatre, in the opening act (not counting narratives produced by the characters), it is likely to occur only when characters visibly slow down their performance or perform using pauses.

Frequency of events

One last concept remains to be examined with respect to narrative time: the notion of narrative frequency. This is the relation between the number of times an event occurs in the story and the number of times it is mentioned in the narrative. "A system of relationships is established between these capacities for 'repetition' on the part of both the narrated events (of the story) and the narrative statements (of the text) – a system of relationships that we can a priori reduce to four virtual types, simply from the multiplication of the two possibilities given on both sides: the event repeated or not, the statement repeated or not" (1980, p. 114).

These four possibilities imply four kinds of frequency relations, which can then be organized into three categories (1980, pp. 114–116):

1 *Singulative narration*: 1N / 1S: Narrating once what happened once.
*n*N / *n*S : Relating *n* times what happened *n* times.
2 *Repeating narrative*: *n*N /1S. Recounting more than once what happened once.
3 *Iterative narrative*: 1N/*n*S. Relating one time what happened several times.

The table opposite summarizes Genette's typology of narrative.

Table 18.2 Summary of Genette's narrative typology

ANALYTICAL CATEGORIES	ELEMENTS ANALYZED	COMPONENTS				
NARRATIVE MOOD	DISTANCE	Reported speech	Transposed speech, indirect style	Transposed speech, free indirect style	Narratized speech	
	FUNCTIONS OF THE NARRATOR	Narrative function	Directing function	Communication function	Testimonial function	Ideological function
NARRATIVE INSTANCE	NARRATIVE VOICE	Homodiegetic narrator	Heterodiegetic narrator	Autodiegetic narrator		
	TIME OF NARRATION	Subsequent narration	Prior narration	Simultaneous narration	Interpolated narration	
	NARRATIVE PERSPECTIVE	Zero focalization	Internal focalization	External focalization		
NARRATIVE LEVELS	EMBEDDED NARRATIVES	Extra-diegetic	Intra-diegetic	Meta-diegetic	Meta-meta-diegetic, etc.	
	METALEPSIS	Breaching of narrative levels				
NARRATIVE TIME	ORDER	Analepsis	Prolepsis	Reach	Extent	
	NARRATIVE SPEED	Pause	Scene	Summary	Ellipsis	
	FREQUENCY OF EVENTS	Singulative	Repeating	Iterative		

Application: "The dairy woman and the crock of milk" by Jean de La Fontaine

In this section we will examine the narrative processes used in a short narrative (a fable) in order to understand how the text is organized and show the relations between narration, story and narrative. As mentioned earlier, analyzing narratological processes is in some ways a textual decoding procedure, and therefore cannot be separated from an auxiliary approach aiming to produce an interpretation.

Table 18.3 "The dairy woman and the crock of milk"

On her head Perrette carried milk in a crock,
Set on a pad so it wouldn't rock.
Her wish was to get off to town with no delay.
Her garb was light and short, her pace was quick;
To move fast, she wore a brief skirt that day,
And flat-heeled shoes were her pick.
Our dairy woman, thus turned out,
Was already thinking hard about
The profit from her milk and how she'd use the money:
Buy a hundred eggs, triple the laying, just no doubt.
With her diligent care, prospects were most sunny.
"It's easy for me", said she,
"To raise chickens 'round my house, I find.
Clever indeed the fox will be
If I'm not left enough to buy the best pig of its kind.
To fatten the hog won't take much bran to my mind:
It'll already be, when I get it, of more than decent size.
When I sell it again, with cash my purse will be lined.
And what's to stop my putting in our stable, a prize
In view of the current cost, a cow, along with her calf?
I can see it frisking in the herd; it makes me laugh!"
With that, Perrette, carried away, kicked up her legs.
The milk spilled; farewell, calf, pig, chickens, and eggs.
The mistress of this wealth, with mournful eye taking leave
Of her fortune thus tossed away,
Begged her husband to forgive,
Instead of beating her that very day.
A farce is what this story became;
The Crock of Milk is now its name.

Who doesn't roam off to Cockaigne?
Who doesn't build castles in Spain?
Picrochole, Dairy Woman, Pyrrhus, all dream lies.
The foolish no more than the wise
Have their fantasies; daydreams hold the sweetest prize.
Seductive illusions sweep reason from our mind:
All wealth belongs to us in our eyes,
Every honor and every beauty we can find.
When I'm alone, I defy the bravest knight ever known;

I travel afar, drag Sophy from his throne.
They make me king, my people cherish me;
Crowns of all the realms rain down on my head.
Should something then happen to restore me to reality,
I'm as before, John Clod instead.

Source: Jean de La Fontaine, *Les fables*, 1668 [trans. N. Spencer]

Using the same order in which we presented the analytical categories of narratology, we can make the following observations about this fable:

Narrative mood

Distance:

There are three degrees of narrative distance used in this fable, making the narrator seem at times very involved in his narrative, and at times completely absent. These variations add diversity to the act of narrating. Some examples follow:

Narratized speech **(narrator is -distant):**

Lines 1–3: The expression "Her wish" implies that a character involved in the narrative act is speaking.

Transposed speech, free indirect style **(narrator is + – distant):**

Lines 22–23: The expression "farewell" reveals the character's words.

Reported speech **(narrator is + distant):**

Lines 12–21: The phrase "said she" and the quotation marks indicate that the narrator is reporting the character's speech verbatim.

The functions of the narrator:

Besides the *narrative function*, which is built into any narrative, this fable manifests three important functions: the *communication function*, the *testimonial function* and the *ideological function*. All three of these can be seen in lines 28–43. While the narrator certifies the truth of the events by presenting this story as a well-known farce (lines 28–29), he ends his narrative by addressing questions directly to the narratee (lines 30–34) and moralizing (lines 30–44).
The effect of this distancing and involvement on the part of the narrator is to bring out and intensify *diegesis* as the narrative mood, the idea being that all narratives should be considered as fictional acts of language, rather than as perfect imitations of reality (*mimesis*).

The narrative instance

Narrative voice:

The fable may be divided into two narrative parts. The first section (lines 1–29) has a *heterodiegetic* narrator: He talks in the third person and he is absent from the story he is telling. In contrast, the second section has an *autodiegetic* narrator. In the instructional discourse found in lines 30–43 we find an involved narrator, speaking in the first person and appearing on stage as a protagonist in his own story.

Time of narration:

We would say that this fable contains *interpolated narration*. The first narrative section (lines 1–29) is presented as *subsequent narration*; the narrator is telling the events after they occurred (indicated by the past tense). Then the last section (lines 30–43) reveals the narrator's *present impressions* of the past story.

Narrative perspective:

This text provides an example of *zero focalization*. The narrator seems to know the words, thoughts, gestures and facts about all the characters, including Perrette. Since the narrator knows that "A farce is what this story became", we can conclude that the perspective is omniscient.

Levels

This fable contains only one narrative level. There is no embedded narrative; the whole text is on the same level. To review the terminology presented earlier, the narrative act occurs at the *extradiegetic* level, whereas the event-story contained in the text is at the *intradiegetic level*.

Narrative time

Order:

We must first determine where the main story begins and ends in order to identify the anachronies. In the present case, we could say that the event-story begins when Perrette starts her trip to market, and it ends in the mocking of the dairy woman as she comes home from her excursion. Within this delineation, two *anachronies* can be distinguished:

(1) An *analepsis*: Lines 5–6 relate an event that happened before Perrette left for market. The *reach* of the analepsis is very short, since the event occurred almost immediately before the beginning of the event-story. The *extent* of the analepsis is *undetermined*, but one would suppose it to be limited, since we don't know how much time this action (getting dressed) took.

(2) A *prolepsis*: Lines 7–21 are a nice example of prolepsis. The dairy woman amuses herself by imagining what will happen after she returns from market with her money. The *reach* of the prolepsis is *undetermined*, as we don't know how much time will elapse between her return from market (the end of the event-story) and the anticipated actions (raising chickens, a pig, a cow and calf, or what have you). The *extent* is*undetermined* as well, because there is no way to know over what time period these predictions extend.

Narrative speed:

The fable includes *three narrative movements* presented in a complex manner:

(1) Firstly, the story of Perrette is a *summary* (lines 1–29); the narrator summarizes the events in a few lines (NT < ST).

(2) Within this summary, we find a *scene* (lines 12–21), in which Perrette is talking to herself. The narrator reports the dairy woman's thoughts in real time. However, we should observe that this scene consists of a *summary* itself, since the protagonist summarizes the anticipated events.

(3) Lastly, lines 30–43 act as a *pause* within the event-story, in that the narrator interrupts the story to offer instructive comments. However, the moral he presents is also illustrated with examples in the form of *summaries*.

Event frequency:

Once again, we need to separate the narrative into two narrative parts.

The first part (lines 1–29) uses the *singulative mood*: what happened once is told once. However, the last part (lines 30–43) provides an interesting example of the *iterative mood*: the narrator relates one time something that may possibly have occurred many times, in many circumstances, and with various protagonists.

19 The anthropic zones

Summary

According to François Rastier, the semiotic layer of social practices can be divided into three anthropic zones: identity, proximal and distal. The identity zone corresponds chiefly to the individual. The proximal zone corresponds primarily to one's fellow creatures. The distal zone is populated with absent, imaginary, or unknown objects (a word to be taken in a broad sense). The zones coincide with two worlds: the obvious world (made up of the identity and proximal zones) and an absent world (consisting of the distal zone). An *empirical* boundary is formed between the identity zone and the proximal zone, and a *transcendent* boundary is formed between the first two zones and the distal zone. Rastier uses the term *fetish* for objects on the first boundary, and the term *idol* for objects on the second boundary (with no pejorative nuances).

For example, the concept of God is unquestionably an idol (with God himself – if he exists – residing in transcendence); cell phones, which allow us to interact with our fellow humans, are fetishes.

To perform an analysis with the anthropic zones, one takes an inventory of the elements (by name and kind) of one or more of the five positions (the three zones and two boundaries); one defines the position(s) of one or more elements; and one records the changes in the inventory and/or positions. Change occurs as a function of the usual factors of relativity: the observing subject (individuals, groups, societies, cultures, etc.), time, space, shifts between elements, transformations in one element, variations in which elements are present, and so on.[1] But one has to remember that these factors can change without any change in inventory and/or position (for instance, two different observing subjects may agree on the position of a particular element). With regard to the trajectories between positions, the possibilities are: travel between zones, travel from one boundary to another, travel from a boundary to a zone or the reverse, and staying put (a preservation operation).

Let us look at a complex example, the famous line of the poet Arthur Rimbaud: "*I* is another". ["*Je* est un autre".] In a simplified analysis, we might say that the *I* in the identity zone is "projected" into the proximal zone with his fellow creatures, or possibly into the distal zone with all things very foreign. This is a change from one zone to another.

Theory

The three layers or domains of practice

In Rastier's view, culture involves three **domains**, although we would add that the most characteristic of these three is undoubtedly the second, where culture comes to reflect upon itself. In an effort to remedy the inadequacies of the ontological dualities (e.g., physical world/cognitive world), Rastier proposes a tripartite scheme: physical domain/ semiotic domain/ mental processes, or cognitive domain (1991, pp. 237–243, 1994, pp. 4–5). This hypothesis is summarized: "a **culture** could very well be defined as a multi-layered system of social practices" (trans. of Rastier, 1994, p. 211). Any **social practice** is a codified activity, involving specific relations between three domains (Rastier, 1994, p. 224), or in current terminology, three **layers**: 1. A ***physical domain*** (or **phenomenal-physical layer**) formed by the material interactions occurring in it. 2. A ***semiotic domain*** (or **semiotic layer**) composed of the signs (symbols, icons and signals, etc.) that are exchanged or employed in it. 3. A ***mental process domain*** (or **(re)presentational layer**) unique to the agents and heavily socialized, in general (Rastier, 1991, pp. 237–243, 1994, p. 4). In this tripartite scheme, the semiotic domain mediates between the physical world and the world of mental processes: the plane of expression (of signifiers) has preferred correlates in the physical domain, and the plane of content (of signifieds) has them in the mental domain (trans. of Rastier, 1994, p. 5). The physical correlates linked to the signifiers are stimuli (Klinkenberg) and the cognitive correlates of the signifieds are mental images (but not in an exclusively visual sense) or multimodal simulacra (Rastier). Next, Rastier (2002, p. 247) further clarified his tripartite scheme by considering it from the perspective of the opposition between ***Umwelt*** – the world unique to individuals – and ***Welt***, as defined by Uexküll (1956):

> The 'internal states' of human subjects are **presentations**, not representations, because they appear in specific interfaces between the individual and his surroundings; however, they do not represent these surroundings or this interface. The substrate of the surroundings (primarily the physical substrate), the ***Welt*** in the background – we will call this the **background world**.[2] In this way, we want to rearticulate the oppositions between the phenomenon and the object, the event and the fact. The **surrounding world** [***Umwelt***] is composed of the presentational layer and the layer of the semiotics of practices. The physical layer does not appear as it is, but as it is perceived, i.e., to whatever degree it has an impact on the presentations (of "objects" or of signifiers [signifieds, too, possibly?]); we have borrowed the term 'pheno-physical' from Thom".
>
> (trans. of Rastier, 2002, p. 247)

The tripartite scheme takes the following form (Table 19.1, trans. of Rastier, 2002, p. 247):

Table 19.1 The three layers, the *Umwelt* and the *Welt*

Surrounding world (*Umwelt*):	(re)presentational layer
	semiotic layer
Background world (*Welt*):	pheno-physical layer

The three anthropic zones

Divisions and anthropic zones

The semiotic layer is characterized by four main **categorial divisions**; the homologies between the zones they articulate define three **anthropic zones** ("anthropic": relating to man, from the Greek *anthropos*, meaning man):

> The semiotic layer of the human *Umwelt* is characterized by four very broad discontinuities or divisions, which seem to be attested in various ways in all described languages, so they may be hypothetically considered as anthropologically significant. [. . .] The homologies between these divisions serve to distinguish three zones: a coincident one, the **identity zone**; an adjacent one, the **proximal zone**; and a foreign or extrinsic one, the **distal zone**. The principal division is the one separating the first two zones from the third. In other words, the opposition between the identity zone and the proximal zone is secondary to the opposition separating these two zones taken together from the distal zone. A distinction is thus created between an **obvious world** (made up of the identity and proximal zones) and an **absent world** (made up of the distal zone). The three zones [. . .] are created, established, populated and constantly rearranged by cultural practices [. . .] The content of the zones is obviously different from one culture to the next, and *a fortiori* from one social practice to the next.
>
> (trans. of Rastier), 2010, pp. 19–20)

To be more specific, the distal zone is "populated with absent, imaginary or unknown objects" (trans. of Rastier, unpublished, 2012). The table below (trans. of Rastier, 2002, p. 249) shows the four divisions and the three zones.

Table 19.2 The four divisions and the three zones

	Identity zone	*Proximal zone*	*Distal zone*
1. Person	I, WE	YOU	(S)HE, ONE, THAT
2. Time	NOW	RECENTLY SOON	PAST FUTURE
3. Space	HERE	THERE	OVER THERE ELSEWHERE
4. Mode	CERTAIN	PROBABLE	POSSIBLE UNREAL

As for the division between persons, note that the third person "is defined by his or her absence from the interlocution (even if physically present)" (trans. of Rastier, 2010, p. 19). In the distal zones of the temporal (or local) and spatial divisions are the elements which have the "defining property of being absent from the *hic et nunc*" (trans. of Rastier, 2010, p. 19), i.e., from the here and now. The distal zone is the only one that is specific to humans, and in this sense, it is characteristic of human culture:

> Compared with animal languages, the distinguishing feature of human language is no doubt the possibility of talking about what is not there: in other words, the distal zone. [. . .] The proximal zone, where one's fellows are recognized as such, is quite likely part of other mammals' *Umwelt*. But the distal zone remains unique to the human *Umwelt*, no doubt because it is founded in language" (trans. of Rastier, 2010, pp. 19–20). "In

short, the distal zone is the source of presentations with no immediate perceptual substrate. In common philosophical parlance, the proximal zone is where the empirical is found, and the distal zone is where the transcendent resides.

(trans. of Rastier, 2010, p. 22)

The two boundaries between zones

There are two boundaries or border areas between the three zones: "the ***empirical* boundary** resides between the identity zone and the proximal zone, and the ***transcendent* boundary** between the first two zones and the distal zone. We have proposed the following names, with no pejorative nuances: ***fetishes*** for objects at the empirical boundary, and ***idols*** for objects at the transcendent boundary". (trans. of Rastier, 2010, p. 22; the opposition between *empirical* and *transcendent* is taken from Rastier, 1992.) Note that in anthropology, a fetish is an object to which magical power is attributed (in psychology, the term "fetishism" refers to a sexual perversion); an idol is the representation of a deity, which is worshipped as if it were the actual deity. The following diagram (trans. of Rastier, 2010, p. 23) shows how the zone boundaries are structured, and correspondingly, the interfaces between zones.

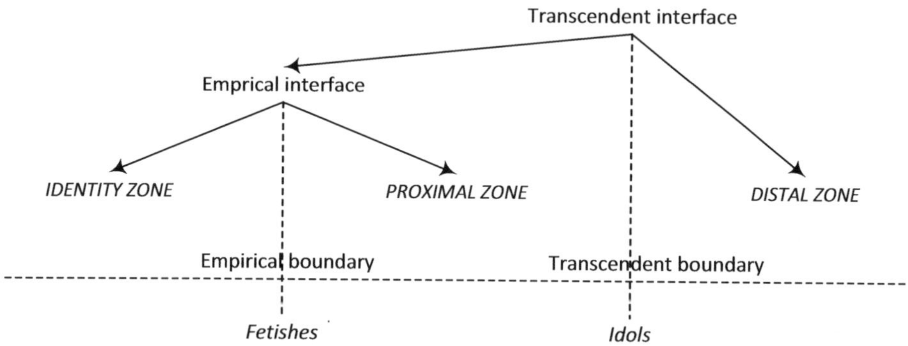

Figure 19.1 Cultural objects and anthropic boundaries

The table below (adapted from Rastier, 2010, p. 22) gives some indicative examples of fetishes and idols, matched to the domains, or layers:

Table 19.3 The mediators between anthropic boundaries

Boundaries Layers	*Empirical boundary*	*Transcendent boundary*
	fetishes	Idols
(Re)presentational layer	fantasies	beliefs
Semiotic layer	signs (words, jewels, currencies, etc.) tools transitional objects (e.g., dolls)	works (works of art, codes, laws, philosophical, scientific and religious theories, ritual objects) instruments (e.g., musical, scientific, rituals)

The table on the previous page presents a typology of cultural objects, which is part of the typology of "things" developed by Rastier (loosely based on a typology by Krysztof Pomian (1996)):

> Let us first distinguish between **natural bodies** [i.e., "any form of materiality, not just solids"], **cultural objects**, and the **waste** produced in the transformation of bodies into objects. The production trajectory goes from the bodies to the waste. **Artifacts** include the cultural objects and the waste: the cultural objects invite an interpretation that makes their production an act of generating meaning; the waste is consigned to meaninglessness. Cultural objects [i.e., "any product of an objectification process that can proceed as such from a social practice: a musical score, for instance"] are in turn divided into three categories: a) **tools** and **instruments**, which are more complex (and also include instruments of communication, such as the media); b) signs (linguistic and non-linguistic: words, symbols, numbers, etc.); and c) **works**, which are a result of elaborating on signs by means of tools. Between signs and works, a difference in complexity can be observed: it is the combined action of tools and signs that produces works. [. . .] They are the end-point of the inherent movement of the human actions that produce them, by creating mediative structures between the proximal world and the distal world: the arts, religions, and sciences.
>
> (trans. of Rastier, 2010, pp. 17–19)

The diagram below (trans. of Rastier, 2010, p. 20) gives a general outline of the typology.

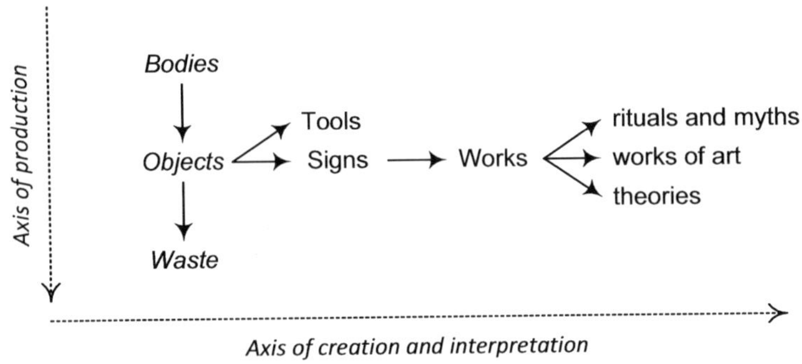

Figure 19.2 Praxeological typology of things

Characteristics of fetishes and idols

Fetishes and idols do not in themselves have any objective property that grants them this semiotic status. The "semiotic decision" (to borrow an expression from Klinkenberg) and the operations associated with it are what give them this status:

> Of course, the fetish, like the idol, has no "objective" physical property that warrants the fascination accorded to it: It simply reifies the fascination attached to it in such an exclusive way that it is decontextualized and becomes an object in itself, emanating an attraction of its own, with no determination. Now, decontextualization is a defining feature of the absolute: that which determines without *being* determined. Thus, a fetish seems to exert power, and exert it effectively, as it trumps all else with the aura that testifies to its mysterious symbolic power.
>
> (trans. of Rastier, 2010, p. 47)

The three characteristics of fetishism are abstraction, generalization and amplification:

> Some time ago, Alfred Binet identified three distinctive features of fetishism as a 'concentration' (1887, p. 107): (1) a tendency to **abstraction**, or detachment of the fetish negates all context (the whole woman

> is in her eyes), and so the fetish object may suddenly become a part (just eyes, not the whole woman); (2) the tendency to **generalization** seems to be the price paid for this abstraction (not those particular eyes, but all eyes); (3) lastly, a tendency to **amplification** leads a shoe fetishist, for example, to value very high heels. The tendency to amplification is rooted in the stylization peculiar to the world of fantasy. [. . .] As one can see, the reifying effects of fetishism closely resemble those of neopositivism: decontextualization, despecification, and an obsessional invasion of objects. Positivism has all the characteristics of a persistent anxiety dressed up as evidence. But while commodity fetishism promoted dollars to idols and stimulated the God market, conversely, the idolatry of Being causes idols to degenerate into fetishes – fascinating little decontextualized objects. Thus the terms and key words that seem to sum up everything, and fascinating objects of hypotyposis, from Achilles' shield to Charles Bovary's cap, which shine before our eyes by virtue of descriptive *enargeia*.
>
> (trans. of Rastier, 2010, pp. 47–48)

Factors of relativity

We would say that the semiotic status of the elements within the anthropic zones is affected primarily by the following variables: which zone they are classified in, where they are positioned in this zone (how close or distant), whether they have fetish and/or idol status, and to what degree they have fetish and/or idol status. For the zones and their boundaries are by no means categorial; they can be scalar, incremental, and have depth: for example, the unreal is undoubtedly more distal than the possible is. One element might be viewed as an idol of greater intensity than another element. Moreover, it is not out of the question, particularly in fictional works, that, all factors of relativity being otherwise constant, one element may belong to two zones simultaneously; or it may be classed as both a fetish and an idol; or it may be both a fetish and a non-fetish-non-idol, or what have you.

An element's status may vary over different cultures and practices, as Rastier pointed out. We should add that it may vary along with any of the factors of relativity, the observer and the time of observation in particular.

These statuses and the factors of relativity can be "real" or else thematized in a semiotic product (such as a news article, a novel, a painting), i.e., incorporated into its semantic content. For example, the real politicians mentioned in a news article and the characters of a novel are thematized observers and the time in which they develop, the time of the story in which they act, is thematized as well. So we must distinguish between real and thematized fetishes and idols. Semiotic products themselves can be fetishes (everyday items, like recipes and news articles) or idols (mythical products, such as novels and essays); whether they are fetishes or idols, semiotic products can thematize (incorporate in their semantic content) both fetishes and/or idols equally well. For example, a news article may talk about newspapers (a fetish thematizing a fetish), or a novel (a fetish thematizing an idol); a novel may talk about newspapers (an idol thematizing a fetish) or a novel (an idol thematizing an idol). Thus one anthropic element may incorporate multiple elements of a status identical to, or different from, its own. For example, Adam Smith's economic theory – an idol, therefore – contains an element that is a hyper-idol (being the superlative idol within this idol of a theory): "the invisible hand" that allegedly regulates the market. This can occur when a "real" element incorporates a thematized element as part of itself. For example, an artwork-idol such as a literary text may talk about fetishes (such as currency and stuffed animals) and idols (such as other literary texts, fictional or not).

Some examples and details follow to clarify fetish/idol status (real or thematized). This status is relative.

(1) The status can change depending on the observer: what is a fetish for one observer may be an idol for another, or neither one for someone else, provided that idols and fetishes are not conceived as an all-inclusive set.

(2) The status can change depending on the time of observation: For a single observer, yesterday's fetish may be promoted to today's idol or yesterday's idol can degenerate to today's fetish; an element that is neither a fetish nor an idol may attain idol status later, and so on. As a rule, a change over time is caused by a transformation in the observing subject and/or in the object, or in the knowledge that the observer has about the object (e.g., he believed the element was an idol because it had "magical powers", which turned out to be an illusion).

(3) Idol/fetish status can also vary along with a change in point of view (general/particular) with reference to the object being observed, the observing subject, and/or the time of observation. Three contrasts can be distinguished with respect to general/particular perspectives: they are whole/part, class/element, and type/token. For example, an object that is an idol *as a whole* may be a fetish (or neither one, just an ordinary element) in one or more of its *parts*; an object that is an idol as a *class* may have one or more *elements* that are merely fetishes or ordinary objects; an object that is an idol as a *type* may be viewed as a mere fetish in one or more of its *tokens*. The same principle applies to the observing subject, considered as a whole or divided into parts (e.g., the id, the ego, and the superego as parts of the psyche), taken as a class or an element (all Westerners vs. a specific Westerner), seen as a type or a token (the average Westerner vs. a particular Westerner). The same principle also applies to time, which can be conceived as a whole or in parts (a particular period vs. its subdivisions), as a class or elements thereof (periods of war vs. a specific period of war) or as a type or a token thereof (periods of war in general vs. a particular period of war). Clearly, the status of a unit can change from one particularity to another: for instance, one unit might be a fetish in one of its parts, and an idol in another part. When the particular characteristics do not match, their content can be echoed on the general level in several different ways. Consider time and whole/part relations. The fact that an element was an idol yesterday, a fetish today, and tomorrow it becomes an idol again can be interpreted simply as a sequence of states each lasting a day (idol → fetish → idol), without situating it in an overall time period lasting three days. Or conversely, it can be carried to the general level, in three basic ways: 1) as an idol-fetish, if one is reporting the ambiguity without weighting it; 2) as more idol than fetish, if one is recognizing the predominance of the idol status; 3) as an idol (simply), if one "rounds" to the predominant value (idol, assigned twice) by discarding the differing value (fetish, assigned once).

(4) Lastly, fetish/idol status can change depending on the inventory of interdefined elements, either in a single temporal position or with a shift in temporal position, and either for a single observer or for a change of observers. What is a fetish relative to a particular idol may be an idol relative to some other fetish. For example, relative to an airplane maintenance instruction sheet, a recipe may be viewed as a work, i.e., an idol, while simultaneously it is viewed as a fetish relative to *In search of lost time* by Proust. This interdefinitional relativity, which brings together at least three elements, can be converted to a scale that gives different weights to the fetish/idol parts within whole elements. Different scales can be used. For example, on a scale from maximum

fetish-ness to maximum idol-ness, a recipe would be somewhere in the middle. On a scale from minimum idol-ness to maximum idol-ness, the instruction sheet would be at the low end (which might correspond to zero intensity).

Synthesis

To perform an analysis with the anthropic zones, one takes an inventory of the elements (by name and kind) of one or more of the five positions (the three zones and two boundaries); one defines the position(s) of one or more elements; and one records the changes in the inventory and/or positions. Change occurs as a function of the usual factors of relativity: the observing subject (individuals, groups, societies, cultures, etc.), time, space, shifts between elements, transformations in one element, variations in which elements are present, and so on.[3] But one has to remember that these factors can change without any change in inventory and/or position (for instance, two different observing subjects may agree on the position of a particular element). With regard to the trajectories between positions, the possibilities are: travel between zones, travel from one boundary to another, travel from a boundary to a zone or the reverse, and staying put (a preservation operation).

The following are some examples of the principal trajectories:

1 From zone to zone: from the identity to the proximal or distal zone, as in the famous line from Arthur Rimbaud's poem: "*I* is someone else" ["*Je* est un autre"].
2 From boundary to boundary: the fetish becomes an idol, which is what happens in the divinization of money or in the hyperbole of advertising.
3 From a boundary to a zone: In the title *God, Shakespeare and me* (Woody Allen), the idol assimilates the zone of his fellows (in one possible interpretation, where God becomes a fellow creature); another example is Jesus becoming a man, making him a fellow creature.
4 From a zone to a boundary: In another possible interpretation of the Woody Allen title, the identity element might become an idol (using irony, the "Me" is put on the same footing as God).[4]

These trajectories produce different effects, which can be serious or funny (which is obvious from the examples).

Application[5]: *The reclining nude* by Magritte

The reclining nude, an oil on canvas by the Belgian painter René Magritte (1898–1967), like any painting, is a work of art, and therefore an idol. Moreover, this work of art is consecrated, or at least it was painted by an artist who is. The point is that there are clearly degrees of idol-ness. The elements depicted – the woman, the objects, etc. – are elements incorporated into the semantic content (signifieds) of the painting, which makes them thematized anthropic elements, not "real" ones (the woman is not a real one, for example).

The subject depicted is Georgette, the painter's wife. Therefore, the painting-idol refers to the identity zone of the producer through the painter, who paints his autobiography indirectly, and it refers to his near proximal zone or his distant identity zone, through his spouse. That is, close relations and dear friends can be accommodated in the distant identity zone or in the near proximal zone. There is no doubt that the level of devotion or egocentrism of the observing subject, who acts as a point of

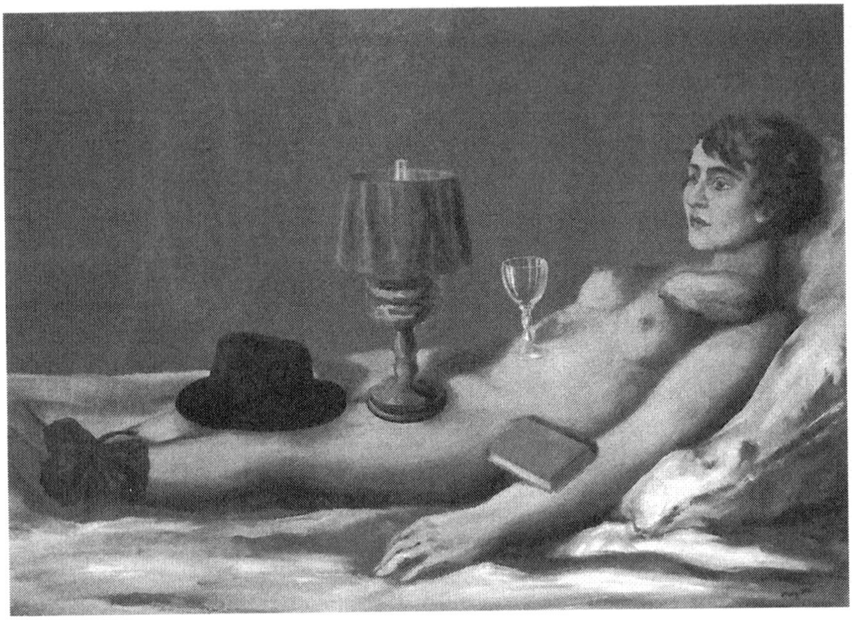

Figure 19.3 The reclining nude (*Le nu couché*)

Source: Magritte (1928)[6]

reference, influences the placement: that is, a more egocentric subject will view his near and dear ones as mere extensions of himself within his identity zone.

The nude woman as represented in the plastic arts is an idol that, like it or not (Magritte did not), symbolizes beauty (with a small 'b') as well as the Beauty that resides in transcendence (with a capital 'B', i.e., esthetic value) – most definitely the latter, at any rate. The female nude also symbolizes Woman (with a capital 'W').

It is well known that Magritte, a surrealist, wanted to represent or evoke what he called "mystery" in his paintings; this was unquestionably a personal idol. Even setting aside Magritte's personal conception of this notion, as a popular idol in art and therefore a collective one, it was undeniably more important to Magritte than to the average producer of art.

The idol-woman is covered with ordinary objects, all of which are fetishes nearby (in contrast to the specialized objects, which are fetishes at a distance – microscopes, industrial tools, and so on). A semantic shock, much valued by the surrealists, is produced by bringing these opposites together. Moreover, the opposition idol/fetish is homologized, i.e., correlated with other oppositions: reality/ideal; poetic/prosaic; human/object; nature (nudity, the stone-like object, the leaf-like (or bow))/culture (the manufactured objects); single/multiple; feminine (woman, bow-like)/masculine (the hat, the painter).[7] This series of homologies amplifies the intensity of the confrontation.

The book depicted in the painting has a special status: If it is the medium for a work, literary or otherwise (which may be inferred from the bedtime reading scenario, reinforced by the lamp and the reclined position of the woman), then it is an idol surrounded by fetishes. The *œuvre*-book also constitutes a metaphorical *mise en abyme* (embedding) of the painting: both are idols, and both are works of art.

While the theme (or isotopy) uniting the objects is a general one – ordinariness – some of the objects are united by a more specific theme: the clothing theme, for instance (the bow and hat), and the fabric theme (the bow, hat, sheets, pillows, the bit of fabric on the pillow in the lower right corner and the lampshade). In short, as with any collection of copresent elements – even the most varied – organizing principles may be found in what initially looks like random odds and ends.

One of the overall effects of this confrontation between an idol and fetishes is an idolization of the fetishes – the source of Magrittian mystery – and a fetishization of the idol: the woman is de-idolized, or objectified. This seems to be a process Magritte uses frequently – at least, the idolization of fetishes is. For example, in *The golden legend* (1958),[8] there are a great number of oversized loaves of bread hovering in the sky, which lends cosmic significance to a typical, everyday object, as ordinary as saying, "Please pass the salt".

The strange, improbable, mysterious, and thus distal quality of the scene is accentuated by an object, embedded as a micro-self-representation (*mise en abyme*): the (at least initially) unidentifiable object sitting on the woman's shoulder. This element is much like numerous other unidentifiable elements found in Magritte's paintings. In a nutshell, this object is an idol, which adds some complexity to the idol/fetish opposition that otherwise seemed so neatly ordered in this painting. It is no longer a simple case of the idol-woman versus the fetish-objects. This unidentifiable object also makes the bit of fabric in the lower right corner seem strange, due to the resemblance between the two; but it could be just a fold in the pillowcase. Another interpretation might say that the object on her shoulder is merely a stone; however, it still contrasts with the other objects in that it is natural and the others are cultural (human-made). The stone is the object that most directly evokes the outdoors in this indoor scene; the hat also does, but to a lesser degree. On that note, many of Magritte's paintings feature stones or objects, animals, or humans. A stone on a beach is certainly not a priori a fetish; if it is picked up and put on display inside, it becomes a fetish, or becomes idol as an object of beauty.

It is well known that the nude is a genre and a theme in two- and three-dimensional art forms. In the Magritte database (*Magritte : toutes les œuvres, tous les thèmes* (Hébert, 2007–2012)), a search on the word "nudité" yields 273 works that contain at least one nude human (nearly always a woman), which amounts to about 14 percent of Magritte's paintings. This makes it an important genre and theme in Magritte's work; and it certainly reveals the fantastical nature of the theme in his work.[9]

The nudity in his pictorial works is not always complete. Firstly, the framing of the subject can make it so only part of the body is shown (e.g., from head to shoulders). Secondly, elements in the world of the painting (objects, clothing, fabric, the subject's hands, etc.) or elements of the enunciation (superposed shapes, etc.) can partially hide the nude body, particularly in the sexuated areas that are fetishes in the anthropic and sexual sense (primarily the breasts and pubis, for the woman). In the painting we are examining, the objects serve in this role of covering nudity: this includes the hat – a man's hat, actually – and especially the lamp, a phallic figure that hides the subject's pubis. As we know, Magritte painted phalluses and sexual situations many times in his works.

If one sees a person nude, unless it is by accident or in some functional situation (a locker room, a medical examination, a massage, someone modeling for a painting, etc.), it means that one is part of that person's distant identity or near proximal zone. That is, as a rule, among close friends and family members, only couples (whether for life or for an evening) have this privilege, with the exception of very young children, who may be seen nude or may see their parents nude, generally speaking. In the painting, since we know that Georgette actually exists (even if she did not pose for this painting – the painter may very well have painted her from memory), nudity becomes an intimate spectacle, displayed even to fellow humans of the distant proximal or distal zones (complete strangers). Moreover, the opposition between the painter and the nude subject is overlain by that between the voyeur and the exhibitionist. The person looking at the painting is also in this voyeur role, which is the case with all nudes in pictorial art, in movies, and so on. The woman is in bed, which increases the degree of intimacy of the scene (identity or near proximal zone). However, the woman is raised up on pillows supporting her, as though in a position not for sex or sleeping, but for an activity (reading, having a drink, daydreaming, etc.).

Notes

1 The same general principles – the inventory of positions, assignment of elements to positions, trajectories, factors of relativity – are valid for some other analytical tools, if not all: the actantial model, the canonical narrative schema, the semiotic square, the tensive model, and others.

2 Translator's note: Rastier's term, *arrière-monde* literally means "back-world", but Nietzsche's term "*Hinterwelt*" is also translated as "back-world." I will simply revert to the German "*Welt*", since it is commonly used in English. For Rastier's term "*entour*" (the "world around" or "surrounding world"), I will use "*Umwelt.*"

3 The same general principles – the inventory of positions, assignment of elements to positions, trajectories, factors of relativity – are valid for some other analytical tools, if not all: the actantial model, the canonical narrative schema, the semiotic square, the tensive model, and others.

4 There is at least one other possible interpretation, in which none of the above (*God, Shakespeare and me*) is engaged in an anthropic trajectory. There is simply a collision between the first two, which are idols to different degrees, and the last, who is merely a being in the identity zone.

5 For an application to visualizations in Tibetan Buddhism, see Hébert, 2019.

6 Hébert, 2007–2012, database number 0282; Sylvester, 1992–1997, vol. I, p. 136.

7 In addition, feminine / masculine incorporates a three-way opposition: feminine (woman, bow) / neuter (lamp, etc.) / masculine (painter, hat).

8 Hébert, 2007–2012, database number 0982; Sylvester, 1992–1997, vol. III, p. 280.

9 See in Hébert, 2007b another analysis of a woman painted by Magritte.

20 A short introduction to semiotics

Summary

Semiotics is the academic field dedicated to the study of signs. A sign (for example, the word "ship") may be recognized by the presence of its constituent parts, which in semiotic theories based on Saussure's, at least, are the signifier (the container, the vehicle form: the letters *s-h-i-p*) and the signified (the meaning or content; the notion conveyed by the signifier: 'a vessel of considerable size for deepwater navigation'). With these concepts, general semiotics allows us to describe any system of signs: texts, images, performances, multimedia productions, traffic signals, fashion, daily life, etc. There are specific semiotic systems (for text, images, multimedia, and so on) that take into account the specifics of each system of signs. This chapter is an overview of general semiotics. In the first section, we define the field of semiotics and the concept of the sign and enumerate the basic concepts and the names of some of the better-known theorists. Then, by analysing a seemingly innocuous object, the traffic signal, we illustrate some concepts of general semiotics – notions such as sender/receiver, sending/transmitting/receiving, channel, context, referent, system, code, redundancy, noise, paradigm/syntagm, margin of safety, seme, isotopy, polysemy/homonymy/synonymy, symbolic/semi-symbolic/semiotic relationships and systems, arbitrary/conventional signs, contiguous/noncontiguous signs, single/repeated signs, successive/simultaneous signs, actualized/virtualized signs, contrast, and so forth.

Theory

Semiotics and the sign: definitions

In a nutshell, semiotics (or semiology) is the field of study that is concerned with signs and/or signification (the process of creating meaning). For several years now, the field of semiotics has been gaining momentum, due to the growth of multimedia, among other things.

Semiotics is not a single theory. There are, in fact, several semiotic theories. Some prominent people are associated with semiotics, including de Saussure, Peirce, Morris, Hjelmslev, Jakobson, Barthes, Greimas, and Eco (the famed author of the novel *The name of the rose*, upon which the movie of the same name is based). Some of the concepts of semiotics are also well known: signifier, signified, referent, paradigm, poetic function, isotopy, actantial model, semiotic triangle, semiotic square, open text, etc.

The notion of the **sign** can be described in several ways. Some definitions are functional: For example, the broadest definition, and one of the oldest, defines the sign as *something that is used in place of something else* (the something else may be interpreted as a signified or a referent, as we will see later). For instance, black is worn at a funeral not just for its own sake; it also signifies death, at least in our culture. Other definitions are based on the presence of the constituent elements of the sign, which vary from one theory to another.

In those theories based on Saussure's (the renowned linguist from Geneva), the sign may be broken down into the **signifier**, which is the vehicle part of the sign (for example, the letters *s-h-i-p*) and the **signified**, which is the understandable part of the sign, or the semantic content associated with the signifier (for example, the meaning of the word "ship"). The signified may be broken down into **semes**. For example, the signified 'ship' contains semes such as /navigation/, /concrete/, etc. An **isotopy** is created by the repetition of one seme. For example, in "There was a fine ship, carved from solid gold/With azure reaching masts, on seas unknown" (Émile Nelligan, "The golden ship"), the words "ship", "masts" and "seas" all contain the seme /navigation/ (as well as others), thus forming the isotopy /navigation/.

The conventional markers shown in the below table allow us to distinguish between (1) the sign (the word) "concrete"; (2) the signified, 'concrete', that it conveys; (3) the signifier associated with this sign, *concrete*, which is composed of the phonemes *k-o-n-k-r-E-t* and the letters *c-o-n-c-r-e-t-e*; and (4) the seme /concrete/ (in 'knife', for example) or the isotopy /concrete/ (in "steel knife", for example). In other places, a single slash may indicate an opposition (for example, life/death). There are other conventions used in semiotics than the markers we will present and use here.

Table 20.1 Conventional markers

"sign" (quotation marks)	*signifier* (italics)
'signified' (single quote marks)	/sememe/ and /isotopy/ (forward slashes)

In the Aristotelian tradition, the sign is broken down into three parts: the signifier, the signified and the **referent**, meaning the concrete thing to which the sign refers (for example, a real horse). In using the terms "signifier" and "signified" for the first two parts of the triadic sign, we are using Saussure's terminology; other terms have been proposed that sometimes correspond to very different theoretical visions. For example, Peirce (a renowned American logician), while part of the second tradition in semiotics, proposed a novel vision (to be presented in the chapter Peirce's Semiotics). The parts of the sign he distinguishes are the **representamen**, the **interpretant**, and the **object**.

Elementary semiotics and traffic signals

As in any other discipline, semiotics reveals the complexity of phenomena that seem simple on the surface. Traffic signals are an example of a simple semiotic system that is far more complex than it seems. We are speaking here of standard traffic signals, not of all the many variations in existence.

Signifiers

The three main signifiers for traffic signals are colors: *green, yellow* and *red.* These signifiers use only one of the five sensory **channels**, that is, only one of the five senses – sight. (This is not the case with olfactory signs, for example.)

Within a single system of signs, signifiers must follow the principle of providing an adequate **safety margin** – and we are not talking about road safety. For example, traffic signals could in theory use these three colors: *dark green, medium green* and *light green.* It is easy to see that the lower safety margin between the signifiers would also decrease safety on the road.

Redundancy and noise

The colors in traffic signals are often associated (or correlated) with other kinds of visual signifiers (which correlate to the same signifieds as the colors), for example, shapes (*rectangle + red, circle + green*, etc.), and positions (*top, middle, bottom* or *left, middle, right*). This correlation produces **redundancy**, which is the process of repeating one signified, either by associating it with several different signifiers or by repeating the sign in which it is conveyed. The purpose of redundancy is to counteract what is called **noise** in information theory, meaning that which impedes or could impede in **transmitting** or correctly **interpreting** (**receiving**) the message that was produced during the act of **sending**. The purpose of redundancy is to ensure that the receiver (the driver or the pedestrian) can perceive the sign with no problem, even when the circumstances are unfavourable (glare, color blindness, distraction, etc.). For instance, why does a telephone ring several times when once would suffice? To ensure that at least one of the repeated signs is perceived.

Signifieds

With each color of the traffic signal we associate one signified that is distinct from the signifieds for the other colors: 'go' for *green*, 'prepare to stop' for *yellow*, and 'stop' for *red.*

Polysemy and synonymy

Polysemy occurs when two or more signifieds are associated with the same signifier.

> NOTE: POLYSEMY AND HOMONYMY
>
> The word "polysemy" has a specific meaning in linguistics, where it indicates a lesser difference between signifieds than in the case of homonymy. For example, the signifier *m-o-u-t-h* may be associated polysemically with two signifieds: 'river mouth' and 'oral cavity'. In contrast, the signifier *d-r-a-f-t* may be associated with two signifieds that are homonymic: 'a current of air' and 'conscription in the armed forces'.

When the same signified is associated with two or more signifiers, it is called **synonymy**, at least in the case of linguistic signs. This would be the case with "dead" and "deceased". Synonyms can also be found in the semiotic system we are discussing, as in the sign composed of *red* + 'stop', which has equivalents, although they are not as prominent: *top* + 'stop' (in a vertical arrangement, the red light is generally located at the top) and *rectangle* + 'stop'.

NOTE: THE IMPOSSIBILITY OF PERFECT SYNONYMY

Perfect synonymy apparently does not exist, at least, not in linguistic systems. This is evidenced by the difference in usage between signs that are synonymous. For instance, "deceased" may be distinguished from "dead" by the fact that it belongs to a higher register of language and that it is used only for humans, except in specific rhetorical usages (we don't normally talk about a dog being "deceased"). The principle of **solidarity** between signifier and signified explains the lack of true synonyms. According to this principle, as soon as we change the signifier, we change the signified, and vice versa. For example, if we change the phoneme *m* in "moose" to a *g*, we change not only the signifier, but also the signified that goes with it (a moose is not a goose).

Symbolic, semi-symbolic and semiotic systems

A system of signs or a relationship between elements of any kind is (1) symbolic, (2) semi-symbolic, or (3) semiotic (the word "semiotic" has a restricted, specific meaning in this context). (1) When one signifier is associated with one and only one signified, we call this a **symbolic system**. Traffic lights and the "language" of flowers are examples of symbolic systems (roses = 'love', tulips = 'friendship', etc.). (2) A system is **semi-symbolic** if an opposition between signifiers corresponds (is homologous) to an opposition between signifieds. Gestures are often semi-symbolic in nature, as in the opposition *vertical movement/horizontal movement*, which is homologous to the opposition 'yes'/'no'. Traffic signals meet this definition partially: while red and green are in opposition as complementary colors, yellow does not have a real opposite in this system. Be that as it may, in other contexts each of these three colors can be part of other culturally defined oppositions (either within one culture or between cultures). For example, red and black are in opposition in several cultures, particularly in Africa. (3) Lastly, other systems may be classified as **semiotic**. Language is such a system.

The sign: arbitrariness and convention

The correlation between a color and its signified is **arbitrary** (unmotivated). Any signifier may in theory be joined with any signified. In order to be correctly interpreted, the sign relies on a **convention**. (In this sense, but only in this sense, is it motivated.) The fact that other cultures and societies (Japan, Australia) correlate *yellow* with 'stop' in their traffic signals proves this point. Our traffic signals are obviously somewhat motivated, since there is a general correlation (or more accurately, a homology) established in our culture between *red/green* and 'harmful'/'beneficial'. (This would not necessarily be the case in other cultures.) This general correlation itself is nevertheless arbitrary, however we may rationalize it. (For example, red could symbolize bleeding, and green the growth of plants; but we can also find associations that go in the opposite direction, as in the color green and illness). Although these associations between signifiers and signifieds are theoretically arbitrary, some constraints do exist, depending on the type of signifier and the situation. For example, it is hard to imagine traffic signals using a black signifier.

Peirce distinguishes three modes of signs: **iconic** (a photograph, or a school crossing sign with a silhouette of a person), **indexic** (signs belonging to the if . . . then . . . type, such as smoke for fire, a cat's tail for the whole cat), and **symbolic** (the word "daddy"). The most arbitrary sign is obviously the symbol, which relies completely on codification: there is no similarity (icon), no contiguity or proximity (index) between "daddy" and the thing it designates. To prove our point, in French, the word used to designate the same referent is "*papa*". One sign may be used in several ways, for example, as a symbol of one thing and an index of another. A traffic signal, for instance, is primarily a symbol, but may also serve as an index for an invisible intersection coming up.

Single/repeated signs and semiotic silence

A sign (1) may be of any duration, (2) may or may not be followed by a silence of any duration, and in the case where a sign is not isolated (a **single sign**), it will yield to another sign or else be repeated (a **repeated sign**).

To illustrate, traffic signals use single signs and repeated signs (blinking lights). In the "language" of traffic signals, a silence would be hazardous (as in the sequence "green light" → no light → "yellow light" → no light → "red light", for instance). The absence of a sign does not constitute a sign in this case, as often happens in other semiotic systems; for safety reasons, there do not seem to be any traffic lights with only one color (as in the hypothetical case where the absence of red would mean 'go', rather than a green light). For similar reasons, someone decided it would be wise to insert an intermediate sign, "yellow light", between the two opposite signs, "red light" and "green light". The yellow light is intermediate in two ways: It is intermediate in time (being in the middle of the sequence, and we shall come back to this) and of course, its meaning is intermediate. In semiotics, it is what we call a **neutral term**, that is, a sign indicating the absence of two opposite terms. Its meaning is 'neither one'.

Simultaneous/successive signs, paradigms and syntagms

All languages are composed of signs and rules, with some degree of constraint on what combinations of signs may be used. Some of these constraints are temporal. Two events (two signs, in this case) can be (1) **concomitant** (they are simultaneous – they appear and disappear at the same time); (2) **successive** (immediately or with a time lapse); or (3) partially concomitant (with one starting later than the other, but before the first one ends).

In the "language" of traffic signals, as in real language, two signs cannot be produced at one time. At least in the oral manifestation of language, phonological reasons explain this rule: It is not possible to pronounce two phonemes at once. With traffic lights, this possibility is excluded for reasons of safety and coherence: the signs may only be produced in succession, with no concomitance and no silence. We can say that the signs are mutually exclusive: only one sign may be **actualized** (present) at a time; the other two must remain **virtualized** (in absentia). This eliminates the possibility of what we call a **contrast**, which is the simultaneous presence of two opposite signs ("red light" and "green light").

A **paradigm** is a set of equivalent virtualized signs, from which one sign is chosen to be actualized in a syntagm. A **syntagm** is a group of signs that succeed each other in time. (For example, a sentence is a group of words, and in this respect, a syntagm; there are other syntagms without temporal succession, such as a painting.)

Traffic signals have only one paradigm, composed of only three signs. They function with a syntagm that necessarily has three temporal and three spatial positions. At each position in time, only one sign is actualized. At each position in space (left, middle and right, if horizontal) only one sign, and always the same sign, is actualized. Undoubtedly for reasons of safety and cost, the option of using one bulb that changes color is not encouraged (although there are pedestrian signals in which the signs "walk" and "don't walk" are located in exactly the same place). Out of all the possible combinations, only one is permitted: "green light" → "yellow light" → "red light" →, and so on. The signs are not equal in duration: The yellow light does not usually last as long as the other two, and the relative duration of the red and green lights is regulated according to the amount of traffic on each road involved. And here we enter into the wonders and the horrors of programming traffic signals, both individually and sequentially (synchronizing them). Semiotics can lead us with no warning into some distressingly mundane realms.

BIBLIOGRAPHY

Aquin, H. (1978), *Neige noire*, Montréal, Le Cercle du livre de France.

Aquin, H. (1995), *Prochain épisode, Édition critique de l'oeuvre d'Hubert Aquin*, tome III, éd. J. Allard, Montréal, Bibliothèque québécoise.

Arcand, R. and N. Bourbeau (1995), *La communication efficace. De l'intention aux moyens d'expression*, Anjou, Québec, CEC.

Baudelaire, C. (1955), *The flowers of evil*, New York, NY, New Directions.

Baudelaire, C. (1975), *Œuvres complètes*, Paris, Gallimard.

Baudelaire, C. (1989), *The parisian prowler: Le spleen de Paris*, Athens, GA, University of Georgia Press.

Baudelaire, C. (1998), *The dog and the perfume*, trans. K. Dixon, Springfield, OH, Wittenberg University, 4 November 2004, http://www4.wittenberg.edu/academics/engl/newpage/paragraf-baud.html

Beer, R. (2006), *Les symboles du bouddhisme tibétain*, Paris, Albin Michel.

Bertrand, D. (2000), *Précis de sémiotique littéraire*, Paris, Nathan.

Binet, A. (2001) [1887], *Le fétichisme dans l'amour*, Paris, Payot.

Bouchard, G. (1917), "Je m'ennuie de la terre", *Premières semailles*, Québec, Imprimerie de l'Action Sociale, pp. 70–71.

Brandt, P. A. (1995), *Quelque chose. Nouvelles remarques sur la véridiction*, Limoges, Nouveaux actes sémiotiques, pp. 39–40.

Burnett, M. (2015), "Guido Molinari" [online], in A. Wilson-Smith (dir.), *The canadian encyclopedia*, 19 May 2019, https://www.thecanadianencyclopedia.ca/en/article/guido-molinari

Céline, L. (1983) [1934], *Journey to the end of the night*, trans. R. Manheim, New York, NY, New Directions.

Clair, J. (1977), "Perspective. Marcel Duchamp et la tradition des perspecteurs", in J. Clair (dir.), *Marcel Duchamp, III, Abécédaire: Approches critiques*, Paris, Centre Georges Pompidou, pp. 126–128.

Courtés, J. (1991), *Analyse sémiotique du discours: De l'énoncé à l'énonciation*, Paris, Hachette.

Courtés, J. (1995), *Du lisible au visible*, Brussels, De Boeck University.

Eco, U. (1988), *Le signe*, Brussels, Labor.

Everaert-Desmedt, N. (1990), *Le processus interprétatif: introduction à la sémiotique de Ch. S. Peirce*, Brussels, Pierre Mardaga.

Everaert-Desmedt, N. (2006), *Interpréter l'art contemporain. La sémiotique peircienne appliquée aux œuvres de Magritte, Klein, Duras, Wenders, Chávez, Parant et Corillon*, Brussels, De Boeck.

Floch, J-M. (1985), "Quelques concepts fondamentaux en sémiotique générale", in *Petites mythologies de l'œil et de l'esprit: pour une sémiotique plastique*, Paris and Amsterdam, Éditions Hadès-Benjamins, pp. 189–207.

Fontanille, J. (1984), *Les points de vue dans le discours*, Doctoral thesis, University of Paris III.

Fontanille, J. (1995), *Sémiotique du visible*, Paris, Presses Universitaires de France.

Fontanille, J. (1999), *Sémiotique et littérature*, Paris, Presses Universitaires de France.

Fontanille, J. (2003), *Sémiotique du discours*, Limoges, Presses de l'Université de Limoges.

Gagnière, C. (1996), *Entre guillemets: petit dictionnaire de citations*, Paris, Robert Laffont.

Gaudreault, R. (1996), "Renouvellement du modèle actantiel", *Poétique*, 107, September, pp. 355–368.

Genette, G. (1972), *Figures III*, Paris, Seuil.

Genette, G. (1980), *Narrative discourse: an essay in method*, trans. J. Lewin, Ithaca, NY, Cornell University Press.

Genette, G. (1982), *Palimpsestes*, Paris, Seuil.

Genette, G. (1983), *Nouveau discours du récit*, Paris, Seuil.

Genette, G. (1988), *Narrative discourse revisited*, trans. J. Lewin, Ithaca, NY, Cornell University Press.

Gervais, A. (1994), *Sas. Essais*, Montreal, Triptyque.

Greimas, A. J. (dir.) (1982) [1972], *Essais de sémiotique poétique*, Paris, Larousse.

Greimas, A. J. (1983) [1966], *Structural semantics: An attempt at a method*, trans. D. McDowell, R. Schleifer and A. Velie, Lincoln, NE, University of Nebraska Press.

Greimas, A. J. and J. Courtés (1982), *Semiotics and language: An analytical dictionary*, Bloomington, IN, Indiana University Press.

Greimas, A. J. and J. Courtés (1986), *Sémiotique. Dictionnaire raisonné de la théorie du langage*, tome 2, Paris, Hachette Université.

Greimas, A. J. and J. Fontanille (1993) [1991], *The semiotics of passions. From states of affairs to states of feelings*, trans. P. Perron and F. Collins, Minneapolis, University of Minnesota Press.

Greimas, A. J. and F. Rastier (1968), "The interaction of semiotic constraints", in *Yale french studies*, 41, pp. 86–105, New Haven.

Groupe μ. (1977), *Rhétorique de la poésie*, Brussels, Complexe.

Groupe μ. (1982), *Rhétorique générale*, Paris, Seuil.

Hébert, L. (1998), "Onomastique, homonymie, paronymie et polyglossie. L'exemple de *Prochain épisode*", *Degrés*, 26–94, Summer, pp. d1–d21.

Hébert, L. (1999), "Schéma de l'interprétation et nombre d'interprétations adéquates", *Semiotica*, 126, 1–4, pp. 97–120.

Hébert, L. (2000), "Analyse des espaces représentés dans la littérature: Le récit du terroir 'Je m'ennuie de la terre' de Georges Bouchard", *Recherches sémiotiques/Semiotic inquiry (RS/SI)*, 19, 2–3, pp. 193–215.

Hébert, L. (2001), *Introduction à la sémantique des textes*, Paris, Honoré Champion.

Hébert, L. (2003), "L'analyse des modalités véridictoires et thymiques: vrai/faux, euphorie/dysphorie", *Semiotica*, 144, 1–4, pp. 261–302.

Hébert, L. (2005), "Typologies et segmentations du temps. Les courbes d'euphorie esthétique", in L. Hébert and L. Guillemette (dir.), *Signes des temps: Temps et temporalités des signes*, Québec, Presses de l'Université Laval, pp. 59–85.

Hébert, L. (dir.) (2007–2012), *Magritte. Toutes les œuvres, tous les thèmes* [online database], Rimouski, Québec, http://www.magrittedb.com

Hébert, L. (2007a), *Dispositifs pour l'analyse des textes et des images. Introduction à la sémiotique appliquée*, Limoges, Presses de l'Université de Limoges.

Hébert, L. (2007b), "Sémantique des affiches. Autour de *Festival mondial du film* de René Magritte", in J. Fontanille (dir.), *Affiches et affichages, Nouveaux actes sémiotiques*, http://epublications.unilim.fr/revues/as/1196

Hébert, L. (2008), "Petite sémiotique du monstre. Avec notamment des monstres de Hergé, Magritte et Matthieu Ricard", in M-H. Larochelle (dir.), *Monstres et monstrueux littéraires*, Quebec City, Presses de l'Université Laval, pp. 121–139.

Hébert, L. (2009), "Autotextualité, intertextualité, architextualité, autoreprésentation, autoréflexivité et autres relations apparentées", in L. Hébert and L. Guillemette (dir.), *Intertextualité, interdiscursivité et intermédialité*, Québec, Presses de l'Université Laval, pp. 71–78.

Hébert, L. (dir.) (2011), "Opérations de transformation dans l'iconographie du bouddhisme tibétain", *Sémiotique et bouddhisme*, *Protée*, 39, 2, pp. 81–94.

Hébert, L. (2014), *L'analyse des textes littéraires: une méthodologie complète*, Paris, Classiques Garnier.

Hébert, L. (2019), "Becoming a Buddha: A semiotic analysis of visualizations in Tibetan Buddhism", in A. S. Kohav (dir.), *Mysticism and meaning: Multidisciplinary perspectives*, St. Petersburg, FL, Three Pines Press, pp. 228–247.

Hébert, L. (2020), *Cours de sémiotique*, Paris, Classiques Garnier.

Hébert, L. and L. Guillemette (2009), "Intertextualité, interdiscursivité et intermédialité", in L. Hébert and L. Guillemette (dir.), *Intertextualité, interdiscursivité et intermédialité*, Québec, Presses de l'Université Laval, pp. 1–9.

Hébert, L., P. Michelucci and É. Trudel (dir.) (2018), *Magritte: Perspectives nouvelles, Nouveaux regards*, Québec, Nota bene.

Ionesco, E. (1960), *Rhinoceros and other plays*, trans. Derek Prouse, New York, NY, Grove Press.

Jakobson, R. (1960), "Linguistics and poetics", in T. A. Sebeok (dir.), *Style in language*, Cambridge, Wiley and Massachusetts Institute of Technology, pp. 350–377.

Jakobson, R. (1963), "Linguistique et poétique", in *Essais de linguistique générale*, Paris, Minuit, pp. 209–248.

Klinkenberg, J-M. (1996), *Précis de sémiotique générale*, Paris, Seuil.

La Fontaine, J. de (1988), *The complete fables of Jean de La Fontaine*, ed. and trans. N. Spector, Evanston, IL, Northwestern University Press.

Low, A. (1992), *Le rêve du papillon*, Saint-Hubert, Québec, Libre Expression.

Mailhot, L. and P. Nepveu (1986), *La poésie québécoise: Anthologie*, Montreal, L'Hexagone.

Martin, R. (1983), *Pour une logique du sens*, Paris, Presses Universitaires de France.

Nelligan, É. (1960), *Selected poems of Émile Nelligan*, trans. P. F. Widdows, Toronto, Ryerson Press.

Piaget, J. (1979), *Le structuralisme*, Paris, Presses Universitaires de France.

Pomian, K. (1996), "Histoire culturelle, histoire des sémiophores", in J-P. Rioux and J-F. Sirinelli (eds.), *Pour une histoire culturelle*, Paris, Seuil, pp. 73–100.

Propp, V. (1970), *Morphologie du conte*, Paris, Seuil.

Rastier, F. (1989), "La tactique", in *Sens et textualité*, Paris, Hachette, pp. 95–102. (Reprinted: 2016, Limoges, Lambert-Lucas.).

Rastier, F. (1991), *Sémantique et recherches cognitives*, Paris, Presses Universitaires de France.

Rastier, F. (1992), "Réalisme sémantique et réalisme esthétique", *Théorie, littérature, enseignement*, 10, pp. 81–119.

Rastier, F. (1994), see : Rastier, F., M. Cavazza and A. Abeillé (1994)

Rastier, F. (1996) [1987], *Sémantique interprétative*, Paris, Presses Universitaires de France.

Rastier, F. (1997) [1989], *Meaning and textuality*, trans. F. Collins and P. Perron, Toronto, University of Toronto Press.

Rastier, F. (2001), *Arts et sciences du texte*, Paris, Presses Universitaires de France

Rastier, F. (2002), "Anthropologie linguistique et sémiotique des cultures", in F. Rastier and S. Bouquet (eds.), *Une introduction aux sciences de la culture*, Paris, Presses universitaires de France, pp. 243–267.

Rastier, F. (2010), "Objets culturels et performances sémiotiques. L'objectivation critique dans les sciences de la culture", in L. Hébert and L. Guillemette (eds. and dir.), *Performances et objets culturels*, Québec, Presses de l'Université Laval, pp. 15–58.

Rastier, F. (unpublished, 2012), *Glossaire*.

Rastier, F., M. Cavazza and A. Abeillé (1994), *Sémantique pour l'analyse*, Paris, Masson.

Sartre, J-P. (1964), *Nausea*, New York, NY, New Directions.

Simonsen, M. (1984), *Le conte populaire*, Paris, Presses Universitaires de France.

Sowa, J. (1984), *Conceptual structures*, Reading, MA, Addison-Wesley.

Stendhal. (1952), *Romans et nouvelles*, vol. 1, Paris, Gallimard.

Sylvester, D. (dir.) (1992–1997), *René Magritte. Catalogue raisonné*, vol. 5, Anvers, Fonds Mercator/Menil Foundation.

Tcheuky Sèngué. (2002), *Petite encyclopédie des divinités et symboles du bouddhisme tibétain*, France, Claire Lumière, n.p.

Tritsmans, B. (1987), "Poétique", in M. Delcroix and F. Hallyn (dir.), *Méthodes du texte. Introduction aux études littéraires*, Paris, Duculot, pp. 11–28.

Uexküll, J. V. (1956) [1934], *Mondes animaux et mondes humains*, Paris, Denoël

Vandendorpe, C. (1994), "De la vérité dans le langage", *Le faux*, *Protée*, 22, 3, Autumn, pp. 7–12.

Zilberberg, C. (2000), "Les contraintes sémiotiques du métissage", *Tangence*, 64, Autumn, pp. 8–24. [Republished on the Web: http://www.erudit.org/revue/tce/2000/v/n64/008188ar.pdf.].

Zilberberg, C. (2002), "Précis de grammaire tensive", *Tangence*, 70, Autumn, pp. 111–143.

Zilberberg, C. (2006), *Éléments de sémiotique tensive*, Limoges, Presses de l'Université de Limoges.

INDEX

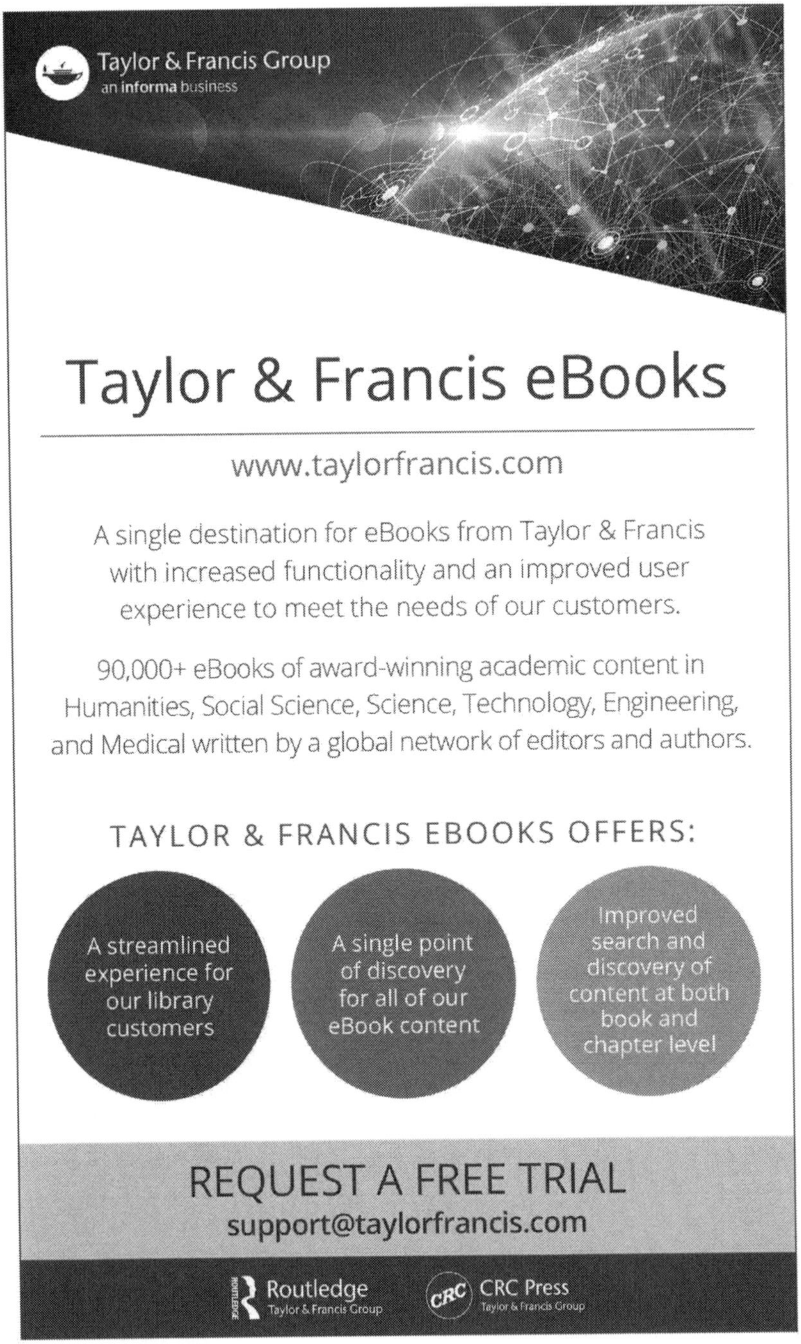

Taylor & Francis Group
an informa business
Taylor & Francis eBooks
www.taylorfrancis.com
A single destination for eBooks from Taylor & Francis with increased functionality and an improved user experience to meet the needs of our customers.
90,000+ eBooks of award-winning academic content in Humanities, Social Science, Science, Technology, Engineering, and Medical written by a global network of editors and authors.
TAYLOR & FRANCIS EBOOKS OFFERS:
A streamlined experience for our library customers
A single point of discovery for all of our eBook content
Improved search and discovery of content at both book and chapter level
REQUEST A FREE TRIAL
support@taylorfrancis.com
Routledge Taylor & Francis Group
CRC Press Taylor & Francis Group

Printed in Great Britain
by Amazon

59866926R00172